ISBN 978-1-332-96400-0
PIBN 10443873

Viola Wynder
Hill Spring
Alberta

The Publications

of the

Yorkshire Parish Register Society

Vol. 14.

Issued to Subscribers for the Year 1902.

The Registers

of

Wath-upon-Dearne

Yorkshire

Baptisms and Burials, 1598—1778

Marriages, 1598—1779

TRANSCRIBED AND EDITED BY

J. W. CLAY, F.S.A,

PRIVATELY PRINTED FOR
THE YORKSHIRE PARISH REGISTER SOCIETY
1902.

W. H. MILNES, PRINTER, WAKEFIELD.

PREFACE.

THE First Volume, containing Baptisms, Marriages, and Burials, consists of three parchment volumes of unequal size bound together. The first has entries from 1598 to 1629, 7½ by 13½ inches; the second, from 1630 to 1652, 9 by 13¾ inches; the third, 1652 to 1724, 6½ by 15 inches. It has been badly bound, the leaves not being in consecutive order. In addition the entries in the third part are very mixed up, so it has been considered the best plan to place them all in their proper yearly order. The edges of many of the leaves are much frayed, which makes the deciphering sometimes difficult.

The Second Volume, also parchment, contains the Baptisms and Burials, 1725 to 1778, and the Marriages, 1725 to 1753.

The Third Volume is solely Marriages, 1754 to August, 1779, and is paper with the modern printed forms.

The thanks of the Society are due to the Vicar (the Rev. H. W. Ward, M.A.) for allowing the Register to be printed and also for the kind way he has assisted the Editor.

J. W. C.

The Register Booke of Wath upon Dearne made in the year of o^r Lord God one thousande fyve hundreth neentie & nyne by John Beard viccar. Thomas Marlott & John Tayller Churchwardens.

Memorand that the 22th day of November 1607 Jo: Bearde, Georg Hoyland, John Addy wth others putt ou^r hands to a certificat for Ann Addy, that she was ffree to be hyred a mayd servant wher she best lyked & had the consent of her ffather & mother to be hyred wth Thomas Adams by Pontefract.

/

October 1598	Baptysed	Jasper the sonne of Nicholas Hunt the xviij^th day
May 1598	Baptysed	Richard the sonn of John Beard viccar of Wath the xiij^th day
	Baptysed	Thomas the sonne of Robte Pulsonn the xxvij^th day
August 1603	Bap.	Jo: Beard vicarij filius 16° die

M^and that the xxix^th day of Maie 1604 William Hepworth of Wath uppō Dearne wth in the countie of Yorke, yeoman had a stall place sett forth in the Church of Wath the highest place and the south syde of the Church nearest the Thornell hall queere to continewe to him & his heares dwellinge in the house wherin he nowe dwelleth in Skyterick.

John Beard viccar of Wath.

The Register booke of Wath sup Dearne wth in the countie of Yorke of all suche psons as have beene maryede baptised & Buried there since the forteeth yeare of the reigne of oure most gratious queene Elizabeth in the yeare of or Lord God 1598.

1598 — 1578

Novembr	Baptised	Nicholas the sonne of Richard Robuck of the Abdye 19° die
	Maried	John Case & Katyren Swallowe eodē die
	Baptised	Richard the soone of Henrie Hill 21 die et sepultus die post
	Baptysed	the daughter of Robt Nailer eodē die et sepultus die post
	Baptysed	George the sonne of Georg Jenkinsonn eodē die
	Buried	Thomas Diconson of Meltonn 28° die
Decemb	Buried	Roger Robinsonn of Wath 17° die
	Maried	Robert Pearsonn and Elizabeth Jubb 19° die
Januarie	Buried	Richard ffostard of Wath 14° die
	Baptised	Williā the sonne of John Taylier 21° die
	Maried	Thomas Hudsonn & Katherē Clay eod̄ die
	Maried	Williā Hepworth and Margret Robucke eodem die
Februarie	Baptysed	the daughter of Williā Prance 11° die
	Baptised	Godfray & grace the sonne & daughter of Lawrence Wade of Swintonn 21° die
March	Baptised	Elizabeth the Daughter of John ffurth of Melton 18 die
	Baptysed	Alis the daughter of John Jepsonn eodē die
	Baptysed	Ursiley the daughter of Thomas Watson 23° die
1599	Baptysed	Grace the daughter of Williā Kytchinmā 25° die
	Baptysed	Rosamond the daughter of John Robts of Wath 30° die
Aprill	Baptysed	Elizabeth the daughter of Wm Hepworth 8° die
	Baptysed	Wm the sonne of Thomas Makin 10° die
	Baptysed	Williā the sonne of Nicholas Mallinsonn eodē die
	Baptysed	Williā the sonne of Thomas Baxter gente 12° day
Maye	Baptysed	Thomas the sonne of John Smyth 4° die
	Baptysed	Thomas the sonne of Richard Mabson 22° die
June	Baptysed	Elizabeth the daughter of Robt Mallinsonn 14° die
Julie	Baptysed	John the sonne of Anthonie Woodworth 8° die
	Baptysed	John the son of Williā of Swintō eodē die
August	Baptysed	Richard the sonne of John Elome 5° die
	Baptỹsed	Grace ye daughter of Wm Barrowe 2° die
September	Buried	Hobsonn de Melton 8° die
	Baptysed	Henrie the sonne of John Wharō 9° die
	Baptysed	Thomas the sonne of Wm Coulbrand 16° die

1599		
October	Baptysed	Alice the daughter of Thomas ffawkes 1° die
	Baptysed	John the sonne of Denis ffroude eodē die
	Baptised	John the sonne of Edward ffrance 10° die
	Buried	Infans . . . . Hill unbapt 11° die
	Baptised	Barraclough eod die
	Baptized	Elizabeth the daughter of Richard Hodgson 29 die
	Bapt	John the (*rubbed out*)
	Baptysed	Ann the daughter of John Turner of Swinton eodē die
Novēmber	Baptysed	Elizabeth the daughter of Robt Neiler 3° die
	Maried	Nicholas Marsh & Ann Pearsonn 18° die
	Buried	the wiefe of John Stable of Meltonn 19° die
	Married	Thomas Booth & Katerine Smith 24° diē
	Buried	infans Richi Beckett de Melton unbapt eodē die
Decēber	Buried	Thomas the sonne of John Addye 1° die
	Buried	Infans Robti Pearson unbaptysed eodē die
	Buried	Widowe Turner of Melton 8° die
	Buried	Widowe Darlie of Newall 10° die
Januarie	Buried	the wief of Thomas Smith 11° die
	Buried	Rich. the sonne of Rich. ffostard de Swinton eodē die
	Buried	Williā Slack of Wath 18° die
	Buried	John Smith de Melton 22° die
	Baptysed	Infans John Dozen de Swinton unbapt 23 die
	Buried	the wief of John Dozen eodē die
	Baptysed	Thomas the sonne of Thomas Mariott eodē die
	Baptysed	Georg the sonne of John Addye 19° die
ffebruarie	Buried	ffayth the wief of Anthonie Wodworth 4° die
	Buried	Williā Saxton of Newall 7° die
	Buried	George the sonne of John Addy 15° die
March	Baptysed	Nicholas the sonne of Williā Croyser 2° die
	Baptysed	Nicholas the bastard sonne of Saunder Wood daughter eodē die
	Buried	an infant of John Cottons of Brāpton 7° die unbap
	Buried	the wief of Cottonn of brampton 10° die
	Baptysed	the daughter of Margret Hudsō kept at Peacoks 16° die
	Buried	the sayde chyld the 17° die
Anno Dom 1600		
	Baptysed	Williā the sonne of Richard Brooke of Swintō 25° die
Aprill	Baptysed	Elizabeth the daughter of George Hoiland 6° die
	Baptysed	Elizabeth the daughter of Richard Newtonn 20° die
	Buried	George the sonne of Wm Praunce 27
May	Baptysed	. . . . the sonne of Thomas Woode of Swintō 4° die
	Buried	John Sayvile gent. 11° die
	Baptysed	Richard the sonne of Ric. Brydley of Swintō 5° die
June	Baptysed	John the sonne of John Leatch de Newall 22 die

1600		
June	Baptysed	Alis the daughter of John Case eodē die
	Buried	Nicholas Paynter of Meltoun xix die
	Baptized	John the sonne (*blank*)
Julie	Maried	Laurence Hicks & ffraunces Hanson xxij^{t} day
	Maried	Thomas Smith & Agnes Hobson xxix^{to} die
August	Maried	Stephen Kay and Agnes Gibson the secunde day
	Baptysed	Lawrence sone of Lawrence Wade of Swintō 10° die
	Baptysed	Robert the sone of Wm Sugdenn eod die
	Buried	Robert White the xvth day
	Baptysed	Jane the daughter of Wm Milner of Swinton 24° die
Sept.	Bur	Widowe Pearson of Meltonn the 27 daye
October	Baptysed	Nicholas the sonne of Rob̄t Pearsonn 19° die
	Maried	Thomas Brook & Elizabeth Seavyle 21° die
	Baptysed	Elizabeth the daughter of Thomas Absonn 26° die
November	Maried	John Stable and Margrett Smith 2° die
	Buried	Henrie Shaw of Houber 8° die
	Baptysed	John the sonne of John ffyrth of Melton 23° die
December	Baptysede	Elizabeth the daughter of John Beard vicar 4° die
	Baptizsed	John the sonne of Nicho. Goodyear base gott 11° die
	Maried	Nicholas Shawe & Grace Smalchar 18 die
	Baptysed	Elizabeth the daughter of Turner of Swintō 24 die
	Baptysed	Elizabeth the daughter of John Taylier 26° die
	Baptized	Thomas the sonne of Nicholas Tindley 27° die
Januarie	Maried	ffrauncis Cosin & Ann England 12° die
	Burial	Isabell Tompson, widowe 12° die
	Baptysed	Richard the sonne of Henrie Hill eodem die
	Maried	William Englande & Elizabeth Shawe 20° die
	Maried	John Gybsonn & Elizabeth Litster eodē die
	Buried	Richard the sonne of John Smalchare 18° die
Februarie	Baptysed	William the sonne of Thomas Menlove of Swinto 8 die
	Buried	Thomas Sherwood of Meltonn 10 die
March	Baptysed	Richard the sonne of John Smalchare 1 die?
	Buryed	Elizabeth Greene? of Melton 4° die
	Buried	Margrett Leatch? vid 19° die
	Baptysed	Ellen the daughter of Robert Harison?
		Anno Domin 1601 Anno Regni dominæ Elizabethæ Reginæ quadragessimo tertio
Aprill	Buried	Widowe Saxtonn of . . . . . 5° die
	Baptysed	Thomas the sone of Jo: Outrã 10° die
Maie	Buried	Widowe Locksmyth of Swinton 16° die
	Baptysed	Cisselie the daughter of Stephe Key 17° die
June	Baptysed	Thomas the sonne of Averye Wright of Newall 2° die
	Maried	William Armitage & Isabel Wainwright 4° die
	Baptysed	Williã the sonne of Williã Barowe of Swinto 9° die

1600

June	Baptysed	John the sonne of Nicholas Tindley 19° die
	Maried	Robert Markiall and Katharine Jonson of Swintō 22° die
	Baptysed	Richard the sonne of Thomas Booth 23 die
Julie	Baptysed	Williā the sonne of Williā Wilsonn 19° die
	Baptysed	Isabell the daughter of John Stable 26° die
	Buried	Elizabeth Rodes of Meltonn 27° die
August	Buried	George Jenkinsonn of Wath 3° die
	Baptysed	Peter the sonne Nicholas Staniland 9° die
	Buried	William Scorer of Wath 16° die
	Buried	John Wombwell of Wath 18° die
	Baptysed	Ann the daughter of John Heaward de Streete 30° die
September	Baptysed	John the sonne of Georg Jenkins of Wath 20 die
Octob^r	Buried	Ann the wief of John Robuck 3° die
	Married	Martin Sloswicke & Isabell Wombwell 8° die
	Married	John Cotton & Margaret Burfeet of Wentworth 11° die
	Baptysed	John the sonne of John Case the xviij^th of October
	Baptysed	Thomas the sonne of Nicholas Shawe xxiiij^th die
	Buried	Richard Cowꝑ of Wath 23° die
Novemb^r	Baptysed	Copley the sonne of Nicholas Hunt 1° die
	Baptysed	Elizabeth the daughter of John Mangall eodē die
	Baptysed	Elizabeth the daughter of Williā Coulbrand eodē die
	Maried	John Sharpe & Katharen ffrickley of Wath viij° die
	Baptysed	Andrewe sonne of Nicholas Mallinson of Wath eodē die
	Baptysed	Marie the daughter of John Roberts of Wath eodē die
	Baptysed	John the sonne of John Tompsonn of Wath eode die
	Maried	Richard Hearinge & Elizabeth Beard 17 die
	Baptysed	John the sonne of Richard Beckett 22 die
	Baptysed	W^m the sonne of Wm Kitchynman eodē die
	Buried	Anthonie Tottingtō of Hoiland 24° die
	Maried	Thomas Headiley & Elizabeth Waynwright eodē die
Decemb^r	Buried	Richard the sonne of Thomas Mallinson 3° die
	Baptysed	Elizabeth the daughter of John Hansonn eodē die
	Buried	a poore beggar who died at the Rodes 24° die
	Baptysed	Alis the daughter of John Peele 3° die
Januarie	Buryed	An infant of Wm Cottom? base gott unbapt 2° die
	Maried	Georg ffoulstō & Katheren Burkes 24° die
ffebruarie	Maried	John Robucke & Margret Blome 2° day
	Baptysed	Elizabeth the daughter of Thomas Wade 4° die Januarij
	Buried	the wyfe of Thomas Wade eodē die
	Baptysed	Elizabeth the daughter of Thomas mallinsō
March	Buried	the said Elizabeth mallinsō 8° die

1600		
March	Buried	Elizabeth the wief of Richard Hearinge 20° die
	Buried	*Margret* the daughter of John Bullye 21 die
Marche	Maried	William Armitage and Dorithie Staniland 13° die
1603-4	Maried	Peter Mallinsom and Dorityhe Elome de Wombwell 12° die
	Maried	Thomas Hudsonn and Alis Darlie de Bramptō eodē die
	Maried	Richard Beardshall of Rawmarshe and Jennett Jessopp 19 die
	Maried	Henrie Tylley and Jennett Nowell de Cowley lane 20° die
	Baptysed	Margrett the daughter Wiłłm Coulbrand 22 die
	Buried	Widowe Rodes of Melton vicesimo tertio die
March	Bapt	Richard the sonne of Thomas Cartwright 3° die
	Buried	the wife of John Dauson of Swinton 14° die
	Buried	Robert the sonne of John Colton quarto die
	Baptysed	Nicho: the son of Wiłłm Wilsō xxviij° die
	Baptysed	Hester the daughter of Nicho : Mallinsō eodē die
	Buried	Richard Ellis eođ die
Anno Domin 1604 in anno secundo Jacobi Regis nostri et &c.		
April	Baptysed	Alis the daughter of Tho Hudsō 17° die
	Buried	the wief Thomas Boultō xxvj^{to} die
	Buried	the wife of John Smalchar eođ die
	Buried	Ann the wief of Jo : Tylley xxvij^{to} die
	Baptysed	Robt the sonne of Jo Smalchar xxv° die
	Buried	the sayd Robte Smalcher xxvjth die
	Buried	John Mabson the ixth of Aprill
Maie	Baptysed	Wiłm the sonne of Geo Hoyland 6° die
	Baptysed	Tho : the sonne of Robte Thackroe 13 die
June	Baptysed	John the sonne of Williā Barrowe of Swintō 3 die
Julie	Baptysed	Richard & Elizabeth the sonne & daughter of Nicholas Tylney of Sandigate
	Buried	Widowe Lowtō of Bramptō the xxth day
August	Buried	Richard Byrkes of Wath 2 die
	Baptysed	John the sonne of James Battersby Smyth of Meltō 5 die
September	Baptysed	Hester the daughter of Nicholas Tompsō 7mo die
	Baptysed	Isabell the daughter of John ffyrth eodē die
	Baptysed	Georg the sonne of Alis Hudson base gott eodē die
October	Maried	Lancelott Briges & Marie Lawtoun septimo die
	Bapt	Godfray the sonne of Richard Brydley 10mo die
	Buried	Infans dicti Richardi Brydley unbaptyzed eodē die
	Maried	Richard Goodale & Katherine Tylney the 28th die
	Maried	John Rodes & Ellen Armsteed 21 die
November	Buried	John the sonne of John Sykes the 3° die
	Baptysed	Grace the Daughter of Richard Beardson 4°
	Baptysed	. . . . . the daughter of John Tompsō of Wath eode die
	Buried	Katharē the wief of Wiłłm Bawdisō ? 9no die

1604

November Buried Wiłłm Tompsō of Wath 23mo
Buried Nicholas Tayler the 31?
December Buried Wiłłm the sonne of Georg Hoyland ij die
Buried John the sonne of William Wilsō the xth
Buried Thomas the sonne of Martin Sloswick 23
Januarie Buried Wiłłm the sonne of Wm Barowe the sixt̃ day
Buried Wiltm the sonne of . . . . Elisonn of Rodes December . . . .
Buried Alis the wief of Thomas Watsonn 21 die
Baptysed Nicolas the sonne of Nicholas Hunt 23 $Decemb^{r}$
Baptysed Wiłłm the sonne of John ffitness 23 die?
ffebruarie Infans of Raphe Hewode y^{e} 23 die
Married Thomas Wattson & Zuzan Ellice 3 die
Married Thomas Boulton & Margrett Rogers 5to die
March Baptysed Thomas the soñe of Margett Tylney bas got 7° die
Baptysed Hester the daughter of Peter Taylier 2 die
Buried Ales the wiefe of Alexand. Wood 12 die
Anno tertio Regni Dom. nostri Jacobi Regis et &c.
Anno Dom. 1605
Aprill Buried Elizabeth Shyers of Newall the forth day
Baptysed Tho: the sonne of Ric Brooke of Swĩto 21th day
Baptysed Edward the soñe of a poore man eodē die
Maie Baptysed Georgie the soñe of Williā Dysō secundo die
Baptysed Joseph the sonne Thomas Boultō nono die
Maried John Dawsō & Ellin Settle duodecimo die
June Baptysed Ann the daughter of John Sykes primo die
Buried Vid Hawksworth of Wath sextō die
Baptysed Peter the sonne of Williā Kytchinmā 29th die
Julie Baptysed Ann the daughter of John Taylier septimo die
Buried Katheren the wief of Rich Goodale nono die
Baptysed Dorythie daughter of Laurence Wade 28° die
August Baptysed Isabell the daughter of Elome y^{e} masō 3° die
Baptysed John the sonne of Nicholas Stanîland 4° die
Baptysed Richard the sone of Rich. Pearsō de meltō 11 die
Baptysed Ann the daught. of John Sharpe eodē die
$Septemb^{r}$ Baptysed Cibill the daughter of John Dawsō 23 die
Maried Stephe Shawe & Grace Hansō 30 die
$Octob^{r}$ Buried Willia Bynnye & Marie Whiteley secundo die
Buried Ann ffaukes the daughter of Tho ffaukes tertio die
Buried Margrett the daughter of Nicho Staniland 8vo die
Baptysed Hester the daughter of Wiłłm Armitage 14 die
Baptysed Margrett the daughter of Tho Barowclughe 21 die
Maried Tho: Mallinsō & Marie Watsō 29no die
Maried ffrancis Eatō & Alis Woode? 30th die
$Novemb^{r}$ Baptysed . . . . of Rich Elisō of Rodes tertio die

1604.

Memorandum that Ann the daughter of John Wharō of West Melto was xv^{th} yeares of age uppo Saint Luke Day in Anno p'dict̃

1605

Willm the sonne of the sonne of the sayd John Wharo was xiij[th] yeares of age the third Sonday in Lent in anno p'dicto

John the sonne of John Wharo abovsaid was of the age of xi[th] yeares of age the feast of Saint Luke in anno p'dicto

Margrett the daughter of the sayd John Wharō was of the aige of eight uppo the feast day of the purificatiō of the virgin Marie in anno p'dict

Memorandu that John Wharō of Westmeltō w[th]in the p'ishe of Wath yeomān was lycensed and authorised by us whose names are hareunto annexed to sett a stall or seat for himselfe and ffamilie in the northsyde of the Church of the Church of Wath under and right before the pulpitt in the yeare of our Lord God 1603 and their to continewe w[th]out disturbance of any p'son in payne of Ecclesiasticall censure.

By us
John Bearde Vicar of Wath
Nicholas Staniland
Robert Watsō — Church
Richard Boore — Wardens
Edmund Sawtrie
Leonard Wilcocks

m[d] that Robtē Watson of Wath was licensed and authorised a place for himself to sit in betwixt Mr. Baxter Stale and the pulpitt the xxvij[th] of Aprill Anno Dnī 1606 by us.

John Bearde, Vicar of Wath
Nicholas Thornhill gen
Raulphe Pearson
Churchwardens

	Married	John Wade & Marie Baxter 13[mo] die
	Baptysed	Willm the sonne of Georg Hoyland eodē die
	Baptysed	Josephe the sonne of John Cottō decimo nono die
	Baptysed	. . . . the daughter of . . . Hurst eodē die
Decembr	Buried	Alexander Wood of Brampto primo die Decembris
	Baptysed	George the sonne of Rich. Mabsō xvi[mo] die
	Baptysed	Sarah the Daughter of Richard Brydley xvii[th] die
	Baptysed	Hester the daughter of Christopher Hurst iiij[th] die
Januarie	Buried	John Hánsō of Wath the third day
	Buried	the wief of Richard Bower secundo die
	Buried	Margrett the wief of Wm Hepworth 3° Decembris
	Married	Robt Burkes and Dorothe Wood 4° Novembris
	Baptysed	Margrett the daughter of Nicho Tylney 26to die
	Baptysed	Elizabeth the daughter of Robert Walker eodē die
	Buried	the wief of Robert Mallinsō 30[mo] die
	Baptysed	Annes? his daughter eode die
ffebruarie	Married	Edmund Sidgwick and Agnes Trivye secundo die
	Baptysed	. . . the sonne of . . . lyinge at Clap : 2 die
	Baptysed	George the sonne of Willia Bynnye basegott sexto
	Buried	the wife of Willm Hinchliffe of Meltō nono die

1605

Marche	Buried	Richard Mabsonn of Wath the tenthe day
	Buried	an infant of Barracloughes of newall nono die
	Buried	John Wade of Meltō decimo die
	Baptysed	Henrie the sonne of Thomas Brome 9no die
	Baptysed	Elizabeth the daughter of ffrances Casse eodē
	Baptysed	Nicholas the sone of John Robuck of Wath 16to die
	Baptysed	Grace the daughter of Tho : Mariott 27 die
	Baptysed	Elizabeth daughter of Martin Sloswicke 19to day

March 25 1606 In Anno Regni Dom. Jacobi Regis nostri Angliæ quarto Scotiæ vero 39 no

	Buried	Williā Absonn of Swintō vicessimo octavo die
Aprill	Buried	Nicholas the sonne of Nicholas Tylney nono die
	Baptysed	Ann the daughter of Raph Hewoode 10mo die
	Maried	John Dobson and Elizabeth Dickinson xxijo die
Maiœ	Baptysed	Margrett the daughter of Nicholas Saxton sexto die
	Maried	Robt Chyld and Agnes Kyrkbie xjmo die
	Maried	John Byrkes & Margrett ffostard eodē die
	Maried	Edward Ellis & Isabell Ley ? decimo octavo die
June	Maried	Williā Chanye ? & vid Coultes the first daye
	Maried	Williā Hepworth and Margrett Watsō 3 die
	Buried	Paule the nylner quarto die
	Married	Robt Mallinsō and Elizabeth Hubburges eodē die
	Buried	vid Wombwell vicessimo octavo die
	Baptysed	Grace the daughter of Williā Coulbrand 8vo die
	Buried	vid Wade of Meltō decimo die
	Baptysed	Alis the daughter of Jo Shawe 22th daye
	Baptysed	Marie the daughter of Rich Wyldsmyth ? 24th die
	Buried	Robt the sonne of Nicho Staniland eodē die
Julie	Bapt	. . . . the sonne of John ffyrth of Melton 9no die
	Baptysed	Thomas the sonne of Tho : Wilkinsō 26to die
	Maried	Nicholas Wade & Margrett Ward eodē die
August	Buried	Bryan ffostard tertio die
	Baptysed	Dorothye the daughter of Henrye Hill 24to die
	Baptysed	Thomas the sonne of John Addye decimo die
	Maried	. . . . . Briges & Ann ffyrth septimo die
	Maried	Robt Cooke & Dorithe Robinsō eodē die
	Baptysed	Margarett the daughter of John Case eodē die
	Baptysed	Elizabeth the daughter of Thomas Booth 24to die
	Buried	Willm the sonne of John Addye the elder 23tio die
	Baptysed	Elizabeth the daughter of Nicho : Tompsō 30mo die
Octobr	Buried	Infans of Dinnis ffrend primo die
	Baptysed	Marie the daughter of William Binnye 4to die
	Maried	Robt Heptō & Dorothie Wade qūito die
	Baptysed	ffrauncis the sonne of John Mr Daylies mylner 5 die
	Married	Willm Dawson & Margrett Tylney 19no die
	Baptysed	Marie the daughter of Tho : Broome gent 29no die
November	Baptysed	Jane the daughter of John Butterworth, Egypt, primo die

1606

	Baptysed	Alis the daughter of Thomas Menlove nono die
	Baptysed	Dorothye the daughter of John Broome eodē die
	Buried	Robt̄t the sonne of Richard Walker of Newall xij die
	Baptysed	Hester the daughter of Robert Pearsō eodē die
	Baptysed	Augnes the daughter of John Beard, vicar 17mo die
December	Maried	William Maykyne and Ann Hogley primo die
	Buried	Marie the daughter of Mr Broome de Brampto 15 die
	Buried	vid. Swallowe de Howber decimo septimo die
	Buried	Elizabeth the daughter of Nicholas Tompsō xxiiij^to^ die
	Buried	Margerie the spinner of Brampto xxvj^to^ die
Januarie	Buried	Raph Hodgson of Wath the 17th day
	Baptysed	Marie the daughter of Roger ffixbie 18 die
	Baptysed	John the sonne of Elome eodē die
	Baptysed	Jaune the daughter of John ffostard daughter base 22 die Decembris
	Buried	Dorithie the wief of John Collinsō 25to die
Februarie	Baptysed	John the sonne of Raphe Cuttes of Swintō primo die
	Baptysed	Thomas the sonne of Richard Beckett eodē die
	Buried	Ann the daughter of Robert Mallinsō secundo die
	Buried	Marie the daughter of Tho: Boultō sexto die
	Buried	John the sonne of Raphe Cuttes 15to die
March	Buried	Elizabeth Diconsō the second day
	Buried	John Pettye the Ancient Hunter tertio die
	Baptysed	Hester the daughter of John Taylier octavo die
	Baptysed	Cicilie the daughter of Richard Tottingtō eodē die
	Baptysed	Elizabeth the daughter of Brya ffostard eodē die
	Baptysed	Jaan the daughter of Ellis de Rodes xxiij^to^ die
	Buried	Marmaduke Medley eodē die
	Buried	. . . . the sonne of Tho: Wood de Swintō 24to die
		March 25th 1607 in anno Regni Dom nostri Jacobi Regis quinto Scotiœ xlmo
Aprill	Buried	Infans Roberti Neiler secundo die
	Baptysed	Betterise the daughter of Robt̄ Watsonne 10mo die
	Baptysed	Ann the daughter of Williā Armitage 19no die
	Baptysed	John the sonne of Williā Croyser eodē die
	Baptysed	Ann the daughter of Rich: Beardsall the 22th daye
Maie	Baptysed	Ann the daughter of John ffitnesse decimo die
	Baptysed	Lewes the sonne of John Cottō 28vo die
	Baptysed	Nicholas the sonne of Peter Taylier eodē die
	Baptysed	Cibill the daughter of Edmund Sidgwicke 26to
	Baptysed	Agnes the daughter of Stevē Kay eodē die
	Buried	John Stable of Melto eodem die
June	Maried	Thomas Rutter & Jane Shawe secundo die
	Baptysed	George the sonne of Nicholas Shawe the xij^th^ day
	Buried	Peter Mallinsō of Wath the twenteth day
	Buried	Margrett the wief of Rich. Robucke 23th die
	Buried	Lewis the sonne of John Cottō the 23th die

1606

Julie	Baptysed	Symō the sonne of Isabell Cattlin base gott 28th die
	Buried	an infant of John Jepsō unbap: primo die
	Baptysed	Williā the sonne of Tho: Brome octavo die
	Buried	. . . . . the wief of . . . . . Joeis (? Joyes) decimo septo die
	Baptysed	Marie the daughter of Williā Hepworth 25to die
August	Baptysed	Trothe the daughter of Thomas Absō 26to die
Septebr.	Baptysed	Thomas the sonne of Nicho: Wade sexto die
	Baptysed	Hester the daughter of Edward Darly 12mo die
	Buried	Jo: Beamonte kyld in Addy Colepitt eodē die
	Buried	Infans Robert Hoptō decimo septo die
	Buried	Infans Isabell Clephā alls Brooke 24to die
	Baptysed	Anthonie the sonne of John Sawtrie 25to die
	Maried	Nicho: ffrankishe & Alis . . . . sexto die
October	Baptysed	Richard the sonne of ffrancis Kettlewell 7mo die
	Buried	Ann Jessopp of Wath widdowe the 9th day
	Baptysed	John the sonne of John Barowclughe 8vo die
	Baptysed	Richard the sonne of Williā Maykyne the 25th die
	Baptysed	Margrett the daughter of Thomas Mallinso 25 die
	Buried	Thomas the sone of Rich: Beckett the xxvijth day
Novembr	Buried	Anthony the sonne of John Sawtrie primo die
	Baptysed	Thomas the sonne of Nicholas Hunt quīto die
	Baptysed	Dorithye the daughter of John Byrkes 14to die
	Baptysed	Margrett & Mary the daughters of Roger Martin 18 die
	Baptysed	Agnes the daughter of Robert Thackroe xxijdo die
December	Buried	Williā Colcke a laborer the 9th day
	Buried	Marie the daughter of Williā Hepworth 18th day
Januarie	Buried	Ann the daughter of Raph Hewood xvito die
	Buried	Ann Bandensō of Swinton 17mo die
	Buried	Vid Chyld of Wath vicessimo quarto die
ffebruarie	Buried	Richard Thackroe of Swintō Septimo die
	Buried	Joseph the sonne of John Cotton 13tio die
	Buried	Dīones the wief of Robt Hearinge 16to die
	Buried	Marie the wief of Launclot Brigges 17mo die
Marche	Buried	Elizabeth ye daughter of Ed ffostard secundo die
	Buried	John son of Nicholas Tylney the 4th March, 1607
	Buried	Tho: the sonne of Nicho Hunt eodē die
	Baptysed	Hester the daughter of Williā Wilsō 11 die
	Baptysed	Marie the daughter of Martin Sloswicke 20mo die

The Register Booke of Wath for this yeare 1608.

Aprill	Baptysed	Thomas the sonne of Tho: Waddy the 27th day
	Buried	Thomas Watsō of Melton eodē die
	Buried	Infans Johis Sharpp the xxviijth die
	Baptysed	Nicho: the sonne of Nicholas Tompsō 18mo die
	Baptysed	Hester the daughter of Tho: ffaukes eodē die
	Buried	Isabell the wief of Williā ffox decimo sexto die

1608

Aprill	Baptysed	Alis the daughter of Rich. Goodale 17mo die
	Buried	. . . the sonne of Williã Burton 29no die
	Baptysed	Margrett the daughter of Tho : Broome gent 26th day
Maiœ	Baptysed	Edward the sonne of John ffirth primo die
	Baptysed	Thomas the sonne of George Hoyland 5to die
	Baptysed	Nicho : the sonne of Jo : Dawsõ eodẽ die
	Baptysed	Richard the son of ffraunces Eatõ eodẽ
	Buried	Williã the sonne of Nicholas ffrankishe 6to die
	Buried	James the sonne of Roger Martin of Howber 29no die
June	Baptysed	Margrett the daughter of Alexander Wood 5to die
	Baptysed	. . . the . . . of Richard Burtõ 25to die
Julie	Buried	the sayd . . . Burtõ the first of Julie
	Baptysed	Thomas the sonne of Tho : Hudson 18th die
August	Bapt.	John the sonne of Williã Dawsõ 3tio die
	Baptysed	Elizabeth the daughter of Jo : Sikes 10to die
October	Baptysed	Thomas the sonne of John Cottõ primo die
	Buried	the sayd Thomas Cotton secundo die
	Maried	Richard Walker & Alis Browne quarto die
	Baptysed	John the sonne of John Robucke nono die
	Buried	Thomas Lee & Marie Hansonn 13th of Septẽber
	Baptysed	Rosomond & Katherẽ the daughters of a begger 16 die
	Buried	Vid Beckett of Meltõ the 23th daye
	Baptysed	Agnes the daughter of Williã Coulbrand eodẽ die
	Baptysed	Ann the daughter Nicho : Saxtõ the 16th day
	Buried	Richard Brydley of Swinto the 24th day
November	Maried	Anthonie Allen & Elizabeth Steele 30th die
	Maried	Steven Eller & Ann Stevenson eodẽ die
	Maried	Roger Stable & vid. Tingle 22th die
	Baptysed	Elizabeth the daughter Xp̃er Hurst 28 die
December	Baptysed	ffayth the daughter of Rich : Wyldsmyth primo die
	Baptysed	Ann the daughter of Williã Dyson quarto die
	Maried	Nicholas Staniland & ffayth Rookbie 13to die
	Buried	Infans of Anthonie Alin unbapt 18th die
	Buried	vid Ellis de Wheele 19th die
	Baptysed	ffayth the daughter of Thomas Brome 25 die
	Baptysed	Alis the daughter of Thomas Mariott eode die
	Baptized	Elizabeth the daughter of Alis Hudsõ base of T.B. 22 die
		Robart the sonne of Robt Mallinsõ of Melton 29 die
	Baptized	Richard the soñe of John Byrks eodẽ die
	. . . . .	the daughter of Tho : Wilkinson eodẽ die
ffebruary	Bapt	ffayth the *(cut off)*
	Maried	Tho : Cleypaun & Elizabeth Key predict
	Maried	Williã Beaumonte & Marie ffoulds the fyfte day
	Baptysed	Alis the daughter of Williã Hepworth 19th die
	Buried	Infans Richardi Beckett unbap. 26th die
March	Baptysed	John the sonne of Williã Walker of Meltõ quinto die
	Buried	Thomas the sonne of James Baudisõ frõ Leo. Wilcockes 16th die

The Register booke of Wath this yeare of our Lord God 1609.

	Baptysed	Williã the sonne of ffrancis Kettlewell vicesimo sexto die
	Baptysed	Elizabeth the daughter of John Shawe eodẽ die
	Buried	Williã Watsonn of Meltõ the 29th of March
Aprill	Baptysed	Richard the sonne of Richard Brouke of Swynton 2 die
	Baptysed	Ann the daughter of Williã Beamont eodẽ die
	Buried	Jennett the wief of Rich: Beardshawe xxviij^{mo} die
	Baptysed	Thomas the sonne of Thomas Brome, gent, 30mo die
	Baptysed	Joan the daughter of John Jepsõ eodẽ die
Maie	Buried	Richard the wief of Thomas Hudsonn Senior 16to die
	Baptysed	. . . . the . . . . of . . . . Hurst April 15th die
	Baptysed	. . . . the sonne of John Barowclughe eodẽ die
	Buried	John Robucke of Wath the xxiiijth day
	Buried	Elizabeth the daughter of Xp̃or Hurst the 25th die
	Buried	Williã Savadge the xxvijth day
	Baptysed	Williã the sonne of Edmund Sidgwicke 5to day
	Baytyzed	. . . . the . . . . of Thomas Diconsonn the 7th day
	Maried	Richard Crosley & Widdowe Hodson eodem die
June	Baptised	Richard the sonne of John Addy Junio^{r} quarto die
	Baptysed	Nicho: the sonne of Williã Maykyn eodẽ die
	Baptysed	. . . . . the sonne of Rob̄t Hoptõ the 29 day
July	Baptysed	. . . . . the daughter of Nicho: ffrankishe nono die
	Bapt	Thomas the sonne of John Beard, vicar, the 18th day
August	Bapt	Henry the sonne of Nicholas Hunt sexto die
	Bapt	John the sonne of John Sharpe eodẽ die
	Baptysed	John the sonne of Rob̄t Pearsonn vicessimo die
	Married	John Taylier and Ann Lowtoun eodẽ die
Septeb^{r}	Baptysed	Rich the sonne of Bryam ffostard the third day
	Baptysed	Thomas son of Tho. Booth the 3 day
	Bap:	Ann the sonne (*sic*) of Richard Browne the tenth day
October	Baptysed	Williã the sonne the sonne of Williã Croyser 10 day
Novemb^{r}	Married	Thomas Wilcockes & Ann Wharo the ffyft day
	Baptysed	George the sonne of John Brooke eodẽ die
	Burried	Marie the daughter of Roger Martin 11 die
	Baptysed	Isabell the daughter of Nicho: Wade 12mo die
	Bapt	Katherẽ the daughter of John Ellisõ eod̄ die
	Married	Tho: Wright and Margaret Stable vicessimo sexto die
	Baptysed	ffayth the daughter of Thomas Absoun eod̄ die
Decembr	Baptysed	Elizabeth the daughter of Nicho: Staniland xiij die
	Baptysed	Hester the daughter of Tho: Lee eodẽ die
Jan:	Baptysed	Williã the sonne of Williã Armitage 17 daye

1609 ffeb:	Buried	Alis the daughter of Thomas Marriott xix^{no} ? die
	Baptysed	Ann the daughter of Robt Greaves a tinker 17 die
	Bur^{d}	Infans Lancelot Brigg unbapt eodē die
	Maried	Edward Crosland and Lucy Thwaytes quinto die
	Bur	Dorythye the daughter of John Byrkes 25to die
	Bapt	Margrett the daughter of Roger ffixby eodē die
March	Buried	williā wainwright de abdy octavo die
	Bur	. . . . . the wief of . . . . . a tinker at Meltō 12mo die
	Bur^{d}	Henry the sonne of Henry Sayvell of Copley fro Meltō hall 13 die
	Bapt	Urseley the daughter of John ffitnesse the 18th die
	Bapt	Rich̄ the sonne of Richard Tottingtō eodē die
	Bapt	Hester the daughter of Anthony Allen 25th die
	Bapt	Jane the daughter of vid̄ Tompson the 23th die
	Baptysed	Anne the daughter of John Tompsonn eodē day

The Regester booke for this yeare nexte cominge beinge 1610 for Wath. fo. 11.

Aprill	Buried	Peter Taylier of Wath the sexteēth daye
	Bur^{d}	the wief of Raphe Briggs of Swintō the xth day
	Bur^{d}	Mary the wief of Thomas Mallinsō the 13th day
	Baptysed	Thomas the sonne of Ed: Crosland the 29th day
Maie	Buried	Ann Pickhaver of Swintō the third day
	Buried	Thom̄as Baxter the elder, gent, the 19th die
	Baptysed	Nicho: the sonne Georg Hopkinson 13th die
	Baptysed	Idithe the daughter of Raph Cuttes primo die
June	Buried	Ann Staniland vid̄ the sexteenth day
Julie	Baptysed	John the sonne of Ann Settle base gott by Thomas Maykyne 29 die
	Buried	James Ramsden of Swintō ultimo die
	Buried	Infans Richardi Walker unbapt tricessimo die
August	Baptysed	ffayth the daughter of Edward Ellis 28th die
Sept.	Bapt	Ann the daughter of Martin Sloswick eodē die
	Bapt	Alis the daughter of John Sawtrie 22mo die
October	Maried	Robert Wiggin and Elizabeth Robinsō 28th die
	Maried	Richard Cuttes & Elizabeth Hepworth eodē die
John {	Maried	Henry wood & Alis Robinsō maie the sixt
Colebrand {	Maried	Peter Robinsō & Isabell Wade Julie 22th
	Buried	Raphe Pearson of Wath the xvth day
Novemb^{r}	Baptysed	Thomas the sonne of John Taylier the mason primo die
	Buried	Henry Tilley of Cowley Lane q̄uinto die
	Baptysed	Henry the sonne of Nicho: Tylney undecimo die
	Baptysed	Thomas the sonne of John ffyrth of melton quarto die
Decemb^{r}	Burried	Infans wil̄l̄mi Maykyne unbapt nono die
	Bapt	John the sonne of Williā Kitchinmā xvj^{mo} die

1610

Decembr Maried Anthony Stable & Ann Peate eodē die
Maried Williā Bodingō & Jennett ffreere secundo die
Buried Williā Hinchliffe of melton vicesimo tertio
Buried Margrett the wief of John Addy thelder 24° die
Buried Isabell the wief of Raph Hodgso vid xxvjto die
Janu Buried Elizabeth woodward of wath quinto die
Buried Isabell Maykyne of Wath widdowe octavo die
Baptysed Williā the sonne of Williā Brome xiijth die
Maried Edward ffostard & mary woode eode die
Buried Alis Peate wyfe of Jobb Peate xvth daie
Baptysed Marie the daughter of Williā dawson vicessimo die
Buried Infans Thomas Hudson unbapt vicessimo Sept die
February Bapt Richard the sonne of Elizabeth Mallinsō base gott tertio die
Buried Marie the daughter of Williā dawson sexto die
Bapt Richard the sonne of Pearse maun the xxvth day
Marche Bapt Alis the doughter of Edmund Sedgwick the third day
Maried Thomas the sonne of John Bearde, vicar, undesimo die in anno primo et mense octavo et hebdomada secunda completa
Baptysed Alis the daughter of Richard Beckett primo die
Baptysed Thomas the sonne of John Cotton decimo septimo die
Buried Bridgett Hogley vicessimo quarto die

The Register booke of Wath for the yeare cominge beinge 1611, as followeth

Maie Maried Robert Yates and Ellin Smalchare quīto die
Baptysed Ann the daughter of Thomas Wilcockes vicessimo sexto die
Baptysed Margrett the daughter of pedler lyinge Hepworth? 30 die
Buried Margrette Casse? de Sheefheld vicessimo die
Buried Raphe Hewoods the Kyngs smyth vicessimo tertio die
Junij Baptysed Lanclott the son of Lanc Brigges primo die
Bur infans dicti Lancloti eodē die
Married Barnabie Hall & Elizabeth Browne ultimo maiœ
Julie Baptysed Williā the sonne Lawrence Hickes xxviijth die
Bur Infans Peter Robinsō vicessimo secundo die
Bur Isabell the wief of the said Peter Robinsō 25to die
August Baptysed John the sonne of Williā Cowlbrand de Swintō undecimo die
Baptysed Alex: the son of Robt Thackwray vicessimo quīto die
Bur Daurithy the wief of Nicholas Woode 28to die
Bapt Elizabeth the doughter of John Birkes ultimo Augusti

1611		
Sept	Buried	Ann the wief of John Jepson quinto die
	Buried	Peter Taylier of Wath octavo die
	Buried	Richard Wyldsmith of Bramptō eodē die
	Baptysed	Lancelot the sonne of Richard Wyldsmyth 22do die
Octob^r	Baptysed	Thomas the sonne of Richard Haghe vicessimo die
	Baptysed	Samuell & Thomas the sonnes Richard Burtō vicessimo quarto die
Novemb^r	Buried	Laurence Teale the 18th day
	Buried	Isabell the daughter of John ffyrth th 24th day
	Buried	a Tinker wch dyed at John Addy house 26th day
	Buried	Alis ffrankishe widdowe the 28th day
	Buried	Jennett the wiefe of James Peacocke eodem die
	Buried	vid. Hanson of Wath the last day
December	Married	Rob̄t Hogley and Ann Sisson the third day
	Baptysed	ffrannces the daughter of Nicholas Saxton octavo die
	Baptized	Rob̄te the sonne of John Dawson vicessimo secundo die
	Buried	John the base sonn of Tho: Maykyne by Ann Settle 23mo die
	Bapt	Thomas the sonne of Williā Hepworth vicessimo sexto die
Jan:	Baptysed	Williā the sonne of John Brome of Bramptō primo die
	Baptysed	ffayth the daughter of Jo: Barrowcloughe 12mo die
	Bur	the sayd ffayth ———— the 28th? day of Jan.
	Baptysed	Grace the daughter of John Addy Junior 19th day
	Bur.	Williā Hepworth of Swintō eodē die
	Bur	Betterice the wief of John Barrowclough eodē die
	Bur	Grace Addy the 23th day
February	Baptysed	Thomas Hurst de Bramptō secundo die
	Baptysed	Richard the sonne of Williā Dawsonn xvi^{th} die
	Maried	Edward . . . . . . and ffrances Watsō eodē die
	Baptysed	Dorithy the daughter of Richard Browne xxi^{th} die
	Buried	Richarde the sonne of John Beard, vicar, ultimo die et in anno quidem ætatis suœ
March	Baptysed	Nicholas the sonne of Stephen Kay of Meltō octavo die
	Buried	vid Ellisonn of the Wheele ultimo die

The Register booke of Wath for this yeare cominge being 1612 as followeth

Aprill	Baptysed	ffranncis the sonne of John Elison de Rodes vicessimo die
	Baptysed	Lanclott the sonne of Nicho: ffrankishe 27mo die
Maie	Bur.	Margerett the wief of John Addy the third daye
	Burried	a vid. of Swinton an Almes woman Ascentiō eve 16 die
	Buried	Ann the wief of Thomas Smyth x^{mo} die
	Bapt	Elizabeth the daughter of Burnabie Hall 21 die

1612		
June	Baptysed	Alis the daughter of Thomas Hudsonn 1mo die
	Baptysed	Margerie the daughter of Tho: Lee 14to die
Julie	Bapt	Margerie the daughter of Georg Hogley nono die
	Baptysed	John the sonne of Willia Maykyne decimo nono die
	Buried	Margerie the daughter of Georg Hogley tertio die augusti
	Baptysed	Williā the soñe of John Brooke vicessimo sexto die
	Bur.	Katharen Taylier widdowe wyfe of ould Peter eodē die
Auguste	Baptysed	John the sonne of John Sykes nono die
	Maried	John Byshopp and Ellin Staniland ultimo die
Septemb:	Bur.	Margrett the daughter of Williā Trivett primo die
	Bapt	Williā the sonne of Alexander Boy of Swintō xiij^th^ die
	Bapt	Georg the sonne of Williā Croyser eod die
	Bapt	Samuell the sonne of Anthony Stable xx^mo^ die
	Bur	Robt Hurst the xxix^th^ day
October	Bur	vid Sherwood of Melton primo die
	Bur	Infans of Rowland ffostard unbap quinto die
	Bur	Ann the wief of Edmund Sidgwicke xiij^th^ die
	Bur	Alis the daughter of the sayd Sidgwicke secundo septembris
	Bapt	Richard the sonne of Williā Bowlson xviij^mo^ die
	Baptysed	John the sonne of Henry Wood xxvij^mo^ die
	Baptysed	Williā the sonne of Williā Lynny eodē die
Novemb^r^	Baptysed	Elizabeth the daughter of Thomas Mariott primo die
	Bur	Isabell the wief of Dinnis ffearnes xvj^th^ die
Decēber	Bur	John Dobson of Meltō the xvi^th^ day
	Bur	Alis ffrance of Melton the sixt day
Janu.	Bur	Georg the sonne of Williā Croyser the third day
ffebruarie	Bur	Elizabethe wief of Edmund Sawtrie the third day
	Bur	Edmund Baconn of Wath the sixt day
	Bur	Robt Scales servant to Wm Coulbrand xxvj^to^ die
March	Bur	Infans Richardi Cuttes unbapt octavo die
1613	Baptysed	Elizabeth the daughter of John Byshop xxxi^o^ die
Aprill	Baptysed	William the sonne of John ffirthe xi^th^ day
	Bur	Elizabeth the daughter of John Byshopp xv^th^ day
	Bur	. . . . the sonne of John Brome the xvi^th^ day
	Bur	John Bearde vicar of Wathe the xxiij^th^ day
May	Bur	an Infante of John Jepson unbaptysed the vth day
October	Baptysed	Jasper the sonn of Nicholas Hunt the xviij^th^ day 1598

The Register booke of Wath upon Dearne continued by Thomas Benson, M^r^ of Artes, Student of Christchurch in Oxford and Vicar of Wath whoe was inducted the seconde of June, 1613

June	Buried	Edward Praunce	28
July	Buried	Richard Haulton	3

1613

July	Bur:	Robert Wood 8
	Bur:	Francis Tomson wyfe of Will: Tomson 12th
	Maried	John Helliwel & Alice Gessop 25
August	Buried	Alexander Wood 2
	Maried	Nicholas Baraclow & Alice Bury 15
	baptised	William Tottingeton ye sońe of Richard Tottingeton 24 of June
	baptised	Tho: Baraclow ye sońe of John Baraclow July 4
	baptised	Roger Waker ye sońe of Lyonel Waker August 29
	baptised	Isabel Wordsworth August 15
	bur:	John Tomson August 24
	bur:	Alice Mallison ye wyfe of Tho: Mallison August 25
	buried	Alice Burkes ye daughter of Richard Burkes Aug. 31
Septem:	bapt	John Addy ye sonne of John Addy 12
	bap	Stephen Brome ye sonne of William Brome 21
	bap:	Richard ye sonne of Nicolas Tomson 26
	buried	Rowland ffoster 30
Octo:	buried	Jenet wade widow 15
	bur:	Jenet ffixbee ye wyfe of Roger ffixbee 19
	baptis:	Jane ye daughter of Thom: Wilcoks 24
Novem	buried	Thomas Booth 10
	maried	Thomas Beale & Jane Hurst 14
Decembr	buried	John a childe ye sonne of John Addy 29
	buried	William Maykin 30
Jan.	buried	John ye sonne of Robert Porson 8
	buried	Richard ye sonne of William Maykin 12
	buried	John the sonne of John Sykes 25
ffeb.	buried	Anne Cutt widow 5
	buried	John Shaw 6
	maried	William Waker & Elsabeth Wood Jan. 30
	maried	Steven Barbar & Dorathie Burks ffeb 6
	buried	Thomas ye sonne of Thomas Benson Mr of Artes vicar of Wath February 18
	baptised	Thomas ye sonne of Roger Stable 13
	baptised	Alice ye daughter of Hugh Hurst 20
	baptised	Isabell ye daughter of Edward Wager 20
	buried	Anne ye wyfe of Edward Wager 27
	buried	Margett ye daughter of Thomas Baraclow 28
March	bur:	Robert Jubb of Swinton the first of Marche
	bur:	Isabell Wager ye daughter of Edward eodem die
	bap:	John ye sonne of John Burkes 6o
	burd	Elsabeth ye daughter of Lawncelot Briggs eodem die
	bur:	a male childe of Nicolas Tilney unbap 14
	bur:	Nicolas ye sonne of Nicholas Tilney 17
	bapt:	Alice Tomson ye daughter of John 20
	bapt:	Richard ye sonne of William Croyser eodem die
Anno 1614	bur	Richard ye sonne of John ffirth March 30
Aprill	buried	John Browne, clarke of Wath 3

1614		
Aprill	buried	Richard Becket 8
	buried	Richard Hage Swin 4
	Baptised	George the sonne of George Hogley Swinton 26
Maye	bur.	Lawrens Wade of Swinton primo die
	bur	Anthonie Woodward of Wath 5
	buried	Elisabeth Scales daughter to John Carr of colie lane suspected to have kild hir selfe 7
	baptised	Jane ye daughter of Tho Abson of Swin: } 15
	baptised	William ye sonne of vid. ffostard of Wath } 15
	bur	Thomas Mallinson of Brampton 19
	baptised	(*blank*)
	buried	Thomas Mallinson of Brampton 19 (*see above*)
June	baptised	John the sonne of Tho: Mariott 12
	buried	Roberte Suggdeane of Swinton 17
	bur	ffaith ye daughter of Tho Abson 24
July	baptised	Richard the sonne of Richard Burton 17
	baptised	Henry the sonne of Richard Dickisón, eodem die
	bur.	Elizabeth the wyfe of Edward Casse 13
	maried	Richard Burfett and widow Tomson 10
	bur.	Christopher Hoyland
Aug	bur.	Helen ye fostar daughter of Robt Marshall of Swin 5
	maried	Robt Beaumont & Elsabeth Newton 7
	maried	Tho: Coe & Alicie Chambers June 29
	bur	Will an infant of Vid ffostard Aug 29
	bap	Willim the sonne of John Jepson August 14
	bap:	William the sonne of Nicholas Shaw August 24
Sept.	Bur	Isabell the wife of Edwarde Ellis the vth day
	Bur	. . . . of John Cotton of Brampton the vith day
	Bur	an Infante of John Bishops unbapt the xiiijth day
	Bur	ffaithe the doughter of Edward Ellis the xvjth day
	Bur	Esther the doughter of Edward Ellis the xvijth day
October	Bur.	Nicholas the sonne of John Robucke the xiijth day
	Baptysed	Susan the doughter of Richard Browne xvith
	Bapt	Hester the daughter of Richard Hobson the viith die
	Baptysed	Bettrice a child basegott of Anne Beardsall wth one Robte eod die
	Married	Raulf Brigges and Ellin Hall the same day
	Bapt.	John the sonne of Richarde Savile of Brampton the xxth day
	Bur	Marie the daughter of Henrie Taylor, cler. ultimo die
Novemb	Bapt	Susanna Lettice the doughter of Thomas Benson M^{r} of Artes and Vicar of Wath the iijth day
	Bapt	Thomas the sonne of John ffitnes the vith day
	Bapt	Alice the daughter of Nicholas ffrankishe the xiith day
	Bur	M^{ns} Margrett the wife of Jasp Blithman esquire at Wentworth the xiiijth day of Nouember 1614
	Bur	Issabell the wife of John Wharome the xxth daye

1614

Novemb	Bur	Mris Aegor the xxjth daye
	Bur	Alice Wood widowe the xxiiijth daye
December	Bur	Roberte Oxleye the vith daye
	Bur	Nicholas ffrankishe the viijth daye
	Married	John Greene And Rosamond Heyworthe the xith daye
	Buryed	the 19 of December Ann Winke?
	bur	the 20 of December Johan Walker fil Mris Walker
Januarie	Bur	Susann the doughter of Richard Browne the xiijth day
	Bur	Willm the sonne of John Jepson the xvijth day
ffebr.	Baptysed	Elizabeth the doughter of Dorithie Smith base gott the ijth day
	Baptysed	Thomas the sonne of Michaell Bowser the vth day
	Baptysed	Henrie the sonne of Henrie Wood the xxiiijth daye
Marche	Buried	widow ffoster the first day of Marche
	Buried	Wm Wilkinson the eight day
	Baptysed	Thomas the sonne of Willm Bawdinson the xijth day
	Baptysed	Issabell the doughter of Alexander Boy eod die

The Register of Wath Church, beginninge March 25, 1615.

Aprill	Baptysed	ffaithe the doughter of Willim Armitage the first day
	Buried	the said ffaithe upon the xixth day of Aprill
	Buried	Wm Burton younger the xxjth day of April
	Baptysed	Thomas the sonne of Nicholas Saxton the vijth day
	Baptysed	Sibilla the doughter of John Brooke eod die
Mar	Baptysed	Katherin the doughter of Elizabeth Smith basegott the second day
	Baptysed	Thomas the sonne of John Tayler the vijth day of Maye
	Buried	George Bunny of Swinton the xxijth day
	Buried	Thomas the sonne of John Teyler the xxiijth day
	Buried	Elizabeth the wife of John Brooke the xxvth daye
	Baptysed	Richard the sonne of Richard Ellisson the xxixth daye
June	Bur.	John Elorne of Melton the xiijth day of June
	Bur	Jennett the wife of Andrewe Wilson the xvth day
	Bapt	Susan the doughter of Wm Hepworth the xxiiijth day
	Bur	Katherin the doughter of Elizabeth Smithe the same day
	Married	Thomas Joyes and Gennett Tillye the xxixth day
Julie	Baptysed	Grace the doughter of Wm Binny the second day
	Baptysed	Hester the doughter of Peter Robinson the xxxth day
August	Married	Thomas Dickinson and Anne Addye the xxvijth day
	Baptysed	Elizabeth the doughter of Edward Wager eod die
	Baptysed	Nicholas the sonne of Robte Beamonte eod die
September	Baptysed	Marie the doughter of John Baracloughe the xxiiijth day

1615

September Bapt. Anthonye the sonne of Anthonie Stable the xxv^th^ day

Bur William Kitchinman the same day

October Bur William Brome the xxviij^th^ of October 1615

November Nicholas sonne of Sr Harye Tayler, Deacon, baptised die primo

Baptysed ffrauncis the sonne of John Baxter of Abdie gen the xix^th^ day of November 1615

Baptysed Elizabeth the doughter of Christopher Hurst xxvi°

Marled John Scholey and Brigeatt Knutton the xxviij^th^

Maried Rich: Hudson and Dorithie Mallinson the xxvi^th^ daie

Decmb. Buried william Hall of Swinton the ix^th^ of December

Bur Thomas Claypam the xiiij^th^ daie

Married Rich: Radford & Elizabeth Hinde the xij^th^ day cū licentiā

Married Thomas Hanson & Joane Wade the last day of December cū lic

Jan: Baptysed Jasper the sonne of John Cotton the vij^th^ daie of Januarie

Baptysed Parsons the sone of Thomas Benson M^r^ of Artes and Vicar of Wath the xxv^th^ of Januarie 1615

Memorandum: That upon the 10th of June 1615 I Thomas ————Benson Mr Artes and Vicar of Wath upon Dearne did geive my free consent and assent somuch as in me did lye, That Henry Savile of ye same parish gentleman, should remove his stall or pew (for the more convenient hearin̄ge of divine service and sermons) from the Ladie Quier unto the uppend of the right hande of the south pte of the bodye of the same Church, next to . . . . his stall. In witnes wherof I have set to my hande the day and yere above written

By me Thomas Benson.

1615

ffebr. Baptysed Matthias the sonne of John Burkes the xxv^th^

Marche Bur Margrett the wife of Wm Croyser the first daie

Bur Elizabeth the wife of Barnabie Hall the xij^th^ daie

Bur Widowe Bawdinson the xiij^th^ daie

Baptysed Jane the daughter of Thomas Swallowe the xvij^th^ day

Bapt Ellin the suposed doughter of Tho: Maykin begotten of the bodey of Anne Settle the same daie wch childe, though shee were borne in Wath; yet was sent & was kept at Boulton; the sixt daye after shee was cristened: by a warrant from Sr Tho: Wentworth & Mr Rookebye; bycause the inhabitants of Wath did make it appeare to them; that the mother of ye sayd childe was borne at Boulton

Buried William Croyser of Wath the xxij^th^ daie

Bapt Elizabeth the doughter of Rich. Lee the xxiiij^th^

1616

The Register of Wath Church beginninge March 25 1616

Aprill	Baptysed	Thomas the sonne of ffrauncis Ellis in Brampton bierlaw the first day
	Married	John Brooke and Barnabie ffarnsworth the xvij^th^ daie
	Baptysed	Susanna the doughter of Robte ffoorde the xxi daie
	Bapt	Nicholas the sonne of John Greene the same daie
	Bapt	Thomas the sonne of Richard Browne the first daie
	Buried	the said Nicholas the xxiij^th^ of Aprill
Maie	Married	John Wilthorpe and Dorithie ffreeman primo die
	Baptysed	Susanna the daughter of John Addie the xxij^th^ daie
June	Baptysed	Richard the sonne suposed of Rich. Hobson base gotten of the bodey of Katherin Smith the iiij^th^ daie
	Buried	Margrett the wife of Thomas Wright the xxvj^th^ day of June
	Baptysed	Elizabeth the doughter of George Hogley the xxix^th^ day
Julie	Married	John Dyson and Jane Teale the vij^th^ of Julie
	Baptysed	Susanna the doughter of John Byshopp the xiiij^th^ of Julie
	Buried	John the sonne of Henry Wood the xxij^th^ day
August	Buried	Elizabeth the wife of Roberte Beaumonte the second daie
	Buried	Issabell the wife of Leonard Wilcockes the vij^th^ day
Septemb^r^	Baptysed	Thomas the sonne of ffrancis Addie primo die
	Buried	Jane the wife of Thomas Richardson Rainburgh tertio die
	Buried	the viij^th^ day Leonard Wilcockes of Swinton
October	Baptysed	Nicholas the sonne of Richard Hudson the xiij^th^ day
	Buried	Christoper Hurst the xvi^th^ day
	Baptysed	Elizabeth the doughter of Edwarde Ellis the xxv^th^ daie
Novembr	Baptysed	Thomas the sonne of Thomas Willcockes the iiij^th^ daie
	Baptysed	Marie the daughter of Humfrey Phessantte the same daie
	Buried	Willm Hodgson piper of Coley lane the vth daie of Novemb^r^
	Buried	Richarde Walker of newall the viij^th^ day
	Baptysed	Susannah the doughter of Nicholas Stanilande the xth daie
	Married	Frances Richardson & Bettrice Boothe the xvij^th^ daie
	Married	Willm Byngley and Grace Addie the xix^th^.
	Buried	. . . . the wife of Edwarde Hurste the same daye
	Married	Thomas Carr & Ales Hodgson the xxvj^th^ daie
	Buried	a poore man one Thomas Cliff the same day
December	Buried	Ales Battersby of Swinton the xix^th^ day
Januarie	Buried	Edwarde Ellis the vij^th^ day of Januarie

1616		
Januarie	Buried	Thomas Dickinson who dyed (as y^{t} pleased God) by the dampe of a coale pitt the xxvth daye
	Baptysed	Jane the daughter of John Baxter the xxxth day
ffeb^{r}	Buried	Jennett Slacke widowe the iiijth day of ffebruary
	Baptysed	Susanna the doughter of Richard Tottington the ixth daye
	Bapt	Barbary the daughter of John Brooke the same day
	Buried	Willm Binnye of Swinton the xiiijth daye
	Buried	Willm Oldfeilde the xvth daye
	Buried	Marye the wife of Roberte Watson the xviijth daie
	Buried	Issabell the wife of Wm Abson of Swinton the xxvth daie
Marche	Buried	Elizabeth Leache the seconde day
	Buried	Susan the doughter of Thomas Willkinson the vijth day
	Buried	Nicholas Wood of Wath the xvijth of Marche
Marche	Baptised	Willm the sonne of Thomas Rookeby, gen the xxth daie
1617.		
Aprill	Baptysed	ffrauncis the sonne of Richard Burton the xiijth day.
	Baptysed	W^{m} the sonne of Richard Cuttes the same daie
	Baptysed	Marye the daughter of John ffitness the xvth daie
	Buried	Roberte Watson of Wathe the xvith daie
	Buried	John Dyson the xxiijth daie
	Buried	Roger Eaton of Brampton the xxiiijth daye
	Buried	Issabell the wife of George Hoylande the xxviijth daie
	Buried	an Infante of Anne Scales unbaptised the xxixth day
Maye	Baptysed	Elizabeth the doughter of Roger Stable the ix^{t} day
	Baptysed	Richard the sonne of Henrie Wood the xith daye
	Buried	an infante of Edmonde Sidgwicke the xiiijth of Maie
	Buried	Jane the wife of John Dyson the xxiijth of Maye
June	Maried	Thomas Waterhouse and Marie Ellis the third day of June
	Bapt	Hester the doughter of John Grene the viijth daie
	Bapt	Elizabeth the doughter of Edward Arthure the xvth daie
	Maried	Tho: Maugham & Barbary Brashawe the xxiiijth daie
July	Buried	Thomas Baracloughe the xjth day
	Baptysed	Elisabeth doughter of Robte Englande the xiijth day
	Married	Alverey Wright & Marye Leake the xvth daie
	Buried	Wm Kitchinman the xxiijth day
August	Maried	Richard Mabson and Margery ffoorde the iijth day
	Baptised	Willm sonne of ffairburne Wilson 31 day
Septemb^{r}	Baptized	John son of Wm Bawdwinson 7 day
	Bur	the said John Bawdinson the xiijth day
	Bapt	Robte the suposed sonne of George Oven the 17th day
	Bapt	Dorithie the doughter of Wm Dawson the 23° daye
October	Baptysed	Ellin the doughter of Richarde Goodheire quinto die
	Baptysed	Elizabeth the doughter of Thomas Mangham eod die

1617

October	Baptysed	Thomas the sonne of Thomas Benson Mr. of Artes and vicare of Wath the xixth of October 1617
	Baptysed	Margrett the doughter of John Carr at Wentworth eod die
	Maried	George Wilcocke and Anne Dickinson the xxith day
	Married	Thomas Jackson & Margrett Watson the 26 Octob
November	Baptysed	Ales the doughter of Lancelott Brigges the second daie
	Buried	Margrett Maugham widowe the xxiijth daye
	Maried	Nicholas Bradforthe & Elizabeth Kay the xxvth day
Decemb	Married	Thomas Wright and Margrett Oldfeild the second day
	Married	Richard Elome & Prudence Pecke (or Peale) the ixth day
	Bur.	Dorithie daughter of Wm Dawson the xth day
	Baptysed	ffrauncis the doughter of James Durham the xiiijth day
January	Buried	Thomas Joyes the xijth of January
	Married	Roberte Scoleffeild and Margrett Hill the xxth day
	Buried	Marie the doughter of John ffirth the xxijth daie
	Buried	Jane Hurst widowe the same daie
ffebr.	Married	Barnabie Hall and Anne Watson the viith day
	Baptysed	John the sonne of Edwarde Wager the xxijth daye
	Baptysed	Wm the sonne of Richard Ellison the same day
	Buried	Edmonde Sawtrie the xxvjth daie
March	Baptysed	Hughe the sonne of Hughe Hurst the vith day of Marche
	Baptysed	ffrauncis the doughter of Richard Elome the xvth daie
	Buryed	Katherin Tomson the xxixth of Marche 1618

The Register of Wathe Church beginge the first of Aprill 1618

1618 Aprill	Baptysed	Marie the doughter of Wm Beamont the xijth day
Maie	Buried	Alverey Paycocke the vth daie
	Baptysed	Agnes the doughter of John Baraclough the tenth daie
	Baptysed	Marie the doughter of Barnaby Hall eod die
	Bur.	an Infant of Tho: Richardson unbaptysed the xvth daie
	Married	John Sugden & Elizabeth Thwaites cū licentia the xiijth day
	Baptysed	John the sonne of Anthony Stable the xxth daie
	Bur.	the wife of Richard Englande the xxiiijth daie
	Bur	Ales the doughter of Lancelott Brigges the xxvijth daie
June	Married	Mr Henrie Tolson and Mris Margrett Savile the xiiijth day
	Married	Thomas Hepworth & Margrett Hurst the xxviijth day

1618

June	Buried	Katherin the wife of Thomas wood the xxixth day
Julie	Married	Thomas Hargrave and Dorithie Senyar the vijth day
	Married	Tho: Cuttes & Mercie Hartley the xijth daie
	Baptysed	Robertē the sonne of Richard Hudson the xixth daye
	Married	Geo Owen (Oven) and Alice Pearson the xxijth day
	Buried	Edwarde Hurste of Coley Lane the xxvjth daie
	Married	Humfrey Brammall & Margrett Ellis the xxvijth daie
1618		
August	Baptysed	Willm the sonne of Roberte ffoorde the second daie
	Baptysed	Nicholas the sone of Rich: Mabson the ixth daie
	Buried	Thomas Baxter of Abdie, gen. the xvijth daie
	Bur.	Nicholas the sonne of Rich: Mabson the xviijth daie
	Bur.	Marie the doughter of John ffitness the xixth daie
	Bur.	. . . . the wife of John Briers the xxxth daie
September	Bapt	Margrett the doughter of Thomas Cuttes the vith daie
	Bur	a poore womans child that died at Henry Hills the vijth daie
	Bapt	W^{m} the sonne of John Addie the xiijth daie
	Married	Alex: ffoster & ffelix Webster the xxth daie
	Baptysed	W^{m} the sonne of George Wade the same daie
	Buried	Thomas Watson the xxixth day
October	Baptysed	W^{m} the sonne of Robte Thackwray the second day
	Bur.	the said W^{m} the third daie
	Baptysed	Elizabeth the doughter of Peter Robinson xith daie
	Baptysed	Thomas the sonne of John Baxter the xviijth daie
	Bapt	W^{m} the sonne of John Cotton the same daie
	Married	Nich: Wood & Marie ffrannce the same daie
	Buried	the *wiffe* of John Sharpe the xxiijth daie of October
November	Baptysed	Anne the doughter of Wm Bawdinson the xvth daie
	Baptysed	Thomas the sonne of Richard Nighingale the xxijth
	Married	Richard Steade & Elizabeth Abson the xxiiijth daie
December	Baptysed	Henrie the sonne of Wm Hepworth the xiijth daye
	Buried	Issebell ffoxe the xiijth daie
January	Baptysed	Thomas the sonne of Thomas Hepworth the xth daie
	Buried	William Rogerson of Howber side the xvth daie
ffebr.	Baptysed	Elizabeth the doughter of Robte Beamont secundo die
	Buried	Lawrence Tottington the iiijth daie
	Buried	Robte fforde the vijth daie
	Buried	Ellin Marriott the sixth? daie
	Baptysed	Margrett the doughter of Rich Lee the xixth day
	Buried	Dorithie the doughter of Richard Goodall the xxijth
Marche	Buried	. . . . the wife of Richard Eller the vth day
	Buried	. . . . the wife of Michaell Stringer the xijth day
	Baptysed	John the soñe of John Jepson the xixth day
	Baptysed	Thomas the sone of Tho: Mangall eođ die
	Bur	Ursleye the doughter of John ffittnes the xxith day
	Bur	Thomas Smith the xxvth daie of Marche
	Bur.	John the sonne of John Jepson the same daie

1619

The Register of Wathe Church from the xxvth daie of Marche 1619

	Bur.	John the sonne of Anthony Stable the xxixth day
Aprill	Buried	Willm the sonne of widow Hoylande the xth day
	Married	Wm Trivett & Ellenor Harrison the xith day
	Baptised	John the sonne of Sr Henry Tayler eod die xith Apr.
	Bur	. . . . the doughter of Alex Boy the xijth day
	Bur	Barbary the doughter of John Brooke the xiiijth day
	Baptysed	ffaithe the doughter of George Oven 28°
Maie	Baptysed	Anne the doughter of Roger Stable the ixth daie
	Married	John Carr and Katherine Wilde the xxvth daie
June	Married	Wm Pearson and Elizabeth ffoorde the vith daie
	Baptysed	Jane the doughter of Launcelott Brigges the xiijth daie
	Buried	Margrett doughter of Rich Lee the 24° day
	Baptysed	Hester the doughter of Henry Tolson gen the xxvijth of June
Julie	Buried	Rosamond the wife of Roberte Haukroyd the first daie
	Buried	Richard Harrison a stranger that died at Sr Henrie Taylers the third daye
	Baptysed	Elizabeth doughter of Wm Dawson the iiijth day
	Baptysed	Elizabeth doughter of Richard Mabson the vith daie
	Baptysed	Anne the doughter of Thomas Marriott the 18
	Married	Richard Eller & Margrett Greene the xxth
	Bur	Anne the doughter of Roger Stable the xxvijth
	Bapt	John son of ffrancis Addye the 25th day
August	Buried	an Infant of Tho: Baxter of Swinton the ixth day
	Bapt	William the sonne of Wm Berrie Clerke Curate of Wathe the xvth daie
	Baptysed	Thomas the sonne of Henry Wood the xvjth day
October	Baptised	Elizabeth the daughter of Thomas Jackson the xth day
	Baptised	Elizabeth the daughter of Richard Holdsworthe xixth daye
November	Buried	Steuen Key the xth daye of this instant
	Buried	Katheryn the wife of William Rogerson the xijth daye
	Maryed	John Turner & Dorothie Crofts the xvjth daye
	Baptized	Richard the sonne of Richard Walker the xxiijth day
	Buryed	an Infant of Brian Barber a stranger the xiiijth (*? xxiiij*th)
December	Buryed	Anne Stable the wife of Anthony Stable the first daye
	Baptysed	William the sonne of Richard Burton the vijth day
	Buryed	Hester the doughter of Henry Tolson gen the ixth day
	Buryed	Nich: Mallinson the xxijth day
	Baptised	Henry the sonne of Thomas Wilcocke the xxvith day
Januarye	Buryed	Nicholas Hunt of Wath the iij^{de} daye

1619

Januarye Baptised William the sonne of a straunger who is a bastard

June 28 1619. I Thomas Benson Batchelor of Divinitie and Vicar of Wath upon Dearne did geive my consente y^{t} Jasp Blythman Esq. and Wm Blythman gent or either of them should build them a stall or pew on ye right hande next to ye South dore of ye chancell of ye parish church of Wath aforesaid, upon condicon that whensoever they two, their wifes and the yssues of either of them two lawfully begotten should departe this life or cease to be Inhabitants within the sayd parish That then and from that day forward the sayd stall remaine wholy in the full and absolute disposition of the vicar of Wath for the tyme beinge

THOMAS BENSON

January.	Baptised	ffraunces the doughter of Nicholas Sandiland ye xvith
	Marryed	Robert Hauslin & Margaret ffoord the xvijth day
	Baptised	William the sonne of William Pearson the xxth day
ffebruary	Baptised	Nicholas the sonne of Richard Tottington the vith day
	Buried	the aforesaid Nich: sone of Rich: Tottington the xth day
	Buried	Richarde Browne the xijth daye of ffebruarie 1619
	Buried	an Infant of Nich: Wood unbaptised ye same day
	Baptised	Elizabeth ye doughter of Elizabeth Mallinson beinge a bastarde the xiijth day
	Married	Edward Dickinson and Mary . . . . the xxvith day
March 1620	Baptysed	Margrett the daughter of ffarburne Willson the xijth daye
	Baptised	Margret the daughter of Richard Eller the xxvith day 1620
	Buryed	Nicholas Sherwodd the xxvijth day of Marche
	Baptised	Richard sonne of Symon Hodgson the 31th of Marche
	Buryed	the wife of John Foster of Swinton the 31 of March 1620

The Register of Wath church 1620 beginninge in Aprill the first.

Hen Tailer & Clarke of Wath } 1620

Aprill	Buried	Issabell late wife of John Browne of Wath the first of Aprill 1620
	Baptised	John the sonne of John Baraclough of Melton ye vijth day
	Buried	Margaret wife of Thomas Hepworth the 11th of Aprill 1620
	Buryed	uxor Eller of Swinton the xvith of Aprill 1620
	Baptysed	Henry the sonne of Richard Lee of Wath the xviijth day 1620
	Maryed	George Hoyland and Elizabeth Hirst the 23 day Apr 1620

1620		
May	Maryed	John Sharp and Margarett Kirkby th 7th May 1620
	Buried	an Infante of John Brooke unbaptized 11 of May 1620
	Baptized	Richard the sonne of Richard Dickinson of Swinton the 27 of May 1620
	Baptysed	Margret daughter of Robert England eod die
June	Baptized	Elizabeth daughter of John Ellis ꝑdict the 8 day of June 1620
	Baptized	Edward sonne of Richard Browne the $xviij^{th}$ day of June 1620
	Baptized	Robart supposed sonne of ffrancesse Popplewell the 21 of June 1620
July	Buryed	John Taylo^{r} of Wath the 7 of Julie 1620
	Buried	the wyfe of Georg Turner of Swinton the 20 day
Aug.	Baptized	An daughter of John Turner of Swinton 13 day
	Baptized	Elizabeth daughter of Willm Tryvye the 30 of August
July	Maryed	John Hunt and Ann ellwood the 30th
Sept	Buried	Ellin wife of Willm Smyth the 30 of September
Octob	Buried	Elizabeth daughter of John Brooke the 2 of Octob^{r} 1620
	Bapt	Thomas sonn of Thomas Richardson the 9th of August 1620
	Baptiz.	Thomas sone of Mychaell Bowcer the 22 of October
	Bapt	W^{m} sonn of Barnabie Hall the 22 of October viz eod die
	Buried	Thomas sonne of Mychaell Stringer the 31° of October an infante
Novembr	Buried	an Infante of Richard Hudson the first of November unbaptized
	Baptized	John sonne of John Baxter gent the 5° of November
	Maried	John Bingley? et Katherina Tryvy 5° Novembris
	Buryed	Willm sonn of Thomas Baxter de abdie the 9 of November
	Baptized	Mary daughter of Thomas Wilkinson the 19
	Bapt	ffrannces sonne of Averey Wright the 22th of Novemb^{r}
	Baptized	Georg sonne of George Owen the 30th of November
Decemb	. . . .	
January	Baptyzed	John sonne of Robart Hauslyne 18 die
	Buryed	Ann wife of Thomas Ellis 19 day a traveller?
January 1620		
	Buried	wydowe Eaton de West melton 25° die 1620
february	Maryed	Richard Eaton and Elsabeth Hudsonn 5° die ffebruarij
1620	Buryed	Jodet wodd wydowe of Wath 8° ffebr 1620
	Buried	two Infants twindles of John Car de Street 10° die unbaptized
	Baptized	Thomas sonn of Thomas Baxter de swinton 4° die febr
	Baptysed	Willm sonne of Willm Bawdwinson 25
	Baptized	Mary daughter of John Sundiforth supposed eod die

1620		
february	Baptiz:	Easter daughter of Nycholas wodd eod die
	Buryed	Katherin wife of John Carr de Coley Lane 21 febr
March	Baptized	Lawrence sonn of George Wade the xviijth day March
	Baptiz:	Robart sonn of Robart Beamount the 22 of March 1620
1621		
Aprill	Maryed	Rich: Robinson and Anne Lorester 8° Aprill
	Maryed	Willm Smyth and Margret barraclough the 15 Ap
May	Baptised	Ann daughter of John Hunt the first of May 1621
	buryed	Richard Croysdall the 9 of May 1621
	buryed	Elsabeth Smyth of Swinton the 11 of May
	buried	Suzan Tottingeton the 25 of May 1621
	Buryed	Ann wife of John Hunt the 6 of May 1621
	Maryed	Thomas Ellis and grace Dawson the 6 of May
	baptized	Wm sonn of Thomas Maugham the 16 of Aprill 1621
	Buryed	Elizabeth daughter of Barnebee hall the 21 of May 1621
	Buryed	Ruben Styringe the 22 of May 1621
	Maryed	Ratcliffe gorrell and Margrett Robarts the 22 of May
	Buryed	Elsabeth daughter of Rychard Lee the 25 of May
	baptized	Ann daughter of Edward Wager the 26
	Buryed	Mrs Thornhill wife of Nycholas Thornhill the 27 of Maie
	Buryed	Ellin Berry the 30 of May 1621 frō West Melton
June	Buryed	xp̃ofer Eller sonne of Richard the first of June 1621
	bap:	John sone of Alvery gollan the 10 of June 1621
	Baptiz	Peter sonn of Henry Taylor clerke the 24 of June
	Maryed	Thomas Popplewell and Alice Loord the 23 of June
	Baptysed	Mary daughter of Willm Robinson the 24 of June
Julie	Buried	Rychard Pearson of West melton the 15 of July
	Baptysed	Dorythy daughter of John Ellis of brampton gent 9 Augustij
	Buried	Ellin daughter of Thomas Wilkinson of Swintō poc de Wath 20
	Buried	John Awtrom of West melton the 30 of August
	Maryed	John Sisson and Margrett Sharpe the . . . . of August
Sept.	Baptysed	ffrances daughter of Roger Armitage the 4th of September
	Buryed	Thomas sonne of John Awtram of Westmelton 7 of Sept
	Bapt	Thomas sonn of Thomas Popplewell the 7 of Sept
	Buryed	Peter sonn of Sr Henry Taylor the 19th of September
	Bapt.	Willm sonn of Rycherd Mabson the 25 of September
Oct.	Baptiz	Willm sonn of James More of Swinton 6 October
	Maryed	Stephen Elam and Ann Burton the 12 of October
	Maryed	Willm Smyth and Elizabeth fixby the 20th of October
No:	Maryed	Nycholas Thornhill and Dorythie Taylor the 13th of No.

1621

Dec. Maryed Thomas England and Johañ Joyes the first of December

Baptiz. John sonne of John Sisson the 27 of December 1621

Januarie Baptized Margrett daughter of Richard goodall Brampton 4 ?

Buryed an Infant of Richard Hudson the 12 Januarie

ffeb Baptysed John sonn of Richard Eaton ffebr 17

Baptysed Thomas supposed sonne of George Hattersfield 25 feb

Bapt Marie (ffrancesse) supposed daughter of Roger Armytage

Maried Thomas Baraclough and Issabell grenwodd 17 febr

Maryed Anthony Howlgate and Margrett Hoyland the 26 febr 1621

Marche Baptized Marie daughter of Robart England the 3 of March

Baptized Humfray sonne of ffrauncis Addy the 3 of March

Baptised John sonne of Richard Burton Swinton the 7 of March

Baptized Richard sonn of Richerd Nelthropp 10 March 1621

1622

Baptized ffrauncis sonne of Richard Tottington March 31 1622

Aprill Bapt Margret daughter of ffarburne Willson of Swinton the 22 Aprill

Buryed Thomas Beamounte of Swynton the 30 Apr.

Maye Maryed Robart ffurnesse and Susaña Anderton the first of May

Buryed frauncis Richardson of Wath the 16 of May

June Baptysed Margrett daughter of Jarvas Browne the 5th of June 1622

Buried Thomas Abson of Swinton the 6 of June 1622

Julie Baptiz Thomas sonn of Thomas Jackson the 13 of May 1622

Bapt Mary daughter of Thomas Ellis of Westmelton 16

Aug Baptiz Margrett daughter of Richard Hobson of Wath 25

Buried an Infant sonne of Richarde Nightengall of Swinton 22

Septemb. Baptiz . . . . daugh of John Ellis of Brampton gent 9 Sept

Baptiz William sonn of John Baxter de abdy 14

Octob. Bapt Elizabeth daughter of Richard Walker eod

Buried Ursula wife of Willm Dyson 10 October

Maried Peter Raventree and Elizabeth Peacocke

Buried Margaret Ogden de Swintone

Buried Humfroy sonn of John Kay October 13

Novemb Baptized Katherin daughter of Richard Hearin 5

Baptiz: Mary daughter of John Wharme 7 No

Baptiz Willm sonn of Anthonie Cowldwell 17 Novemb

Baptiz James sonne of Mychaell Stringer of Swinton eod

Bapt. Barbary daughter of Peter Robinson 3 Nov

Baptiz Thomas sonn of Thomas Richardson 10 N.

Buried Thomas sonn of Thomas Richardson 21 Nov.

1622		
Novemb	Bapt.	Zara daughter of John Car de Cooley Lane
	Maryed	Thomas Smyth and Mary Bloome 19 November
	Bapt	Ann daughter of Richard Eller de Swinton Nov
	Buryed	Peter sonn of Wm Kitchiman the 23 of November
December	Marryed	Emanuell Armfeild and Mary Hanson the 24 December
	Buried	Beaumonte wife the xvth daie
	Baptized	Thomas sonn of John Wodhead 29 December
Jan	Bapt	John sonn of Jarvas Smyth of West Melton 6 January
	Buried	Thomas Scales the 12 Januarye
febr.	Buryed	Wyllm sonne of Robart ford the first of ffebruary
	Maried	Peter Bayliffe and Mabell Smyth the fourth of febrũ
	Baptized	Isabell daughter of Roger Stable the xixth ffebruary
	Maryed	Henry Kay and Eliz : Taylo^{r} 9th of ffebr 1622
	Maryed	George Yates and Rosamond Waggstafft 12 febr
	Buried	an Infante of Thomas Wilcocke de Swinton 19
Marche	Buryed	Thomas Wodd of Wath the 4 of Marche 1622
	Baptiz :	Edward Spurins Edwardi Ward 2 Marcij
	Baptiz	Ann daughter of Wm Tryvie eod̄ die
	Buried	Thomas Rychardson of Rainburgh 18 March
	Baptized	James sonne of James More de Swinton 20 die
	1623	
	Baptized	Marie daughter of John Byshopp Clerke 26 March
April	Buried	Thomas Hudson of Brampton thelder 4 Aprill
	Buried	Dorithy daughter of Thomas Hanson 2 Ap
	Buried	. . . . daughter of Wildsmith wife the 20 of Aprill 1623
	Buried	Wm Brooke de Wath eod̄ die
	Buryed	John Slater of Wath the 23 of Apr
	Buried	Grace Malinson the 26 of Apr
May	Buried	an abortive or infant of Samuell Wortley the 9 of Apr ?
	Baptiz	Katherin daughter of Peter bayliffe the 20 Apr
	Buried	george Smith a poore man of Bolton the xith of May
	Buried	Elsabeth Hodgeson of Wath the xiith of May
	Buryed	Issabell daughter of Crosland wife de Street 16 of May
	Buryed	Elizab daughter of John Ellis of Brampton, gent 22
	Baptiz	Rychard sonn of Thomas Baraclough the xviijth
June	Buryed	Alice wife of Thomas Coo the 2 of June
	Bapt	Elizabeth daughter of Hugh Hirst of Brampton May 9
	Buryed	Adam Awbrey a begger of Mexbrough the 31 of May
	Bur.	Ellin the wife of John Dawson the fifte daie
	Bur.	Margrett the doughter of Rich : Goodale the xijth daie

1623

July	Maried	Samuell Wortley and Grace Abson the 20th of Julie. 1623
		Witnesses herof Hen: Taylor, Clerke.
		Am: Wortley, ar; Nicholas Tilney, yeoman.
		Thomas Sattartwheff, yeoman.
		Mychaell Halliday, James More, Elsabeth Steade.
Aug.	Buried	Elsabeth daughter of Michaell Bowcer Julie 2° Etat 8°
	Buryed	Elizabeth Jubb of Swinton the 15 of Julie
	Baptized	Añ daughter of Witlm Robinson 2° July
	Baptiz	Ann daughter of Barnabie Hall 20 Julye
	Buryed	John Cotton the iith of August 1623
Sep.	Buryed	Wydowe Wade of Newall the 19th of August
	Baptized	Wyllm son of Thomas Baxter Aug: 13
	Maryed	John Hunt and Marie Barlawe the 10th Aug
Sept	Baptiz	Jasper sonn of george Yates the 18 of Sept
	Buried	the wife of Launclot Briggs the 23 of Sept
	Maryed	Willm Barraclough and Jane Craggs the 17 Sept
Octob.	Buried	Willm Smyth and the wife of Rich. Ellis primo die
	Baptiz	Rychard sonne of Willm. Bawdwinson of Swinton 5°
	Buryed	Widowe Wodd of Swinton the 17 of October
	Buried	vid Walker of Westmelton eod die
	Maryed	Rychard Hilton and Ann fforde the 19 of Octob
	Buried	Margret Child of Westmelton sister unto John Sawtre wife 26 Octo
Nov:	Baptized	Elizabeth daughter of Ratcliffe Gorrell 5°
	Maryed	John ffearnes and Ann Denby the 9° of November
	Buried	Thomas Waterhouse of Newall the 15 of Novemb
	Buryed	Robert ffrankesse of brampton the 19 of Nov 1623
	Maryed	Thomas Coo and Ann Margesson the 23 of No
Decem.	Buried	Ralph Malinson a poor traveller 15 December
	Buried	an Infant of Henrie Kay the 14 December 1623
	Buryed	a child daughter of Thomas Eller de Swinton 17 die
	Buryed	Ellen wife of John Case de Hoober 20 December
	Buried	Thomas base soñe of Thomas England daughter de Coley lane 23
Jan.	Buried	John ffreeman de Roides 14 Januarye
	Maryed	Thomas Ulley and Grace Maryott 10 Dec 1623
	Maryed	John flinte and Ann Martin the 11 of Dec 1623
	Buryed	Uxor Walker de Westmelton the 17 of December
	Buryed	James sonn of James More the 15 ? of Jan. 1623
	Baptzd	Richard sonne of Richard Ellar de Swinton 19 Jan
	Buried	Nicholas Thornhill de Wath gent 24 of January
	Buried	Willm sonn of Willm Bawdwinson the 17 January
Feb	Buryed	Nycholas Tilney of Wath the tenth day of ffebr 1623
	Baptysed	Ann daughter of Rychard Lee the 15 of ffebr. 1623
	Buried	an Infant of Saumell Wortley the 14 of ffebruary
	Buryed	Rychard sonn of Wm Bawdwinson the 16 of ffebr. 1623

1624		
Feb	Baptized	George sonn of George Wade the 28 (or 29) of ffebruary
	Buried	Katherin foxe the ix day of februarie 1623
	Buryed	uxor Nayler wife of Robert Nayler 16 ffebruary
March	Buried	Richard Beardsall de Wath the 5° of March 1623
	Baptized	Dorythie daughter of Richard Eaton the 7 March
1624		
Apr.	Buryed	Margret wife of Henry Hill the 13 of Aprill
	Buryed	an Infant of Jarvas Smyth of Westmelton the 14 of Aprill
	Bapt.	Thomas sonn of John Sisson the 15 of Apr
	Buried	Spurius filius Rogeri fixby an infant the 17 of Aprill
	Buriid	Ellin daughter of Roger fixby the 16 of Apr
May	Bapt.	George sonn of Thomas Wilkinson de Swinton the 15 of Aprill
	Maryed	Launclot Briggs & Ann foster the 2 of May 1624
	Baptized	Henry sonn of Robart Hawslin the 9 of May
	Buried	Robart Beamount of Wath the 10 of May 1624
	Maried	Humfrey Jackson and Elizabeth Robarts the 9 of May 1624
	Maried	Richard Chappell and Alice Beardsall 30
	Buryed	Wiłłm Tryvie of Wath thelder the 22 of May
	Baptyzed	Alise daughter of Thomas Mangall the 16 of May
	Buried	vid Styringe de Wath 26° May 1624
	Baptysed	Richard Marshall sonn of Wm Marshall the 29 of May 1624
	Maryed	Richard Robinson & Mary Waterhouse 25 May
June	Maryed	John Dawson and Martha foster the 8 of June
	Maryed	Robart Green and Katherin fox the 10 June
	Maryed	Richard Sha and Grace Sawtree the 6 June
	Maryed	Wiłłm Booth and Katherin Barraclough the 6 June
	Baptized	Sara a basterd of Roger fixby his daughter the 29 May
	Bapt	Anna daughter of Rychard mabson the 13 June
	Baptized	Thomas sonn of Thomas Penyston the 20 June 1624
	Baptiz	Ann daughter of Nicholas Stanyland the 28 of June
Julie	Baptiz	Margret daughter of John Hunt the 4 day of Julie 1624
	Maryed	Wyłłm Grenewodd and Alice Jepson the 4 of July
	Maryed	Henry Wharā and Margrett Pearson the 6 of July
	Buried	the wife of Thomas Adderschurch the 11 of Julie
Aug.	Bapt	John sonn of John Car de Cooley lane primo Augustij
	Bapt	Richard son of Wiłłm Baraclough eod die
	Baptized	Ellin daughter of John Sharpe the 15 of August
	Maried	John Skailes & Jenet Brayton the 22 day of Aug 1624
Sept.	Baptiz	Mychaell sonne of Mychaell Bowcer the 5 of September
	Maryed	Mychaell Bysbie and ffaith Adams the 29 Aug

1624

Sept. Maryed George Barraclough and Elizabeth Brooke 12 sep
Baptiz Elizabeth daughter of George Hintch 21° Sept
Baptiz Grace daughter of Willm Binglee de Swinton 25 Sept
Buried Agnes Whară de West Melton the 30 of September 1624
Maried Thomas Robinson and Jenet Sha the 30
Buried Eliz daughter of Georg Hintch of Mexbrough 30 Sept

October Baptized Mary daughter of John Baxter gent the 10th of October
Maried George Smith and Ester Thompson the 17 October
Baptized Thomas sonne of Thomas Rawlin the xth of October
Baptized Thomas sonne of John Ellis of Brampton 12th of Octob
Baptiz. Robert sonn of Robte England the 7 of Octob
Bapt. Dorythie daughter of Willm Greenwodd the 7th Novemb
Baptized ffraunces and Willim sonns of Launclot Briggs the 16th of Nov
Maryed Willm Stones and Dorythie Thornhill the 18th of Decemb 1624
Maryed Richard Maryott and Elsabeth Robarts 21 of November

Md that Nicholas Sha of Hoober in pish of Wath, yeoman, was admitted and licensed by us whose names are hereunder written to set a stall or seat made of his pp charges for himselfe and other his owne familie in the south side of the church of Wath adioyninge upon Sr Thomas Wentworth stall or pew in the upper end of the South alley ther viz in the year of our Lord God 1624 the xixth of November and ther to contynue without disturbance of any pson in paine of Eccclesiasticall Censure.

Hen Taylor, Clerke
John Baxter
Robarte Hawslyn

Buried John Jepson of Westmelton the xijth of December

Jan Buried Ann Scales of Swinton the first of January
Buryed Mr Mapples of the Abdy the 3 of Jan
Baptiz. Elsabeth daughter of Richard Hilton the 4 Jan
Baptiz Willm sonn of Anthony Holgate of Rawmarsh the 6 Jan
Buryed an Infant of John Barraclough the 10th of Jan.
Buried old Mr Mapples the 3 of January 1624
Buryed Peter Robinson the 19 of January 1624
Buryed a wanderinge begger Cotton the 10 of Jan
Baptized Willm sonn of Henry Cotton the 19 January
Baptized Rychard and Mary gemini children of Nycholas Wodd the 22°
Baptiz: ffrauncis sonn of ffrancis Addy the 23 January

1625 *Jan*	Baptiz	Agnes daughter of Rychard Nelthropp the same day
	Baptiz	Elizabeth daughter of Henry Kay the 3 of January
	Baptiz	Mary and Rychard gemini of Nycholas Wodd the 26 of Jan
	Maryed	John Case and Agnes Kempe the 6 of ffeb
	Baptiz	Jane daughter of Thomas Sha eod̄
	Buryed	John newall brother to Tho: England wife the 16 of ffeb
	Buried	Em̃ wife of Richard Burfet the 24 of ffeb
	Buried	Kathrin Carter the 20 of febr.
	Buryed	Thomas Alderschurch the 27 ffeb
March	Baptiz	Wiltm sonn of Wm Booth the 6th of March
	Baptiz	Mary daughter of Humfray Jackson the 13 March
	Buryed	Jane wife of Wm Baraclough the 10 of March
	Buryed	James Heathcote servant to Mr Jarvas Smythe the 14 of Mch
	Baptiz	Georg sonn of George Jenkinson the 20 of March 1624
1625	Bapt and buried	Richard sonn of James More the 29 March
April	Bapt	John sonn of Thomas Wade the 11 of Aprill 1625
	Buryed	the wife of Thomas Cartwright the 22 of Aprill 1625
May	Buryed	Margret daughter of Wiltm Armytage the 15 day of May 1625
	Maryed	Wm Barraclough and Elisabeth Johnson the 15 of May
	Buryed	Anthony Yates the xth day of May 1625
	Buryed	vid̄ Ward mother to Nicholas Wade wife of West Melton 3 of
	Buryed	George sonn of Richard Nelthropp of Wath the 6 May
	Bapt	Elisabeth daughter of George Wade of Swinton the 27 of May
	Baptized	Richard grandchild to Wiltm Burton wife of Swinton the 29 of May
June	Bapt	Rychard and Tho: gemini sonns of Rich goodall of Brampton the 7 June
	Bapt	Thomas sonn of George Barraclough of Wath the 7 of June 1625
	Buryed	Elsabeth wife of Henrie Kay of Wath the 13 of June 1625
	Maryed	John Barlawe and Ann Smyth the 24 of June 1625
	Maryed	Rychard Hogley and Dorythie Wade the 6 of June 1625
	Maryed	Wm Huggell and Ellin Watson the 19 of June
	Buryed	Elzabeth wife of Henry Kay the 20 of June 1625
	Buried	Thomas Sha of the Abdy, Coleyer, the 21 of June
Julie	Baptized	John sonn of Thomas Johnson the 17 of Julie
	Baptiz	George son of Thomas Wilcocke the 20 of Julie

1625		
Aug	Bapt	Rosamond daughter of Thomas Jackson the 3 of Aug
	Maryed	Nycholas Malinson & Katherin Brydley the 4 of August
	Bapt	Richard basterd of Rychard Middleton the 10th
	Buryed	Ellin wife of John Blacksmith of Swinton 14 August
	Maryed	Henry Turner and Elsabeth Malinson 14 August
	Buryed	Rosamonde wife of George Yates the 19 August
	Baptiz:	Mary daughter of Henrie Wharā the 24 of Aug
	Baptized	Elizabeth daughter of Samuell Wortley the 24 of Aug
	Bapt	Edward sonn of Edward Wager the 28 Aug
	Buryed	faith wife of Nycholas Stanyland the 31 Aug
Sept	Bapt	Willm sonn of Willm Tryvie the 4 September
	Baptized	An daughter of Willm Robinson the 21 of Septemb
	Baptiz:	Thomas sonn of Rychard Maryott the 25 of Sept
	Buried	a poore traveller dying at Brampton hige packman gate 29 Sept
	Buryed	a daughter of Rychard Lee Easter by name the 27 of Sept
Oct	Buryed	the 4 of October Tho: sonne of Rychard Browne
	Baptiz:	Alice daughter of Rychard Sha the 2 October
	Buried	Alice wife of Richard Tottington the 12 of Oc^{r}
	Maried	Thomas Cartwright and Ellen ffrannce the 10 of Oc.
	Bapt	. . . . sonn of Mychaell Stringer of Swinton the 25 September
Novemb^{r}	Baptized	William the sonne of Richard Walker the xvijth daie
	Buried	ffrancis the sonne of Lancelott Brigges the xxvith daie
Dec.	Bapt	Thomas ye sonne of Thomas Newton ye 18th December 1625
	Bapt	Elizabeth ye daughter of Tho: Mangham ye 25th Dec. 1625
Jan	Bapt	Willm ye sonne of Richrd Herring ye 8th Januarye
	Jan 14	W^{m} ye sonne of Richrd Herringe was buried
	Jan 15	Richardus filius Richardi Eaton bapt
	Jan 19th	Richardus filius Rich. Eaton sepultus
		Nicholaus filius Johannis Case de Howbar bapt eod die
	Jan 22	Willmus Dyson & Elizabetha Booth matrimonio coniuncti
	Jan 29	Maria filia Jobis Sissanne baptizata
		Christopher Barrowcloughe & Anna Brooke matri coniuncti
	ffeb 2	Ellinora filia reputata Johis Holland & Elizabethæ Newton
	ffeb 4°	Nichas filius Jo. Case de Howbar sep
	ffeb 16°	Willmus fil Willmi Greenewood bapt
	Martij 3°	Elizabetha Darley de Brampton sepult

1626

Martij 5° Ellinora filia reputata Johis Holland & Elizabethæ Newton sep

" Hester fil Jo: ffearne baptizata

The Register Booke of Wathe for ye yéare 1626.

Martij 26	Richardus filius Xpoferi Barrowcloughe bapt
Martij 28	Alverius Wright sepult
Martij 31	Hellena filia Petri Baylye bapt
Aprilis 2°	Elizabetha Yates de Brampton bapt
April 9°	Johannes filius Thomæ Baxter bapt
Apr: 11°	Mayareta filia Thomæ Barrowcloughe bapt
Apr. 12°	Richardus Burton sepult
April 2°	Anna filia Gervasij Smith gen bapt
Ap: 25°	Robtus fil reputatus Robti Bushel et Mariœ Wood bapt
Junij 4°	Elizabetha filia Gulielmi Pearson sepult
Junij 5°	Thomas Darley de Melton sepult
Maij 25°	Johannes filius Nicolai Mallinson bapt
Junij 10°	Johannes filius Johannis Hunt bapt
	Robtus Cartwright et Katherina ffalconer matrim coniunt
Junij 12°	Wmus fiilius Willelmi Wilson sepult
	Maria Leake eod die sepult
	Johannes filius Johannes Ellis, gen bapt eod die
Junij 30°	Michaell Woodhead sepult
Junij 25°	Gulielmus Broome sepult
Junij 27°	Thomas Bingley et Anna Taylor matrimonio coniuncti
Junij 30°	Johannes Owtram sepult
	Anna fil Barnardæ Hall eod die sepult
Julij 2°	Jacobus fil illegitimus Johannis Gillot et Janæ ffoster bapt
Julij 16°	p'dcus Jacobus filius Johannis Gillot et Janæ ffoster sep.
Julij 17°	Dorothea vidua relicta Thomæ Darley sepulta
Julij 25°	ffrancisca filia Johis Wharram bapt
Aug. 20°	Anna filia Richardi Newton baptizata
Aug. 24°	Rosamunda uxor Johts Greene sepulta
Aug. 30°	Anna filia Richardi Newton sepulta
Sept 6°	Georgius filius Wmi Dyson sepultus
Oct. 3th 1626	Mrd that the bridge commonly called the Vicars bridge was by Rie Burfett and Geo: Jenkinson, Constables of Wath bought of Robt Pearson of Wath: for the wch was pd 3s the day and yeare abovesaid and 6d pd to Rich. Nellhoppe for setting the same

The m'ke of + Rich Burfett — The mrke of + Geo: Jenkinson

Oct 10th	Troth filia posthuma Richdi Burton bapt
Octo 14th	Johannes Johnson de Swinton sepultus
Octo 15th	Maria filia Emmanuelis Armfeild bapt
Octo 29°	Johannes Greene et Elizabetha Slacke matrimonio coniuncti

1626

Novem : 9°	Thomas fil illegitimus Wm Bingley et Annæ Athye sep
Novemb. 14°	Thomas Shepherd et Joanna Yates matrimonio coniuncti
	Rosamunda Baxter eod die sep
Novembris 19°	ffranciscus fil Wiłłmi Bawdwinson bapt
Novembris 21°	Hen : Wilkinson et Beatrix Robinson mat coniuncti
Novembris 23°	Johannes Hoyland et Maria Butler matr. coniuncti
Novembris 26°	Leonardus fil Wiłłmi Pearson bapt
	Nicholaus Sharpe et Constantia Short mat coniuncti
Januarij 28°	Richardus fil Johannis Carre de Coley lane bapt
ffebr. 22°	Thomas Wilkinson fil. Henrici Wilkinson bapt
Martij 4°	Henricus fil. Leon. Turner bapt
Martij 11°	Jones fil Nicholai Wood bapt
Martij 23°	Kathrina fil Richardi Mabson bapt

The Register booke of Wath sup Dearne for the year 1627.

Aprill	Buried	Margrett the wiffe of Willim Smithe the first of Aprill
	Buried	Robt Smith the vij° daie of Aprill
May 4th	Baptized	Williã the sone of William Dison the 4th of May
	Baptized and buried	Thomas the supposed sonne of Thomas Harrison & Anne Sharpe base begotten
May the 16th	Baptized	Elizabeth the daughter of William Booth
		Elizabeth the daughter of Richard Burfett eodem die
May the 24th	Buried	William the sonne of Barnabie Hall
May the 27th	Baptized	Thomas the sonne of Elizabeth Addy Base begotten
June the 9th	Buried	Margaret the wiffe of John Sharpe
June the 29th	Baptized	Margaret the daughter of Richard Eaton
	Baptized	Thomas the sonne of Nicholas Sharpe the 8th July
July the 25th	Buried	Troth the daughter of Richard Burfett
July the 29th	Baptized	James the sone of Robert Hausline &
		Thomas the sone of Robert England eodem die
August the 6th	Baptized	Jane the daughter of John Greene
August the 13th	Maried	Simon Hodgson & Elizabeth Smith
August the 21th	Baptized	John the sone of Henry Towlson gent
September the 16th	Baptized	Richard the sone of Richard Mariott } eodem die
	Baptized	John the sone of Nicholas Pearson } eodem die
	Baptized	Thomas the sone of Henry Kay } eodem die
September 19th	Baptized	George the sonne of John Ellis gentleman
September 30th	Baptized	Sara the daughter of Laurence Wade } eodem die
	Maried	Thomas Harrison & Anne Sharpe } eodem die
	Buried	Thomas the sone of Henry Kay } eodem die

1627

October 1th	Buried	an infant of George Jenkinsons
	Buried	Anne the wife of George Jenkinson
October 11th	Baptized	Elizabeth the daughter of Richara ffoster
	Baptized	Jane the daughter of Samuell Wortley gentlman
November 9th	Buried	Henry the sonne of William Lee
November 11th	Baptized	Edward the sonne of Rich. Newton
	Baptized	Dorithy the daughter of John Case
November 13th	Maried	Gilberb Robucke & Margaret Wood
November 25th	Baptized	Henry the sone of John Baxter gentlman
December 3th	Buried	Elizabeth the daughter of Robert Naylor
December 6th	Buried	William ffox
December 6th	Maried	Ralph Hattersley & Elizabeth Hill
December 9th	Baptized	William the sone of William Soresby
Dec 16th	Baptized	William the sone of John Sisson
21th	Buried	Dorithy the daughter of John Case
January 3th	Buried	William the sone of John Sisson
Jan: 5th	Buried	Jennet Wood of Wath
Jan: 12th	Maried	Thomas Neuison & Dority Hole
13th	Baptized	Elizabeth daughter of Jarvas Smith gent
14th	Maried	Ralph Jillott of Darfield & Esther Hurst
16th	Buried	John sone of William Kitchinman
18th	Baptized	William sone of Georgie Thornton
27th	Baptized	John the sonne of William Robinson
February		Richard the sonne of ffrancis Addie and Elizabeth the daughter of Richard Shaw eodem die
February 10th	Baptized	Margaret the daughter of Ralph Hattersley
February 21th	Buried	Alis the wife of Henry Wood
February 23th	Maried	Robert Winder & ffrancis Hill
February 26th	Buried	Elizabeth the daughter of Jarvas Smith, gent
March 9th	Baptized	Katherine the daughter of Richard Sylvester
March 12th	Buried	Thomas Sheppherd of Brampton
March 16th	Baptized	Jane the daughter of George Barraclough George the sone of Thomas Blacksmith eodem die
March 20th	Buried	Jane the wife of Thomas Sheppherd
March 23th	Baptized	Robert the sonne of Ratcliffe Gorrall

The Register Booke for Wath sup Dearne 1628.

March 25th	Baptized	Henry the sone of Ralph Jellot?
March 27th	Buried	Henry the sonne of Ralph Jellot
Aprill 3th	Buried	Richard Ellison
Aprill 25th	Buried	Anne . . . . . .
Aprill 27th	Buried	an infant of Nicholas Mallinson
May 1th	Baptized	Troth the daughter of John Ellis

1628

May the 11th	Baptized	Wiłł the sone of Barnabie Hall	eodem die
	Baptysed	Joane the daughter of Alis Walker base begotten	
	Buried	Henry the sone of Henry Towlson gentleman	
May 29th	Baptized	Henry the sone of John Hunt	
May 31th	Buried	Will Wharā	
June 1°	Baptized	Thomas the sōne of Richard Hilton	
June 7th	Buried	ffrances Elles de Wheale	
June 8th	Baptized	. . . . the daughter of Thomas Wilcocke	
June 15th	Baptized	Rosamond the daughter of Simon Hodgson	
June 22th	Married	John Meddley & ffrances Martin	
	Baptized	Thomas the sone of Thomas Johnson eod̄ die	
	Maried	Peeter Setle and Elizabeth Hodgsonn July the 1 die	
	Buried	Jane the daughter of Thomas Carr the 2° day	
1628			
July 4 die	Burried	the wife of John Hunte	
22th	Married	Alexander Shaw & Alice ffaux	
27th	Baptized	John the sone of Thomas Jackson	
August 3° die	Baptized	Issabell the daughter of Gilbert Robucke	
31 die	Baptysed	Marie the daughter of Henry Kay	
September 14th	Baptysed	Jaspar the sone of Thomas Harison	
18th	Buried	Helen the daughter of John Sharpe	
27th	Buried	Thomas the sonne of Nicholas Sharpe	
29th	Buried	John Peate	
October the first	Buried	Jasper the sonne of Thomas Harrison	
2 day	Buried	John Ellyson of the Roydes	
4 day	Buryed	Alice? the daughter of Nicholas Wood	
11 die	Buryed	Ann the daughter of Wiłł Robinson	
19 die	Married	Richard Seluester & Hester Taylor	
29	Buried	Susanna the daughter of John Addye	
eodem	Buried	Williā the sonn of Barnabie Hall	
Novemb 4	Buried	Hester the daughter of John Fearnes	
4th	Buried	Wiłłm the sonne of Williā dison Junior	
9th?	Baptized	Thomas the soñ of Tho: Cutt of Swinton	
16th	Baptized	Richard the sone of Richard Pearson	
23d	Baptized	Richard the sone of Richard Thakchraw	
29	Buried	Ann Tingle	
29	Buried	an infant daughter of Mr Ellis of bramton unbaptized	
December 3	Buried	Rob̄t Naylor December the 3	
23d	Baptized	Robert the sōne of Richard Walker	
1628			
Jan 4	Married	Henry Drable & Dorithy Sharrowe	
11th	Baptized	Wm the sone of Wiłł Trivy	
13th?	Maried	Henry Johnson & Mary Hurst	
January	Buried	Elizabeth Dobsonne of Melton xx day widow Etatis 67	

1628

xxij	Buried	Katherine the daughter of Wilł Coulbran of Swinton. Her age 22 years
xxvi	Buried	Jennitt the wife of Wiłł : Wilson
xxvii	Maried	Richard Tyass of Boulton & Margerett Tillney of Wath
xxviii	Buried	Katheryne the wife of Alexander Mariatt Etat 30
xxix	Maried	Richard Tillney and Rosamonde Roberts
xxix	Maried	Richard Ramsden & ffayth Wildsmith eodē die
Februarij	Bapt :	Rich : the soñ of Rich Mabson, Sureties Mr Ralph Copley : Robt Hauslin the 2d day
	Maried	Wiłł Huntla & Rosomond Elliss 3 day
viii	Bapt	Issabell ye daughter of Wiłł greenwood of Melton sureties Issabell Wade & Dorothie Firth Tho Hudson
xii	Buried	an Infant of Mr Jaruiss Smith of Melton unbaptized
xiii	Buried	John the son of Mr Henery Toulson clerke Etate 1 et demid
xv	Maried	Wilł Sharpe of Barnber & Ann Peate. Buried Nicholas Stainland eodē die
	Baptized	Helen the daughter of Peter Shetle eodem die
xix	Baptized	Ann the daughter of Anthonie Stable of Melton etat 7
xxii	Bapt :	Anna the daughter of John Carr of Cola lane Suerties —
xxii	Buried	widow Smith etat 70
March iii	Baptiz :	Ann the daughter of John Greene et sepultus quartō die
ix	Buryed	Henry Hill of West Melton Etat 70
x	Buryed	Ellinor the wife of Wiłła Triuie etat, &
	Baptized	Anne daughter of Wiłł Wharā
xi	Buryed	Robart Hauslin of Wath
xiii	Buryed	William the soñe of William Trivie
xv	Baptized	Anne the daughter of William Dyson iunior
xviii	Buried	Margarett Collinson of Wath
Incipit Aprilis		
Aprill	Buried	Margarett the wife of Thomas Wright 1629
	Baptized	Richard the sone of William Pearson eodē die
	Married	Robt Cutt & Isabell Robarts
	Baptized	ffrancis the sone of Samuel Wortley, gentleman
	Baptized	Jaspr the sone of Nicholas Mallinson
	Buried	Alice Beckett widow
	Married	Christopher Warde & Eedeth Hill
	Buried	Thomas Hudson of Brampton
	Baptized	Margaret the daughter of Peter Bayly
	Baptized & Buried	William ẏ sone of Nicholaŝ Pearson & an other sone

1629

April Married Thomas & Margarett Hauslin wid. the third day

Baptized Wm. Nicholas Sharpe the xijth day

Memorandū that William Hoyland of Wath upon Dearne in the County of Yorke, Tanner, was licensed & authorysed by us whose names are hereunder written to sett a stall in the North Alley against the pullpitt there to stand, & remaine wthout any disturbance or molestaeōn by any one in paine of Ecclesiasticall Censure anno domini 1630.

Ralph Goodyeare Curate

John Addye
Richard Silvester } Churchwardens 1630
William Wharā his m'ke

1629 ?

Octob^r	Baptized	Anne the daught^r of William Soresby the 4th day
	Baptized	Grace the daughter of Richard Sylvester 14th day
	Baptized	Cicily the daughter of Barnaby Hall the 18th day
	Buried	William Robinson eodē die
Novemb^r	Baptized	Margaritt the daughter of Ralph Jellott the 1 day
	Buried	John the soñe of John Baxter gentleman ye 22th day
Decemb^r	Married	Richard Eelom & Isabell Stable the 1 day
	Baptized	Hester the daughter of Richard Tilney the 20th day
	Buried	a pedler woman of Rotheram the 26th day
January	Buried	Hugh Hirst the 2^d day
	Buried	John Baxter gentleman the 3^d day
	Baptized	Elizabeth daught^r of the said John Baxt^r ye 17th day
	Buried	Henry the sōne of the said John Baxter the 24th day
	Baptized	Jane the daughter of a Colliar of Swīton moore id the 24 ?
ffebruary	Baptized	Elizabeth the daught^r of John Ellis, gent, the 3^d day
	Baptized	Richard the soñe & Hester ye daught^r of John Wharā ye 24th
	Baptized	Elizabeth ye daughter of Richard Heaton the 28th
	Baptized	ffraunces & Jane the daughters of Ratcliffe Gorral eodem die
March	Buried	Elizabeth the daught^r of John Baxter aforsaid the 1st day
	Buried	Jane the daughter of Ratcliffe Gorrall the 3^d day
	Buried	ffrances the daughter of the s^d Ratcliffe the xiij
	Baptized	Thomas the sonn of Richard Ramsden ye 14th
	Baptized	Thomas the sonne of Thomas Blacksmith the
	Buried	Willm Dyson the 15th day
	Buried	Simon Hodgson the 17th day
1630	Buried	Thomas Cartwright the 20th day
May	Baptized	Elizabeth daughter of Richard Eerlam ?
	Buried	(*Nil*)
	Married	Richard ffletcher & Joanna Steade the 18th

1630 *May*	Baptized	the daughter of Ralph Hatt^{r}slay the 23th day
	Buried	Thomas ye sone of John Barraclough the 30th day
	Buried	Willm Dawson the 27th day
June	Baptized	John and George ye sones of George Barraclough 29th day
	Married	Richard Heaton & Hester Pearson the first day
	Buried	Anne the daught^{r} of William Wharā the 4th day
	Buried	John the soñe of George Barraclough the 4th day
	Buried	the wife of John Leach the 28th day
July	Buried	John ffosterd the 6th day
	Baptized	ffrances the daught^{r} of Nicholas Pearson the 21th day
	Baptized	Thomas the soñe of Thomas Cutt eod die
	Buried	a poor wench wch Mr Wortley kept the 31st day
August	Baptized	Robert the soñe of John Lewin the 6th day
	Baptized	Letice the daught^{r} of Christopher Barraclough the 8th day
	Baptized	Jane the daught^{r} of Thomas Baxter the 13th day
	Baptized	Anne the daught^{r} of Richard Shaw eodē die
Septemb^{r}	Baptized	Isabell the daught^{r} of Gilbart Robucke the 5th day
	Married	James Adams & Hester Wilson the 29th day
Octob^{r}	Baptized	Henrie the soñe of Jarvas Smith the 3 day 1630
	Baptized	Hest^{r} the daught^{r} of Henry Tolson the 4th
	Buried	the said Hest^{r} the seaventh day
	Buried	Jane the daught^{r} of Alice Walker eodē die
	Buried	Humphrey Skirrawe the 25th day
	Baptized	Elizabeth the daught^{r} of William Robinson eodē die
Novemb^{r}	Married	Thomas Hudson & Hester Armatage the 2^{d} day
	Baptized	Lucie the daught^{r} of George Jenkinson the 21th
	Baptized	Elizabeth the daught^{r} of John Greene eodē die
	Buried	George Armefield the 24th day
December 1630	Baptized	Thomas the sonne of Georg Hinch Swinton 28
5th	Baptized	Richard ye sonne of George Wade of Swinton 5th
	Baptized	Nicholas the soñe of Thomas Tilney eodē die
	Buried	widow Taylier ye 22th day
	Buried	Hester the daughter of John Wharā ye 25th
January	Buried	Richard Tilney of Wath 6
	Buried	Nicholas Taylior the 28th
	Married	Mr Jasp Hunt & Mrs Grace ffullwood ye 4th day of January
February	Married	George Leach & Mary Wood ye i day
	Married	Wiłł^{m} Barbar & Elezabeth Benson ye 3 day
	Married	Alexander Marriott & Sara Ransley ye 6th
	Buried	an infant of Thomas Hudson unbaptized 15th
	Married	Wiłłm Wharā & Lucie Heaton ye 21th day
	Baptized	Elizabeth ẏ daughter of Richard Heaton 27th
	Buried	Anne ye daughter of Thomas Cutt ye 28th
	Baptized	John ye soñe of Henry Kay ye 2^{d} day

1630

February Baptized Helen the daughter of Witt^m Dison eodē die

Memorandū A license und^r the hands of Mr Doctor Benson was sho . . and alowed dated the 8th of December anno domini 1630. Whereby Peter Man of Wentworth and in the ꝑish of Wath, gent. is licensed to eate fleshe meate of such kinds onely as are admitted by his Maties lawes upon Fridays Sat^rdayes Wednesdayes and all other fasting dayes duringe his time of Infirmity and ꝑ sent sickness:

Ralph Goodyeare, Curate
The m'ke of
W.P.
William Pearson Churchwarden

1630-1

Baptized Anne the daughter of Richard Nelthroppe 7^e 13th of March
Baptized ffrances ye daughter of John Ellies
& Thomas ye sonne James Adams eodē die
Buried Alice ye wife of Witt̃m Soresby the 21th day

Incipit Annus 1631.

Buried Elizabeth the wife of Robart Smith the 28th day
Buried Thomas the soñe of Thomas Johnson the 30th day

May Baptized William the soñe of Laurence Wade the first day of May
Baptized Robart the soñe of Richard Hill the 8th day
Buried Robart Cutt of Swinton the 18th day
Buried John Leach the 28th day

June Buried Vid: Praunce the fifth day of June
Married Thomas Chapman & Hester ffaux the 13th day
Buried John Winder the 15th day
Buried James Adams the 23th day

July Married Williã Carr & Elizabeth Slosewicke the 17th of July

August Baptized Samuell the sone of John Ellis, gent, the 9th day August?
Baptized Rosamond the daughter of Richard Walker the 28th

September Maried Robart Swift & Elizabeth ffosterd the fourth of September
Baptized John the soñe of Anthony Holgate the 15th day
Buried an infant of Thomas Hudsons unbap: the 20th day
Baptised William the sone of Gilbart Robucke eodē die

October Baptized Elizabeth the daughter of John Carr the 2 of Octob^r
Buried a Bastard of Thomas Hudsons the 13th day
Baptized John the sone of Richard Pearson the 24th day
Buried Widow Abson the 27th day
Married George Mallinson & Mary Robarts the 30th day
Buried Vid. Trivy the 31th day

November Baptized Jasꝑ the soñe of Jasꝑ Hunt the first day of November
Baptized Anne the daughter Williã Wharã the 14th
Buried an infant of William Wharã unbaptized the 15th day

1630-1		
November	Baptized	Anne the daughter of Alexander Marriott the xxth
	Baptized	Anne the daughter of Emanuell Armefield the xx . . .
	Baptized	Anne & Jone the daughters of Thomas Jackson eod die
	Buried	Anne Swallow the 30th day
December	Buried	Gilbart Robucke the third day of December
	Buried	two infants of Thomas Chapman unbapt the 13th
	Baptized	Stephen the soñe of Nicholas Wood the 18th day
	Buried	Lawrence Brown the 23th day
	Buried	vid : . . . . the 24th day
	Buried	Jone the daughter of Thomas Jackson the 25th
	Baptized	Thomas the soñe of Richard Eller the 30th day
	Baptized	James the soñe of Thomas Maughã eodẽ die
January	Buried	the said Thomas the 3 of January
	Baptized	Richard the soñe of Richard Eller the 9th of January
	Buried	the said Richard the 10th
	Baptized	Williã the soñe of Richard Mabson eodẽ die
	Baptized	Anne the daughter of Charles Cawthorne the 16th day
	Married	William Trivy & Helen Hoyle eodẽ die
	Buried	vid. Tilney the 20th day
	Buried	the wife of John Brooke the 30th
February	Baptized	John the sone of William Carr the fifth of February
	Baptized	Anne the daughter of Nicholas Sharpe the 6th of ffebruary
	Baptized	Richard the soñe of Thomas Leach the same day
	Buried	Widow Kay the 20th day
March	Baptized	George the soñe of Williã Hoyland the 4th of March
	Buried	Hester Robinson the 6th day
	Baptized	Elizabeth the daughter of Ralph Jellott the 16th day
Incipit Annus 1632		
April 15th	Baptized	Elizabeth the daughter of Williã Pearson
April 22th	Buried	an infant
May i	Baptized	Anne the daughter of Samuell Wortley, gent.
	Baptized	Helen the daughter of Godfray ffoster eodẽ die
May 9th	Baptized	Elizabeth daughter of John Ellis of Wath
May the 12th	Baptized	Ralph the soñe of Thomas Hudson
May 19th	Buried	the said Ralph Hudson
June 2.	Baptized	John the soñe of John Parratt
July the 7th	Baptized	John the soñe of Thomas Blacksmith
July the 8th	Baptized	Richard the sonne of Robart Swift
August 4th	Baptized	Jone the daughter of Radcliffe Gorrall
August 18th	Baptized	Thomas the sonne of Richard Heaton of Brampton
25	Baptized	Anne daughter of John Sisson
27	Buried	Jane sister to Nicholas Wade wife
Sept 3	Baptized	Nicholas soñe of Nicholas Pearson
9	Buried	Mary wife of Martin Slosswicke
15	Buried	John Barraclough
29	Baptized	John soñe of Richard Eelam

1632

Octob[r] 16th Baptized Williã sonne of Humphray Jackson
16th Married John Smalchayre & Elizabeth Tompsõn
20th Baptized Tobias the sonne of John Ellis, gent.
25th Baptized Elizabeth the daughter of Richard Hill
Novemb[r] 3 Married Nicholas Tompson & Elizabeth Ransley
10th Baptized Henry the soñe of Richard Shaw
15th Baptized Williã the soñe of George Mallinson
20th Buried the said Henry Shaw
24[th] Baptized John the soñe of a tincker
29[th] Married Robart Lile & Alice Sawtry

Memorandũ the 2 of Aprill, 1633: John Carr of Wath was licensed by us whose names are here under written to reedifie a stall in the north alley w[ch] hee usually hath sitten & to continue there w[th]out molestacõn of any one in paynes of ecclesiastical censure. Radulphus Goodyear, minister, John Sison, Jarvas Smith, Humphray, Jackson.

December Baptized Elizabeth daughter of Thomas Harrison y[e] 5th
Buried Williã the sonne of George Mallinson 8th
Baptized Thomas sonne of Williã Trivy the 15th
January Buried Williã sonne of Humphrey Jackson the 7th day
Buried John Goodyeare the 9th
Baptized Annis daughter of Thomas Cutt the 13th
Buried Nicholas Shaw the 19th
Married Richard Pearson & Anne Stable 27th
Baptized Thomas the sonne of Widowe Jenkinson the 30th day
Feb Buried Mr Ambrose Wortley the 4th day
Married George Shaw & Alice Robinson the 13th
March Baptized Richard sonne of Richard Heaton the 10th
Baptized Jane daughter of Jarvas Smith gent: 17th
Baptized Anne daughter of Richard Thackrow 21th

Incipit Annus 1633.

March Baptized Thomas soñe of Lawrence Wade 25th day
Buried Thomas Billam the 26th
Aprill Buried an infant of Thomas Benson unbap: the 5th day of Aprill
Buried William Darely the 22th day
Baptized Grace the daughter of Mr. Jasper Hunt the 30th day
May Married Cotton Horne & Elizabeth Autrã wth a licence the 3[d]
Baptized Hester the daughter of Williã Wharã the 12th
Baptized Williã soñe of Williã Carr the 26th day
June Baptized Tobias the sone of Richard Tottington & Arbella the daughter of Thomas Hudson the 23th day
Baptized Dorcas the daughter of Williã Pearson 30th
Juy Married Williã Bilingley & Elizabeth Richardson the 9th
Buried ould Marshall of Swinton the 20th
Baptized Thomas the sonne of George Greenhough 21th

1633

August	Married	Mathew Browne & Helen Dickinson the 4th day
	Baptized	Margarett the daughter of Willm Soresby *18*th
	Baptized	Elizabeth daughter of Robt Lile the 25th day
Septembr	Baptized	Isabell daughter of Mathewe Browne the i day
Octobr	Baptized	Henry soñe of Henry Kay the 14th day
	Buried	the said Henry the 19th day
	Baptized	Williã sone of Christopher Barraclough 20
Novembr	Married	Williã Gawtres & Edith Brookesbrough ?
	Baptized	Humphray soñe of Humphray Jackson
	Baptized	George soñe of George Mallinson
December	Baptized	Helen daughter of Peter Bayliffe the 8th day
	Buried	Margaret wife of the said Peter Bayliffe
	Buried	the said Helen the 22th
January	Buried	Williã Broome the 3 day
	Baptized	Jarvas soñe of Jarvas England the 6th day
	Baptized	Margarett daughter of John Carr the 13th day
	Baptized	Martine soñe of Willia Iredall the 20th day
	Buried	a man found dead of Hoober the 21th day
	Baptized	Thomas soñe of Richard Pearson the 27th day
ffebru	Baptized	Nicholas soñe of Nicholas Sharpe the 3d day
	&	Thomas soñe of Thomas Leach eod̄ die
	Buried	Richard Horner the 16th day
March	Baptized	Dianas the daughter of Ralph Hattersley 10 ?
	Baptized	William the soñe of Richard Shaw eodẽ die
	Baptized	John the soñe of Williã Haynton the 17th
1634		
	Buried	. . . . the wife of Thomas Hanson 27th
Aprill	Baptized	Hester the daughter of Nicholas Tompson 6
	Baptized	Hester the daughter (sic)
	Baptized	(*blank*)
May	Buried	an infant of Thomas Hepworth the 3th day
	Married	Henry Wood & Margarett Soresby the 4th day
	Buried	Anne daughter of Williã Coulbrand the 18th
June	Married	Richard Carr & Elizabeth Maughã the first
	Baptized	John the sone Richard Slacke the 8th
	Buried	John Tilney the 12th day
	Buried	Elizabeth Hunt widow the 21th day
	Married	Ralph Hattersley & Ann Broome the 29th
	Baptized	Elizabeth the daughter of Henry Yates
	&	Elizabeth daughter of John Smalchayre the 13th day

Memorandũ That the thirteenth day of Aprill 1634 Willm Dyson of Wath upon Dearne was licensed to sitt in a stall in the North Alley of the wch hee hath already bestowd cost accordinge to the directions of the commissioners in the wch hee hath usually sitten. Witnes our hands the day of date above said

Radulphus Goodyeare ministrũ ibid
Gervase Smyth
E.A.
Emmanuell Armefield

1634

Memorandū That the 13th of April, 1634 was licensed to sett up a stall in wch the marriages useth to sitt when any is) one of Mr. Wortleys. Emanuele Armefield & John Carr of Coley lane, of the wch they have bestowed . . . . accordinge to the Commissioners directions witness our hand the day & date above

Radulphus Goodyeare ministrū ibid
Gerves: Smyth
Emanuell + Armefield. Humphredi Jackson

Memorandū That the 20th of May 1634 Richard Pearson of Wath upon Dearne was licensed and authorized to Reedifie & make upp a stall in the Lady quiar in wch his forfathers hath usually sett & there to stand & Remaine wthout any Disturbance or molestacon of any one in payne of Ecclesiasticall Censure by us whose names are hereundr written.

Radulphus Goodyeare ministrū ibid.

July	Baptized	Ann the daughter of William ffreeman the 6th day
	Baptized	William the sōne of Jarvas Smith gent the 12th (off Septem (*Inserted*)
	Buried	an infant of Richard Wells unbaptized the 27th
August	Baptized	Grace daughter of Willia Soresby the 2d
	Baptized	James the sōne of Richard Pearson the 9th
Septe	Baptized	Alice daughter of Nicholas Pearson the 13th day
	Buried	a poore man a stranger the 15th day
	Baptized	John sone of William Gawtres the 22 day
October	Buried	an infant of Anne Sunderland base begott the first day
	Buried	the said Ann Sunderland the 20th day
	Buried	Elizabeth wife of Richard Walker the 23th day
	Married	Josuah Maud & Anne Herringe the 27th day
Novembr	Baptized	Richard sōne of a colliar of Swinton moreside the first day
	Baptized	Abraham the sōne of Edmund a colliar of Swinton the 8th day
	Married	Thomas Tilney & Jane Slack the 17th
	Buried	an infant of Richard Mabson the 18th day
	Baptized	Rosomond daughter of Thomas Johnson (*rubbed out*)
	Buried	a stranger the 23th day
December	Buried	Richard sōne of William Barraclough the first day
	Baptized	Ralph sōne of Ralph Gillott the 6th day
	Baptized	Isabell daughter of John Sison the 15th day
	Buried	Elizabeth wife of Nicholas Darely the 20th day
January	Baptized	Richard sōne of Richard Hill the 11th day
	Baptized	Samuell the sone of Samuell Wortley, gent, the 28th
	Buried	Thomas Biltcliffe the 30th
	Buried	Elizabeth wife of Nicholas Tompson 31th

1634

February	Buried	ould Mabson wife the fourth day
	Buried	a poore man the eleventh day
	Baptized	Richard sōne of Peter Jessopp the 15th & Willia sone of Thomas Jackson eođ die
	Buried	the said Richard the 17th day
	Baptised	Richard sone of a poore man 22th day
March.	Buried	Mihil Stringer the 6th
	Baptized	the sonne of Richard Nelthorp
	Batpiz	the daughter of Godfrey Fosterd
	Buried	Katheran the wife of Richard Liuitt
	Buried	Elizabeth the wife of George Hoyland January 28th

1635 In cipit Annus.

March	Baptized	Nicholas soñe of Henry Wood, March 25th
	Buried	an Infant of Ralph Hattersley the 29th
Aprill	Baptized	Isabell daughter of Richard Eelam 5th
	Baptized	Elizabeth daughter of William Carr 19th
	Baptized	Susan daughter of Laurence Wade the 20th
	Baptized	Jane daughter of Thomas Blacksmith 27th
May	Baptized	Robart soñe of Robart Swift May the 3d
	Baptized	Anne daughter of Richard Westrin the 10th
	Buried	John Sawtree the 26th
	Buried	the said Nicholas soñe of Henry Wood 30th
June	Baptized	John soñe of Richard Mabson the 21th
	Baptized	Anne daughter of William Pearson 28th
July	Baptized	Alice daughter of John Wharã the 17th
	Baptized	John the soñe of Walker nithe Shaw 24th
	Baptized	William soñe of William Brooke the 31th
August	Baptized	Thomas sone of Richard Tottington 23th
	Baptized	Anne daughter of Richard Pearson the 30th
	Buried	Widow Marshall the 31th
	Baptized	Katherine the daughter of Mathew Browne of Melton eođ die
September	Baptized	Ralph soñe of George Jenkinson the second
	Buried	the said Ralph the 6th day
	Baptized	Hester daughter of Richard Heaton 27th
	Buried	Joane Eelam the 30th
October	Buried	Elizabeth Eelam the 12th
	Married	John Hogley & widow Barraclough the 20th
	Buried	the said Thomas Tottington the 21th
	Married	William Swall & Elizabeth Birks the 27th
	Buried	Nicholas Darely the thirtieth day
November	Buried	an infant daughter of Nicholas Mallinson the first
	Baptized	Helen daughter of Henry Kay the 3d
	Buried	Thomas Booth the 5th
	Married	William Beckett & Widow Biltcliffe the 15th
	Baptized	Elizabeth daughter of Thomas Tilney the 20th
	Married	Thomas Hudson & Isabell Wade the 27th
	Baptized	Elizabeth daughter of Jarvas England the 30th

1635		
December	Baptized	Rosamund daughter of John Greene the 6th
	Buried	John Dawson the 10th
	Buried	an Infant of George Bensons the 15th
	Baptized	William son of John Parrake the 27th
January	Baptized	Helen the daughter of William Wharã the 17th
	Baptised	Thomas the soñe of Thomas Mirefeild eod die
	Buried	John the sone of John Smalchayre the 18th
	Baptized	Nicholas the sone of Thomas Harrison the 20th
	Baptized	Dorithy daughter of the Pedler the 25th
February	Buried	George Benson the 11th Feb.
	Buried	John the soñe of Richard Mabson the 14th
	Baptized	Hester the daughter of Thomas Hudson the 15th
	Baptized	David the soñe of a poore man at Tottingtons 19th ?
	Baptized	Helen the daughter of William Trivy the 25th
	Buried	an infant of John Ellis the same day
March	Buried	Widow Mabson the first day
	Buried	the aforesaid soñe of Henry Yates
	Buried	widow Biggland eod die the second day
Incipit Annus. 1636		
Aprill	Buried	Richard Tottington the ninth day
	Buried	Thomas the soñe of Nicholas Saxton the 17th day
	Buried	the soñe of George Yates the 18th day
	Baptized	ffrancis the soñe of Richard Thackerawe the 24th
	Buried	Elizabeth daughter of Thomas Marriott the 25th
May	Baptized	Thomas soñe of Richard Eelam the 8th day
	Baptized	Elizabeth daughter of William Swallow eod die
	Baptized	Elizabeth daughter of John Ridiough the 15th day
	Baptized	George & Robart the sonnes of John Tinsley the 12th day
June	Baptized	John the soñe of William ffreeman the 7th day
	Buried	. . . . the soñe of John Wharam the 12th day
	Baptized	Grace the daughter of Thomas Burton the 19th
	&	Richãrd the soñe of Richard Shaw eod die
	Buried	William the son of Jarvas England
	Baptized	Jane the daughter of Richard Slacke the 24th
July	Baptized	William the sone of William Iredale the 3 day
	Baptized	William the soñe of John Beard the last of September
1636		
October	Buried	ffrancis Gawtre the wife of John Gawtre October the thirteenth
	Married	Ralph ffoords and Anne Stafford of Darton October the 27th
	Buried	Elizabeth Wildsmith Nom̃ber the first
	Baptized	John Lile the son of Robt Lile November 13th
	Maried	Thom: Longley & Jane Cuttes November 13th
	Baptized	Tho: Pearson the sonn of Richard Pierson November the 24th

1636

Baptized Elizabeth Carter daughter of Robert Carter November the 26th

Baptized Will Carr the sonn of John Carr December the 4th

December Betterris daughter to John Lewin baptized December the twentie one

Baptized John the sone of Thomas Robinsone of Brampton the 27th day of December

1637 ? *1636/7*

Jan Buried John Carre the 13th day of this instant January

Baptized Henry Yates the sonne of Henry Yates of Brampton January 13th

Baptized Henry the sonne of George Hinche the 22th day of January

Buried Grace Greenhough the wife of Thomas Greenhough the 25th day of January

Baptized . . . . the sonn of Henrie Wood the 30th day of January

ffebruarie Baptized Elizabeth daughter to Thomas Jackson the 12th of ffeb

Baptized Elizabeth daughter to Expofer Baraclough the 12th of ffeb.

March Buried Marie Armfield the first day of March

Baptized John the sonn of Ralph Gillat the fift of March

Baptized Elizabeth the daughter of Nicholas Peerson March the fift

Baptized Willia son of Edmund Brooke of Swinton March the 12th

Baptized Richard son of Richard Eller of Swinton March the 12th

Baptized Elizabeth daughter of . . . . Arundell of Swinton March the 19th

Baptized Elizabeth daughter of John Ellis of Wath March the 19th

Baptized Elizabeth daughter of Richard Shaw of Wath March the 19th

Baptized Elizabeth daughter of Expofer Barraclough March the 19th

1637

May Married Thomas Greenwood of the ꝑish of Rotheram and Doritie ffirthe the eighteenth day of May

Buried Elizabeth Greenhaugh May the tenth day

Baptized Marie the daughter of Richard Hill May 21th

Baptized Ann the daughter of Joseph Bristow? May 21th

June Baptized Mary the daughter of Samuell Wortley June the eleventh

Baptized Williā the son of Edward Daile June the 21

Baptized Robert the sonn of Richard Heton June the 2

Baptized Easter the daughter of Richard Heton June the 2

Baptized Garvas the son of Garvas Enilandes (*England*) June the 2

1637		
June	Baptized	Williã the son Wiłł Gawtresse June the 4th
July	Buried	John Sharp July the first
	Buried	Elizabeth ffox July 25
August	Baptized	Ellen the daughter of Thomas Tilney the tenth day of August Año Dom̃ 1637
	baptized	Catherau the daughter of Thom: Longley the 20th day
	baptized	Williã the sonn of Mary Wood the 27th
	baptized	Elizabeth the daughter of Will: Walker the 27
	baptized	Mary the daughter of Thom.: Leach 27
September	baptized	Jasper the sonn of John Sissan September the tenth
	buried	Jaruis the son of Jaruis England the 13th
	buried	Barbary the daughter of Peter Robbinson the 16th day
	baptized	Mary the daughter of Lawrence Wade the 17th day
	baptized	Ellen the daughter of Williã Car the 17th day
	baptized	Ellen the daughter of George Yates the 24th day
November	baptised	Ellen the daughter of Georg Malison the fift day of Nouember
	baptized	Ursella Bely daughter of Peter Bely the fift day
	married	Robt̃ Cheriholme & Dorithie Bisby the fift day
	buried	Mabell the wife of John Carr ye 8th day
	buried	Elizabeth ye wife of Williã Pearson the 8th day
	buried	an infant of Samuell Burtons the same day
	buried	Elizabeth the wife of John Helam the 15th day
	baptized	Humphrey the sonn of Thom: Blacksmith 19th day
	buried	Nicholas Beomont the 25th day
	Baptized	Nicholas the son of Richard Peerson 9ber 26th bur: the 27th
	baptized	Richard the sonn of John Green Nouember 26t
	Baptized	Margrett the daughter of ffrancesse Carr Nouember 3d
December	Baptized	Williã the sonn of Godfrey ffoster December 24th
Jany	Baptized	Thom: the son of Williã Swallow Jan: the 7th
	Baptized	John the son of Matthew Brown Jan: 7th bur: ye 10th
	Buried	Elizabeth Marriott the 20th
	Baptized	John the soñe of Robert Robinett the 21th
	Married	Richard Nickolson & Jane Widder eođ die
	Married	Godfray Bintcliffe & Winifred Broome 22th
	Baptized	Elizabeth daughter of William Burton ye 28th
	Baptized	William the soñe of George Barraclough eođ die
ffeb.	Buried	Thomas the sone of the said William Swallow 5th
	Buried	William the sone of the said Barraclough the 6th
	Baptized	Robart the sonne of Richard Eelam the 11th day & Elizabeth daughter of Thomas Hudson eođ die
	Buried	Thomas Baxter the 18th day
	Baptized	Thomas the sone of William Brooke the 20th day
	Buried	the said Thomas the 21th
	Buried	ffrances the daughter of Jarvas England the 22th

1637		
March	Baptized	Jane the daughter of George Greenehough 4th
	Buried	Richard England the 15th day
	Baptized	John the sone of Thomas Mirrefield the 18th
	Buried	vid. Elam & Jasp the sone of John Sisson 24th
1638 Anno	Domini.	
March	Baptized	Sara the daughter of Adam Earle the 27th & Thomas the sone of Thomas Johnson eod die
	Buried	Thomas Hawkay eod die & ffrancis daughter of Ralph Hatt'sley eod die
	Buried	John Sisson the 28th day
	Buried	Elizabeth Heaton the last day
Aprill	Baptized	Thomas the sone of Robart Carter the first day
	Buried	Widow Baxter & late wife of Thomas Baxter the 4th day
	Baptized	Helen the daughter of Nicholas Mallinson the 8th day
	Married	ffortune Shackersley & Elizabeth Tottington eod die
May	Buried	an infant of Richard Eller of Swinton the second day
	Baptized	Richard the sone of Henry Slaeke the 16th day
July	Baptized	George the sonne of Robart Swift the 8th day
	Buried	Elizabeth wife of John Broome the 9th day
	Buried	Margarett the wife of William Marshall
	Baptized	Elizabeth the daughter of Emanuell Armefield Curate the 15th day
	Baptized	Rosamond the daughter of Ralph Goodyeare the 22th day
	Buried	widow ffixby the 28th day
	Baptized	William sone of William ffreeman the 29th day & Sara the daughter of Alexander Mariott eod die
August	Buried	John Broome the vith day
	Baptized	Helen the daughter of Thomas Liversage the xixth day
	Buried	Elizabeth the wife of Robert Thackrawe the xxijth
	Buried	the said Robert Thackrawe the xxixth day
Sept.	Married	John Baldricke & Elizabeth Dyson the ijd
	Buried	Sr ? Coldwell the 15th day
	Baptized	George the sone of George Heasleaste xvjth
	Married	Richard Thomson & Mary Pheasant the xxiijth
	Buried	an infant of William Wilson, unbaptized, the 30th
Octobr	Married	Richard Townend & Anne Hage the 14th day
	Baptized	Katherine the daughter of Humphray Jackson, & Elizabeth the daughter of Peter Jessopp the xxviij
	Buried	Widow Skiddmore the xxxith day
November	Baptized	William the sone of John Riddiough the xith
	Baptized	William the sone of a cobler of Swinton the 18th
	Baptized	Katherine the daughter of Samuell Burton the xxvth day

1638

November	Baptized	Samuell the soñe of Thomas Burton the 30th
December	Buried	John the soñe in law to John Lambert ye vth day
	Baptized	Jarvas the soñe of Richard Slacke ye ixth
	Buried	an infant of Richard Shaw ye xvith
	Baptized	Thomas the soñe of William Pearson the xxxth day
January	Baptized	ffrances the daughter of Edward Dale the vith day
	Baptized	Elizabeth daughter of Richard Hencoyte ye xiijth
	Baptized	Richard the soñe of Richard Nicolson ye xxth
Februarye	Baptized	William the soñe of Richard Wells ye xth day
	Baptized	Mary the daughter of John Beard the xvijth
	Baptized	Ralph the soñe of Richard Pearson the xxiiijth
	Baptized	Rosamond the daughter of Ralph Hattrsley pred die
	Buried	an infant of Henry Yates ye xxvith
March	Baptized	Anne the daughter of William Swallow the third day
	Baptized	Rosamond the daughter of Richard Eller the xth day
	Baptized	Mary the daughter of John Lambert the xvijth
	Baptized	Margaret the daughter of John Baldrigge the xxiiijth day

1639 Incipit Annus.

April	Baptized	Nathaniel the sone of Mr Crosland Aprill the 11th
	Baptized	Mary the daughter of William Trivy the 14th
	Baptized	John the soñe of Thomas Filney the 23d
	Baptized	John the soñe of Thomas Harrison the 28th
May	Married	William Makin & Margaret Pearson May the first
	Baptized	William soñe of Richard Pearson the 5th
	Buried	Helen the wife of Thomas Cooe the 6th
	Buried	Thomas the soñe of William Pearson the first day
	Buried	Anne the wife of the said William Pearson

1639

August	Baptized	Anne the daughter of Nicholas Kay the 4th
	Baptized	Thomas sonne of John Carr the 11th day
	Buried	Elizabeth daughter of Jasp Hunt gent the fifth of June
	Baptized	Nicholas the sone of the said Jasp the sixth day
	&	Elizabeth the daughter of John Coulebrand eod die
Sept:	Buried	Henry Turner the 8th day of September
	Baptized	Mary daughter Ralph Jellot the 9th
	Baptized	Richard the sone of Richard Tompson the 30th day
	Buried	Robert Clay the 31th
Octobr	Buried	Nicholas Wood the 4th day
	Baptized	Nicholas the sonne of William Wilson the 16th daye
	Baptized	Jaine the daughter of Nicholas Pearson ye 20th
	Baptized	William the sone of William Brooke the 27th
Novem:	Baptized	Thomas the sone of Samuell Wortley gent the 12th
	Married	John Ward and Jane Wilcocke the 15th
	Buried	Anne the daughter of Robt Swift the 16th
	Buried	. . . . . . the daughter of William Soresby the 27th
	Buried	George Greenhough the 30th day

1639

Decembr	Baptized	John the sone of Matthew Baxter the first day
	Baptized	John the sone of Richard Hill the 29th
Janu :	Baptized	Jane the daughter of Ralph ffoards the fifth day
	Married	John Stockdale & Mary Wood the 12th
	Married	Robt Jepson & Margaret Carr the 14th day
	Married	Robt Jackson & Elizabeth Shaw the 28th
ffebru :	Baptized	Anne ths daughter of John Tinsley the first day
	&	Buried an infant of the said Johns the same day
	Baptized	Jobn sone of George Leach the second day
	&	Grace & Anne the daughters of Edmnnd a Colliar eod die
	Buried	Mrs Helen Tolson the same day
	Buried	Rodger Martin the 13th day
	Baptized	Margarett the daughter of Thomas Jackson 9th
	Buried	Margarett the wife of Williã Soresby the 20th
	Baptised	Nicholas sonne of William Carr the 23th
	&	Henry sone of Richard Shaw eod die
	&	Jane the daughter of William Maykin eod die
March	Baptized	Mary the daughter of George Mallinson the eighth day
	& Isabell the daughter of thomas Hudson	
	& John the sone of Richard Heaton eod die	
	Baptized	Ruth the daughter of George Shaw the 12th
	Baptized	Elizabeth the daughter of George Brooke the 22th day
	Baptized	Hester the daughter of William Greenwood the 24th
	Buried Richard the sone of Richard Marriott	

Incipit Annus 1640.

	Buried	the said Hester the 31th day
Aprill	Baptized	William the sone of Thomas Walker the 5th day of Aprill
	Baptized	Alice daughter of John Flint
	Buried	widow ffrankish the 13th of Aprill
	Buried	an infant of George Barracloughs the 22th day
	Buried	Buried John Hunt the 25th day
May	Baptized	Thomas the sone of Thomas Liũsage the 3 day
	Buried	George Wilcock the 5th day
	Baptized	. . . . the daughter of Henry Wood ye 10th
	Married	Jervas Miller & Mary Baxter the 14t day
	Baptized	Anne the daughter of Jervas Arendale eod die
	Buried	ffitnes wife of Swinton the 17th day
June	Married	Nicholas Crosland & Edith Beaumont the first day
	Married	Thomas Lockewood & Mary Clarke eod die
	Baptized	Helen the daughter of Adam Earle the 7th day
	Buried	widow ffreeman the 11th day
	Baptized	Anne the daughter of Henry Shaw 21th
July	Baptized	Grace the daughter of Thomas Blacksmith the 14th
	Married	Robert Longbottome & Anne Jubb the 27th
August	Buried	Thomas ffaux the 10th day
	Baptized	William the soñe ot Alexander Thackrowe the 16th day

1640

August	Buried	the said William the 26th day
	Baptized	Anne the daughter of Richard Thackrowe 30th
	Buried	the said Anne the 31th day
Septem	Baptized	John the son of John Ward the 6th day
	Buried	Elizabeth England the 13th day
	Buried	Sara daughter of Alexander Marriott the 23th day
Octobr	Married	Nicholas Dawson & Rosamond Scales the 4th
	Baptized	Henry the putative sone of Richard Hill 11th
	Baptized	Katherin the daughter of Richard Mallinson the 18th day
	Buried	Alice ffrankish the 20th day mother of the said Henry
Novembr	Buried	Katherin the wife of Nicholas Mallinson the first
	Baptized	Anne the daughter of Robt Longbottome the 7th
	Baptized	Hester the daughter of Mathew Baxter the 8th day
	Buried	Nicholas Tompson the 10th day
Decembr	Baptized	Thomas the sone of Emanuell Armefield the sixth day
	Baptized	Elizabeth the daughter of Mr Crosland the 18th day
	Buried	Widow Booth the 20th day
	Buried	Widow ffostar of Swinton the 20th day
January	Baptized	John the soñe of John Wright the first day
	Baptized	Elizabeth the daughter of William Gawtres the 10th day
	Baptized	Mary the daughter of Peter Bayliffe the 17th day
	Married	William Soresby & Elizabeth Wade 21th day
	Buried	Nicholas Morton the 22th day
ffeb. :	Buried	Elizabeth the daughter of William Gawtres the 10th
	Buried	John Brooke the 20th day
	Baptized	Thomas soñe of Godfray Biltcliffe the 23th
	Buried	Ursula the wife of John ffirth the 27th day
	Buried	John Gibson the 28th day
March	Buried	an infant of Edward ffirth base begott the 2 day
	Buried	John the soñe of Thomas Tilney the 4th day
	Baptized	Anne the daughter of Thomas Cooe, 10th
	Baptized	Anne the daughter of Henry Yates the 17th day

Incipit Annus 1641

	Buried	Lionell the soñe of Robart Chappell the 28th of March
	Buried	John Case the 29th
	Baptized	John the soñe of John Ellis the 30th day
Aprill	Baptized	Nicholas the soñe of Nicholas Dawson the 4th day
	Buried	the above said John Ellis the fifth day
	Buried	George Mallinson soñe of George Mallinson eod̄ die
	Buried	John the soñe of John Wright the 10th day
	Baptized	Richard the soñe of Richard Pearson the 12th day
	Baptized	William the soñe of Henry Yates the 14th day
	Buried	Elizabeth the wife of Robart Swift the 17th day
	Buried	the above said Robart soñe of Richard Pearson the 24th day

1641

Aprill	Baptized	Alice the daughter of Thomas Mirrefied the 25th day
	Baptized	William the soñe of Samuel Burton the 27th
May	Buried	Thomas Poplewell the second day of May
	Married	Nicholas Maykin & Alice Walker the 4th
	Baptized	William the soñe of William Seton the 9th day
	&	Thomas the soñe of Richard Eelam
	&	Elizabeth the daughter of John Marriott eod̄ die
	Buried	widow Ellison eod̄ die
	Married	Gilbart Houlmes & Dorothy ffrankish eod̄ die
	Married	John Hallott of the pish of Ecclesfield & Elizabeth Waide of the pish of Wath wth a licence the 12th day of May
	Buried	Elizabeth the daughter of the said John Marriott the 13th day
	Baptized	Joãny the daughter of Jarvas England the 20th day
	Buried	the said Joãny the 22th day
	Married	Edward ffirth & Ursula the 28th day
	Married	Thomas Bawdison & Elizabeth Edeson the 30th
June	Buried	Ralph the sõne of Richard Pearson the 4th day
	Baptized	Jane the daughter of Thomas Tilney the 6thday
	Married	Richard Walker and Alice Slacke the 20th day
	Buried	Ellen Tottington the 23th day
	Baptized	Richard the sõne of William ffreeman the 24th day
	Buried	John the sõne of Edmund Brooke the same day
	Buried	Widow ffaux the 25th day
	Baptized	Eideth the daughter of Godfray ffostard the 27th
July	Baptised	Alice the daughter of Robert Saundrson the 4th day
August	Baptised	Grace the daughter of Alexander Marriott the first day
	Baptized	Elizabeth the daughter of John Beard eod̄ die
	Buried	William Ceton the 4th day
	Buried	Elizabeth the wife of John Wharã the 8th day
	Buried	Henry the sone of Richard Shaw the 12th day
	Buried	Thomas Leach the 14th day
	Baptized	Ralph the soñe of John Eelam the 15th day
	Baptized	William the soñe of John Couldebrand the 24th day
	Baptized	Thomas the soñe of Alexander Thackrowe the 29th
	&	Jane the daughter of Jarvas Milner eod̄ die
	Buried	Mr. Henry Savile the 30th day
Septembr	Baptized	Margarett the daughter of James Wilcocke the 23th of Septembr
Octobr	Married	Rodger Stocks & Anne Armitage the 5th day
	Buried	Peter Jessop the seaventh day
	Buried	Helen Harper the 9th day
	Married	Lancellott Briggs & Mary Moore the 27th day
	Buried	an infant of Nicholas Pearson unbaptized the last day
Novembr	Married	William Wordsworth and Anne Wood
	Buried	Anne the wife of Mathew Baxter the 12th day
Janu.	Buried	an infant of Robt Liles the second day

1641

Janu.	Buried	Henry Henry Kay the 16th day
	Baptized	Humphray the sone of William Gawtres the 20th day
	Buried	John Birks the 22th day
	Baptized	William the soñe of Thomas Bawdison the 23th day
	Baptized	John Preston the 29th day
	Baptized	John the soñe of John Baldrigge the 30th day
ffebruary	Buried	Widow Shaw the third day
	Married	Henry Tilney & Helen Kellam the 7th day
	Buried	Nicholas Mallinson the 8th day
	Buried	2 infants of Mr Jasp Hunt unbaptized eod̄ die
	Baptized	Margaret the daughter of Samuell Wortley gent the 15th day
	Baptized	Elizabeth the daughter of William Bridelay the 20th day
	Baptized	Nicholas the soñe of Nicholas Kay eod̄ die
	Buried	Joane the wife of John More the 25th day
Marche	Buried	William Hoyland the first day
	Buried	Jane the wife of William Cobbacke the third day
	Baptized	ffrancis the soñe of William Carr the 6th day
	Buried	widow Gibson eod̄ die
	Baptized	Thomas soñe of Gilbart Houmes the thirteenth day
	Baptized	Jane the daughter of William Swallow eod̄ die
1642	Incipit Annus	
	Baptized	John the soñe of Ralph ffoards the 27th of March
	Buried	an infant of William Brooke of Swinton eod̄ die
Aprill	Buried	ffrances the daughter of Peter Bayliffe the third day
	Baptized	Ralph the soñe of Richard Pearson of Wath the 7th
	Baptized	Thomas the sone of John Ellis of Wath the 10th die
	Buried	John ffirth the 17th day
	Buried	Ralph the sd sonne of Richard Pearson eod̄ die
	Baptized	Mary the daughter of Adam Earle the 24th day
	Baptized	Anne the daughter of Edward Dale the 25th day
	Married	John Peate & Elizabeth Carneley eod̄ die
	Buried	Mr Crosland curate of Swinton the 29th day
May	Buried	Mrs Coldwell of Swinton the 7th day
	Baptized	Henrie the sonne of Rich Walker of Wath
	Baptized	William the sonne of Nicholas Maykin of Wath
	Buried	Hellen the daughter of Thomas Tilney of Wath
	Baptized	Thomas the sonne of Thomas Teylor of Wath
	Buried	Elizabeth the wife of Henrie Teylor, clerke
	Married	George Steele and Anne Sloswick
	Baptized	Richard the sonne of Richard Nicholson
	Buried	Margarett the daughter of James Willcock
	Baptized	Amie the daughter of Rich: Tompson of Wath
	Buried	Elizabeth the daughter of Matthew Baxter
	Baptized	Hester the daughter of Willm Kempe of Wath
	Baptized	Elizabeth the daughter of Willm Ellison of the Roydes

1642		
May	Buryed	Thomas Greenehough of Wath
	Baptized	Henrie the sonne of Henrie Tilney
	Buried	the said Henrie Tilney junior
	Buried	Widdowe Martin of Brampton Byerley
	Buried	John Tinsley of Hoober
	Baptized	John the sonne of Edward ffirth of Melton
	Baptized	Rosamond the daughter of Gervis England of Brampton
	Baptized	Grace the daughter of Rich : Pearson
ffebru 27th	Buried	John the sonne of William Wharme of Melton
	Buried	Richard sonne of Richard Hutchinson de Newall
	Buried	Widdowe Shawe of Melton
	Buried	Richard the sonne of Robert Tompson
	Baptized	Allice daughter of John Golland of Melton
	Marled	Samuell Doncaster & Elizabeth Goodall
	Baptized	Elizabeth the daughter of Lancelott Briggs de Swinton
	Buried	Widdowe Bridleye of Swinton
	Baptized	2 Twynnes of a Coblers
	Baptized	George the sonne of Thomas Walker of Swinton
	Baptized	Margarett the daughter of Wiłłm Brooke
	Bapt.	Thom. ye sonn of Godfrey Bintleife May 17th 1644
	Bapt.	Emanuell ye sonne of Tho : Hirst of Brampton febr. the 1643
	Bapt.	Rich. ye sonne of Wiłłm Maykin Novemb. 18th 1642
	Bapt.	Easter ye daughter of Adam Earle Aprill the 10th 1645
	Bapt.	George ye sonne of Rich : Pearson Sept. 14th 1645
	Bapt.	Margarett ye daughter of John Colbrand Septem : the 21th 1644
	Bapt.	Ann ye daughter Xstopher ffoulston Novemb : 24th 1644
	Bapt.	Henry the sonne of Wiłłm Brooke October 3^d 1645
	Bapt.	William the sonne of Henrye Tilney Jan : ye 1643
	Bapt.	Nich : the sonne of John Wright July ye 12th 1643
	Bapt.	Henry the sonne of Joh : Wright June the 15th 1645
	Bapt.	David the sonne of Gervis Hinchliff the . . 1645
	Baptized	Henrie the sonne of Rich : Hill ffebr 25th 1644
	Baptized	Joseph the sonne of Rich : Hill Octob : 30th 1642
	Baptized	Mary the daughter of John Mariot August the first 1643

M^d The Visitacōn of the plague began in Swinton June the 27th 1646 & continued untill the 5th of October of the same year duringe wch time 59 ꝑsons dyed thereof.

M^d Ringing of the bell at eight of ye clock at night & six at morn was begun March ye 25th in the begining of the year 1646

ꝑ me Nich : Hunt clericum
pochialem ibiđ.

1643

Baptized Ann the daughter of Ric. Heaton May 7th 1645

Md Mr Thomas Benson Mr of Artes & now vicar of Wath preached his first sermon here upon Sunday the 25th of July 1647

Md The Pulpitt was remoued from the uppermost piller on the north side of the bodye of the church A° 1646 unto ye place where it now standeth next under the Arch divideing the bodye of the church from the quere

Baptized Thomas ye sonne of Marke Hagg Mr of Artes & Vicar of Wath June 22 1645
Baptized Willm ye sonn of Jervis England eod. die
Baptized Willm the sonn of Thomas Plats Octob 31th 1645
Baptized Easter ye daughter of Jasper Hunt gent . . . the . . 1644
Baptized Elizabeth the daughter of Joh Baldrick November the 14th 1644
Baptized Elizabeth the daughter of Ralfe Fordes August 6th 1644
Maryed Rich: Baracloug & . , . . December ye 21th 1645
Baptized Ann daughter of William Carr October the 14th 1644
Maryed Francis Baxter & Anne Tinley Octob 20th 1645
. . . . Emie the daughter of Bryan Hirst Decemb 15th 1646
Maryed Francis Baxter & Anne Tinley October

Md that upon the 30th day of November 1645 Nicholas Hunt was chosen Parish Clerke of Wath upon Dearne by Marke Hagge Mr of Artes and Vicar there with full consent of the whole pish, Rich Heaton & John Baldrick being the churchwardens.

November 1645
Buried 27th John Addie, pish clerke of Wath
Maried 28 William Rodwell and Elizabeth Mallinson
December 1645
Maried 2th John Sisson and Mariē Jackson
Buried 6th John Robucke of Wath
Maried 8th Henrie Yates and Anne Bintliffe
Maried 9th John Addie and Elizabeth Smyth
Baptized 9th Rosamonde the daughter of George Mallinson
Maried 18th John Taylor and Anne Harrison
Baptized 19th Anne the daughter of John Ellis
Baptized 21th Nicholas the sonne of ffrancis Carre of Brampton
Buried 25th the said Nicholas the sonne of ffra: Carre
Buried 28th Marie the daughter of John fflinte of Hooberside
Buried 31th An Infant of William Cusseworthe of Brampton unbaptized
Bapt Ann daughter of Peter Bayliffe eodem die
January 1645
Baptized 22th William the sonne of Thomas Liversedge
February 1645
Buried iith Anne Dyson daughter in lawe of John Baldrick
Buried 15th Thomas the sonne of Thomas Teylor
Buried eod die Grace the daughter of Robert Lile of Westmelton
Baptized 23th William the sonne of John Warde of Westmelton
Baptized eod die Marye the daughter of John Gollande of Westmelton

1645

March 1645	
Baptized 12th	Anne ye daughter of Tho Wilcock iunior de Swinton
Buryed 14th	Grace Dawson aľ Ellis of Westmelton
Buryed 18th	Thomas Blacksmyth of Swinton
Incipit annus 1646	
[*Buryed?*] 28th	Dorothye Broome of Brampton
Aprill 1646	
[*Buryed?*]	Robert Eller of Swinton
Buryed 16th	. . . the daughter of Margarett ffixbye, illegtime procreat
Baptized 21th	Nicholas the sonne of Henrie Tilney
May, 1646.	
Buryed 17th	Isabell the wife of Thomas Hudson of Brampton
Buryed 28th	George the sonne of Richard Pearson of Wath
June 1646	
Maryed 8th	Thomas Eller & Hellen Cosine of Swinton
Buryed 11th	William the sonne William Brideley of Swinton
Buryed 24th	William Maiken
Maryed 25th	Leonard Wood and Sara Wadsworth of Sheffield
Buryed 27th	Michaell Kirkbye of Swinton
Buryed 29th	Alice the wife of the said Michaell Kirkbye
Buryed eod die	Elizabeth the wife of James Moore of Swinton
Marled eod die	Robert White & Mary Ellis
Maryed 30th	Henrye Wilcock & Marye Lewin
Baptized 13th	Alice the daughter of Willm Silvester a stranger yt lay at Swinton
Baptized 2th	Anne the daughter of Richard Baraclough
July 1646	
Baptized 2th	Jane the daughter of John Teylor of Wath
Buried 10th	Elizabeth Cutte of Swinton
Buryed 12th	Marye the wife of Robert White of Melton
Buryed eod die	James Moore of Swinton
Buryed eod die	. . . the daughter of ffrancis Hogley of Swinton
Buryed eod die	. . . the daughter of Lancelott Briggs of Swinton
Buried eod die	Rich : Nightingale of Swinton
Buryed eod die	. . . the wife of the said Richard
Buryed eod die	Edward the sonne of John Lewin late of Swinton
Buryed eod die	. . . the . . . of Jarvis Arundell of Swinton
Buryed 15th	Bryan Hirst of Swinton
Buryed eod die	. . . Wilkinson de Swinton
August 1646	
Maried 4th	Nicholas Goodyear & Alice Beckett
Baptized 14th	Jane the daughter of John Heape of Wath
Baptized 18th	Margaret the daughter of William Kente of Wath
Baptized 30th	Jane the daughter of ffrancis Baxter of Abdie, gent.
September 1646	
Maryed 1st	Jervis Bosvile de Edlington & Mary Stringer de Whiston
Baptized eod die	John the sonne of Thomas Hirst of Brampton
Maried 8th	Allexander Hattfeild of Ranfeild, cleric, & Alice Tinley of Wentworth Wood

1646

Baptized 24th	William the sonne of Henrie Yates of Wath
Baptized 28th	John the sonne of John Sisson
Buryed 29th	Grace the daughter of Richard Pearson of Melton
October 1646	
Maried primo die	John Hoyland & Anne Slacke
Baptized eod die	John the sonne of Thomas Tyas of Newall
Baptized 28th	Anne the daughter of John Pate of Wath
November 1646	
Baptized 3d	Hellen the daughter of John Baldrick of Wath, Church-warden
Baptized 5th	Anne the daughter of Godfrey Shells of Swinton
Maryed eod die	Robert White & Alice Boardman
Baptized 8th	Anne the daughter of John Flinte
Baptized 26th	Susan the daughter of Ralph ffoardes
December 1646	
Baptized 3d	Sara the daughter of Edward Milner of Rainber
Maried the same day	Humphrey Addye & Anne Jenkinson of Swinton
Bapt 10th	Elizabeth the daughter of Tho: Taylor of Wath
Bapt eod die	Hellen the daughter of Christopher ffoulston of Brampton
Bapt the 13th	Thomas the sonne of Rich: Ball of Wath
Baptized 17th	George the sonne of William Carre of Wath
Maried 22th	Valentine Tine & Jane Wood of Swinton
Maried eod die	Richard Baraclough & Beterice Wright of Wath
Buried 25th	Nicholas the sonne of Henrie Tilney of Wath
Baptized 26th	Katherin the daughter of John Ledger of Wath
January 1646	
Buried 4th	Hellen the daughter of Henrie Kaye of Wath
Maried 12th	Henrie ffirth of Swinton & Sarah Gelat
Baptized 14th	Dorothie the daughter of Henrie Sanderson
Buryed 23th	Allexander Maryott of Wath
Baptized 24th	Willm the sonne of Thomas Mirfin
ffebruary 1646	
Baptized 2d	Gervis the sonne of Robert Lile
Buried eod die	Anne the wife of John Teylor
Baptized 6th	Anne the daughter of Robert Longbottom
Maryed 10th	William Bowser & Elizabeth Hinch of Swinton
Baptized 14th	John the sonne of Mr Mark Hagge Vicar of Wath
Baptized eod die	Michaell the sonne of Michaell Slack of Brampton
Buryed 16th	John the sonne of William Maykin of Wath
Maried eod die	Gervas Arundell & Sarah Man of Swinton
Bapt 28th	Susana the daughter of John Bcarde of Wath
Bapt eod die	Hellen ye daughter of Willm Brydley of Swinton
March 1646	
Baptized 2d	George the sonne of Thomas Longley of Swinton
Marled eod die	Thomas Brooke & Katherin Herringe
Buried 3d	Henrie Tillney of Wath
Baptized 13th	Thomas the sonne of ffrancis Carre of Brampton
Buried 15th	Cicilie the wife of Adam Earle of Wath

1646

Buried eod die An Infant of William Cliftons of Wath unbaptized

Incipit Annus 1647

Aprill 1647

Baptized 5th Margarett the daughter of Rich. Hill of Melton

Baptized eod die Easter the daughter of Rich : Pearson of Wath

Buried 6th John ye sonne of John Readihough slaine wth a waine of Tho : Coes of Wath

Buried 19th Anne the daughter of Sam : Wortley, gent.

May 1647

Baptized 15th Easter the daughter of George Drable

Buried 17th John the sonne of Mr Marke Hagg, vicar of Wath

Baptized 4th Richard the sonne of Rich : Elison of the Royds

Buryed 27th Widdowe Willson of Swinton

Buryed 30th Anthonye Stables of Melton

June 1647

Baptized primo die Richard the sonne of Richard Peck of Wath

Baptized 8th Anne the daughter of Thomas Tilney of Wath

Baptized eod die Hellen the daughter of Richard Shawe of Wath

Baptized 13th Marye the daughter of Richard Baraclough of Wath

Baptized eod die Margarett ye daughter of George Brook of Wath

Baptized eod die Anne the daughter of Thomas Walker of Swinton

Maryed 18th Thomas Hudson & Elizabeth Stables

Baptized 22th Mary the daughter of George Foulston

Baptized eod die Henrie the sonne of Henrie Wilcock of Swinton

Baptized 24th Ann the daughter of Robert Gepson of Melton

Maryed 28th Michaell Bowser & Elizabeth Wade of Swinton

Buryed 30th Henrye the sonne of Henrye Wilcock of Swinton

July 1647

Buried 5th William Iredall of Coley lane

Buryed 7th Katherine the wife of John Colbran of Newall Grange

Baptized 10th William the sonne of Thomas Addye of Swinton

Baptized 18th William the sonne of Robert White of Brampton

Buried 22th Edyth ye wife of Rich : Pearson of Melton

August 1647

Baptized first Elizabeth the daughter of Allex. Thackerey of Swinton

Buryed 14th An Infant of William Cussworth of Wath, unbaptized

Baptized 16th Grace the daughter of Lancellot Briggs of Swinton

Buryed 18th Elizabeth the wife of ye sayd William Cussworth

Baptyzed 19th Thomas the sonne of Nicholas Dawson of Wath

Buried 27th Nicholas Telyer of Wath

September 1647

Buryed 2d John Colbrande of Newell Grange

Baptized 12th Edward the sonne of Edward Firth of Melton

Maryed 23th William Willson & Margarett Mayking of Wath

Buryed eod die Margarett the daughter of George Brooke of Wath

Buryed 26th Susan the daughter of John Beard of Wath

Baptized 28th Frances the daughter of Thomas Willcocke of Swinton

October 1647

Baptized 17th Elizabeth the daughter of Humphrey Addye of Swinton

1647

Buried eod die Anne ye wife of ye sayd Humph: wth an Infant of hers unbaptized
Buried 25th Elizabeth the wife Francis Kettlewell of Hooberside

November 1647

Maryed 4th Thomas Tilney alias Rearsbie and Anne Meller
Baptized 21th William the sonne of Thomas Platts
Maryed 23th Robert Stables & Margaret Litster
Buryed 24th Thomas Mirfin of Wath
Baptized 28 Jonathan the sonne of Gervase Hinchliffe of ye Abdie
Buryed 29th Katherine the widdowe of Robert Wilton
Buryed eod die Thomas the sonne of Thomas Platts of Wath

December 1647

Maryed 2^d^ Nicholas Birks & Anne Broadbent of Wath
Maryed 10th William Herringe of Billingley & Elizab Iredalle of Coley Lane
Baptised 12th Hellen the daughter of Thomas Coe of Wath
Baptised 19th Elizabeth the daughter of John Wells of Newall
Buryed 26th Robert Bushell of Swinton

January 1647

Buried 2^d^ Rosamond the daughter of Tho: Jackson of Wath
[*Buried* 5th] Rich. the sonne of Rich Peck of Wath
[*Buried* 8th] Richard Pearson of West Melton
Buryed 9^h^ Jane the wife of John Parre of Wath
Baptized eod die ffrancis the sonne of Rich. Heaton of Brampton
Baptized 10th Elizabeth the daughter of John Wells of Newall
Maryed 20th Adam Earle & Alice Shawe of Wath
Maried 21th Parker Barnard & Martha Houle of Britheside

February 1647

Baptized 3^d^ Gervase the sonne of William Carniley of West Melton
Buryed 13^h^ Jane the daughter of John Greene of Wath
Maried 15th John Taylor & Alice Preist
Buryed 18th William Stones of Wath
Buryed 20th Elizabeth the wife of Richard Eller of Swinton
Maried 24^h^ William Cussworth & Margaret Wilcock
Buried 26th Widdowe Hirst of Brampton

March 1647

Baptized 9th Richard the sonne of Rich. Hutchinson of Newall
Buryed 13th Nicholas Saxton of Newall
Baptized 19th Godfrey the sonne of Samuell Doncaster of Brampton
Baptized eod die John the sonne of Rich: Baraclough of Wath

Incipit Annus 1648

Buryed 30th John Browne of Wath—Good ffryday

Aprill 1648

Baptized 2^d^ Elizabeth the daughter of John Wright of Wath
Buried 3^d^ Hellen the wife of Mathew Browne of Melton
Buried 9th Easter the daughter of Tho: Hudson of Brampton
Buried 10th Martha ffoster of Wath widdowe
Buried 13th Mary the wife of William Broadley who died at Swinton

1647

Baptized 16th	Anne the daughter of Henrye Yates of Wath
Baptized eod die	Anne the daughter of Ralph Hattersley of Wath
Buryed 26th	John Greene of Wath
Baptized 27th	Edward the sonne of Jervase Millner of Westmelton
May 1648	
Buryed	. . . . [*no name*] . . . . of Swinton
Baptized 28th	William the sonne of Nich Key of Westmelton
Baptized 31th	William the sonne of Richard Kitchinman of Wath
June 1648	
Baptized 4h	Bernard the sonne of Marke Hagg, Vicar of Wath
Buryed 10th	William the sonne of Rich Kitchinman
Buryed 16th	An Infant of Malas Pearson ye yonger of Westmlton unbaptized
Buryed 21th	the daughter of Robert Ante of Swinton
Maryed 22th	John Armitage & Anne ffreeman
July 1648	
Buryed 4th	The wife of George Scoales of Theefhole
Baptized 16th	Jane the daughter of Thomas Hague alias Brook of Wath
Maried 23	Nicholas Adamson & Elizabeth Nightingale of Wentworth Chapelrie
Baptized 31th	Mary the daughter of Willm Clifton of Wathe
August 1648	
Maryed first	Thomas Marriott & Dorothie Graye
Maried 3d	Gervase Hanson & Hellen Tillney of Wath
Buryed 8th	Francis Carre alias Flower of Brampton
Baptized 13th	Elizabeth the daughter of Thomas Burton of Swinton
Maryed 17h	Edward Foweather & Mary Denbigh
Buryed 24th	An Infant illegitime proceat a filia La: Briggs & Gulielmū Cussworth
Maryed 31th	William Broadley & Katharine Carniley
September 1648	
Baptized 3d	Easter the daughter of William Willson of Wath
Baptized 9th	William the sonne of William Briggs of Brampton
Buryed 24th	Anne the daughter of Wm Shemeld drowned at Kilnhurst
October 1648	
Buryed 2d	John the sonne of William Robinson slaine with a waine of Tho Tilneys
Baptized 5th	Thomas the sonne of Nicholas Birkes of Wath
Baptized 7th	Elizabeth the daughter of Henry Wilcock of Swinton
Buryed 9th	The sayd Elizabeth
Buried eod die	Godfrey Foster of Wath
Baptized 11th	Elizabeth the daughter of Thomas Liversedge of Wath
Bāptized 15th	Elizabeth the daughter of Robert Stables of Melton
Baptized 22th	Elizabeth the daughter of Thomas Addye of Swinton
Buryed 28th	Widdowe Birkes of Wath
Baptized 29th	Richard the sonne of Willm Gawtresse of Wath
November 1648	
Baptized first	Samuell the sonne of William Boy of Swinton

1648

Baptized 12th Richard the sonne of Adam Earle of Wath
Baptized 20th William the sonne of William Broadley of Wath
Maryed 28th Francis Hogley & Elizabeth Heaton
Buried 29th William Beckett of Wath
Maryed 30h Robert Hudson & Grace Pyeman

December 1648

Buryed 3d Widdowe Wright of Melton
Baptized 10th Thomas the sonne of Francis Baxter de Abdy, gent
Buryed 11th Willm Smyth a souldier wounded at Pontefract Leaguer
Maryed 14th George Wilkinson & Joane Robinson of Swinton
Buryed eod die An Infant of John Telyers unbaptized
Baptized 12th William the sonne of William Thrift of Melton
Baptized 17th Lucye the daughter of John Bearde of Wath
Baptized eod die Anne the daughter of John Addye of Swinton
Baptized 20th Elizabeth the daughter of Michaell Bowser of Swinton
Baptized 30th Dorothie the daughter of Thomas Hirst of Brampton

January 1648

Buryed 3d Dorothie the daughter of Thomas Hirst of Brampton
Baptized 19th Anne the daughter of William Smyth of Swinton
Baptized 22th Humphrey the sonne of John Sisson of Melton
Baptized 27th Jane the daughter of William Brooke of Wath
Buried 28th Jane the daughter of Ralph Hattersley of Wath
Maryed eod die Richard . . . . & Isabell . . . . of Wakefeild
Baptized 29th William the sonne of William Cussworth of Wath

ffebruarie 1648

Baptized ffirst Elizabeth the daughter of Christopher Foulston of Brampton
Maryed 6th James Clayton & Ester Tilney
Maryed 7th Edward Foster & Grace Bingley of Swinton
Baptized 12 Jane the daughter of William Brooke of Wath
Buryed 13th John the sonne of Lawrence Wade of Melton
Buryed eod die John the sonne of William Michchell a wandering begger
Buryed 17th Elizabeth the daughter of Christopher Foulston of Brampton
Baptized 25th George the sonne of Lawrence Wade of Swinton
Buried eod die John Sisson of Melton
Buryed eod die Jervase the sonne of Jervase Milner of Melton
Buryed 26th Anne the wife of Mr Marke Hagg of Wath

March

Buryed 2d Richard the sonne of Rich: Pearson of Melton
Buryed eod die An Infant of Godfrey Bintliff of Brampton unbaptized
Baptysed 19th George the sonne of George Brook of Wath
Baptysed 22th Margarette the daughter of Thomas Tilney of Wath

Incipit annus

Baptysed 28th Mary the daughter of Lawrence Robinson of Newall
Marled eod die Thomas Barber & Anne Robinson
Maryed February the 25th John Hunte & Elizabeth Fitz of Wath

Aprill 1649

Baptized ffiirst Marye the daughter of Thomas Tyas of Newall
Buryed 2d An Infant of Willm Wades of Swinton unbaptized

1648

Baptized 8th Elizabeth daughter of George Foulston of Brampton
Baptized eod die Elizabeth daughter of John Sheapheard of Melton
Buryed 14th William the sonne of John Colbrand late of Newall Grange
Baptized 15th Katherin the daughter Anne Robinson illegitime procreata
Buryed 18th Nickolas Wade of Melton
18th Mary the daughter of John Ellis of Wath
24th Thomas the son of Richard Hill of Melton
Buried? 26th Katherin the daughter of Anne Robinson
Baptized 27th Tobias the sonne of Michaell Slack of Brampton
Baptized 29th Margarette the daughter of Jervase Hanson nata post mortem patris
Baptized eod die James the sonne of Ralph Foards of Wath

Md Thursday the 27th of Aprill 1648 Anthonye Sawdrye ꝑish clarke of Harrwood delūded unto Wm Colbrand of Swinton, John Baldrick of Wath & to me Nich Hunt Thirtye & Six poundes 30li. whereof were to be letten at xvjd ꝑ pound upon treble securitie to such inhabitants wthin the Towne of Wath as should be of good reporte & had occasions to imploy the same. And the intrest thereof was unto the Schoolmaster of Wath ffor the time being to be pd him at daie Christmas for the teaching of fower poore children of the Towne of Wath and twoo of that ꝑte of Swinton wch belonged whollye thereunto the other 6li was for repayre of West Melton Towne Cawsway 2li for repayre of ꝑte of Ardsley lane 2li to the poore of Brampton Byerley 1li 6s 8d to ye poore of Wath xs & to the poore of Swinton 3s 4d wch money wth certaine lands given by the sd Anthony by his last will and allso confirmed by deed unto ye Inhabitants of Bra: Bierley for maintainance of six pore children at Schoole wth the yearely Rent thereof to be pd to ye Schoolmaster as afforesaid if it were from time to time and at all times for ever imployed to yt onely use and to returne unto the heires of ye sd Anthony wthin one yeare & a day after ye same was otherwise imployed

Nich. Hunie John Baldrick
Wm Colbrand.

May

Baptized 6th Elizabeth the daughter of Willm Rodwell of Melton
Buryed 7th Elizabeth the widdow of Nicholas Tilney of Wath
Buryed eod Elizabeth the daughter of Willm Rodwell of Melton
Buryed 9th Frances ye daughter of Helen Dobson of Melton
Buryed 10th An Infant of the sd Frances unbaptized illegitime procreata

June 1649

Baptized 4th Edward the sonne of Edward Milner of Rainber
Maryed 7th William Teylor & Edith Whittles
Baptized 16th . . . . . of Valentine Tine of Swinton
Buryed 23d Thomas Oxley of the Roydes
Buryed 24th Mr Jasper Hunte of Wath

July 1649

Maryed 5th John Teylor & Isabell Stables
Baptized 15th William the sonne of Thomas Marriott of Wath

1649

August 1649

Buryed 9th	. . . . the wife of William Whittaker of Hoober side
Buryed 11th	Thomas Stables of the Brigge
Baptized 20th	Anne the daughter of Rich Pearson of Wath

September

Buryed 5th	Edmund Carver servant to John Marsden of Melton
Buryed 8th	Elizabeth the daughter of Tho Liversedge of Wath
Maryed 19th	Thomas Jackson & Margarett Killam of Wath
Buryed 20th	Thomas Mangham of Wath
Buryed 21th	William the sonne of William Broadley of Wath
Buryed 27th	An Infant of Nicholas Pearson iunior de Westmelton unbaptized

October 1649

Baptized 2d	Anne the daughter of John Pate of Wath
Baptized eod die	Anne the daughter of John Warde of Melton
Baptized 8th	Elizabeth the daughter of John Golland of Melton
Baptized eod die	Henrye the sonne of George Heaslehurst of Wath
Buryed? 12th	Jane the daughter of John Taylor of Wath
Buried? 16th	Hester the daughter of Mr. Jasper Hunte

November 1649

Maryed first	Charles Hill & Hellen Kente
(*rubbed out*)	Robert the sonne of Robinet of Wath.
Buryed 17th	Roger Stables of the Bridge
Maryed 19th	Anthony Stables & Susanna Holdsworth of Melton
Buryed 27th	Two infants of Thomas Wilcock of Swinton, unbaptized
Baptized 25th	Anne the daughter of John Ledger of Wath
Buryed 30th	James the sonne of Ralph ffoards of Wath
Baptized eod die	Henrye the sonne of Henry Sanderson of Hooberside

December 1649

Buryed 2d	Two infants of William Wades of Swinton unbaptized
Baptized 6th	Lancelott the sonne of Lancelott Briggs of Swinton
Buryed 14th	The sayd Lancellott
Maryed 15th	Guy Hague & Elizabeth ffox
Baptized 17th	Francis the sonne of James Clayton of Wath
Bapt 18	. . . . the . . . . of Henry Wilcock
Buryed 25th	Richard Herring of Wath
Baptized 26th	Margaret the daughter of William Carniley of Melton
Baptized 28th	William the sonne of Alexander Thackwrey of Swinton

January 1649

Baptized 17th	Richard the sonne of Christoph: Foulston of Brampton
Baptized eod die	Sloswick the sonne of William Carre of Wath
Buryed 18th	Edwarde the sonne of Edwarde Milner of Rainber
Baptized 31th	Jane the daughter of Richard Shawe of Wath

February 1649

Baptized ffirst	Magdalen the daughter of John Rushbrook a stranger
Buryed 6th	Richard Tompson of Wath
Baptized eod die	Marye the daughter of Thomas Teylor, of Wath
Buryed 7th	Richard Eller of Swinton

1649

Baptized 10th	George the sonne of William Wade of Swinton
Buried 14th	. . . . the wife of Roberte Robinette of Wath
Buryed 21th	Thomas Johnson of Wath
Buryed 26th	. . . . the wife of Tho. Wilcock of Swinton
March 1649	
Baptised 24	David the sonne of Ralph Hattersley, of Wath
Incipit Annus.	
Baptised 25	Richard the sonne of Robert Lile of Melton
Aprill 1650	
Buryed 6th	Henry Wharram of West Melton
Buryed 11th	Edith Sisson of West Melton
Baptised 14th	Helen the daughter of Mathew Broune of Melton
Buryed 17th	Elizabeth Pearson of West Melton
Buryed 21th	Margarett the wife of Henry Wharram of Melton
Buryed 22th	Anne Hudson of Brampton
Baptised 23th	Jervase the sonne of Nathan Elison of Swinton
May 1650	
Buryed 19th	Thomas Brook of Wath
Baptised 23th	Elizabeth the daughter of John Hunt of Wath
Buryed eod die	Elizabeth the daughter of George Wilkinson of Wath
June 1650	
Buryed 15th	James Hawsline of Wath
Buryed 24th	Anne the wife of John Carniley of Wath
Maryed 28	John Cawthorne & Mary Crosley
Baptized 30th	Hellen the daughter of William Broadley of Wath
	the sonne of Thomas Bloome baptized 16 day of June 1650 fr Melton
July 1650	
Baptised 15th	Elizabeth the daughter of Thomas Hirst of Brampton
Buryed 26th	Thomas Elam of Hoober Syde
August 1650	
Baptized 8th	Marye the daughter of John Teylor of the Brigge
Baptized 20th	Elizabeth the daughter of Jervas Milner of Melton
Baptized 25th	Thomas the sonne of Thomas Hudson of Brampton
Buryed 31th	An Infant of John Teylors of Wath unbaptized
September 1650	
Baptized first	John the sonne of William Teylor of Wath
Baptized 8th	Thomas the sonne of Thomas Plattes of Wath
Baptized 10th	Marye the daughter of Jervase Arundell
Baptized 12th	Alice the daughter of Nicholas Pearson Junior of Melton
Baptized 22d	John the sonne of Anthony Stables of Malton
Baptized 29th	Elizabeth the daughter of Thomas Coe of Wath
October 1650	
Baptized 9th	Robert the sonne of Robert Hudson of Newall
Baptized 17th	Francis the sonne of Thomas Liversedge of Wath
Buryed 24th	Edward Bruerton a Bedlam drowned at ye vper Knowbuck bridge

1650

November 1650	
Buryed 12th	Robert Ushey the servant of Michaell Slack
Baptized 21	Richard the son of Gorge ffoulston of Coley lane
Buryed first	Jeremy Kempe of Wath cuius nomeñ supra scriptu esse oportuit
Baptized 24th	Betterice the daughter of Rich. Baraclough of Wath
Baptized eod̄ die	Nicholas y^{e} sonne of Rich. Tomson natus post morte patris
Baptized 25th	Jane the daughter of Mich : Slack of Bramton
Maried 26	Thomas Holland & . . . .
Baptized eod̄ die	Frances the daughter of Thomas Jackson iunior of Wath
Bapt 23$_{th}$	Eliz. the daughter of Godfrey Bintliffe of Brampton
December 1650	
Buryed 5th	Widdowe Hudson of Wath
Maried 10th	Mr William Wood & Mrs Isabel Raynie
Baptized eod die	Crispianus the sonne of John Marsden of Melton
Baptized ii	Helen the daughter of Katherin Brook post mort patris.
Baptized 13	John the sonne of Richard Hutchinson of Newall
Buried eod die	Margarett the wife of William Wilson of Wath
Baptized 27th	Nicholas the sonne of Thomas Tilney of Wath
Januarie 1650	
Baptized 2^{d}	Richard ye sonne of Richard Kitchinman of Wath
Buryed 5th	Samuell Burton of Swinton
Baptized 23th	Adam the sonne of Adam Earle of Wath
Baptized 28th	Elizabeth the daughter of William Boy
Maryed 30th	Thomas Baraclough & Elizabeth Greene
ffebruarie 1650	
Baptized 2^{d}	William the sonne of Guy Hague of Wath
Buryed 8th	Isabell Elam
Baptized 13th	Marye the daughter of William Smyth of Swinton
Baptized eod̄ die	Marye the daughter of Humphrey Addye of Swinton
Baptized eod̄ die	. . . . the . . . . of . . . . a Begger at M^{r} ffitz
Buryed 21th	Mary the daughter of Humphrey Addye
Buryed 22th	William Elam of Hoober Syde
Buryed 25th	Easter the daughter of Adam Earle.
March	
Buryed ffirst	Thomas Baraclough of Wath
Baptized 2^{d}	Mary the daughter of Lancellott Brigges of Swinton
Baptized iith	Thomas the sonne of Michaell Bowser of Swinton
Buryed 16th	Thomas the sonne of Francis Hogley of Wath
Buryed 19th	Samuell the sonne of William Boy of Swinton
Baptized 20th	. . . . the suposed . . . . of Wm Pepper by Anne Baraclough
Buryed 23th	the sayd
Baptized 24th	John the suposed sonne of Wm Battie by Grace Marstine
Aprill 1651	
Buryed 4th	William Boys of Swinton
Baptized 20th	Robert the sonne of Gilbert Holmes of Melton

1628

Buried 22th	Grace the daughter of Richard Beamont of Swinton
Baptized 24th	Thomas the sonne of William Cussworth of Wath
May 1651	
Baptized 2^{d}	John the sonne of John Hutchinson of Swinton
Buryed 3^{d}	Richard Lee of Wath
Buryed 11th	Mary Freeman of the Roydes
Buryed eod die	Elizabeth the wife of Geo: Baraclough of Wath
Buryed iith	Widdow Wilkinson of Swinton
Buryed 19th	Alice the daughter of Edw. Milner of Rainber
Maryed 20th	Robert Oxley & Helen Foster of Wath
Baptized 24th	Helen the daughter of Robert Stables of Melton
June 1651	
Buryed 3^{d}	Mary the daughter of Hugh Allen of the Roydes
Baptized 4th	Thomas the sonne of Georg Wilkinson of Swinton
Baptized 22th	Thomas the sonne of John Beard of Wath
Baptized 26th	Hannah the daughter of Jervase Hinchliffe of the abdye
Baptised 27th	Emma the daughter of John Fitz of Wath
July 1651	
Buryed 4th	John Parre of Wath
Buryed 7th	Richard the sonne of Adam Earle
Baptized 17th	Humphrey the sonne of Nicholas Birkes of Wath
Buryed 27th	Elizabeth the wife of William Colbrand of Swinton
Maryed 29th	Mathias Birkes & Marye Herring of Wath
Bapt. last	Margarett daughter of Tho: Bawdison of Swinton
August 1651	
Buryed the 8th	Thomas Lee of Wath. Thomas Lee of Wath (*sic*)
Buryed the 9th	Thomas Burgan of Wath
Baptized 12th	Marye the daughter of John Wright of Wath
Buryed the 16th	Marye the daughter of John Wright aboves^{d}
Buryed the 28th	Thomas Mariott of Wath the elder
Buryed 3^{d}	Isabell the wife of Thomas Baraclough late of Wath
September 1651	
Baptized ye 7th	Anne the daughter of Wm Briggs of Brampton
Baptized ye 9th	Thomas the sonne of Ralph ffoardes of Wath
Buryed ye 21th	Widdowe Dawson of Wath
October, 1651.	
Baptized ye 9th	Sarah the daughter of William Gawtresse of Wath
Buryed eod die	Jane the daughter of Michaell Slack of Brampton
Buryed ye 10th	Alice the widdowe of Nicholas Saxton of Newall
Baptized 22th	William the sone of John Pate of Wath
Baptized eod die	Thomas the sonne of Georg Wikcock of Melton
Baptized 26^{h}	Agnes the daughter William Carniley of Westmelton
Buryed 30^{h}	William the sonne of William Rodwell of Melton
November 1651	
Buryed 6th	Francis Eaton of Wath
Buryed 7th	Margarett the wife of Thomas Jackson of Wath
[*Rubbed out*] 9th	Margaret the daughter of Henry Hawslin of Wath
do eod die	Anne the daughter of Thomas Baraclough of Wath
do 23th	Elizabeth the daughter of Thomas Holland of Newall

1651

Buryed 27	William Sanisthwait of Hooberside
Marryed the 27th	Geo? Smalls & Katherine Walker
December 1651	
Baptized 10th	Jane the daughter of George Brook of Wath
Maryed 11th	Edward Browne & Mary Wilkinson
Baptized 14^{h}	Helen the daughter of Nicholas Kay of Melton
Januarie *1651*	
Bapt 11th	William the sonne of Thomas Tyas of Newall
Bapt eod die	William the sonne of John Hunte of Wath
Bapt 12th	John the sonne of William Eliston of Wath
Baptized 23^{d}	Elizabeth the daughter of ffrancis Hogley of Wath
Buryed eodem die	Mr Thomas Benson Master of Arts & Vicar of Wath
Februarie 1651	
Baptized 4th	Richard & Nicholas sonnes of Richard Pearson of Wath
Baptized eođ die	Richard the sonne of Helen Lambe suposed to be begoten by Tho Neylor
Buryed 5th	Thomas the sonne of Georg Wilcock of Melton
Baptized 29th	William the sonne of francis Baxter of the Abdie gent
March 1651	
Buryed 13th	Matthewe Browne of Melton called by a by name Ployden
Buryed 21th	Robert the sonne of Robert White of Brampton
Anno 1652	
Buryed 28th	Anne the widdowe of Jeremye Kempe of Wath
Baptized eod die	Thomas the sonne of Tho Jackson of Wath iunior
Aprill 1652	
Baptized 5^{t}	Anne the daughter of Tho Bloome of Melton
Buryed 8th	Jane the daughter of Richard Peareson of Wath
Buryed 16th	Anne the daughter of Tho Bloome of Melton
Buryed ye 24th	Elizabeth ye widdowe of Robert Pearson of Wath
Baptized 27th	Anne the daughter of William Smyth of Swinton
Baptized 28th	Isabell & Ester the daughters of John Warde of Melton
Buryed 30th	. . . . the wife of John Nelson of Coaley lane
May 1652	
Baptized 9th	Nicholas the sonne of Mathias Birkes of Wath
Baptized 11th	Andrew the sonne of Ralph Smyth of Wath
Buryed 19th	John Nelson of Coaley lane
Buried 29	Alexander the sonne of Alexander Thackerowe
June 1652	
Baptized 4th	Jane the daughter of Henry Wilcock of Swinton
Buryed 5th	Anne the daughter of John Warde of
8th	Anne the daughter of Edward Milner of Wath
10th	Anne the daughter of
Baptized 15	Richard the sonne of Wm Broadley of Wath
Buryed eođ die	Jane the daughter of Henry Wilcock of Swinton
27	Richard the sonne of Edward Browne
Buryed	An Infant of John Teylors of Wath, unbaptized
July 1652	
Baptized 4th	Thomas the sonne of Guy Hague of Wath

1652	
Buryed 8th	Helen the daughter of William Iredalle of Coaley Lan
Baptized 25	Georg the sonne of Gervaise Milner of Melton
Baptized eod die	Susan the daughter of Lawrence Robinson of Newall
August 1652	
Buryed 4th	Elizabeth ye wife of William Dawney of Swinton
Bapt 12th	John the sonne Sheapgard of Melton
Buryed 25	Thomas the sonne of Richard Cussworth of Wath
Bapt 26th	Elizabeth the daughter of John Teylor of the Brigge
Sept 1652	
Buryed 4th	Thomas the sonne of Thomas Plattes of Wath
Bapt 5th	George the sonne of John Fittz of Wath
Buryed 6^{h}	Thomas the sonne of Richard Ramseden of Brampton
Buryed 7^{h}	Nicholas the sonne of Richard Tomson of Wath
Maryed 14^{h}	John Raughton & Rosamonde Jackson
Buryed 18	Helen the daughter of Thomas Brooke ōf Wath
Baptized 26th	William the sonne of William Beaumount of Swinton
Maryed 23th	Richard Robinson & Dorothie Nelthroppe of Wath
Baptized 29th	Elizabeth the daughter of Robert Hudson of Newall
October 1652	
Baptized 12th	Anne the daughter of Wm Teylor of Wath
Buryed 18th	Richard Pearson of Wath
Baptized 26th	Sarah the daughter of William Wade of Swintoñ
Buried 31th	John the sonne of John Wright of Wath
November 1652	
Baptized 7th	Mary the daughter of Thomas Webster of Swinton
Buryed 24th	An Infant of James Claytons unbaptized
Buryed 25th	An Infant of Rich Baracloughs unbaptized
Baptized 28th	Thomas the sonne of Edward Foster of Swintoñ
December 1652	
Buried 3^{d}	Helen the daughter of William Broadley of Wath
Torn off	John Fearnes of Wath
"	Thomas Coe of Wath
"	Anthonye the sonne of Anthonye Stables of Melton
"	Joshua the sonne of Geo. ffulston of Coaly lane
Januarie 1652	
"	. . . . the daughter of John Baldrick of Wath

A Register of all the Christ*enings* & Burialls within the parish of Wath (the Chapellrie of Wentworth excepted) and allsoe of all such mariages as have beene & taken effect there from the nine twentith day of September 1653, according to the tenor of the Act of Parliament in that case made and prided bearing date the ffower & twentith day of August in the yeare of our Lorde 1653.

Anno 1653		
Octob:	Maried 20th	ffrancis Swift of this pish and . . . . . . of the pish of Darfield. Ri. Tolson
Novem:	Maried 17th	John Baraclough of this pish with Anna Baxter of the pish of Darfield Ri. Tolson

1653

Novem : Maried 24th John Kellam with Anne Liversedge both of this pish. Ri. Tolson
Maried eod die Robert Lewin of the pish of ffelkirk with . . . . Wilcock of this pish, Ri. Tolson
Maried 30th Thomas Jackson of this pish with Betterice Moore of the pish of Bolton. Ri. Tolson

Jan : Maried 17th George Browne of the pish of Hathersedge with Helen Gray of this pish. Ri. Tolson

ffebr. Maried 17th William Broadley with Anne Lume late of this pish

Anno 1654

March ffrancis the sone of Richard Addy of Swinto baptized the last of March (*inserted*)

Aprill Baptiz 6th Humphrey the sonne of Thomas Jackson the yonger of Wath
Buried eod die John Wharram of this Towne of Wath
Buryed 9th An Infant of Humphry Addies of Swinton unbaptized
Baptiz 11th Richard the sonne of Richard Watson of Swinton
Bapt. 15th Grace the daughter of Robert Longbottom of Wath
Baptiz eod die Richard the supposed sonne of Robert Ant of Swinton
Baptiz 24th John the sonne of Richard Kitchinman of Wath
Buried 25th Eliz : the Widdow of Edward Milner of Heatfeild Woodhouse who dyed here

May Maried 6th ffrancis Stead of the pish of Darfeild & Eliz : Wilkinson of this pish
Bapt 7th Mary the daughter of Robert Stables of Melton
Buried 8th William Swallowe of Wath
Baptiz : 15th Marie the daughter of Willm Carniley of Melton
Buryed 30th William the sonne of Xtopt Baraclough
Buryed eod die Sarah the daughter of Xtopt ffulston of B . . .

June Buried 9th John Carniley of Wath
. . . . the sonne of Robert Hudson
Elizabeth the daughter of Robert Lile of Melton
Bap : 18th Anne the daughter of Lancellot *Brigges*
Bur : 20th Richard the sonne of Xtopher ffulston Brãpton
Baptiz 25th George ye sonne of Geo : Chappell of Brampton
Bapt eod die Helen the daughter of Charles Hill of Swinton

July Buryed 23d Elizabeth the daughter of John Ledger of Wath

August Baptized William ye son of Thomas Hepworth of Wath the 28th day of July 1654
Buried 4th Richard the sonne of Richard Walker of Wath
Bapt 8th Edward the sonne of Ralph Smyth of Wath
Buried 13th Mary the daughter of Edward ffirth of Melton
Buryed 14th Dinah the wife of Lawrence Wade of Swinton
Buryed 15th Valentine Tine of Swinton

st	Buryed 31th	Thomas Mabson of Wath
mber	Maried 7th	Thomas Hopton & Dorothie Chapell both of Swinton Ri Tolson
	Maried 25th	Robert Rawlin & ffrancis Burton both of this pish Ri Tolson
	Maried 28	Arthur ffaybie? & Anne Barraclough both of this pish
er	Buried 2d	Anne the widdowe of Georg Steel of Kimberworth
	Maried	William Brooke & Alice Mangall both of this pish
	Maried 16th	Willm Brooke and Alis Mangall both of this pish before me Dar. Wentworth
		John Baraclough and Marie Mirfeild were maried before me the 18th day of October Dar. Wentworth
m	Buried 10th	Alice the wife of John Taylor Wath
	Buryed 7th	John Wood of Wath
ber	Buried 3d	Jane the wife of Tho Tilney of Wath
	Bapt 14	Margery the daughter of Tho Casse of Swinton
	Bapt 14	Hellen the daughter of Willm Smyth of Swinton
	Bapt 16	Mary the sonne (*sic*) of Edward Browne of Wath
	Bapt 18	Roger the sonne of Arthur ffixbie of Wath
	Bapt 18	Henry the sonne of Mark Rawlin of Wath
ry	Bapt 11th	Alice the daughter of Geo ffulston of Coaly lane
	Bapt 14th	Margaret the daughter of Robert Hudson of Newall
	Buried 19th	Margarett the daughter of the said Robert
	Baptized 20th	Thomas the sonne of Michaell Boulton of Swinton
	Buryed 30th	Richard the sonne of John Geffery of the Shawe
ary	*Maried* 4th	Thomas Elam & Isabell Ward both of this parish
	. . . .	. . . . . the . . . of Wm Tomson of Melton Ri Tolson
	. . . .	. . . . . the sonne of W Beaumont of Swinton
	Buried	Mary the daughter of (*torn off*)
	Bapt 17th	Jane the daughter of John (*torn off*)
e	Bapt first	Anne ye daughter of Rich. Tolson of Wath
	Bapt eod die	Anne ye daughter of Tho: Pheasant of Swint*on*
	Bapt 2d	Elizabeth ye daughter of Willm Brodley of Wath
	Bapt 4th	ffrances ye daughter of John Kellam of Wath
	Bapt eod die	Mary ye daughter of Tho: Addie of Swinton
	Bur. 14th	ffrances the daughther of John Kellam of Wath
	Maryed 20th	James Earnshawe of this pish & Elisabeth West of the pish of Silkston before me, Ri Tolson
	Buried 28th	Rosamond the daughter of Tho Hudson of
	Buried 31th	John Peat of Melton

Anno 1655

	Bapt 5th	Mathew the sonne of John Jackson of Wath

1655

	Buried 22th	An Infant of John Jeffereyes of Shawwood? unbapt
	Buried 29th	Richard *Mariot* ? of Wath
	Bapt eod̄ die	William the sonne of Wm Teylor of Wath
May	Bapt	Richard son of Richard Walker the 10th day
	Maried 22	Thomas Beaumont & Helen Saterthwart both of this ꝑarish before me
	Maried 29th	Robert Skargill of the ꝑish of Bolton & Anne Shawe of this ꝑish before me R. Tolson
	Buried eod̄ die	Anne the wife of Tho Bloome of Melton
	Bapt 30th	Joshuah sonne of Thomas Bloome of Melton
June	Buryed 2d	Thomas Greene of Melton
	Bur. 17th	Eliz. the wife of John Parratt of Melton
	Bapt 18th	John the sonne of John Ledger of Wath
July	Bapt 22th	Jane the daughter of Tho: Eller of Swinton
	Bapt 23th	John the sonne of John Teylor of the Brigge
	Buried 31th	Anne Lee of Wath
	Baptized 14	Robert sonn of Richard Carr of Cooley lane
	Bapt 31th	John the sonne of John Pate of Melton post mortem patris
	Bapt eod̄ die	John the son of Willm Brooke of Wath
Septembr	Buryed 4th	Mary wife of Thomas Teylor of Wath
	Bapt 6th of August	Georg sonne of Thomas Hopton of Newall
	Buryed 5th	John Stockdalle of Wath
	Buried 11th	Betterice the widdowe of Henry Wilkinson of Wath
	Buryed 25th	John Carre of Rainber
	Bapt 21	Samuell the sonn of Willm ffarburne of Swinton
	Bapt 28	. . . . the sonne of Steeven Wood of Wath
Octob.	Maryed the 8th	Roger Browne of the ꝑish of Rotherham and Dorothye Greenwood of this ꝑish
	Bapt 10th	Thomas the sonne of Georg Chapell of Brampton
	Bapt 23th	John the sonne of Nicholas Birkes of Wath
	Bapt eod̄ die	. . . . the sonne of . . . . Lewin of Melton
November	Bapt 4th	Jane the daughter of Thomas Barraclough
	Maried 10th	Richard Tuckman of the ꝑish of Hucknall in the countie of Derbie & Ann Nevile of this ꝑish by me Dar Wentworth
	Maryed 20th	William Greene of this ꝑish . . . . of the ꝑish of Peniston
	Maryed	Georg: Hattersley & ffrances Collier both of this ꝑish by me according to the Act of Parliament in that case provided Dar Wentworth
	Maryed 21th	Nicholas Hudson of this ꝑish & Rosomonde Vicars of the ꝑish of Darfeild according to the Act of Parliamt in that case made by me Ri Tolson

1655

	Maryed 26th	Thomas Taylor of this parish & ffayth Bisbye within the Parish of Bolton were married According to the Act of Parliamt in that Case Made and Provided By Mee Ri Tolson
December	Maried 24th	Georg Hoyland & Mary Wade both of this pish according to the Act of Par in that case made and pvided By me Ri. Tolson
	Buried 30th	ffrances Kettlewell of Hoober side
January	Buryed 13th	Richard Eaton of Brampton
	Bapt 25th	ffrancis the sonne of Nich: Tilney of Wath
	Bapt 31th	Elizabeth daughter of Adam Earle of Wath
ffebruary	Buryed 3d	The wife of Georg Gray of Wath
	Buryed 8th	Anne daughter of Thomas Baraclough of Wath
	Bapt 12th	Robert sonne of Robert Hudson of Newall
	Bapt 14th	Richard sonne of Ralph Smyth of Wath
	Buryed 20th	Helen daughter of Charles Hill of Swinton
	Buryed 23th	Edward Hill of Swinton Moore
March	(*Nil*)	

1656

Aprill	Bapt 10th	Elizabeth the daughter of Mathias Birks
	Bapt 17th	Ane the daughter of Richard Addy of Swinton
	Buried 18th	Elizabeth daughter Wm Brodley of Wath
	Bapt 20th	Mary daughter Robert Walker of Swinton

be it Remembred that the tenth day of Aprill 1656 Lawrence Wade of Wath in the West Riding of the County of Yorke was sworne Register for the said towne (beinge chosen to the said office by the consent of the inhabitants of the said towne) accordinge to a late Act of parliamt.

before mee
Wm Beckwith

	Maryed 29th	Robert thompson and Susan flint both of this pish accordinge to the act in that case pvided
May	. . . . 6th	borne and Baptiz thomas son of thomas Willcocke of Swinton
	. . . . 6th	Willm Skyers of Darfeild pish and dorothie . . . . of the pish of Wath accordinge to the act
	18th	Buried Ann the wiffe of Hugh Shaw of Wath
	Maried	Willm Willson and Margery Mabson both of this pish accordinge to the act in case
	Baptiz 27th	thomas the sonn of Willim Hinch of Swinton
	Buried 31th	Nicholas pearson of Melton
June	Baptiz. 1d	Willim the son of Willim broadley

Baptizd the same day John the son of ffrancis Addy de Swinton
Buried the same day Alice Wharram of Swinton widdow

	Baptiz: 3d	Ann the daughter of Henry Willcocke of Swinton

1634

June	Baptiz: 5th	John the sonn of Richard Watson of Swinton
	Baptiz 14th	Elizabeth daughter of John Jefery of Swinton
	Buried 18th	Robert Thackwray of Swinton
	Maried 24th	Willm Willson and Margarey Mabson both of
June 1656 vizt		the pish of Wath accordinge to the Acte of pliament in that case pvided By me Tho: Westbye

A regester of all mariages Bellongginge to the Pish of Wath.

August the 26th 1656	Maryed Thomas Baxter husbandman and Elizabeth Hill, Spinster both of the pish of Wath with the consent of their friends accordinge to the act in that case pr'vided. Tho: Westby
November 7th 1656	Maryed George Gray of Wath, widdower and Mary thompson of Adwicke upon Dearne widow accordinge to the act in that case pr'vided
Desember 15th 1656	Maried Hugh Shaw of Wath ffellmonger and Mary Dodson of the same pish spinster with the consent of theire friends accordinge to the Acte in that case p'vided. Tho: Westby
December 18th 1656	Maryed John Car of Wath butcher and Mary fferam of the same towne and pish spinster by the consent of their friends accordinge to the act in that case p'vided.
June 15th 1657	Maryed Humphrey Jackson and Elizabeth Tinker by consent of theire friends accordinge to the act in that case p'vided.
October 20th 1657	Maryed Thomas Wade and An Crofton both of this pish by the consent of their friends accordinge to the act in that case p'vided.
Desember 7th 1657	Maryed Thomas Heaton and Mary Wiggffull both of this pish by the consent of their friends accordinge to the act in that case provided.
Aprill 24th 1660	Maryed Richard Robinson and Jane Slacke.

A Register of Baptismes.

Baptized 26 June 1656	Grace the daughter of John Blacksmith of Swinton
the same day	Thomas the sonn of Thomas Hepworth of Wath
the 27th of July	John the sonn of John Kempe of Wath
the 31th of July	Helen the daughter of Thomas Jackson of Wath
24th of September	Jervis the sonn of Nathan Ellison
November 30th 1656	Thomas the sonn of Thomas Holland of Newhall

1656

Desember 14th 1656 John the sonn of George Chappell of Brampton
same day John the son of Nickolas Hudson of Newhall
December 18th 1656 Thomas the son of Thomas Wade of Swinton
December 21th 1656 Richard the son of Christopher ffoulston de Brampton
December 30th 1656 Grace the daughter of Willm Bingley yonger in Swinton
same day John the son of Thomas Cutt of Swinton
January 4th 1656 An the daughter of Thomas Tyas of Newhall
January 18th 1656 Elizabeth the daughter of Willm Skyers
ffebruary 5th 1656 Jane the Daughter of Jervas Arandalle
ffebruary 3th 1656 Elizabeth daughter of John Marstin of Wath
ffebruary 9th 1656 Willm the soone of Willm Brooke of Wath
March 5th 1656 William the son of Thomas Blakeman
March 7th 1656 Richard the son of Mr Richard Tolson of Wath
1657 . . . . . William the sonn of William Smith of Swinton
March 27th or 28th 1657 . . . . . the daughter of Thomas Hudson of Brampton
April 16th 1657 Mary the daughter of Edward Greene
May 26th 1657 Grace the daughter of Thomas Addy of Swinton
June 21th 1657 Thomas the sonn of John Bramhery of Swinton
July 2th 1657 Sarah the daughter of Thomas Bullas of Swinton
July 26th Jaan the daughter of Robert Hill of Melton
the same day Rosamond the daughter of Humphrey Addy of Swinton
August 8th 1657 Martha the daughter of George Jenkinson of Wath
September 10th 1657 Hellen the daughter of George Hoyland of Wath
de eadem Esther the daughter of Edward ffosterd of Swinton
September 27th 1657 Michaell the son of James Stringer of Swinton
November 15th 1657 John the son of John Hogley
November 19th 1657 Samuell the son of Michaell Bouser of Swinton
July the last 1657 Thomas the son of Thomas Baxter of Melton the last day
July 17th 1657 . . . . . Tupman of Wath
November the 9th 1659 John the son of Thomas Baxter of Melton

1659

same day maried John Parret? and Janet Leach
Baptised the 7th of August 1660 Joseph the sonne of Thomas Bloome of West Melton
Bapt Jaane daughter of Thomas Hepworth the 24^{h} day of May anno dom 1659

1659

December 1658 Baptized Thomas the son of Thomas Heaton of Brampton the 8th day

December 1658 Baptized ye 10th Elizabeth the daughter of Lancelot Briggs of Swinton

Aprill 4th 1658 Baptized Hellen the daughter of Thomas Elarr of Swinton

Aprill 8th 1658 Jane daughter of Wiłłm Skyers

Aprill 13th 1658 Baptiz: An the daughter of Thomas Jackson of Wath

May 2th 1658 Baptized Easter the daughter of Robert Stablles

September 8 1658 Baptized John the son of Thomas Willcock of Swinton

January 27th 1658 Baptized Mary the daughter of Richard Addy of Swinton

ffebruary 13th 1658 Baptized Joshuah the son John Sheppard of Mellton

March 10th 1658 Baptized Thomas the sonne of Wiłłm Wood of Swinton

March 13th 1658 Baptized .... the .... of Wiłłm Sourby of Wath

March 22th 1658 Baptized Robert the sonn of Thomas Cutt of Swinton

Same day Baptized .... the daughter of Henry Willcoke of Swinton

May 16th 1659 Baptized Mary the daughter of George Hoyland of Wath

June 22th 1659 Baptized Hellen the daughter of Ralph Smith of Wath

July 17th Baptized George Shaw & Thomas Shaw sons of John Shaw of Newhall

Novembe 27th 1659 Baptized ffrancis the daughter of Wiłłm Smith of Swinton

Januarye ye first 1659 Baptized Hellen the daughter of Mathew Birkes of Wath

July 3d Baptised Ann the daughter of Richard Carr of Cooley lane

March 27th 1660 Baptized Thomas the son of Thomas Nickollson of Swinton

Aprill the 15th 1660 Baptized James the sonn of James Clayton of Wath

Aprill 29th 1660 Baptized Wiłłm she son of Wiłłm Willson of Wath

May 31 1660 Baptized Sarah the daughter of Edward ffosterd of Swinton

June 7 1660 Baptized John the son of Henry Winder de Wath

June 24th 1660 Baptized Jasper the son of Richard Kitchingman

de eadem Baptized .... the son of John Wright

Jully 17th Baptized Mary the daughter of Richard Oxlley of Wath

September 9th 1660 Baptized Richard the sonn of Thomas Hudson of Brampton

September 16th 1660 Baptized Robert the sonne of Ralph foard of Wath

September 23th 1660 Baptized .... the sonne of Wiłłm Thompson of Wath

Septemberr 30th 1660 Baptized nemīah the sonn of Lawrence Wade of Swinton

de eadem Baptized .... the sonne of Wiłłm Cusworth of Wath

October 21th 1660 Baptized John the sonn of James Stringer

October 28th 1660 Baptized Richard the son of John Jacson

de eadem and Richard the sonn of Richard Robinson

1660

November 11th 1660 Baptized William the son of John Hogley of Wath
November 15th 1660 Baptized Thomas the son of Thomas Jenkinson
November 5th 1660 Baptized Richard the son of Willim Redyhaugh and Allice the daughter of Willm Beckitt

Baptized Ann daughter of Anthony Stables the 26th day of August Anno domini 1656

Baptized Abell son of Anthony Stables the 20th day of July 1660

Bapt. Georg son of Thomas Hepworth november the 18th 1660

A Register of Burialls.

June 19th 1656 Gartwright wiffe of Richard Hutchinson de Newhall
August 15th Buried Richard sonne of Richard beamont of Swinton
October 31th 1656 Buried An Metcalffe of Swinton the younger
November 4th 1656 Buried an Infant of Willim wood of Swinton
November 6th 1656 Buried Robert Walker of Swinton
November 15th Buried Margarett the wiffe of Willim Green
November 19th Buried An the daughter of Willim Green
Desember 5th 1656 Buried John Beard of Wath
Desember 21th 1656 Buried Ann the wiffe of Christopher ffoulston de Brampton
Desember 30th 1656 Buried Hellen Bishopp of Swinton
March 2th 1656 Buried Marie the daughter of Willim Thompson of Wath
March 6th 1656 Buried Nicholas Hopkinson of Swinton.
March 7th 1656 Buried Ann the daughter of Richard Tolson of Wath
March 18th 1656 Buried Alice Slinger of Swinton widdow
Aprill 6th 1657 Buried Joshua the son of Lawrence wade of Swinton
May 7th Buried Edy the daughter of George Jenkinson of Wath
June 28 1657 Buried Hellen the daughter of Thomas Jackson of Wath
August 6th 1657 Buried Willim Bingley of Swinton
Augt 18th 1657 Buried Elizabeth wade the daughter of thomas wade of Swinton
Same day Buried Willim Colbrand of Newhall Grange
August 20th 1657 Buried James . . . . from the house of Willim Smith in Swinton
September 11th Buried Jane the wiff of John Browne of Swinton
September 24th 1657 Buried ffrancis the wiffe of George Sherwin?
October 4th 1657 Buried John Browne of Swinton
Desember 7th 1657 Buried Mary Sisson of Mellton widdow
Aprill 7th 1658 Buried Jane the daughter of thomas Ellar of Swinton
July 1658 Buryed ffrances the sonn of Thomas Tinley? of Wath
September 3d 1658 Buried Robert Skyars of Mellton
Same day Buried Jervas Yngland of Brampton
September 27th 1658 Buryed widdow Sisson of Mellton
September 29th 1658 Buried Samuell Ellam of Wath

1658

October 10th — Buryed Thomas Jackson of Wath

November 29th 1658 Buried Martha the daughter of George Wilkinson of Swinton

November 30th 1658 Buryed Plats wiffe of Wath

Buried Richard Mabson of Wath

Desember 6th 1658 Buried Thomas Linley of Wath

de eadem Jane the wiffe of Richard nickollson of Wath

January 28th 1658 Buryed Joseph the sonne of Jerviss Hincthcliffe of Abdy

March 25th 1659 Buryed Willim Wade of Swinton

Aprill 2th 1659 Buried Elizabeth the wiffe of Michaell Bouser of Swinton

June 25th 1659 Buried Roger Smith of Swinton

July 25th 1659 Buryed George and thomas sons of John Shaw of Newhall

Jully 29th 1659 Buryed . . . the wiffe of the same John Shaw

. . . . day of October 1661 John Marstin was chosen parish Clarke of Wath upon Dearne by Joseph Ludlam Mr of Artes and Vicar of Wath with full consent of the pish, John Carr and Richard Walker then Churchwardens, for Wath, Nicholas Pearson & George ffoulstone for the Bierley, Thomas Webster for Swinton

1661

Baptized Ellen the daughter of John Tayler of Wath the last day of August 1661 (*Inserted*)

Octob ye 4th Buried Nicholas Huntt, Late Clarke of Wath

Octob ye 6th Baptized francis the sonne of francis Bristow of Street

Octob ye 10th Maryed Richard . . . . and Mary Beardshaw, of Hoyland

Octob ye 15th Buried Elizabeth the daughter of Marke Rawlin of Wath

Octob ye 20th Baptized francis the sonne of Richard Tupman, of Wath

Octob ye 26th Baptized Easter ye daughter of Michael Gessop, of Wentworth

Novembr ye 4th Buried Widow Crowder of Lee

Novembr ye 14th Maried John Skargill & Hellen Dyson

Novemb ye 19th Buried Thomas Taylor from Newall a stranger

Novemb ye 21th Maried Richard Bell & Widdow Swallow

Novemb ye 28th Maried Willm Readyhough & Elizabeth ffoster

eodem die Baptized Anne ye daughter of Willm Wood of Swinton Junr

Decembr 12th Buried . . . Bingley widdow of Swinton

Decem ye 15th Baptized Henry sonne of Henry fayram Wath

Decem ye 19th Buried Beatrice ye daughr of Robt Skargill Wath

Jany ye 9th Baptized Mary ye daughter of John Brooke of Wath

Eod die Baptized Willm the sonne of Richard Elam of West Melton

Jany ye 14th Buried Robt Stables of West Melton for which John Loughton? were troubled

16

Jan ye 19th	Baptized	John ye sonne of Guy Hague of Wath
Jan ye 26th	Baptized	Olive the daughter of Willm Kettlewell of Hoober
ffebruary first	Bapt.	Easter ye daughter of Willm Smith of Swinton
the 12th	Buried	Nicholas Hunt sonne of Jaspar Huntt of Wath
the 19th	Buried	an Infant of . . . of Swinton. Illegitimate
the 20th	Buried	John ye sonne of Nicholas Birkes of Wath
the 23d	Baptized	Mathew the sonne of George ffoulston of Coaley lane
eodem die	Bapt	Thomas ye sonne of Edward ffawether of Cortwood
March 2d day	Bapt	Richard ye sonne of Raphe Smith of Wath
Mar ye 7th	Buried	Margret ye wife of Robt Ant of Swinton
Mar ye 8th	Buried	James Durham of West Melton, Etatis . . .
Mar ye 16th	Bapt	Mary ye daughter of Hugh Shaw of Wath
eodem die	Bapt	Lancelot sonne of Lancelott Brigs of Swinton
Mar ye 10th	Married	John Kemp & Ann Tilney
eodem die	Buried	. . . . the wife of Richard Addee of Swinton
Mar yo 22th	Buried	Easter ye daughter of Willm Smith of Swinton and with her 2 infants
1662		
Mar ye 25th	Buried	. . . . the wife of . . . . Tim of Abdie
eodem die	Buried	Georg ye sonne of George Jenkinson of Wath jun
Mar ye 31th	Baptd	. . . . ye sonne of John Parrat of Newall
eodem die	Bapt	Ann ye daughter of Tho: Heaton of Brampton
. . . .	Buried	Mary ye wife of John Wormall and with her two infants unbaptized
. . . .	Bapt	Margarett ye daughter Henry Winder of
	Bapt	daughter of Michaell Bouzer of Swinton
Apr ye 22th	Bapt	Joseph ye sonne of Willm Bingley of Swinton
Apr ye 26th	Buried	. . . . ye daughter of Michaell Bowzer of Swinton
May ye 28th	Buried	. . . . ye daughter of Robert Stables of Melton
June ye 6th	Maried	Nicholas Gills and Grace Huntt
June ye 10th	Married	Hughe Allen and Sarah Smith
June ye 24th	Bapt	Nicholas the sonne of Nicholas Birkes of Wath
July ye 2d	Buryed	Widdow Bowzer of Swinton
July ye 3th	Baptized	Elizabeth the daughter of Robert Heaton of Wath
July ye 13th	Baptized	Elizabeth the daughter of Thomas Hopton of Newall
Baptized ye 17th July		Thomas and John the sonns of John Kay of Wath

Memorandum that ye 12th day of May 1662 I Joseph Ludlam Maister of Arts and Vicar of Wath upon Dearne did with the consent of the Churchwardens then being gave free consent that Richard Walker the younger of Wath affores:d Tanner should Build him one Litle Stall or pew on the Right hand of the Chancell of the pish Church

1662

of Wath afforesd Adioyneing to a Stall built by Mr Jasp Blithman Esqr and Mr Willm Blythman gent upon condicion that whensoever that his wife and the issues of their two bodyes Lawfully begotten should depte this life or cease to be Inhabitants wthn the sd pish that then and from that day forward the sd Stall shall Remaine wholy in the full and absolute disposition of the Vickar of Wath for the time beinge

Joseph Ludlam, Vicar
Nicholas Pearson, George × ffoulston, John Carr, Richard Walker — Churchwardens.

Buried July ye 22th	Mary wife of John Kay of Wath
Baptiz. July ye 29th	. . . . ye daughter of Henry Willcock of Swinton
Baptiz. August ye 10th	Isabella ye daughter of John Taylor of Tingle Bridge
Maried August ye 12th	Robert Ant & Issabella Beaumont
Baptized August ye 17th	Willm ye sonne of Willm Roebuck of Upper Hauge
Baptized August ye 24th	Sarah ye daughter of John Shaw of Newall
Buryed	Henry Winder of Wath
Septem Buryed ye 12th	. . . . the sonne of Willm Brigges Bramp
Buried ye 16th	Robt Longbotham of Brampton bierley
Baptized ye 18th	Mary ye daughter of George Robinson of Wath
Buried ye same day	Edithe Golland of Brampton bierley Widdow
Baptized ye 26th	Margret ye daughter of Ralphe ffoardes of Wath
Buried ye 29th	a pore man dyed at Henry Winders
Married ye sixth of October	John Turner & Ursula Wood
Baptized ye 2d	Martha ye daughter of Richard Oxley of Wath
Baptized ye 2o of Novem.	Thomas ye sonne of Willm Redihaugh of Newhall
Eodem die Bap	Jane ye daughter of John Kent of Wath
Bapt ye 9th of November	Richard the suposed sonne of . . . . Base gotten of the body of Elizabeth Kay of West Melton
Buried ye 19th of Novembr	Sarah the daughter of Adam Earle of Wath
Maried ye 25 of Novembr	~~John Hoyland & Sarah Tod~~
Eodem die	Jonas Maude & Sarah Wood
Maried ye 27th	ffrancis ffirth & Anne Sissons
Buried ye same day	Richard Walker ye elder of Wath
Buried ye 8th of December	Katherine wife of Thomas Rawlin of Wath
Maried ye 11th of December	Willm Booth & Mary Wilkinson
Bapt ye 14th of December	Katherine ye daughter of Marke Rawlin of Wath
Bapt ye 18th of Decemb.	Willm ye sonne of Willm ffarburn of Swinton

1662

Buried ye 3° of January	John Cawthorne of Swinton
Bapt ye 4th	Anne ye daughter of Willm Sowerby of Wath
Buried the 5th	Margret the daughter of Widdow Windor
Bapt. ye 8th	Mary the daughter of John Loriter of Wath
Buried ye 12th	Anne the wife of Richard Tupman of Wath
Buried ye 14th	Jaane the wife of Adam Mitton of Wath
Buried ye 19th	Elizabeth the wife of John Ellis of Wath
Bapt 27th	Elizabeth the daughter of Thomas Skales of Swinton
Buried ye 29th	Elizabeth the daughter of Robt Heaton of Wath
Buried ye first of ffebrary	Hester ye daughter of Thomas Hudson of Bra
Baptized ye 12th day	Elizabeth the daughter of Richard Carr of Coley lane
Baptized ye same day	James ye sonne of Thomas Jenkinson of Wath
Baptized ye same day	Thomas ye sonne of Willm Rushforth of Wath
Maried ye 26th day	Thomas Collier & Dorothy Sikes
Baptized ye 3° day of March	Richard the sonne of Richard Marshall of Street
Buried ye 22th of March	John ye sonne of Robert Skargill of Wath
Baptiz ye 14th day of March	John the sonne of John Cawthorn of Swinton post mortem patris
Buried ye 21th day	ye saide John

Anno Domini 1663

Baptized ye 5th of Aprill	Rosamond y daughter of Willm Tompson of Wath
Baptized ye 28th of Aprill	ffrances the daughter of John Kempe of Wath
Baptized ye 3^{d} of May	Anne the daughter of John Jackson of Wath
Baptized ye 4th of June	Elizabeth the daughter of Edward Browne of Wath
Buried ye 8th of June	Susanna the wife of Thomas Topham of Wath
Baptized the 14th of June	John the sonne of Willyam Booth of Newall the younger
Baptized the 2^{d} of July	Maudlin the daughter of Thomas Hepworth of Wath
Buried ye 10th day of July	John Redihaughe of Newall
Baptized ye 16th day of July	Easter the daughter of George Jenkinson of Wath the younger
Buried the 21th day of July	Richard Tupman of Wath
Buried the 28th day of July	Rosamond the wife of Nicholas Dauson of Wath
Baptized the 30th day of July	Mary the daughter of Nicholas Gills of Wath
Buried eodem die	Seth Shepley of Swinton
Maried the 6th day of August	Nicholas Cromocke and Easther Gorrill

1663

Baptized ye 9th day of August	Willyam the sonne of George Chaphell of Brampton
Buried eo dem die	An Infant of James Stringers of Swinton unbaptized
Buried ye 13th day of August	the sayde Willm the sonne of the sayde George Chaphell
Maried ye 20th day of August	Thomas Adamson and Mary Hogley
Baptized ye 23th day of August	Anne the daughter of Willm Becket of Melton
Buried the 13th day of September	John Kent of Wath
Baptized ye 24th day of September	Henry the sonne of John Kay of Wath
Maried eodem die	Willm Shaw and Hellen Tinley with a Lycence
Baptized the 11th day of October	John the sonne of Robert Lewin of Melton
Baptized the same day	Richard the sonne of Thomas Tyas of Newall
Baptized thy^e^ first day of November	Jane the daughter of Jonas Maude of West Melton
Buried ye 5th of November	ffrances the daughter of John Kemp of Wath
Buried ye 10th of November	Mary ye wife of Mathew Birkes of Wath
Buried ye 20th of November	Esther the daughter of Willm Brooke of Wath
Buried ye first day of December	ffrancis ffayram Wath
Buried ye 4th of December	Margret the wife of Marke Rawlins of Wath
Buried ye 17th of December	Nicholas Gills of Wath
Baptized ye 16th of December	Martha daughter of Willm Skyres of Lee
Baptized the 20th of December	John the sonne of Willm Athy of Boulton
Buried ye second day of January	Jane the daughter of Jonas Maude of Melton
Buried ye 5th of Januarie	Thomas Topham of Wath
Baptized ye 6th of Januarie	John Turner of Wath (*sic*)
Buried ye 7th of Januarie	the saide . . . .
Baptized ye 15th of Januarie	Elizabeth the daughter of Richard Elam of Melton Junior
Baptized the 31th day of January	Willyam the sonne of Thomas Bullas of Swinton
Baptized eodem diē	Hellen the daughter of John Barraclough of Wath
Buried the 6th day of ffebruary	John the sonne of John Warde of Melton
Buried the 7th day of ffebruary	Willyam Briggs of Brampton
Buried the 10th day of ffebruary	Willyam the sonne of Widdow Carr of Rainber
Buried the 12th day of ffebruary	John the sonne of Guy Hague of Wath
Baptized ye 15th day of ffebruary	Rebeccka the daughter of George Hoyland of Wath
Baptized ye 18th day of ffebruary	Easther the daughter of William Cusworth of Wath
Baptized the same day	Jonas the sonne of George ffoulstone of Coley Lane

1664

Baptized the 6th day of March	John the sonne of John Morley of Boulton
Buried the 9th day of March	Elizabeth the daughter of Richard Addy of Swinton
Buried the 10th day of March	Margret Baylife of Wath, widdow
Baptized the 13th day of March	Joseph the sonne of ffrancis Tustan (or Tuftan) of Marsbrough cū Rotherham
Buried the 20th day of March	Elizabeth the wife of Guy Hague of Wath
Incipit Annus 1666	
Baptized the . . day of Aprill	. . . the . . . of John Tinsley of Hoober
Buried the 13th day of Aprill	. . . Leach of Newall.
Buried the 19 of Aprill	Lawrence Wade of Swinton
Baptized the 21th day of Aprill	Easter the daughter of George Broodheade of Melton
Buried the 26th day of Aprill	Thomas Rawlins of Wath
Buried eodem diē	Thomas the sonne of Guy Hague, Wath
Buried the 5th day of May	Mary the daughter of one Thomas Denton of Marsbrough cū Rotheram a stranger
Baptized eodem die	Mary the daughter of John Houlgate of Wath
Baptized the 8th day of May	Willm the sonne of John Shaw of Newall
Buried eodem die	Elizabeth Robinson of Wath vidue
Buried ye 16th day of May	John Jagger of Brampton
Baptized ye 19th day of May	ffrances the daughter of Robert Skargill of Wath
Baptized ye 22th day of May	John the sonne of Robert Hudson of Newall
Buried the 23d day of May	Grace the wife of Willm Tayler of Wath
Baptized the 26th day of May	Anne the putative daughter of . . . Raysin of Doncaster base begotten of Alice Haslehurst of Wath
Married the 30th day of May	John ffreeman & Sarah Hill
Married the second of June	Josias . . . . and Jane Sheimeild
Buried the 4th of June	Jane the daughter of Willm Cussworth of Wath
Baptized the 12th day of June	Elizabeth the daughter of George Robinson of Wath
Baptized eodem die	Anne the daughter of Nicholas Cromacke Brampton bierley
Married the 16th day of June	John Howet and Elizabeth Shaw
Buried the 24th day of June	the sonne of John Parratt of Newall
Buried the first day of July	John Ledger of Wath
Married the 15th day of August	Adam Mitton and Alice Roe
Buried the 16th of August	John Warde of Melton
Baptized the 28th day of August	James the sonne and Anne the daughter of Raphe Smith, Twins born
Buried the second day of September	Willyam the sonne of Nicholas Maychin of Wath
Baptized the 4th day of September	Jonathan the sonne of Richard Walker of Wath

1664

Baptized the same day Willyam the sonne of Willm Elam of Melton

Baptized the 22th day of September John the sonne of Richard Oxley of Wath

Married the 27th day of September Richard Nichols and Ellenn Earle

Baptized the 4th day of October Anne the daughter of John Kempe of Wath

Maried the 6th day of October Willm Robinson and Anne . . . .

Baptized the 9th day of October Thomas the sonne of Willm Robucke of Brampton

eodem die Elizabeth the daughter of Willm Redihaugh of Newall

Baptized the 13th day of October John the sonne of Henry ffayram of Wath

Baptized the 20th day of October Ann the daughter of Willyam Bingley of Swinton

Baptized the 23d day of October . . . . of Robert Pitt of Linthwaite

Buried the 11th of Nouember (*nil*)

December the 12th Anno Domini 1664

Buryed Issabell Stables of Melton the 12th day

Buryed Issabell the wife of Richard Ellam of Melton the 17th day

Buryed Laurence Wade of Melton the 27th day

Buryed Wid: Heaton of brampton the 28th day

January 1664

Buryed John Wright of Wath the first day

Buryed John Marstin of Wath the 6th day

Buryed Joane the wife of Ric: fostard the 8th day

Baptized John the son of John Brooke of Wath the 12th day

Buryed William Booth of Newall eodem die

Buryed Wid: Bintlife of brampton the 13th day

Baptized Ann the daughter of John Kirke of Swinton the 15th day

Buryed Tho: Hopton of Newall the 21th day

February 1664

Marryed Guy Hage and Grace Cut the second day

Buryed John son of Robert Lewin of Melton the 3d day

Buryed Elizbeth daughter of Rich: Ellam of Melton and Rosamond Ingland of brampton the 5th day

Buryed Trauth Nuby of Abdy the 13th day gentlewō

Buryed Wid Carr of Rainber the 23th day

Buryed Mary daughter of Lancelot Briges of Swinton the 27th day

March 1664

Baptized Mary the daughter of John Turner of Wath the 5th day

Baptized Thomas the son of Robert Ellam of brampton the 9th day

Baptized William & John sons of John Parrat of newall the 16th day

Buryed those 2 children the 22th day

Incipit annus 1665

Baptized William son of William Sourby of Wath the 28th day

Baptized Mary the daughter of Marke Rawlin the 29th day

Robert Hill received lycence to be Clarke the sixt of Aprill 16 yeare 1665

1665

Aprill 1665

Baptized George son of Thomas Jenkinson of Wath the second day
Baptized ffrances daughter of William Rushworth of Wath the 16th day
Baptized Ann daughter of John Loriter of Wath the 18th day
Buryed William Triuy & William Fixby the 19th day
Buryed Jane Marstin the 21th day
Baptized Easther daughter of Henry Hawslin the 23d day
Baptized William son of William Ward of Swinton, Jun. the last day

May 1665

Buryed Sarah the wife of Jonas Maude the 5th day

June 1665

Maryed John Carr & Ann Skyers the 15th day
Buryed an infant of Lancelot Briges unbaptized the 17th day
Buryed a son of Ralph smith the 20th day
Maryed John Amery & Ann Fostard the 23d day
Baptized John the son of John Taylor of Wath the 25th day

July 1665

Buryed wid: barraclough the 21th day
Baptized Ralph son of James stringer of swinton the 23d day
Baptized Jane the daughter of Thomas Baxter of brampton the 25th day

August 1665

Buryed Ellizabeth daughter of John Taylor the 5th day

September 1665

Baptized Easter the daughter of francis Addy of swinton 10th day
Baptized Elizabeth the daughter of John Kay of Wath the 23d day

October 1665

Marryed William hoult & Ellizabeth Marstin both of this ꝑish
Baptized Martha the daughter of Nich.: birkes of Wath the 10th day
Marryed Nich: dawson & Jane Richardson the 17th day

November 1665.

Marryed Mathew Birkes & Ann Pogmore the second day
Baptized Thomas son of Thomas Jessop of Melton the 5th day
Marryed Beniamin Saunderson & Ann Coothe 7th day
Baptized Mary the daughter of Tho Pearson of Swinton the 12th day
Marryed Thomas Mallinson & Allis Smith the 16th day
Baptized Elizabeth the daughter of Henry Willcocke of Swinton the 20th day
Buryed William Booth of Newall the 23d day
Baptized Martin the son of William Tomson of Wath the 26th day
Buryed Issabella wife of George broadhead the 27th day
Marryed John Stead and ffrancis Shaw the 28th day
Marryed Thomas Kaworth and Grace Marriot eodem die
Marryed Samuell Birkes & ffrancis Pearson ultimo die
Baptized John the son of Mathew Crosse of Swinton eod die

December 1665

Buryed an infant of William Beckits of Melton, unbaptised the 5th day
Baptized Jane the daugher of John Kempe of Wath the 7th day
Buryed Nathan Ellison of Swinton the 18th day

1665

Buryed the said Jane the 23d day
Buryed Ellizabeth the wife of John Addy of Swinton the 28th day
January 1665
Baptized Mary the daughter of William Cettlewell the 11th day
Buryed Ursilla the wife of Edward firth the 30th day
ffebruary 1665
Baptized Jane the daughter of Richard Ellam the first day
Marryed John Heaton & Mary Howden the 8th day
Buryed Richard Oxley of Wath the 19th day
Maryed Thomas Tinley & Rosamond Mallinson the 20th day
Maryed Thomas Hartley & Ann Shaw the 27th day
March 1665
Baptized John the son of George Jenkinson of Wath ye 2 day
Baptized Ann the daughter of Richard Robinson of Wath ye 11th day
Baptized Mercy the daughter of Rich Carr of Coley lane ye 16th day
Buryed a daughter of Wid: Kents of Wath eod die
Buryed Thomas Wade of Swinton the 20th day
Buryed Wid: Kent of Wath the 23d day
Incipit Annus 1666
Baptized Nicholas the son of John Shaw of Newall the 25th day
Baptized Rebeckah the daughter of Elizabeth Litster of Rotherham base begot eodem die
Aprill 1666
Baptized William the son of William Redihough the first day
Baptized George the son of Richard ffletcher of bawtry the third day
Buryed Elizabeth the wife of Humphray Jackson the 12th day
Baptized John ye son of John Jackson of Wath ye 26th day
Baptized Elizabeth daughter of John Amery of Wath ye 16th day
May 1666
Baptized Ellizabeth daughter of John frost the 3d day
Maryed Edward ffirth & Susana Stables the 14th day
Baptized Mary ye daughter of Thomas Ellis of Newall ye 18th day
Buryed Ann the wife of the said Thomas Ellis ye 19th day
Baptized William ye son of Thomas Heaton of brampton the 24th day
Buryed Thomas Colbrand, gentleman, of Newall grange ye 28th day
June 1666
Marryed Robert Smith & Joane Hattersley the 3d day
Buryed Thomas burton the first day
Baptized Joane ye daughter of Nicholas Cromacke of Melton ye 10th day
Baptized Mercy ye daughter of Thomas Cut of Swinton ye 17th day
Buryed an infant of William Iredales unbaptized the 19th day
July 1666
Baptized Peter ye son of Jonas Maude of Melton ye first day
Buryed Sarah the wife of William Iredale ye third day
Baptized William the son of James Stringer ye 8th day
Maryed Richard ffosterd & Elizabeth Readyhough ye 16th day
Baptized Hellen daughter of Godfrey bawdison ye 22th day
Buryed George broadhead the 27th day

1666

Baptized Ruthe ye daughter of George Wilkinson of Swinton ye 29th day
Baptized Elizabeth daughter of Thomas triuye of Wath eodem die
Buryed . . . . ye wife of Thomas Triuye eod die
Baptized Thomas son of Samuell Cotes, gentle, of Wath had by Susannah his wife ye 23d day of July

August 1666

Baptized Martha ye daughter of George ffoulston of Coley lane ye second day
Buryed an infant of Thomas Mallinson unbaptized ye 10th day
Baptized Matthew son of Matthew Birkes of Wath ye 12th day
Buryed Elizabeth daughter of Mathew Birkes ye 16th day
Buryed Ralph Marstin of Wath ye 20th day

September 1666

Baptized John ye son of John Carr of Wath ye 9th day
Baptized Ann ye daughter of William Skyres of Lee ye 13th day
Buryed an infant of Joseph Hansons unbaptized ye 24th day
Buryed Guy Hague of Wath ye 25th day
Buryed Rosamond ye wife of Joseph Hanson ye 26th day
Baptized Mary ye daughter of Richard Kitchinman ultimo die

September 18th 1666 Memorand that James Clayton of Wath, yeoman, was Licensed & authorised by us whose names are añexed to Inioy one seate bought of Robert Ant beinge betwixt the seate of Mr Baxter & the place where the pulpit formerly stoode in the yeare of our Lord 1666 and there to continue without disturbance of any pson in paiñe of Ecclesiastical Censure.

Joseph Ludlam, Vicar de Wath
Robert Hill, Clarke
Thomas Tilney
William Heward } Churchwardens
George Shaw

Memorandū that the right honorable William Earle of Strafford did give wood to make our Bell frames anno domini 1666 and they was made by Edward Ratlife and Thomas his son and was finished ye 28th day of September 1666

James Clayton
Thomas Tinley
William Heward } Churchwardens
George Shaw
William Bingley

Memorand that Wath Church Steeple & the body of the Church was pointed & finished in August & September Anno domini 1669

John Kaye
John Jackson
John Elam } Churchwardens
Humphrey Jackson

October 1666

Baptized Ann ye daughter of Beniamin Saunderson ye 7th day
Baptized Elizabeth ye daughter John Stead of Wath ye 9th day

1666

Baptized Elizabeth ye daughter of Richard Marshall ye 11th day
Buryed Grace ye wife of Marke Rawlin ye 12th day
Maryed Nathaniell Nayler of ye ꝑish of Wakefeild & Margarete Shimeild of this ꝑish the 22th day
Buryed Margaret ye wife of Edward Crosley eodem die
Buryed Easther Wharam the 23d day
Buryed Richard Hutchinson ye 24th day

November 1666

Baptized John ye son of William Beckit of melton ye first day
Buryed Henry Shaw of Coley lane ye 11th day
Maryed John Rushworth & Ellizabeth Heaton ye 26th day
Baptized Richard ye son of Robert Scargall of Wath ye 27th day

December 1666

Baptized Gilbertus son of William Robucke ye first day
Buryed Richard Ellam senr ye 3d day
Buryed Margaret Wade of Swinton eodem die
Maryed Henry Cowꝑ and Mary Watson the 6th day
Buryed Robert Dawson from brampton ye 8th day
Bapt John ye son of Tho: Hartley of Wales ye 9th day
Buryed a stranger which was found dead in Wath feild ye 15th day
Maryed William Ganithry & Sarah Milners ye 20th day
Buryed one wid: child the 21th day
Baptized Mary ye daughter of Tho: Tinley of Wath ye 26th day

January 1666

Buryed a daughter of Richard Ellison of royds ye first day
Buryed Ann ye wife of William Wade of Melton ye 9th day
Buryed William Sawrby the 11th day
Baptized Mary ye daughter of William Bingley ye 15th day
Buryed wid Coo of Wath the 20th day
Baptized Ellizabeth ye daughter of Richard niccols of Wath ye 22th day
Baptized John ye son of George Robinson of Wath ye 27th day

ffebruary 1666

Maryed Humphray Jackson & Ann Leach the 14th day
Buryed a child of John houlgate ye 16th day
Baptized John ye son of John tingley ye 17th
Maryed Joseph hanson & Mary Booth the 19th day
Baptized Margaret daughter of John Heaton of Wath ye 24th

March 1666

Baptized Edward son of Edward Wood of hoober top ye 5th day
Baptized Elizabeth & Susanah daughters of John Wormald of West Melton ye same day
Buryed Elizabeth one of the twins ye 9th day
Baptized Matthew the son of Thomas Jenkinson of Wath the 10th day
Buryed John Brumhead & a Child of James stringers ye same day
Buryed a Child of William Redyhoughes ye 22th day
Buryed a Child of George Jenkinson ye 23d day
Baptized Mary a daughter of George Chappell ye 2— (*torn off*)

1667

Incipit Annus *1667*

Buryed Richard Robinson of Newall & ye wife of Thomas Sca Swinton ye 26th day
Buryed Thomas son of Jarvis Parkin ye 27th day

Aprill 1667

Buryed wid Brumhead ye second day
Buryed a Child of Rich: Citchinmans ye 3^d day
Baptized Edmond son of Ralph Crowder ye 5th day
Buryed ye s^d Edmond ye 7th day
Maryed Thomas Hutchinson & Elliz: ffostard the 9th day
Buryed a daughter of Henry Hinch of rotherham the 16th day
Buryed John Brooke of Wath ye 18th day
Buryed a Child of John Turners the 22th day
Baptized Richard son of John Baraclough the 28th day
Buryed George haslehurst & a Chiid of George Hoylands the 29th

May 1667

Baptized Thomas son of John Bellamy the 12th day
Buryed Jaine daughter of Thomas Baxter the 14th day
Maryed William Barkinshew & Ann Shells the 16th day
Baptized Mary daughter of William Sawrby the 19th day
Maryed Thomas Boulton & Elizabeth Wells the 28th day

June 1667

Baptized the child of John Bellamyes the 9th day
Buryed Ann wife of John Jackson the 12th day
Buryed ffrancis Addie of Swinton the 16th day
Baptized Richard son of John Kempe the 23^d day
Buryed a daughter of Humphray Addies ye 25th
Baptized Ann daughter of John houlgate the last day

July 1667

Buryed Mary wife of lanclot Briges the first day
Buryed Stephen Barber the 4th day
Buryed Humphray Jackson the 13th day
Buryed William Tillney the 17th day
Buryed Joane ye wife of George Willkinson the 18th day
Buryed Adam Earle the 23^d day
Buryed Sarah daughter of Roger Browne the 26th day
Buryed a Child of Mathew Birkes ultimo diè

August 1667

Baptized Mary daughter of Matthew birkes ye 11th day
Buryed Nicholas Birkes eodem die
Buryed William Wade the 14th day
Maryed Richard Gorril and Ann Carr the 15th day
Buryed Mathe birkes, eodem die
Buryed Ellin broadhead the 16th day
Baptized John son of Thomas Ellis of newall the 18th day
Buryed Alis Greenwood and an infant of Richard Hills unbaptiz 29th day

1667

September 1667

Baptized Willm son of Robert Elam the first day
Buryed Wid: Oxley eodem die
Buryed Wid: Wood the 3d day
Buryed John Smith wife the 10th day
Baptized Elizabeth daughter of William Cusworth the 17th day
Baptized Elizabeth daughter of Thomas Hepworth the 26th day
Buryed William son of Joseph Ludlam, vicar of Wath ye 27th

October 1667

Baptized Elizabeth daughter of Thomas Mallinson of Melton ye 8th day
Buryed Elizabeth daughter of Thomas Hepworth ye 10th day
Buryed Thomas Boulton of Newall ye 14th day
Buryed Dorothy Jeffry of Melton ye 17th day
Baptized William son of John Loriter the 15th day

November 1667

Buryed Easther the wife of Nicholas Cromacke the 4th day
Buryed John Wells the 9th day
Baptized Easther daugher of John Turner the 10th day
Buryed Edward Crosley the 11th day
Buryed Ralph Hattersley the 18th day
Buryed Ann Wright & Roger ffixby the 23d day
Baptized Humphray Addy son of Widd: Addy of Swinton natus post mortem patris the 24th day
Buryed A Child of widd: Birkes the same day
X Maryed John Beale of the pish of Tankersley & Ellin Carr of this pish the 28th day

December 1667

Buryed Thomas Hudson the 2d day
Baptized Ellin daughter of John Kay the 8th day
Maryed John ffirth & Ann houlmes the 9th day
Buryed an infant of the sd Ann base begot by the sd John ffirth the same day
Maryed William Haman & Easther Shells the 12th day
Buryed Ellin Doncaster the same day
Buryed John son of Thomas Wade the 17th day
Baptized John son of Edward Browne the 22th day
Buryed an infant of Edward ffirths unbaptized the 26th day

January 1667

Baptized Mary daughter of Thomas Hutchinson ye 5th day
Buryed Ann Pearson the 16th day
Baptized Ann daughter of William Elam the 12th day
Buryed a child of Robert Elams the 14th day
Baptized William son of Matthew Crose the 16th day

february 1667

Buryed a child of John Skiers unbaptized the 9th day
Buryed Ales the wife of William ffenton the 14th day
Buryed . . . . the wife of Mathew Crosse the 15th day
Baptized William son of John Carr the 16th day

1667
Buryed a child of John Bramwiths the 25th day
March 1667
Baptized Thomas son of John Parkin of Swinton the first day
Buryed A child of John Kempes of Wath the 12th day
Buryed Elizabeth wife of John Skiers of Swinton the 13th day
Buryed a child of Georg Jenkinsons the 19th day
Maryed John Smith & Elizabeth Baldricke the 23d day
Buryed Wid: Wade of Swinton eodem die
Incipit Annus 1668
Buryed Margaret the wife of Robert Hill the 25th day
Buryed Thomas More of Wath the 26th day
Buryed Joane wife of Richard Robinson ultimo die
Aprill 1668
Baptized John son of William Wood of Swinton the second day
Baptized Elizabeth daughter of Robert Heaton ye 3d
Buryed John Skiers of Swinton the 11th day
Buryed Sarah the wife of William Cawthry eodem die
Baptized Hannah daughter of Richard Walker the 12th day
Buryed John Marriot the 15th day
Baptized William the son of Thomas Triuy the 19th
Maryed Richard ffreman and Mary Hill the 23d day
May 1668
Buryed James Crosley the 7th day
Buryed fforton Shackleton wife eodem die
Buryed ffrances wife of John Parrat the 20th day
Baptized Anthony son of Willm Readyhough the 24th day
June 1668
Buried Elizabeth daughter of John Carr of rainber ye 7th
Marryed Robert Amery & Edith ffostard ultimo die
March the 20th 1667 Memorand that Richard Bell of Wath upon De was licensed & authorized by us whose names are herof u written to set a stall in the lady quire and there to stand & rem without any disturbance or molestation by anyone in pain Ecclesiasticall Censure Anno Domini 1667

Joseph Ludlam, Vicar
Georg Hoyland
Richard Tilney
John Laughton
Richard Casse
} Churchwarden

July 1668
Buryed Ellen wife of William Shaw the 4th day
Buryed ould briges wife the 11th day
Baptized Richard son of Richard Gorrill the 12th
Baptized John son of William Skiers the 30th day
Baptized Elizabeth daughter of Robert Lewin eodem die
September 1668
Buryed Georg Jenkinson, senior. the 3d day
Baptized Elizabeth daughter of John Shaw eodem die

1668
Maryed John Dawson & Mary Barber the 22th
Baptized Ann daughter of Willm Haman the 23d day
October 1668
Maryed Nicholas Bower & Allis Lee the 15th day
Baptized William son of George Hoyland the 20th day
November 1668
Maryed Henry Wright & Allis Saunderson the 12th day
Baptized John son of Phillip ffint the 15th day
Buryed a child of Thomas Tilneys the 26th day
Buryed a child of Jarvis Slackes the 29th day
December 1668
Baptized Grace daughter of Thomas Scales the 27th day
January 1668
Baptized Jaane daughter of Wm. Tomson the 3d day
Baptized Willm the son of John Parrat the 10th day
Buryed John son of William Beckit the 18th day
Buryed William Warde son of Widd: Warde the 19th day
Baptized Jaane daughter of Richard Addye of Swinton the 21th day
Maryed Jonathan Sheppeard & Katherine Marriat with a licence the 30th day
Buryed Thomas Woodcocke eodem die
ffebruary 1668
Maryed John Walker & Elizabeth Boulton the 4th day
Baptized Margaret daughter of Thomas Wade eodem die
Buryed Willm Shemeild the 5th day
Baptized Ann daughter of Thomas Popplewell the 7th day
Buryed Scotch Jaane the 11th day
Baptized John son of John Smith the 12th day
Baptized William son of Thomas Hartley the 21th day
Maryed John Sisson & Margaret Tilney, Joseph Wagstaffe and Mary ffoulston, George Tinsley & Elizebeth Shaw the 23d day
Buryed William Wadsworth the 27th day
March 1668
Buryed Jaane the wife of John Kempe the 6h day
Baptized Ann daughter of John ffrost the 7h day
Buryed Rosamond wife of Thomas Tilney rhe 8h day
Baptized Edward son of John Elam & John son of Richard Carr the 11th day
Baptized John son of John Amery the 14th day
Baptized Oumphray son of John Laughton the 18th day
Buryed Elizabeth daughter of John Addye of Swinton the 24th
Incipit Annus 1669
Baptized William son of Edward Wood the 25th day
Aprill 1669
Maryed Thomas Cawthorne & Dorithy Hopton the 12th day
Baptized ffraunces daughter of Christopher Moore the 22th day
Buryed George Robinson eodem die
Baptized John son of John ffirth the 23d day
Buryed Mr Samuell Wortley of Barnesley eodem die

1669

Buryed a Child of Robert ffayrams the 29th day

May 1669

Maryed Alexander Meridall & Elizabeth Wood the 6h day

Buryed a child of William Woods of Swinton the 10th day

Buryed Elizabeth wife of Oumfray Jackson the 11th day

Buryed a child of Widd: Addyes of Swinton which was kild with a waine the 12th day

Buryed Thomas Scales the 13th

Buryed Hannah daughter of George Wilkinson the 20th day

Maryed William Addye & Allis Walker the 25th day

June 1669

Maryed Robert Hill & Jaane Hunt the first day

Baptized Ann the daughter of James Stringer eodem die

Buryed Widd: Eller of Swinton the 4th day

Baptized Witlm son of William Cettlewell the 10th day

July 1669

Maryed ffrancis Tottingeton & Jaane Robinson the 20th day

August 1669

Baptized Elizabeth daughter of Thomas Sowerby the first day

Baptized Ellin daughter of Robert Scargall the 8th day

Buryed a child of John Allats the 10th day

Buryed Mary Land the 17th day

Baptized John son of Richard Marstin and Hannah daughter of Humphray Jackson the 22th day

Maryed George Walker & Jaane Haslehurst the 24th day

Baptized Katherine daughter of Richard Marshall the 26th

September 1669

Buryed an infant of Richard Hills unbaptized the 7th day

Buryed Ann the wife of Oumphray Jackson the 12th day

Baptized Jaane the second daughter of Thomas Baxter eodem die

Buryed an infant of Mr Tobias ffowler scholemaster of Wath unbaptized the 19th day

Baptized Thomas son of Henry ffayram the 21th day

Buryed the said Thomas the 22th day

Buryed Robert Heaton eodem die

Baptized William son of Thomas Jenkinson the 23d day

Baptized Elizabeth daughter of Jonas Maude the 26th day

October 1669

Baptized Thomas son of Henry Wright the first day

Buryed the sd Thomas the 12th day

Baptized Mary the daughter of John Parkin the 14th day

Buryed Dorothy wife of Thomas Casse the 15th day

November 1669

Baptized Mary the daughter of John Sisson the 5th day

Baptized Ann the daughter of Thomas Mallinson the 9th day

Baptized John the son of John Hicke the 14th day

Baptized Judeth the daughter of John Carr of Wath the 16th day

Buryed Ann Wilcocke of Swinton the 21th day

1669

Baptized Richard son of William Beckit eodem die
Buryed Nicholas Hudson of Newall the 22th day
Baptized Mary the daughter of Henry Hawslein the 28th day
December 1669
Baptized Elizabeth daughter of Robert Hill ꝑish Clarke the eyght day
Buryed Mary Wood of Swinton the 14th day
Baptized Sarah daughter of Richard Niccals the 16th day
Baptized Jaane daughter of Thomas Hutchinson the 19th day
Buryed Alis the wife of Nicholas Maykin ultimo die
January 1669
Baptized George son of George Tinsley the 9th day
Buryed Dorithy the wife of Robert Elam the 11th day
Buryed Widd: Jackson the 28th
Baptized ffrancis son of ffrancis Carr the 30th day
ffebruary 1669
Buryed . . . . the wife of John Crosse the 4th day
Baptised Thomas son of Thomas Ellis the 9th day
Buryed Samuell Beckit the 11th day
Buryed ffrancis son of ffrancis Carr the 12th day
Baptized John son of Samuell Shaw the 16th day
Buryed Widd: Stables of the Bridge the 17th day
Baptized Joshua son of Ralph ffords the 19th day
Buryed the sd Joshua the 20th day
Buryed Richard Citchinman the 21th day
Buryed Willm son of John Loriter the 25th day
March 1669
Baptized Thomas son of Richard Elam the 3d day
Baptized Jaane the daughter of Richard Tilney the 8th day
Buryed Widd: Marstin the 12th day
Incipit Annus 1670
Baptized Elizabeth daughter of John Loriter the 27th day
Baptized Ratcliffe son of Richard Gorrill ultimo die
Aprill 1670
Buryed a child of John Loriter the first day & another the 8th day
Buryed one . . . Wright which came in a carte? to Wath the 10th day
Baptized Susannah daughter of John Kay the same day
Buryed George son of Henry Willcocke the 23d day
May 1670
Buryed Elizabeth wife of William Robucke the 8th day
Buryed a child of Humphray Jacksons the 14th day
Buryed Richard son of Rich- Carr the last day
June 1670
Maryed William Hill & Allis Jessop the 16th day
Buryed Easther daughter of William Cussworth the last day
July 1670
Maryed Robert Elam & Rebeccah Mirfin the 7th day
Maryed Richard Barber & Mary Elison the 19th day
Baptized Thomas the son & Mary the daughter of Richard Hill the 20th day

1670

Baptized John son of John Steade the 28th day

August 1670

Maryed Robert Singleton & Ann Woodhead the first day

Buryed Sarah wife of Hugh Allen eodem die

Maryed Joseph Hamshay & Allis Armitedge the 4th day

Buryed Richard Malinson the 20th day

Baptized Richard the suposed son of George Smith of Thunerclife the 21th day borne of Mrs Greene

Buryed ffortan Shackelton eodem die

Buryed Elizabeth wife of Richard Bell the 12th day

Buryed Widd: Carr of Wath the second day

September 1670

Buryed Rich: ffostard the 13th day

Buryed Elizabeth Sourby the 14th day

Buryed John shaw the 16th day

Buryed the wife of George Shaw the 26th day

Buryed a Child of Darcy stones the 27th day

Buryed Widd: Ployden ultimo die

October 1670

Buryed Widd: Greenehough the 3d day

Baptized Ann daughter of Thomas Huit the 4th day

Buryed Jaane wife of Marke Rawlin the 5th day

Buryed Mary Walker of Swinton the 6th day

Buryed a Child of ffrancis Tottingetons the 7th day

Buryed Thomas Beard the 15th day

Buryed George Shaw the 19th day

Buryed Elizabeth ffostard of newall the 20th day

Buryed ffaith the wife of John Taylor the 22th day

Buryed Edith Wiggin the 24th day

Buryed Martha daughter of one . . . Wallis a stranger eode

Buryed Elezabeth wife of Thomas Jenkinson the 29th day

Baptized Mary daughter of Richard Robinson the 30th day

November 1670

Buryed Ann daughter of Willm Bingley the second day

Baptized Thomas son of Thomas Tilney the 3d day

Buryed a child of Richard Addyes the 4th day

Buryed Widd: Thrift the 14th day

Baptized Ann daughter of John Elam the 17th day

Buryed Margaret Carr of brampton the 20th day

Buryed Ellen daughter of Elizabeth Swallow eodem die

Buryed A Child of Thomas Triuie the 22th day

December 1670

Buryed Ann the wife of Anthony Aneley the second day

Buryed George Tinsley the 6th day

Buryed Ann the Widd: of John Wharam the 12th day

Buryed a child of John Ameries eodem die

Buryed a child of Edward Brownes the 18th day

Baptized John the son of John Carr of Rainber the 23d day

1670
Buryed the said John the 25th day
January 1670
Buryed Elin the wife of Richard Niccoles the second day
Buryed Mary the wife of Thomas Jessop the 5th day
Buryed ffrancis the wife of George Jenkinson 6th day
Buryed George Winter the 8th day
Buryed Thomas son of Thomas Tilney the 9th day
Buryed . . . . the wife of Alexander Thackerow the 18th day
Buryed a child of William Tomsons the 29th day
ffebruary 1670
Buryed a child of Ralph ffoards the 20th day
Buryed Richard Shaw the 24th day
Buryed one steward wife of barnsley the 26th day
March 1670
Baptized Ellin daughter of Henry ffayram the 5th day
Baptized Richard son of Mathew Crosse the 9th day
Buryed the sd Ellin eodem die
Buryed John Iredall the 12th day
Buryed John Houlgatt the 18th day
Buryed Ann Birkes widd: the 23d day
Buryed a child of Henry Hawselins the 24th day
Incipit Annus 1671
March
Buryed a child of William Elam the 30th day
Buryed Thomas Addye of Swinton ultimo die
Buryed Ann Elis eodem dīe

Memorand That Thomas Wade of West Melton. yeoman, was authorized by us whose names are here unto annexed to Inioy one stalle standlnge on the south side of the Church of Wath sup Dearne beinge exchanged by him the said Thomas Wade & Wim Cottle of Newall in the yeare of our lord 1670 and there to continue & be belongeinge unto his house in west Melton afore said in paine of Ecclesiasticall Censure

Joseph Ludlam, vicar
John + Smith his marke, ffrancis Carr, Richard Gorrill — Churchwardens

Aprill the second 1671
Memorand That Richard Gorrill of Coley Lane in the pish of Wath was licensed & authorised by us whose names are here under written to build one stalle in the lady quire & there to stand & remaine without disturbance or molestation by any one in paine of Ecclesiasticall censure.

Joseph Ludlam, vicar
John + Smith his marke, ffrancis Carr, Thomas Wade — Churchwardens.

1671

Memorand that Henry Walker, gent, was authorized by us whose names are here unto annexed to Inioy one stall standinge on the north side of the midale alley in our pish Church of Wath sup Dearne beinge bought of Mr. Samuell Wortley of Swinton and there to continue & be belongeinge to his house in Swinton afforesaid in paine of ecclesiasticall Censure.

April 1671

Maryed Henry Coop & Mary Wightman the 24th day

Maryed John Turton & Mary Baraclough the 25th day

Buryed Elizabeth wife of Joseph Ludlam Mr of Arts & Vicar of Wath eodem die

Buryed Mary hall the 26th day

Buryed Nicholas Dawson the 28th day

Buryed Thomas Sisson the 29th day

Baptized William son of Robert Beamont of Nether hoyland eodem die

May 1671

Maryed Thomas Archdall & Margaret Hill the second day

Buryed Henry Hauslin the third day

Maryed Edward Brocke & Sarah Staneie ? the 25th day

Buryed Sarah daughter of Thomas Wilcocke the 27th day

June 1671

Baptized Ann daughter of Joseph Hamshay the 3d day

Bnryed Thomas Kirkeby the 8th day

Maryed ffrancis Whiteley & Ann More the 11th day

Buryed Mary the daughter of John Loriter eodem die

Baptized Issabella daughter of Willm Elam the 18th day

Buryed Margaret Stables the 20th day

Maryed Thomas Preistley & Ann Carr 16 22th day

Buryed a Childe of Thomas Triuye eodem die

July 1671

Maryed Thomas Clarckeson & Ann ffreman the second day

Baptized George son of Edward Wood eodem die

Buryed a Child of Richard Robinsons eodem die

Buryed Thomas Jenkinson the 14th day

Buryed William Tomson the 25th day

August 1671

Maryed Edward ffirth & Katherine Walker the first day

Baptized Hester daughter of William Haman eodem die

Baptized Elizabeth daughter of John Loriter the 20th day

September 1671

Maryed William Rhoades & Grace Elison the 5th day

Maryed Jonathan Hill & Elizabeth Barker the 11th day

Buryed ffrancis Baxter of Abdye eodem die

Buryed Mary wife of Henry Wilcocke the 16th day

Buryed Ann the wife of Godfrey Shells the 18th day

Baptized John the son of Edward Otley & George the son of George Durdie the 24th day

Buryed John Ellis of Wath eodem die

1671

Baptized Thomas son of Robert Hill pish Clarke the 24th day

October 1671

Buryed a Child of Nicholas Wrights unbaptized the 6th day

Baptized William son of John Heaton the 8th day

Baptized Jaane daughter of Thomas Robinson Junior of Nether Hoyland the 16th day

November 1671

Buryed Mary Stables the 5th day

Baptized Thomas son of Widd : Tomson the 12th day natus post mortem patris

Buryed ffrances daughter of Thomas Wilcocke the 15th day

Buryed Mary daughter of John Sisson the 26th day

Buryed Ralph Smith the 28th day

December 1671

Maryed Richard Wood & Sarah Iredale the 7th day

Buryed a Child of Widd : Winters eodem die

Maryed William Iredale and Jane Roome the 12th day

Buryed a Child of Mark Rollens the 13th day

Buryed Thomas son of Nicholas Maykin the 14th day

Baptized Edward the son of Edward ffirth Junior the 17th day

Buryed A servant of Thomas Wade the 18th day

January 1671

Buryed Widd : Booth the 4th day

Baptized Mary daughter of John Smith the 7th day

Maryed Nicholas Maykin & Allis Cuttall the 15th day

Baptized John the son of John Sisson the 30th day

ffebruary 1671

Buryed John the son of William Cusworth the second day

Baptized John son of Nicholas Willson eodem die

Buryed the said John the 3d day

Buryed Thomas Heaton eodem die

Maryed William Parrat & Elizabeth Tinsley the 6th day

Buryed a Child of Matthew Crosse the 9th day

Baptized Elizabeth daughter of John Carr of Wath the 11th day

Buryed Katherine the daughter of Widd : Pate eodem die

Maryed William Adamson & Dorithy Cutt the 15th day

Baptized ffrances the daughter of Elizabeth Sheppeard base begott the 18th day

Buryed Mary the widd : of Thomas Heaton eodem die

Maryed Thomas Gooddall & Elizabeth Stables the 20th day

Buryed Margaret ffixbye the 23d day

Buryed a Child of Anthony Aneleyes the 27th day

March 1671

Buryed . . . . the daughter of Widd : Wadsworth the 3d day

Baptized Grace the daughter of Thomas Wade of West Melton the 6th day

Buryed Mary the wife of John dawson the 19th day

Incipit annus 1672

1672

Aprill 1672

Buryed William Soreby the 3^d^ day

Baptized Hellen the daughter of Thomas Tilney the 4th day

Maryed William Booth & Elizabeth Rollin the 8th day

Baptized Thomas the son of ffrancis Carr the 9th day

Buryed Widd: Shaw the 11th day

Baptized Hester daughter of John Rollin of Nether Hoyland the 14th day

Baptized Thomas son of Robert Scargall the 25th day

Buryed Thomas Carr of Brampton eodem die

June 1672

Baptized John son of John Parkin the 8th day

July 1672

Baptized Margaret the daughter of Richard Tilney the 5th day

Buryed Elizabeth daughter of Jonas Maude eodem die

Maryed William Smith & Elin Shaw the 23^d^ day

August 1672

Baptized Hanah the daughter of Richard Carr the first day

Buryed Emanuell son of Widd: Carneyley the 7th day

Buryed an infant of John Elam the 14th day unbaptized

Baptized Thomas son of Thomas Malinson the 18th day

Buryed the daughter of John Parkin eodem die

Buryed Easther the wife of James Clayton the 19th day

Buryed the wife of John Lambert the 29th day

September 1672

Baptized Sarah the daughter of Thomas Hutchinson the 8th day

Baptized William son of John ffrost the 15th day

Maryed John Poules & Ann Jessop the 26th day

Baptized Joseph son of Thomas Hartley the 29th day

October 1672

Buryed William son of William Brooke the 3^d^ day

Baptized Mary the daughter of Thomas Huit the 6th day

Buryed Robert Hudson eodem die

Buryed John Parrat senior the 10th day

Baptized Ann daughter of Thomas Broadhead the 20th day

Buryed Joseph Hanson the 25th day

November 1672

Maryed Thomas Hattersley & ffrances Hobkinson the 10th day

Baptized Edward son John ffirth eodem die

Buryed Elizabeth wife of John Jackson the 13th day

Buryed the wife of John Allott the 15th day

December 1672

Baptized Bridget the daughter of Thomas Triuye and Martha daughter of Henry Wright the first day

Buryed the wife of Richard Beamont eodem die

Maryed John Bloome & Jaane Brooke the 3^d^ day

Baptized Christopher the son of John Kay the 5th day

Buryed Martha daughter of Henry Wright the 7th day

Baptized William son of Richard Marshall the 10th day

1672

Baptized Grace daughter of Nathaniell Naylor the 12th day
Buryed John Baraclough the 16th day
Buryed Jaane daughter of Richard Tilney eodem die
Buryed Ellis wife of Henry Wright the 19th day
Buryed Marke Rollin the 21th day
Buryed Richard Thackerowe of Swinton the 24th day
Baptized William son of Richard Gorrill the 26th day
Baptized Richard son of Robert Hill, pish clarke, the 27th day
Buryed Jaane wife of the said Robert Hill eodem die
Buryed a Child of Widd: Smith the 29th day
Buryed a Child of Widd: Hages ultimo die

January 1672

Baptized William son of Josias Wadsworth the 12th day
Baptized Elizabeth daughter of Thomas Elis eodem die
Buryed Jaane wife of ffrancis Tottingeton eodem die
Baptized Joseph son of Richard Hill the 19th day
Baptized Thomas son of Mathew Crosse the 26th day
Maryed Richard Sale & Ann Addye the 30th day
Baptized Sarah daughter of Richard Townend, gen of uper hoyland ultimo die

ffebruary 1672

Buryed John Smith the 7th day
Maryed Robert Hall & Ellen Bradley the 11th day
Buryed Nicholas Morton the 14th day
Baptized ffrances daughter of Richard Bell the 16th day
Buryed Easther Hudson the 18th day
Buryed William Taylor the 21th day

March 1672

Buryed Thomas Younge the second day
Buryed ffrancis Yates the 7th day
Buryed dorythy Brooke the 10th day
Buryed Henry Wilcocke the 16th day
Baptized Elizabeth daughter of William Iredale the 20th day
Baptized Easther daughter of Nicholas Wright & Katherine daughter of Phillip ffiint the 23d day

Incipit Annus

Aprill 1673

Maryed Henry Wright & Mary Birkes. John Allot & Ellin Tomson. George Carr & Ann Wilcocke the first day
Baptized William son of Thomas Binclife the 13th day
Baptized Richard son of Richard Elam the 24th day

May 1673

Baptized Sarah daughter of John Hurst the 11th day
Baptized George son of George Carr the 15th day
Baptized John son of John Parrat the 18th day
Baptized Henry son of William Parrat the 29th day

June 1673

Buryed Lawrence Robinson the first day

1673

Maryed John Jackson & Jaane Shaw the 5th day
Baptized William son of ffrancis Carr the 8th day
Maryed Richard Cooe & Mary Hanson the 12th day
Maryed William Steare & Elizabeth Dyson eodem die
Baptized Abigall daughter of George Hoyland eodem die
Baptized John son of John Carr of rainber the 23° day
Maryed Richard Niccols & Mary Jub the 24th day
Baptized Richard son of Thomas Tilney eodem die

July 1673

Baptized John son of William Smith the 3d day
Buryed a child of William Parrats the 10th day
Baptized Elizabeth daughter of William Beckit the 14th
Maryed Godfrey Matheman & Ruth Shaw the 17th day
Baptized Robert son of Darcy Stones the 20th day
Buryed Elizabeth widd of Thomas Addye the 23d day

August 1673

Maryed John Gawtrees & Easther Goodison the 14th
Maryed Thomas Marsh & Easther Pearson the 18th
Baptized Jaane daughter of Nicholas Carr the 27th
Buryed the sd Jaane the 30th
Baptized Jaane daughter of Jonas Maude ultimo die
Baptized Mary daughter of Joseph Hamshey eodem die

September 1673

Buryed Godfrey Bawdison the 27th

October 1673

Baptized Thomas son of William Haman the 16th day

November 1673

Baptized William son of Richard Niccolls the 25th day
Maryed Richard Beaumont & Mary Carr the 27th day

December 1673

Buryed Jarvis Parkin the 22th day

January 1673

Baptized Thomas son of John Sisson the first day
Baptized John son of Robert Hill, ꝑish clarke, the 11th day
Maryed ffrancis Tottington & Margaret Jessop the 15th day
Baptized Thomas son of Richard Beamon eodem die
Buryed an infant of John Elam unbaptized the 17th day
Maryed Michaell Croft & Allis Pearson the 29th day
Buryed Humphray Jackson the 30th day

ffebruary 1673

Maryed Thomas Roggers & Ann ffulston the 5th day
Buryed John the son of Robert Hill, ꝑish clarke, the 9th day
Baptized Skiers Carr son of John Carr of Wath the 10th day
Baptized Thomas & Ann twins of John Bloome eodem die
Buryed John Kempe the 12th day
Maryed Jarvis Bely & Sarah Smith the 19th day
Buryed a childe of George Chambers a tinker eodem die
Maryed Robert Bingley & Sarah Skirtley the 26th day

1673

Buryed Thomas son of John Bloome the 27th day

March 1673

Buryed Jonas Maude the 14th day

In cipit Annus 1674

Buryed Ann daughter of Alexander Thackrow the 27th

Buryed Albert son of William Robucke the 29th

Aprill 1674

Baptized Henry son of Thomas Rogers the 2d day

Buryed George Hoyland the 3d day

Buryed a childe of Richard Robinson eodem die

Baptized Jaane daughter of John Loriter the 5th day

Buryed Elizabeth wife of Thomas Baraclough eodem die

Baptized Elizabeth daughter of Thomas Wade the 9th day

Buryed Richard fflint eodem die

Baptized George son of George Wade of Swinton the 11th day

Buryed ffrances durham the 18th day

Buryed the said George Wade the 25th day

Baptized Thomas son of Thomas Gooddall the 26th day

Baptized John son of John Heaton eodem die

May 1674

Baptized Elizabeth daughter of Richard Marsden ye 9th day

Buryed William son of John Heaton the 15th day

Maryed Samuell Burton & Elin ffulston the 21th day

June 1674

Baptized John son of John Hill the 7th day

Maryed Alexander Meridall & Ann Soreby the 8th day

Bapt Ann daughter of Richard Tilney eodem die

Maryed Thomas Baraclough & Jaane Hage the 11th day

Buryed a child of Widd: Hudson of Newall the 19th day

Buryed Nicholas Pearson the 20th day

Baptized Grace daughter of William Rushforth the 26th day

July 1674

Baptized Mary daughter of John Allot the 19th day

August 1674

Bapt George son of Godffrey Matheman the 20th day

Bapt Willm son of Willm Parrat the 23d day

Bapt Mary daughter of John Gawtress the 30th day

September 1674

Bapt Mary daughter of Thomas Baxter of Abdye, gent the 3d day

Bapt Elizabeth daughter of Nicholas Carr the 22th day

Bapt Elizabeth daughter of Josias Wadsworth the 27th day

October 1674

Burd Allis wife of Robert White the 6th day

Bapt Robert son of William Elam & Mary daughter of Gilbert Wood of Wentworth the 11th day

Burd Widd: Beckit the 14th day

Baptized Ellin daughter of William Bingley the 22th day

1674

December 1674

~~Baptized~~	William son of Richard Bell the 3^{d} day
Maryed	Thomas Eller & Mary Coe the 10th day
Bapt	Robert son of Robert Hill ꝑish Clarke the 14th day
Bur	Christopher ffulston eodem die of Swinton
Bapt	George son of William Addye the 20th day
Baptized	Elizabeth daughter of William ffoster the 17th day
Bapt	Thomas son of Jervis Bely the 27th day
January 1674	
Bapt	Willm the son of Willm Wadsworth the 10th day
Marr^{d}	Nicholas Pearson & Ann Carneyley the 14th day
Bur^{d}	Mary wife of Hugh Shaw the 30th day
Bapt	Mary daughter of John Kay ultimo die
ffebruary 1674	
Bapt	Sarah daughter of John Parkin the 4th day
Bapt	Hanah daughter of Thomas Tilney the 7th day
Bur^{d}	Grace wife of John Elam of Grange eodem die
Bur^{d}	Jaane Warde of Swinton the 12th day
Bur^{d}	an infant of Thomas Hutchinson unbapt the 14th day
Bapt	Elizabeth daughter of the s^{d} Thomas eodem die
Bapt	Thomas son of Samuell Burton the 18th day
Bapt	Thomas son of Richard Addye the 20th day
Bur^{d}	Elizabeth daughter of Thomas Hutchinson the 26th
March 1674	
Bapt	John the son of Richard Gorrill the 4th day
Bur	Richard son of Robert Hill, ꝑish clarke, the 13th day
Bapt	Ann daughter of Robert Wharam the 18th day
Bapt	Richard son of Thomas Malinson the 21th day
Bur	Thomas son of Samuell Burton the 22th day
Incipit Annus 1675	
Aprill 1675	
Bur	Ann daughter of Richard Tilney the first day
Bapt	Ann daughter of John Dixon the 16th day
Bur	Abigall daughter of Widd : Hoyland the 22th day
Married	Thomas Wiggin & Ann Pate the 27th day
May 1675	
Mar	Robert Tyas & Eliz : Sheppeard the 13th day
Bapt	Mary the daughter of Thomas Hartley the 9th day
Bapt	Mary daughter of William Smith & Elizabeth daughter of Thomas Eller & Mary daughter of Thomas Poplewell the 16th daie
Bur^{d}	Robert son of Robert Hill, ꝑish clarke, the 24th day
Bapt	Jonathan son of Nicholas Wilson the 25th day
June 1675	
Bur	an Infant of ffrancis Tottingeton unbapt the 28th
Bapt	Mary daughter of George Wade of Swinton the 29th
July 1675	
Bur	Ann daughter of John Allott the 25th day

1675

August 1675
Bapt Joseph son of ffrancis Carr the 12th day
September 1675
Burr John Taylor of the bridge the 4th day
October 1675
Bapt Thomas son of John ffirth the 10th day
Bapt Mary daughter of John Bloome the 17th day
Bapt Mary daughter of Willm Coe of Upr Hoyland the 24th day
Bapt ffrances daughter of John Jackson the 28th day
November 1675
Bur an Infant of Henry Wright's unbapt the 22th day
Marr Nicholas Beardshaw & Katherine Hage the 25th day
Bapt Samuell son of Samuell Burton eodem die
December 1675
Bapt William son of William Iredall the 9th day
Bapt Jaane daughter of Thomas Baraclough the 15th day
Bur Jaane wife of Thomas Baraclough the 16th day
Bapt Jaane daughter of Thomas Huit the 26th day
January 1675
Bapt Thomas son of Robert Tyas the first day
Bapt John son of Richard Beamont the 16th day
ffebruary 1675
Marr Richard Hogley & Ann Yates the 3d day
Bapt Mary daughter of Godfrey Mattheman the 12th day
Bur Beteris the wife of Richard Baraclough the 16th day
Bapt Sarah daughter of John Gawtress the 22th day
March 1675
Bur Mary daughter of Godfrey Mattheman the 4th day
Bur the sd Sarah daughter of John Gawtress the 14th
Incipit Annus 1676
Mard Thomas Sharpe & Mary Kirke the 26th day
Mar Nicholas Tilney & Mary Tilney the 30th day
Aprill 1676
Mar Thomas Baraclough & Elizabeth Parkin ye 6th day
Bur the wif of William Wood senior the 15th day
Bapt John son of Nicholas Pearson the 16th day
Bapt Richard son of Richard Hill the 25th day
Bapt Ann daughter of George Carr the 27th day
Bur an infant of Humphray Sissons unbapt eodem die
May 1676
Bur Elizabeth daughter of Humphray Jackson ye 11th day
Bur Elizabeth wife of Humphray Sisson the 15th day
Bapt Thomas son of Thomas Baxter of Abdie, gent, the 18th day
Bur Robert Ant the 19th day
July 1676
Bapt Thomas son of Thomas Hutchinson ye 13th day
Burd Thomas Cettlewell the 19th day
Mard Robert Roids & Elizabeth Addie the 20th day

1676

Mar^{d} Thomas Holmes & Elizabeth Jessop the 30th day

August 1676

Bur^{d} the wife of Willm Brooke of Swinton the 2th day

Bur^{d} Widd: Shemeild the 8^{d} day

Bapt^{d} Mary the daughter of Phillip fflint the 13th day

Mar John Bagshaw of Great Huckley in the pish of Hope gentl & Elizabeth Coats of this pish gent the 22th day

Bapt Jaane daughter of Thomas Sharpe the 27th day

Bapt Mary daughter of Nicholas Wright ultimo die

September 1676

Bur The s^{d} Mary the first day

Bapt Mary daughter of Thomas Lambert the 5th day

Bapt ffrances daughter of Robert Hill pish Clarke ye 7th day

Bapt Thomas son of Edward ffirth Junior the 10th day

Bapt Grace daughter of John Loriter the 14th day

Bur Richard son of John Bramwith the 17th day

Bapt Elizabeth daughter of John Bramwith the 17th day

Bapt Elizabeth daughter of Robert White ultimo die

October 1676

Bur^{d} Ellin the widd: of Lawrence Wade the second day

Mar Tho: Booth & Ellin Kay the 5th day

Bapt Jaane daughter of Thomas Tilney eodem die

Bapt Michaell son of Joseph Wadsworth & Ellin daughter of William ffostard & Mary daughter of George Leach the 15th day

Bur^{d} Thomas Soreby the 17th day

Bur^{d} a child of William Elam the 29th day

November 1676

Mar^{d} Robert Pinder & Ann Bisbye the 9th day

Bapt Ann daughter of Nicholas Tilney eodem die

Bur a bastard child which came from Swinton of one Elizabeth Parkin the 19th day

Bapt William son of ffrancis Tottington the 22th day

Bapt Ann daughter of John Sisson the 28th day

Mar^{d} William Bell & Mary Tayler ultimo die

December 1676

Bur^{d} Thomas son of Alex: Thackray the first day

Bapt Dorithy daughter of Thomas Holmes the 7th day

Bapt Hester daughter of William Rushforth the 12th day

Bapt Judith daughter of Robert Wharam the 14th day

Bur an infant of Thomas Broadheads unbapt eodem die

Bapt Thomas son of Thomas Gilbert the 17th day

Bur William Brooke the 22th day

Bapt Darcye son of Darcye Stones the 26th day

Bur^{d} Thomas son of Thomas Gilbert the 27th

Bapt Richard son of John Trickitt ultimo die

January 1676

Bapt Richard son of Godfrey Matheman the 18th day

Bapt Mary daughter of Thomas Wade the 30th day

1676

ffebruary 1676

Bapt Ann daughter of Thomas Triuie the 11th day

Bapt Dorithie daughter of Margaret Hill base begot ye 12th day

Mard Wllliam Bentley & Elizabeth Houlmes the 13th day

Mard John Beckit & Ann Longbotham eodem die

Burd Mary daughter of Thomas Wade the 14th day

Burd Widd: Shaw the 16th day

Bapt Elizabeth daughter of Nicholas Wilson the 18th day

Bapt Mary daughter of Thomas Malinson the 27th day

March 1676

Bur George Wilkinson the first day

X Bapt John son of Nicholas Carr the 4th day

Bur Timothy Wade eodem die

Bapt John son of William Beckit the 6th day

Bapt Elizabeth daughter of Richard ffulston the 8th day

Bapt Ann daughter of John Carr of Hoober the 12th day

Burd Lucie wife of Hugh Allen the 13th day

Incipit Annus 1677

Bapt William son of John Kay the 25th day

Bapt Ann daughter of William Addie of Swinton the 29th day

Aprill 1677

Bapt George son of Jarvis Bely of Wath the first day

Bapt Richard son of John Heaton the 12th day

Bur Ann daughter of William Addie the 23d day

Bapt Elizabeth daughter of John Hurst the 13th of May

Aprill the 17th 1677

Memorand that Edward Wood & Phillip fflint was licensed & authorised by us whose names are here unto annexed to build one stall adioininge to the west end of the stalls in the middle alley & there to stand & be to them and their owne proper use in paine of Ecclesiasticall censure

Joseph Ludlam, vicar
Richard Walker
William Yates
Robert Wharam } Churchwardens
George ffulston
John Addie

Memorand that Thomas Hutchinson of Newall was licensed & authorized by us whose names are here unto annexed to build one stall at the west end of the midle alley joineing to Edward Wood & Phillip fflint stall & there to stand & be remaineinge unto his house in Newall in paine of Ecclesiasticall censure

John Ludlam, vi ar
Richard Walker
William Yates
Robert Wharam } Churchwardens
George ffoulston
John Addie

1677
June 1677
Bur Dorithy daughter of Margaret Hill the 4th day
Bur Jaane wife of Richard Casse the 5th day
Bapt Dorcas daughter of Thomas Morton the 12th day
Mard Thomas Carr & Mary Hoyland the 18th day
Mard William Richardson & Elizabeth Elison the 19th day
Bur an Infant of William Bentley the 23d day
Bur Dorcas daughter of Thomas Morton the 26th day
Bapt Mary daughter of Joseph Nailer of hoyland & Thomas son of Richard Tilney & Mary daughter of John dison of Lee the 28th day
July 1677
X Bapt Hanah daughter of ffrancis Carr primus die
Bapt Joseph son of John Parkin of Swinton the 5th day
Bapt Joseph son of John ffrost the 15th day
Mard William Knight & Elizabeth Scoales the 17th day
August 1677
Bur William Bingley of Swinton primus die
Bapt William son of George Wade of Swinton the second day
Burd Elizabeth wife of Thomas Tyas & Robert White eodem die
Bur William Haman of Swinton the 28th day
September 1677
Bupt Jaane daughter of Thomas Warde of Swinton the 11th day
Bur Seabastin Child the 18th day
Bapt Easther daughter of William Bell the 20th day
October 1677
Mard ffrancis Clayton & Mary Hoyland the 2d day
Burd Mary wife of William Casse the 4th day
Mard Thomas Elam & Bridget Hunt the 9th day
Burd Thomas Poplewell the 21th day
November 1677
Mard Thomas Jessop & Elizabeth Shaw the 8th day
Burd Thomas Gooddall the 10th day
Bapt Thomas son of Robert Pinder the 25th day
Burd Alis wife of Adam Dawson eodem die
December 1677
Burd Robert Tomson the 4th day
Burd Jaane daughter of Thomas Tilney the 14th day
Burd Thomas Baxter of brampton the 17th day
Bapt Ann daughter of Willm Smith the 26th day
Bapt John son of John Wadsworth of Wath the 27th day
January 1677
Bapt Hanah daughter of John ffretwell of the Shaw the 5th day
Bapt Mary daughter of Thomas Elam the 24th day
Bapt Nicholas son of Nicholas Wright the 26th day
Bapt Mary daughter of William Knight the 27th day
Burd the sd Nicholas Wright ultimo die

1677

ffebruary 1677

Bapt Richard son of John Hill of Swinton the 5th day
Burd William Roebuck of brampton eodem die
Bapt Margaret daughter of Nicholas Pearson the 8th day
Burd William Wadsworth of Newall the 12th day
Bapt Thomas son of John Jackson of Wath ye 14th day

March 1677

Bur 2 Infants of William Bentley unbapt the 5th day
Bapt Ann daughter of of Robert Tyas of Newall the 10th day

Incipit annus 1678

Bapt John son of Thomas sharpe the 28th day
Bur Widd Gorrill eodem die
Bapt Elizabeth daughter of Thomas Carr of Wath ultimo die

Aprill 1678

Bapt Thomas son of Thomas Harteley the second day
Mard Richard Baraclough & Dorithy Nicholson the 4th day
Burd John Addye a solger of Swinton the 7th day
Burd Joseph Ludlam Mr of Artes & the Vicare of Wath the 18th day

May 1678

Bur Mary wife of Jonathan Heward of greasebrough the 12th day
Bap the daughter of Richard Beamant the 17th day
Bapt Elizabeth daughter of John Lile the 30th day

June 1678

Bapt Richard son of Richard Bell the 13th day
Bapt Thomas son of Margaret Bawdison base begotten the 16th day
Bapt Ann daughter of Thomas Tilney the 27th day

Memorand that Mr John Twittey did preach his first Sermon in Wath Church the 16th day of June anno dom. 1678 and had possession of the sd Church liuered unto him by Mr Heaton & Mr Stones of Darfeild

Preached his last Sermon on X'mas-day 1724. wch happened so to be on ye failing of his sight (*Inserted*)

Departed this life Jan 9th about 9 a clock in ye Forenoon 1728

July 1678

Burd Ann Willcocke the 5th day
Bapt Thomas son of Thomas Morton the 28th day
Burd one Hannah Hinchliffe which came into Brampton byer with a pass the 29th day
Bapt Easther the daughter of John Blome the 29th day

September 1678

Bapt Jaane daughter of George Carr the 13t day
Mard Thomas Willson & Elizabeth Boy the 19th day
Bapt Mary daughter of Thomas ffostard of Swinton the 22th day
Bapt Matthew son of John Birkes of Swinton the 24th day

October 1678

Mard Charles Loriter & Elizabeth Thursbye the first day
Mard John Robinson & Susanah Robinson the 22th day
Mard John Bingeley and Jaane Ward the 24th day

1678

Bapt Sarah daughter of George Leach of Swinton ye 27th day

November 1678

Mard Thomas Lancaster & Mary Tyas the 5 day

Mard William Wainewright & Ann Smith the 7th day

Bapt Mary daughter of Thomas Wade of Melton ye 14th day

Bapt Thomas & William sons of Nicholas Tillney of Wath the 23th day

Bapt John son of Tho Jessop the 24th day

December 1678

Bapt Ann daughter of Tho: Lambert of Swniton the 21th day

Bapt Mary daughter of Richard ffulston of Brampton the 26th day

January 1678

Bapt Jaane daughter of Darcye Stones the 14th day

Bapt Jaane daughter of Thomas Baxter of abdye the 16th day

Bapt Elizabeth daughter of Mathew Crosse the 18th day

Bapt Mary daughter of Richard Niccolls the 28th day

ffebruary 1678

Bapt Margaret daughter of George Wade of Swinton the 15th day

Bapt Elizabeth daughter of Thomas Huit the 24th day

Mard Joshua Bingley and Ann Wade the 27th day

Bapt Ann daughter of Jarvis Bayley eodem die

March 1678

Bapt Margaret daughter of Thomas Eller the 2d day

Bapt Elizabeth daughter of John Robinson the 16th day

Incipit annus 1679

Bapt Mary daughter of William Bell the 27th day

Bapt Sarah daughter of Grace Hawslin base begotten by one John Steele eodem die

Aprill 1679

Bapt Elizabeth daughter of Richard Hill of Melton primus die

Bapt Jasper son of John Sisson of Brampton the 4h day

Bapt Ellin daughter of William Iredall the 21th day

May 1679

Bapt William son of Robert Wharam the first day

Mar Daniell Twigge & Elizabeth Gibson the 4th day

Bapt Ann daughter of ffrancis Clayton the 11th day

Bapt Mary daughter of Edward Wood the 14th day

Bapt William son of John Parkin of Swinton the 22th day

Bapt Hester daughter of John Loriter the 25th day

June 1679

Bapt Ann daughter of Phillip fflint primus die

Mard Samuell Parkin & damaris Thomson of thorpe the 10th day

Mard William Wells & Ruth Wilbye the 24th day

August 1679

Bapt Jaane daughter of Godfrey Matthewman the 28th day

September 1769

Mard Richard Shaw & Ellen Smith the 25th day

December 1679

Mar: Matthew Speight of the Parish of Darfield & Margaret Rushby of this Parish the 11th day (*Inserted in wrong page*)

1679

October 1679

Bapt Thomas son of Thomas Lancaster the 16th day

Bapt Catherine daughter of George Seclair of Cortwood the 19th day

Bapt Mary daughter of Richard Marshall of street the 23d

Bapt Nicholas son of John Carr of boober the 26th day

Bapt William son of William Bentley eo dem die

Nov: 1679

Baptizd Mary the Daughter of John Firth the 25th Day

Baptizd Sarah the Daughter of Thomas Wilcock of Swinton the 27th day

December 1679

Baptizd Thomas the son of Alice Mallinson of West Melton in the Parish of Wath the 7th day

January 1679

Mar: Jonathan Taylor of the Parish of Rotherham & Ann Bullos of Thorp-Hasley in the Parish of Wath cum Licentiā the 29th Day

Mar. John Twittey Vicar of Wath and Ann Hoyland of the same Town the 22d day

ffeb. 1679

Baptizd. Sarah Daughter of Thomas Rogers the 8 day

March 1679

Baptizd. Nicholas son of Thomas Tilney the 4th Day

Burials.

April ?

Burd Elizabeth Wild a Cripple brought in a Cart the 9th day
Recd Affidavit the 10th day

Bur Ann daughter of Jarvis Bayley the 26th day
Recd the Affidavit the 28th day

May 1679

Bur. Margaret daughter of George Wade the 16th day
Recd Affidavit the 17th Day

Bur Joseph Hoyland the 22th Day
Recd Affidavit the 27th Day

Bur an Infant of Richard Hutchinson ultimo die unbaptized

June 1679

Bur John son of John Allott the 22th day
Recd Affidavit the 24th day

Bur Thomas Bramwith the 24th day

July 1679

Recd the affidavit the first day

Bur. ffrances wife of Richard Hill the 26th day

August 1679

Recd Affidavit the second day

Bur. Ann daughter of ffrancis Clayton the second day
Recd Affidavit the fifth day

Bur Rebecka Hoyland the 4th day
Recd Affidavit the fith Day

Bur Grace Child the 7th day
Recd Affidavit the 13th day

Bur Thomas Holland & Grace Briggs the 26th day
Recd their Affidavits the 28th Day

1679

September 1679

Bur William Brooke the second day
Rec^{d} the Affidavit the 8th day

Bur. Richard Walker Jun the 14th day
Rec^{d} Affidavit the 19th day

Bur Thomas Mallinson & Elizabeth daughter of John Loriter the 21th day
Rec^{d} Affidavits the 26th day

Bur. Richard son of Dorithy Addye & John son of Hanah Hinchliffe & ffrancis Morton the 22th day
Rec^{d} their Affidavits 26th day

Bur^{d} Catherine Smith the 28thday

October 1679

Rec^{d} the Affidavit the third *day*

Bur^{d} Elizabeth wife of Thomas Holmes the 12th day
Rec^{d} the Affidavit the 18th Day

Bur^{d} Ellin Jackson the 16th day

Bur^{d} ffrances daughter of Robert Hill the 19th day
Rec^{d} their Affidavit the 20th Day

Novembr 1679

Bur^{d}: Mary the wife of Francis Cleyton the 7th day of November
Rec^{d} her Affidavit the 13th Day

Bur: Hannah the Daughter of Robert Pindar the 9th Day
Rec^{d} the Affidavit the 15th day

Bur: Ursula the wife of Rich: Slack the 21st
Rec^{d} Affidavit the 27th day

Bur. Mary daughter of John Firth of Melton the 24th Day
Rec^{d} Affidavit the 29th day

Bur: Robert Hill Clarke of Wath the 25th Day
Rec^{d} Affidavit the 29th Day

December 1679

Bur: John son of William Beckett of West Melton the 11th day
Rec^{d} Affidavit the 18th Day

Bur: Mary the Daughter of John Allott of Wath the 14th day
Rec^{d} Affidavit the 20th Day

Bur: Paul Capper a vagabond person the 19th Day
Rec^{d} Affidavitt the 24th Day

Bur: Mary the Daughter of Thomas Hewett of Melton the 21st Day
Rec^{d} Affidavitt the 26th Day

Bur: at Wath Thomas Ward of Swinton in Mexbro Parish the 29th Day

January 1679

Rec^{d} Affidavit the 2^{d} Day

Bur: John Wadsworth the 1st Day
Rec^{d} Affidavit the 5th Day

Bur: Gilbert Holmes & Eliz: Hudson of Melton the 14th day
Rec^{d} Affidavitts the 16th Day

ffebruary 1679

Bur Matthew Crosse the 26th Day
Rec^{d} Affidavit the 4th Day of March

1680

Incipit Annus, 1680
March
Baptizd Nicholas the son of Nicholas Carr the 30th Day
Aprill 1680
Baptizd Mary the Daughter of John Heaton the 6th Day
Mar. John Jenkinson & Barbary 13th day
Baptizd Nicholas son of Nicholas Pearson ye 15th day
Baptized John the son of George Wade of Swinton the 6th Day of May
May 1680
Baptized John ye son of Jervis Bayly ye 23th day
Baptized John the son of Tho: Elam of Melton ye 23th day
Baptized Darcy ye son of Tho: Midleton of Swinton ye 22th day
July 1680
Baptized Mary ye Daughter of Thomas Sharpe 22th
August 29 1680 Baptized Godfrey son of Wm ffostard
Septemb. 5 1680 Baptized Ann Pitt a Bastard child
Sept: 12 Baptized Sarah Daughter of John ffrost
Sept: 19 Baptized Olive Daughter of Daniell Twigge
Octob: 17 1680 Baptized Mary ye daughter of Joh: Robinson
Oct: 19 Baptized ffrances Daughter of Wm Smith
Octob. 1680
Baptized Elizabeth daughter of Wm Wells ye 28th
November 1680
Baptized Jane Daughter of John Jackson ye 9th day
Baptizd Eliz: daughter of George Leach ye 14th day
Baptizd Thomas son of Thomas Carre Decembr 9th
December 1680
Baptizd John son of John Dyson 15th day
Baptizd Ann daughter of Thomas Harteley 19th
Baptizd Joseph son of John Bloome ye 19th day
Jan: 1680
Baptized Ann Daughter of Richard Watson 6th day
February 1680
Baptized Robt the son of Robt Wharam ye 1st day
Baptized Ann Daughter of Tho: Wilkinson ye 10th day
Bap: Margarett Daughter of Will: Wilson ye 22th day
Baptizd Elizabeth Daughter of John Firth ye 27th day
Baptizd Catherin daughter of Nich: Wright ye 28th day
March 1680
Baptized Sarah daughter of Thomas Lambert ye 5th

Marriages

Septemb. 1680
Maryed M Joseph Green & Mrs. Alice Walker ye 28
Mar: Robt. Mirfin & Ann Jackson eodem die
Oct: 19 Maryed Thomas Cutt & Elizabeth Slack
Octob: 21 Maryed John Arundall & Helen Tinsley
Incipit Annus 1680

1680

Aprill
Bur: Ann Daughter of Widd: Crosse the 4th Day
Recd Affidavit the 8th Day
Bur: Robt Lyall of West Melton the 14th Day
Recd Affidavit the
Bur: Nicholas son of Nicholas Carr the 17th Day
Recd Affidavit the 24th Day
Bur: John Taylor the 25th Day
Recd Affidavit the 28th Day
Bur: Nicholas Pearson of Melton the 30th Day

May 1680
Recd Affidavit the third day
Bur Thomas Bullos of Swinton the 20th Day
Recd Affidavit the 25th Day

June 1680
Bur: John ye son of Thomas Jessop ye 1st Day
Recd Affidavit the 3d Day

July 1680
Bur: Margaritt Eller the 18th Day
Recd affidavit the 20th day
Bur: Ann Broadhead the last day
Recd Affidavitt the 9th day of August

August 1680
Bur: Ann Winscomb the 28th day
Recd Affidavitt the third Day of September

September 1680
Bur: Samuell Wortley the 3d Day
Recd Affidavitt the 8h Day
Bur: Richard Hey the 27th Day

October 1680
Recd Affidavitt the 3d Day
Bur: Mary daughter of John Eaton the 9th Day
Bur: Margarett ffosterd ye 10th day
Recd both Affidavitts the 13th day

November 1680
Bur: Christopher Moor 9th Day
Recd the Affidavitt 11th Day
Bur: John son of Mr. John Twittey 25th Day
Recd Affidavitt ye 1st of Decemb.
Bur: Catherin Smith the 28h Day
Recd Affidavit ye 1st day of Decemb.

December 1680
Bur: Lancelott Briggs the 4th Day
Recd Affidavitt the 10th Day
Bur: John Shepherd the 12th Day
Recd Affidavit 15th Day
Bur: Thomas young child of Thomas ffosterd 12 day
Recd Affidavit the 19th Day

1680

Bur: Mary Smith the 18th Day
Recd Affidavit the 23d Day
Bur: Wm ffrith a vagabond person ye 30th day
Recd Affidavitt ye last Day
Jan: 1680
Bur: Richard Hill ye 5th Day
Recd Affidavit 10th Day
Bur: Thomas Hammond ye 29th
Recd Affidavit 2d Day February
Bur: John Beckitt & Godfrey son of William Fosterd the 21st Day
Recd Affidavit for Godfrey ffosterd ye 23th Day
Recd Affidavit for John Beckit 28 day
Bur: Wm Beckitt the 26 Day
Recd Affidavit the 28 Day
March 1680
Bur: John Sisson the 1st Day
Recd Affidavit 5th Day
Bur Catherin Wright wife of Nicholas Wright the 1st day
Recd Affidavit 7th Day
Bur: Catherin daughter of Nicholas Wright 3d day
Recd Affidavit 7th Day
Bur: Mary wife of Henry Wright 4th Day
Recd Affidavit 7th Day
Bur: Ann Wilcock the 7th Day
Recd Affidavit 11th Day
Bur: Sarah Lambert the 8th Day
Recd Affidavit 11th Day
Bur: John Jackson 9th Day
Recd Affidavit 15th Day
Bur Richard Slack 15th Day
Recd Affidavit the 22th Day
Bur Elizabeth daughter of John ffirth 15th Day
Recd Affidāvit the 22th Day
Bur Catherin Leiger the 22th Day
Recd Affidavit the 26th Day
Aprill 1681
Baptized Mary daughter of James Linsley 2d Day
May 1681
Baptized William ye sonne of Tho: Baxter ye 3d day
Baptized John ye sonne of Robert Tyas the 15th day
Baptized John ye sonne of Robert pinder ye 23d day
July 1681
Baptized Richard ye sonne of Rich: ffoulston ye 28th day
August 1681
Baptized James ye sonne of Edward Wood ye 14th day
Octobr 1681
Baptized Elizabeth daughter of John Eaton ye 4th day
Baptized Jane daughter of John Arundall ye 9th day

1681

Novemb: 1681

Baptized John son of George Chappell ye first day

Decemb. 1681

Baptized Hannah daughter of William Yates ye 10th day

Baptized Thomasin daughter of Thomas Trivye ye 29th day

January 1681

Baptized Sarah daughter of Robert Pinckney ye first day

Baptized Sarah daughter of George Carr ye 10th day

Baptized Thomas son of Robert Lupton ye 14th day

February 1681

Baptized Jane daughter of Thomas Wil(*son*) ye 16th day

Baptized Elizabeth daughter of Thomas Holmes ye 19th day

Baptized Richard & William sons of Robert Brown ye 22th

Baptized Ann daughter of Andrew Smith the 27th day

March 1681

Baptized Ann the daughter of William Iredall the 5th day

Baptized Esther the daughter of Nicholas Carr ye 12th day

Marriages

Aprill Ann Dom 1681

Maryed Robert Brown & Elizabeth Thacker 5th day

Maryed Robt Lupton & Sarah Gawtrey ye 10th day

Marryed Andrew Smith & Margarett Carnaly the 15th day of May Ann Dom 1681

Marryed Nicholas Wright & Elizabeth Moore the 7th Day of July Ann Dom. 1681

July 1681

Marryed Thomas Holland & Mary Wadsworth ye last day

Marryed Robert Torr & Sarah Carniley the 18th Day of Octob Ann Dom 1681

Marryed Thomas Sharpe & Jane Sheppard ye 3^d^ Novemb (81)

Marryed Thomas Haslhurst & Isabell Cowme the 13th day of Novemb 1681

ffebr 168½

Maryed Joseph Hague & Elizabeth Walker

Ann: Dom: 1681

Bur: Ann Addye daughter of Rich: Addye the 28th of March Ann: Dom: 1681

Aprill 1681

Rec^d^ Affidavit ye 1st day

Bur: Mary Sharpe ye 16 of April

Rec^d^ Affidavit 24th day

Bur: Mary daughter of James Linsley ye 14th day

Rec^d^ Affidavit the 22th Day

May 1681

Bur: Hannah Booker ye 15th Day

Rec^d^ Affidavit ye 22th Day

Bur: Elizabeth Beckitt ye 16th Day

Rec^d^ Affidavit the 17 day

Bur: George ffulston ye 24th day

Rec^d^ Affidavit ye thirtyth Day

1681

June 1681

Bur: Ann ffoarde 2^{d} Day
Rec^{d} Affidavit 8th Day

Bur: Thomas Tyas & John Eaton 8th Day
Rec^{d} their Affidavitts 15th Day

Bur Hellen Hill 30th Day
Rec^{d} her Affidavit the 3^{d} Day of July

July 1681

Bur: Thomas Cawthern the 7th Day
Rec^{d} Affidavit the 14th Day

Bur: Ann the wife of John Carr of Hoober ye 8th Day of August
Rec^{d} Affidavit the 14th Day

Bur: Margaritt wife of ffrancis Tottington ye 9th Day
Rec^{d} Affidavit the 16th Day

August 1681

Bur Nicholas son of Thomas Tilney ye 24th Day
Rec^{d} Affidavit the 29th Day

Bur: Eliz: Jessop the 13th day of September, 168
Recd an Affidavit the 17th Day

Octob 1681

Bur: Jane daughter of John Arundall y^{e} tenth Day
Recd Affidavit y^{e} 17th Day

Bur: Sarah daughter of John Hurst y^{e} 20th Day
Recd Affidavit y^{e} 23th Day

November

Bur: Elizabeth wife of Nicholas Kay first Day of November 1681
Rec^{d} Affidavit y^{e} 4th Day

January

Bur: Robt Scargill the first day of January 168$\frac{1}{2}$
Rec^{d} Affidavitt 5th Day

Bur: Ruth wife of Godfrey Mathewman y^{e} 7th day
Rec^{d}. Affidavitt 10th Day

Bur: Sarah wife of Tho: Trivye the 8th day
Rec^{d} Affidavit y^{e} 10th Day

Bur Skiers son of John Carr of Hoober y^{e} 14th day
Rec^{d} Affidavit y^{e} 19th Day

Bur Thomasin daughter of Thomas Trivye y^{e} 21th day
Rec^{d} Affidavit y^{e} 23^{d} Day

Bur: Thomas son of Richard Elam Feb: 3^{d} 1681

ffebruary 168$\frac{1}{2}$

Rec^{d} Affidavit the 10th Day

Bur: Henry Wright the 13th Day
Rec^{d} Affidavit the 15th Day

Bur: William Lewin & Thomas son of Robt Lupton the 15^{t} Day
Recd Affidavit the 19th Day

Bur: Elizabeth wife of Robt. Browne the 22th day
Rec^{d} Affidavit the 28th Day

Bur: Richard & William sons of Robt Brown the 26^{h} day
Rec^{d} both Affidavits the 28th day

168½

Bur: Adam Dawson ye 28th day

March 168½

Recd Affidavit ye 4th Day

Bur: Dorothy Daughter of Thomas Holmes ye 13th Day

Recd Affidavit ye 18th Day

Bur: Agnis wife of Thomas Morton ye 16th day

Rec^d Affidavit ye 22th Day

Bur: Esther wife of Ralph Gillott the 25th Day

Baptisems for ye yeare 1682

March 1682

Baptized Anne daughter of William Bentley ye 26th Day of March

Aperill 1682

Baptized William ye sonne of Tho ffosterd ye 11th day

Baptized Joseph ye sonne of Joseph Halmshaw & Martha ye 17th day

May 1682

Baptized Samuell ye sonne francis Carr ye 18th day

Baptized Mary ye daughter of Nickholas Tilney ye 23th day

Baptized Isack ye sonne of George Wade ye 25th day

June 1682

Baptized John the sonne of Rich: Hutchinson ye 23th day

July 1682

Baptized Mary daughter of Robert Bingley ye 2th day

Baptized Johnathan ye sonne of Mr. John Twitty vic. at Wath ye 14th day

Baptized Richard ye sonne of francis Tottington ye 23th day

September 1682

Baptized ffillip ye sonne of Phillip fflint ye 3th day

Baptized Richard ye sonne of Henry Wright ye 17th day

Baptized William ye sonne of Richard Watson ye 18th day

October 1682

Baptized William ye sonne of William Kemp ye 1th day

Baptized Anne ye daughter of John Arrundall ye 8th day

Baptized Matthew ye sonne of John Birkes the 12th day

Baptized Katerine ye daughter of Tho: Sharp ye 23th day

November 1682

Baptized Robert ye sonne of John Perkin ye 9th day

Baptized John ye sonne of Thomas Holand ye 12th day

January 1682

Baptized Ann ye daughter of Tho: Elam ye 28th day

ffebruary 1682

Baptized Elizabeth ye daughter of Jervis Bayly ye 1th day

Baptized Nickholas ye sonne of Tho: Hopkinson ye 5th day

Baptized Sarah ye daughter of Will: Wells ye 15th day

March 1682

Baptized Richard ye sonne of James Linsley ye 7th day

Baptized Elizabeth ye daughter of Robert Wharam ye 8th day

Baptized Godfrey ye sonne of Edward Wood ye 15th day

Marriages

July 1682

Maryed William Baxter & Mary Walker ye 5th day

1682

Maryed James Bettony and Ruth Pearson ye 25th day
August 1682
Maryed James Hanley and Anne Popelwell ye 3d day
October 1682
Marred ffrancis Hanley and Margery Crose ye 5th day
ffeb. the 6th 1682
Marryed then John Aneley & Ann Barraclough
Maryed Robt Carr & Jane Clarkson the 15th Day
Incipit annus 1682
March . Recd Affidavit y 27th Day
Aprill 1682
Bur Dinah ffrost the 14th Day
Recd Affidavitt the 20th Day
Bur: Sarah Daughter of George Carr the 16th day
Recd Affidavitt the 23d Day
Burd Elizabeth Wild the 28th
Recd Affidavit the 5th of May
Burd Thomas Epworth of Wath & John Crosse the 30th Day
Recd their Affidavitt the 5th of May
May 1682
Bur. William son of Nicholas Tilney of Wath the 25th
Recd Affidavitt the 30th Day
June 1682
Buryed Matthew son of John Birks of Swinton the 6th Day
Recd Affidavitt the 13th day
Buryed Susannah ffirth the 7th day
Recd Affidavitt the 10th Day
Bur: Beatrice Wilcock of Swinton the 11th Day
Recd Affidavitt the 13th Day
Bur: Nicholas Maykin the 22th Day
Recd Affidavitt the 24th Day
Bur: Margarett Coldwell the 18th July
Recd Affidavit the 22th Day
Bur Mary Bradbury a stranger that at dyed Mrs Barbers of Swinton the 23th
Recd Affidavit the 29th Day
Bur William Baxter the 29th Day
Recd Affidavit the 4th of August
Bur Thomas Popplewell the 8th Day
Recd Affidavitt the 12th Day
Bur: Mary daughter of George Leach the 24th Day
Recd Affidavitt the 29th Day
Bur: Mary wife of William Bell the 12th of Septembr
Recd Affidavit the 18th Day
Bur: Mary wife of Thomas Carr the 29th day
Recd Affidavit the 5th day of October
Bur: Dorothy wife of Wm Carr the 14th day
Received Affidavit ye 20th day
Bur Hesther daughter of John Bloome the 26th day
Recd Affidavitt the last day

1682

Bur Catherin daughter of Thomas Sharpe the 10th day of Novembr
Recd Affidavitt the 15th day

Bur: Thomas son of Tho Morton ye 24
Recd Affidavit ye 29th of Novembr

Bur William Bell of Wath the 21st day
Recd Affidavit the 23th day

Bur: Sarah Arandall and Mary Bell the 22th day
Recd Affidavits the 26th Day

Bur. Ann daughter of Thomas Lambert the first day of December
Recd Affidavitt the 3d day

Bur William son of Wm Kempe the 1st day of December
Recd Affidavitt the 6th day

Bur: Nicholas son of John Carr of Hoober ye 13th day January
Recd Affidavitt ye 25th Day

Bur: Rich Walker of Wath the 25th Day
Recd Affidavitt ye 27th Day

Bur: Ann ffint ye 29th day
Recd Affidavitt the 4th Day of ffebruary

Bur Gregory ye son of Rich Tolson Esqre ye 14th Day of ffebruary
Recd Affidavitt the 19th Day

Bur: Michaell Wadsworth the 17th Day
Recd Affidavitt the 23th Day

Bur Margarett Watson the 15th Day of March 1682
Recd Affidavit ye 18th Day of ye same month

Bur: Jane Arundall the 15th day of March
Recd Affidavit the 19th Day

Bur: Mary Oxley the 16th Day
Recd Affidavitt the 21th Day

June: 3d 1683
Married then Thomas Amcoate & Mary Craggs

Octob 23d 1683
Marryed then William Carniley & Ann Carr of this Parish wth License by the Rural Deane at Hooton Robberts

Nov. 5th 83.
Married ffrancis Robbinson & Elizabeth Tyas

Nov: 19th
Marryed John Sheppard & Martha Iziott

Nov: the 22d 1683
Marryed Thomas Wilkinson of the Parish of Mexburge & Elizabeth ffoulston of Wath par

Nov 26th 1683
Marryd then Thomas Gawtrey & Mary Baxter both of ye Parish of Wath

Jan 22d 83
Marr: Edw: Smith & Sarah Baley both of Parish of Wath

Bur: Susãñah Bawdison the 8th Day of April 1683
Recd Affidavit the 14th Day

Bur: Mary daughter of Richard ffoulston the 7th
Recd Affidavit the 14th Day

Bur: William Broomskin the 15th Day
Recd Affidavit the 20th Day

1683

Bur: John son of Widd Pearson of Melton the 17th Day
Rec^{d} Affidavit the 21th day

Bur: John Parkin of Swinton & Ann Lyall of Melton ye 9th Day of May
Rec^{d} Affidavits 13th Day

Bur: John son of Richard Mastin the 17th Day
Rec^{d} Affidavit ye 20th Day

Bur: Elizabeth daughter of Nicholas Carr the 25th. Day
Rec^{d} Affidavit the 30th Day

Bur: Elizabeth daughter of Thom: Holmes 1st of June
Rec^{d} Affidavit the 5th Day

Bur: the 1st day of June
Rec^{d} Affidavit the 6th Day

Bur: Samuell son of ffrancis Carr ye 6th Day
Rec^{d} Affidavitt the 11th Day

Bur: Richard son of John Eaton the 10th Day

Bur: Elizabeth daughter of John Eaton ye 15th Day
Rec^{d} both Affidavitts the 16th Day

July 1683

Bur. William son of John Kay de Wath ye 4th day
Rec^{d} Affidavitt the 9th day

Bur: ffrances Kempe the 26th Day

Bur: Elizabeth daughter of Gervase Bayley ye last Day
Rec^{d} Affidavit the 1st day of August

Bur Elizabeth Doughter of Gervase Bayley ye 3^{d} Day

August

Bur Jane Daughter of Widdow Baxter the 4th day
Rec^{d} Affidavit the 11th day

Bur . . . . son of John ffoardge the 5th Day
Rec^{d} affidavit the 11th Day

Bur: Catherin wife of Edward ffirth the 13th day
Rec^{d} Affidavit ye 17th Day

Bur: Helen daughter of Darcey Stones the 13th of Octob^{r}
Rec^{d} Affidavit the 18th Day

Bur: Dorothy Broadhead the 16th day
Rec^{d} Affidavit the 19th Day

Burr: Alice wife of Nicholas Goodyer the 22th day
Rec^{d} Affidavitt the 27th Day

Bur: Alice Jagger the 26th day
Rec^{d} Affidavitt ye 30th Day

Bur: Gervase Bayley the 3^{d} Day of Novemb:
Rec^{d} Affidavit concerning his Burial in Woollen the 9th day

Bur. Esther wife of John Gawtrey the 10th
Rec^{d} Affidavit ye 17th Day

1683

Bur: ffaith Taylour of Wath the 14th
Rec^{d} Affidavitt the 20th day

Bur: Ellen daughter of Wm Smith the 19th day
Rec^{d} Affidavit the 20th Day

1683
Bur. Ellen wife of Wm Smith 10th day of Decembr
Recd Affidavit the 14th Day
Bur Nicholas son of Widdow Pearson ye 12th Day
Recd affidavit the 17th Day
Buryed John son of Widdow Bayley ye 21st day ?
Recd Affidavit ye 27th Day
Bur: Beatrice Moody de Wath ye last Day of January
Recd Affidavit ye 5th of February
Feb 20th 83 Bur: Sarah wife of Edward Smith
Recd affidavit 24th day
March 12 Bur William son of John ffirth
Recd affidavit 16th day
March 17th Bur: Charles Hill of Swinton
Recd affidavitt the 23th day
Incipit Annus 1684
May 1684
Baptized William ye sonne of Thomas Wilkinson ye 15th day
June 1684
Baptized William ye sonne of Thomas Cussworth ye 12th Day
Baptized John ye sonne of Thomas Baxter ye 13th day
July 1684
Baptized Susana ye daughter of William Addy ye 10th day
Baptized Mary ye daughter of Richard ffoulstone ye 29th day
August 1684
Baptized Anne ye daughter of George Wade ye 16th day
Baptized Martha ye daughter of Thomas ffosterd ye 29th day
Baptized Mary ye daughter of Thomas Huit ye 31th day
Baptized William ye sonne of Thomas wilkinson Junr ye 31th day
September 1684
Baptized Anne ye daughter of John Sheppard ye 11th day
Baptised John ye sonne of John Twitty vic. de Wath ye 29th day
October 1684
Baptized Thomas ye sonne of John Arundall ye 12th day
Baptized Mary ye daughter of ffrancis Carr ye 12th Day
Baptized Johnathan ye sonne of Thomas Gawtresse ye 16th
Baptized Thomas ye sonne of francis Robinson ye 19th day
Baptized Jervis ye sonne of William Karnilley ye 24th day
November 1684
Baptized Elizabeth ye daughter of Tho: Roebuck ye 18th day
Baptized Jane ye daughter of Joseph Bingley ye 30th day
December 1684
Baptized Thomas ye sonne of Richard Hutchinson ye 24th day
Baptized Thomas ye sonne of John Hill ye 29th day
January 1684
Baptized William ye sonne of Nickolas Carr ye 1th day
Baptized Elizabeth ye daughter of Andrew Smith ye 10th day
Baptized Anne ye daughter of Tho: Hartley ye 11th day
Baptized Anne ye daughter of James Linsley ye 11th day

1684

ffebruary 1684

Baptised Richard son of Rich: Watson ye 5th day

Baptized Ann daughter of Thomas Hopkinson 5th day

Bapt John son of Hen: Wright and Ann daughter of Robt Wharam ? 12th

Baptised John the son of Joseph Robbinson ye 22 day

Bapt Rich: son of Robt Ellis ye 8th of March.

March. 1684

Bapt John ye son of Robt Bingley ye 22^d^

Bapt John ye son of Joseph Robbinson ye 22^d^ (*see above*)

1684

March 30th 84	Marr.	William Oates & Ann Hole b^th^ of Wath par
May ye 20th 84	Marr.	Robert Ellis & Mary ffosterd both of Wath par
September ye 3th 84	Marr.	Tho Robuck & Sarah Wright both of Wath par
November ye 6th 84	Marr.	Samuel Sikes of ye par of Anston & Anne Smith of this parrish
November ye 18th 84	Marr.	John Bell of ye par of ffellchurch and Margret ffosterd of this parr
January ye 29th 84	Marr.	Joshay Sharp of ye parr of Rotherham & Anne Stables of this parr
ffebr ye 5th 84	Marr.	Gervase Lyall & Mary Parkin both of this parish
12th	Marr^d^	ffrances Bozor & Esther Bingley both of this parish
19th	Marr^d^	Rich: Gawtrey & Ann Walker both of this parish
26th	Marr^d^	Wm Smith & Ann Bayley both of this parish

1684

Sept 29th	Bur:	Thomas Taylour of Wath
Oct 4th		Rec^d^ affidavit the . . . . Day
Oct 26 84	Bur.	Elizabeth daughter of Wm Wells Rec^d^ affidavit ye last day
Dec 6 84	Bur:	Alice Lyall of Melton Rec^d^ affidavit ye 11th Day
Dec: 14th	Bur:	W^m^ son of Michaell Ellis a Travell^r^ Rec^d^ Affidavitt the 19th day
Dec: 17th	Bur.	ffrances Robbinson Dec. 19th Rec^d^ affidavit
Jan: 3^d^	Bur	Esther Lassiter Jan: 5th Rec^d^ affidavit
Jan: 12th	Bur:	Henry Haslehurst Jan: 17th Rec^d^ affidavit
Jan: 15th	Bur:	Elizabeth Addye Jan 20th Rec^d^ affidavit
Jan: 18th	Bur	Eliz Smith Jan 24th Rec^d^ affidavit
Jan 21th	Bur:	Richard ffletcher Jan 23th Rec^d^ Affidavit
Feby 8th	Bur:	Richard Elam Feb 13th Rec^d^ Affidavit
9th	Bur:	Ann Butterworth Feb 14th Rec^d^ affidavit
9th	Bur:	John Watkinson Feb 15th Rec^d^ affidavit
13th	Bur:	daughter of Robt Wharam Feb 15th Rec^d^ affidavit
18th	Bur:	Alexander Thackerey ? Feb 22th Rec^d^ affidavit
20th	Bur	Jane wife of Jo: Kay } Feb 24th Rec^d^ affidavit
21th	Bur:	Robt Oxley of Wath }

1684

March 7th 84 Bur: Ann wife of John Twittey, vicar of Wath Recd affidavit ye 11th day

12 84 Bur: Wm Wilson Recd affidavit 15th day

Bur: Wm Kettlewell Recd affidavitt

18th Bur: Ann Browne Recd affidavit March 21th

20th Bur: James Stringer Recd affidavit March 23th

Aprill 1685.

Bapt Ann daughter of Sam: ffarburn 2d of April

Baptized Elizabeth daughter of Thom: Tilney 12th

Baptiz: Mary daughter of John Birkes 21st

Bapt: Esther daughter of Robt Carr 26th

July 85.

Baptisd Margarett daughter of Phillip fflint 9th

Thomas son of Thomas Holmes 12th

August 85.

Bapt Edmund son of Geo: Wade 12th

Thomas son of Wm Knight & Anthonie son of Archilaus Hoyland 16th day

Octob 85.

Bapt. Thomas son of Wm Smith 1st day

November 1685

Baptisd Elizabeth ye supposed daughter of John Sheppard ye 8th day

Bapt Mary daughter to Godfrey Matheman 19th

Bapt: Jane ye daughter of Nich: Tilney 26th day

December 85

Bapt Richard the son of Richard Gawtrey 6th

Bapt Ann daughter of Wm Smith 24th

Bapt Mary daughter of Daniel Twigge 27th

Jan: 85

Bapt Sarah daughter of Robert Lupton 20th

Bapt Elizabeth daughter of Thom: Lancashire 31th

March 85

Bapt Thomas son of Thomas Broadhead 14th

March ye 2d 1685

Memorand that Thomas Ellis was Licensed & Authorized by us whose names are underwritten to build One stall in the South Alley adjoineing to the Closett which doth belong to the Mannor House of the Earle of Strafford & there to stand and be to Him and his proper use under pain of Ecclesiastical censure.

Jo: Twittey Vicar de Wath

John Key
Thom: Ellis
John Trickit
Tho: × Bintliffe } Churchwardens

March 2d 1685

Memorand that John Key was Licensed & authorized by us whose names are underwritten to build one stall in the North Alley adjoyneing to

1685

the stall of Nicholas Carr and there to stand and be to Him and to his proper use und' pain of ecclesiastical censure

Joh: Twittey vic̃ de Wath
John Key
Tho Ellis
John Trickit
mck Tho × Bintliffe } Churchwardens

June 11th 85 Marryed Edward Smith & Eliz: Amorie
15th Marr: Godfrey Mathewman & Mary ffawill
23 Marr Thomas Broadhead & Marg^t Tottington
25 Marr: Joseph ffarrow & Marg^t Rhodes
Octob 20th Marr: Matthew Jackson & Sarah Tilney
Novemb 10th Marr: Seth Gascoign & Magdalene Hepworth
10th Marr: Thomas Barwicke & Ann ffoulston
19 Marr: John Smith & Eliz: Sorbie
March 27th Bur & Ralph Gillott ffoulston } Rec^d Affidavitts Aprill 4th
30th Edw: son of John ffirth Recd Affidavitt Aprill 5th
31th Bur ffranc Tottington Rec^d Affidavit April 6th
Aprill ye 23th Bur Bridget Hicke Rec^d Affidavit Aprill 29th day
26th Bur Dinah ffrost Rec^d Affidavit ye 3^d of May
27th Bur Marg^t Smith Rec^d Affidavit ye 3^d of May
May ye 31th Bur: . . . . . daughter of Geo. Wade Rec^d Affidavit ye 6th Day of June
July 26th Bur: Alice Bawdison Rec^d affidavit July 31th day
July ye 28th Bur Mary daughter of Jo: Birkes of parish Mexburg Rec^d Affidavitt 2^d of August
August 2^d Bur: Nicholas Goodyer Rec^d affidavit 6th day
17th Bur: Mary Stockdall Rec^d affidavit 23^d day
Edmund son of Geo: Wade Rec^d affidavit 25th day
Dec^ber 24 Bur Ann wife of Wm Smith Rec^d affidavit Jan 1st
Dec: 24 wife of Wm Kempe Rec^d affidavit Jan 1st
Feb^r 1st Bur John Hutchinson of Newhill Rec^d affidavit 7th day
March 11th Bur Nicholas Kay of Melton Rec^d affidavit 16th day
March 16 Bur Thomas son of Rich. Hutchinson Rec^d affidavit 22^d day
March 18 Bur: Thomas son of Tho: Brodhed Rec^d affidavit 22^d May
Aprill the 1st 1686

Memorand: that ffrancis Carr of Wath was Licensed & authorised by us whose names are underwritten (through Liberty first granted by Jasper Blythman Esqr Impropriet or of Tythes of ye parish) to erect one stall or Pew: in the Chancell of ye psh Church of Wath adjoyneng on ye seates of the right Honoble Wm Earle of Strafford north of Nicklas Tilney west & there to stand & be to Him & his prop^r use und^r pain of ecclesiastical censure

Jo: Twittey. Vic̃ Wath
Adam Earle
Tho Gautresse
John Elam
John Blome } Churchwardens.

1686

Incipit Annus 1686

March 1686.

Baptised Joshuah son of Joshuah Sheppard ye 26th day of March

Baptised Thomas son of Thomas Elam 28th day

Baptised John son of George Lyall 30th day

Aprill 1686

Baptised John son of Edward Smith 6th day

Baptised Joshuah son of John Bloome 9th day

Baptised Ann daughter of Thomas Amcoate 11th day

Baptised Esther daughter of Robt Wharam 13 day

May 1686

Baptised Samuell son of Edward ffirth 2^d^ day

June 1686

Baptised Elizabeth daughter of Sam: Burton second day

Baptised William son of George Carr 24th

Baptised Elizabeth daughter of Robt Pindar 29th

July 1686

Baptised Thomas son of Joseph Bingley first day

August 1686

Baptised Mary daughter of Matthew Jackson 12th day

Baptised Mary & Marg^t^ daughters of John Arundall 22^d^ day

September 1686

Baptised Mary daughter of Wm Richardson 12th

Baptised Elizabeth daughter of Robt Winter 12th

Baptised Robt son of John ffoardge 15th ?

September 19th Baptised George son of Seth Gascoign

October 10. Baptised Mary daughter of Thom: Tilney

24 Baptised John son of John Sheppard

24 Baptised Elizabeth daughter of Pete Mawde

28 Baptised William son of Thom Sharpe

November 4th Baptised Thomas son of Thomas Lockwood

16 Baptised Ann putative daughter of John Cawthorn

23 Baptised William son of John Birkes

28th Baptised Jonathan son of Thomas Hasle Hurst

December 11th Baptised Sarah daughter of John ffeather

19 Baptised Margaret daughter of Edward Wood

(1686-7)

January 2^d^ Baptized Thomas son of Robt Ellis

13 Baptised Martha daughter of Godfrey Mathewman

13 Baptised Thomas son of Humphrey Jackson

27 Baptised Elizabeth daughter of Thom: Lambert

February 1st Baptised Martha daughter of Thomas Wilkinson

3 Baptised John son of Thomas Cusseworth

6 Baptised Isabell daughter of Wm Smith

8 Baptised Thomas son of Thomas Wilkinson

13 Baptised Ellen daughter of Wm Carniley

March 14 Baptised Thomas son of Geo: Wade

15 Baptised John son of Sam: ffarborn

1686

Marriages.

Aprill 6th 1686. Marr. Wm Smith & Alice Hudson
May 11. Marryed Rich: Scales & Mary Ragg
25 Marryd Wm Kemp & Mary Yates
June 29 Marryd. Edward Martin of ye Parish of Ouston & Ann Jackson of this Parish of Wath
Septemb: 17. Marryd George Bell & Francis Scargall
October 3. Marryd Thomas Cutt & Grace Bateman both of this parish
28. Marryd Richard Kay & Mary ffox

1686

March 27 Bur: John son of Robt Bingley Recd affidavit 30th
Aprill 7th Bur: Hannah daughter of Nich: Morton Recd affidavit 13th day
20th Bur: Grace Guy Recd affidavit 26th
24th Bur: Richard son of Thomas Pennington Recd affidavit
29 Bur: Elizabeth wife of John Geffrey Recd affidavit May 11d
May the 19th 86 Buryed Mary wife of Rich: Foulston Recd affidavit May the 23d
20th 86 Bur: . . . son of Joseph Halmshaw Recd affidavit the 27th day
27 Buryed Marg wife of Edward Butterworth Recd affidavit last day
June 10th 1686 Bur: Gervase Longley Recd affidavit ye 17th
27th Bur: Eliz daughter of Thomas Tilney Recd affidavit July 3d
July 3d Bur: Wm Knight Recd affidavit 8th
Septemb: 2d Bur: Jane wife of John Bloome Recd affidavit 8th
12 Bur: Ellen Holland widd Recd affidavit 18th
Octob: 4 Bur: George son of Seth Gascoigne Recd affidavit 9th
30th Bur: Elizabeth Tompson Nov 3 Recd affidavitt
Feb: 15 Bur: Mary daughter of Tho Gessop
Feb: 15 Bur: Thomas son of Tho: Wilkinson 18 Recd affidavit
March 16 Bur: Michaell Bozor 19 Recd affidavitt
18 Bur: Thomas son of Geo: Wade 25 Recd Affidavit

Decemb 27th 1686

Memd that Mr Marshall of Street is lawfully possessed of a Seat in ye Body of our Church (having purchased the same of Richard Tilney, formerly of this parish, & placed with consent & approbacon of Dr. Watkinson Chancellor) adjoining to the Pew or Stall of Rich Tolson Esq east there to stand & be unto him and to his House under paine of Ecclesiasticall censure.

Jo: Twittey Vic de Wath
Andrew Smith
Thoos Cusworth
Humphrey Jackson his mark
John Tinsley + mark
} Churchwardens

1687

Memorandum that Richard Gorrill of Brampton Birely is lawfully possessed of a Seate scituate upon the South Alley & adjoyneing to the Seate or Pew of Richard Tolson Esq there to stand & to be unto him, & to his house under paine of Ecclesiasticall Censure.

Jo : Twittey Vic. of Wath

William Jackson
Robert Binlay
Richard Carr
Rich : Gorrill
} Churchwardens

Christenings for 1687

Aprill	9	Baptized	Catherin daughter of Hugh Ellison
May	19	Bapt	Elizabeth daughter of John Dyson & Eliz daugh of Jos : Haumshaw
	23	Bapt	John son of Edward Browne
	23		Eliz : daughter of George Bell
June	25	Bapt	John son of Wm Wells
July	20	Bapt	Jane daughter of James Linsley
August	4	Bapt	Sarah daughter of Tho : Robucke
	14	Bapt	Elizabeth daughter of Rich Kay
	21	Bapt^d^	William son of Thomas Rufforth
Septemb^r^	8	Bapt	Elizabeth daughter of Thom : Broadhead
	13	Bapt	Barbarah daught of Nich Tilney
	18	Bapt	Sarah daughter John Elam
Octob^r^	1	Bapt	Edward son of Thomas ffostard
	13	Bapt	Sarah daughter of Archilaus Hoyland
	20	Bapt	Nicholas son of Nicolas Car
	22	Bapt	Eliz daughter of Wm Smith
	22	Bapt	Jane daughter of Seth Gascogine
Decemb^r^	8	Bapt	ffrancis son of Robt Bingley
	27	Bapt	Jonathan son of John Frost
Jany^y^	9	Bapt	Mary daughter of Nich : Morton
	28	Bapt	Hanna daughter of Robt Carr
ffeb^y^	2	Bapt	Ann daughter of Rich : Gawtresse
	9	Bapt	Thomasin daughter of Thom : Gawtresse
	19	Bapt	John son of Thom : Eller
	23	Bapt	William son of Phillip Flint
	27		Mary daughter of John Lile

Marriages for Year abovesaid *1687*

April	18	Marr.	Thomas Pearson & Hannah Walker
July	28	Marr.	Michaell Harvey & Ellen Baraclough
Novemb	5	Marr.	John Frost & Elizabeth Hilton
	6	Marr	John Sheppard & Jane Mote
	18	Marr	John Holland & Ann Dodson
	24	Marr	Ambrose Hoyland & Marg^t^ Marshall
Decemb	1	Marr	Richard Foulston & Ann Linley
		Marr	ffrancis Fowler & Elizabeth Carr

1687.

March 25 Bur : Eliz : wife of Wm Bentley. Rec^d^ Affidavitt 30th

1687

April 6 Bur: Ann daughter of Robt Lewin. Recd affidavit 11th day
Sept 1 Bur: Nich son of Wm Kemp. Recd affidavit 7th
Sept 19 Bur: Barbara daughter of Nich Tilney. Recd affidavitt 23
20 Bur: Martha Arandal. Recd affidavit 25
Bur John Geffray
Nov. 2 Bur: Alice Earle of Wath Novemb 26 Recd affidavit
Jany ye 6 Bur Robt Winters Jan 12 Recd affidavit
27 Bur John Tinsley Jan 30 Recd affidavit
Feb. 1 Bur Sarah Hanley Feb 5 Recd affidavit
Feb 2 Bur: Hannah Carr Feb 8 Recd affidavit
Feb 8 Bur: Richard Cosse Feb 12 Recd affidavit
Feb 10 Bur: Richd son of wid Mallison Feb. 15 Recd affidavit

Ann dom. 1688 Baptisms for ye Yeare 1688

May 6 Baptized John son of Rich: Watson
20 Baptizd Susannah daughter of Godfrey Mathewman
June 19 Bapt Beatrice daughter of Joseph Bingley
July 19 Bapt John son of Robt Wharam
August 3 Bapt Ann daughter of Mich Harrop
9 Bapt Elizabeth daughter of Daniel Twigge
12 Bapt Mary daughter of Robt Tyas
14 Bapt John son of Matthew Jackson
28 Bapt George son of Mrs. Baxter
Septemb: 23 Bapt John son of Will: Kempe
23 Bapt Ann daughter of Tho: Wilkinson
4 Bapt John son of Robt Lupton̄
Bapt John son of Thomas Sharpe
Bapt Edmund son of Will: Roebucke.
Novemb̄ 6 Bapt Richard son of Rich: Foulston
11 Bapt Richard son of Thomas Amcoate
18 Bapt Elizabeth daughter of John Hill
20 Bapt John son of John Arundall
Febry 3 Bapt Richard son of John Birkes
26 Bapt Alice daughter of Robt Ellis
28 Bapt John son of John Kay
March 17 Bapt Margt daughter of Richard Kay
19 Bapt Nicholas son of Nich Tilney
20 Bapt John son of Tho: Lambert
21 Bapt Jonathan son of Will: Bentley

Marriages in ye yeare 1688

Aprill Marryed Robt Bingley & Elizabeth Watkinson 17th day
May Marryed Wiiliam Roebuck & Mary Bingley 1st day
Marryed John Kay & Elizabeth Wright 6th day
Marryd Jasper Kitchaman & Eliz: Inman 17th day
Marryd John Trickitt & Jane Higgins 29th day
June Marryed Wiłł Wood & Sarah Pilley 4th day
Marryed Rich. Jackson and Esther Tilney 12th day
July Marryed Wiłł Jackson and Elizabeth Earle 19th day
Octobr Marryed Wiłł Shaw & Elizabeth Briggs 18th day

1688

November Marryed George Hague & Mary Shaw 4th day
Marry^d^ Martin Tompson & Elizabeth Lewin 6th day
Marry^d^ Thomas Guest & Mary Parr 29th day
February Marryed Samuell Broadbent and Elizabeth Hopton 7th day

1688

March 26 Bur Mary Hartley. Rec^d^ affidavit last day
29 Bur: Eliz: wife of Jon Hurst. Rec^d^ affidavit 1st day of April
April 16 Bur: Widdow Brāwith de Swinton. Rec^d^ affi. 22^d^
May 16 Bur Martha wife of Tho Wilkinson. Rec^d^ both Affida 24 and John Addy of Swinton same day
June 4 Bur: Richard son of Rich ffoulston. rec^d^ aff 8
15 Bur: M^s^ Brooke. Rec^d^ affidavit 18
August 26 Bur: Ellen White. Rec^d^ affidavit 31
Octob. 7 Bur. Ralph ffoardge Rec^d^ affid. 12
Novemb. 13 Bur: wife of John Lyall Rec^d^ affid 16
Bur son of John ffoardg. rec^d^ affid. 17
Decemb: 13 Bur: Mary Rawlin Rec^d^ affidavit 16
24 Bur: William Wade de Swinton. rec^d^ aff 29
January 7 $168\frac{8}{9}$ Bur Isabell daughter of Geo: Chappel Rec^d^ aff: 14
15 Bur: William Addy de Wath. Rec^d^ affid. 17
27 Bur: Elizabeth daughter of Wm Cusworth de Wath Rec^d^ affid Feb 2^d^
31 Bur: Hannah Carr of y^e^ p^sh^ of Wath. Feb. 6 rec^d^ aff.

Christenings y^e^ Yeare 1689

Aprill 4 Bapt Jane daughter of Thom Haslehist
7 Easter daughter of Jasper Kitchaman
12 Joseph son of Thom: Cussworth
19 John son of Rich: Jackson
21 Sarah Daughter of Will Carniley
May 6 Bapt: Rebecka daughter of Robt Carr
8 William son of Wm Jackson
19 Edward & William sons of Edward Smith
19 Joseph & Sarah son & daughter to Edward Wood
20 Marg^t^ daughter of John Shepperd
23 Elizabeth daughter of Wm Wells
June 16 Bapt. Eliz: daughter of Thomas Holmes
July 7 Bapt. Jonathan son of John Thropp
21 John son of Martin Tompson
23 Anne daughter of Thom: Baxter of
August 3 Bapt. John son of Thomas Baxter of Bramton
Septemƀ 8 Bapt. William son of Wm Smith
9 Susana daughter of Godfrey Matheman
18 Rich: son of Wm Richardson
24 Bapt. Eliz: daughter of Geo: Wade.
31 Bapt. Francis son of Archilaas Hoyland
8. Mary daughter of John Elam of Melton
Novemb 1 Joseph son of Robt Pindar

1689

November 22 Bapt. Ann daughter of Geo: Bell
29 Bapt John son of Wm Addy de Swinton
January 13 Bapt. Marg^t^ daughter of John Trivie de Brampton
15 William son of John Kampsall
Feb^ry^ 16 Thomas son of Rich. Foulston
March 2 Thomas son of John Holland
9 Esther daughter of Rich. Booth
13 Sarah daughter of John Hirst

Note that the Marriages the yeare 1688 and ye yeare 1689 are Inscribed next Page

Memorand

That ye clock was set up in Wath church between Monday ye first and Saturday ye sixth of November in ye year 1714
Novr 4th John Twittey Vic

Marriages in ye year 1689.

Aprill	Marryed	Thomas Hartley & Mary Casson 1th day
	Marryed	Edward Roberts & Grace Earle 29th day
May	Marryed	John Thropp & Elizabeth Winter 8th day
June	Marry^d^	George Hopton & Sarah Foulston 27th day
September	Marry^d^	John Elam & Anne Burley the 1st day
November	Marry^d^	George Ropehar & Isabell Taylor 5th day
December	Marryed	Thomas Fowenther & Sarah Copley 8th day
	Marry^d^	Luke Ogle & Mary Dutton 6th day
	Marr^d^	Wm Watkinson & Ana ffarborne 25th day

Burials 1689

Aprill 5 Mary wife of John ffoardge April 11 rec^d^ affid.

1689. Most probably being same page as August 16, 1689.

May ye 9th	Bur:	Jane wife of Robt Carr de Wath May 11th Rec^d^ affidavitt
May 23	Bur:	Joanna Elam de Melton. Wid May 28 rec^d^ affid
June 11	Bur:	William son of Edw: Smith 14th rec^d^ affid
July first	Bur:	John son of Edward Smith Rec^d^ affidavd ye 7th day
July 24	Bur	Nicholas son of Nich: Carr 31th rec^d^ affid.
August 8	Bur:	Hannah supposed daughter of John Cawthern Aug 11 Rec^d^ affidavitt
Eodem die	Burr	Jon̄ sō of Martin Tompson 14 rec^d^ affidavit
Aug 15.	Bur:	John son of Robt Lupton Aug 19 Rec^d^ affidavitt
August 16. 89	Bur:	John son of Thom: Sharp 26 rec^d^ affid
Aug^st^ 17	Bur:	Ann daughter of John Carr de Hoober 24 Rec^d^ affidavit
Aug^st^ 29	Bur:	Thomas Sheath apprentic in Wath. Sep^br^ 5 Rec^d^ affidavit
Sept: 19	Bur.	Dorothy Cawtherne. 26 affidavit made
Octob: 20	Bur:	Marg^t^ Daughter of Jon Trickit 25 Rec^d^ affidavit
Octob: 31	Bur:	Eliz Wade of Swinton Novemb 6 rec^d^ affidavit
Novemb. 17	Bur:	Thomas son of Thomas Ellis 19 rec^d^ affidavit
Decemb^r^ 19	Bur:	Edward ffirth de West Melton 24 Rec^d^ affidavitt
Jan	Bur:	wife of Tho: Baraclough. Rec^d^ affidavit

1689

ffeb^r 17. 89 Bur : George son of Mr Baxter of 23 Rec^d affidavitt
ffeb. 21 Bur : George Wade de Swinton. 27 rec^d affidavit
March 4 Bur : Richard son of Wm Richardson. March 10 Rec^d affidavit

Baptisms in ye Year 1690.

Aprill. Baptis^d John ye son of Thomas Lockwood 6th day
Bapt Sarah daughter of Thomas Hartley 22th day
May Bapt William son of Matthew Jackson 28th day
June Bapt Mary daughter of Thomas Gawtreys 26th day
July Bapt Elizabeth daughter of Hugh Ellison 3^d day
Bapt Mary daughter of Thomas Wood 13th day
Bapt Ann daughter of Rich : Jackson 24th day
Bapt Jonathan son of Thomas Sharpe 29th day
Septemb̄ Bapt Francis̄ son of Nicholas Carr 7th day
Bapt William son of Martin Tomson 9th day
Bapt Ann a Bastard child of Eliz : Gooddall 9th day
Bapt Susannah daughter of Joseph Tomson 28th day
Novemb. Baptis^d Martha daughter of Nich : Morton 2^d day
Bapt Mary daughter of Edward Brown 6th day
Bapt Mary daughter of Joseph ffoulston 13th
Bapt Esther daughter of Nich Tilney 23^d day
Decemb^r Bapt Thomas son of John Hudson 27th day
Bapt Mary daughter of Will̄ Watkinson 28th
January Bapt Jasper & John sons of Jasper Kitchaman 1st
Bapt Thomas Heaton Wharam son of Rob_t Wharam 1st day

1690

Aprill 16 Bur : George Haslehurst de Wath. Rec^d affidavit
April 25. 90. Bur John son of John Eaton. Rec^d Affidavit 2^d day of May
April 27 Bur : Edward son of Edw : Smith. Rec^d affidavit May 3^d
May 8 Bur Ann wife of John Aneley Rec^d affidavit
25 Bur : William son of George Carr. Rec^d affidavit June 1st
June 1 Buryed Elizabeth daughter of Wm Smith. Rec^d affidavit
16 Buryed Elizabeth daughter of James Linsley Rec^d affidavit 23
22 Bur : Jane daughter of James Linsley Rec^d affidavit 24th
26 Bur : Eliz : wife of Edward ffirth Rec^d affidavit 2^d of Aug^st
July 2^d Bur : Richard Tolson Esqr. Affidavit made for his Burial in Wollen eo die.

Baptisms in ye Year 1691

Aprill Baptis^d Mary daughter of Rich Watson ye 5th Day
Baptis^d Ann daughter of Wm Kempe 12th day
Baptis^d Sarah daughter of Michael Harop 17th day
Baptis^d John son of Peter Mawde 19th day
Baptis^d Mary daughter of Thomas Amcoate 29th day
May Baptis^d Elizabeth daughter of Jo : Arandal of Hoober 3 day
Baptis^d Grace daughter of Robt Lupton 24th day

1691

June	Baptis^{d}	Ann daughter of John Frost ye 7th day
	Baptis^{d}	Sarah daughter of Thomas Fosterd 14th day
July	Baptis^{d}	John son of John Hurst } 26th
	&	Matthew son of Wm Jackson }
August	Baptis^{d}	John son of Godfrey Mathewman 13th day
	Baptis^{d}	John son of Edward Smith ye 16th day
	Baptis^{d}	Sarah daughter of Phillip Flint 25th day
Septemb^{r}	Baptis^{d}	Ann daughter of John Thropp ye 13
	Baptis	W^{m} son of Archie Hoyland 22^{d}
October	Baptis^{d}	Sarah daughter of Wm Bentley 4th
	Baptis^{d}	John son of John Wilcocke ye 28th
December	Baptiz	Sarah daughter of Nehemia Wade 9th day
Januarie	Baptiz^{d}	Mary daughter of Richard Jackson 4th day
	Baptiz^{d}	Thomas ye son of Thom: Haslehurst 30th day
	Baptiz^{d}	Susanna daughter of Thomas Broadhead 30th
Februarie	Baptis^{d}	Adam son of Adam Earle ye 2^{d} day
	Baptis^{d}	Ann daughter of Richard ffoulston 18th day
	Baptis^{d}	Will son of Wm Carniley ye 21th day
	Bãptis^{d}	Sarah daughter of John Kay jun^{r} 24 day

Marriages in ye year 1691.

April	Maryed	Matthew Hague & Mary Hutchinson 14th day
May	Maryed	Adam Earle & Dorothy Sheppard ye 21th
July	Mary^{d}	William Hoyland & Mary Baxter 7th day
September	Mary^{d}	Robt Foardge & Mary Eller 29th day
October	Mary^{d}	Charles Longley & Sarah Bullows 22th
	Marr:	William Rodes & Olive Viccars 29th

May ye 11th 1691

Memorandũ that Robt Bingley of Wath was Licensed & Authorized by us whose names are underwritten to erect one Pew or Seate on the South side of the ffont in ye body of the Church & there to stand and be to Him and his proper use uuder paine of Ecclesiastical censure.

John Twittey. Vic. de Wath
ffrancis Carr } Churchwardens
John Gawtrey }

Burialls 1692

Aprill 25	Buried	William Yates de Wath
May 8	Buried	Grace Daughter of Richard Addy
May 14	Buried	Samuell son of Mr Robbinson de Wath
May 16	Buryed	Robt Lewen de Melton
June 26	Buryed	William ffosterd de Wath
Juy 16	Buryed	Robt Ellis de Wath
August 4	Buryed	John Kay de Wath
October 30	Buryed.	Ann daughter of Mich Harrop, Swinton
Decemb̃ 14	Bur.	Humphrey a Servt Boy to Robert Cutt
ffeb^{ry} 14	Bur.	Elizabeth wife of Jasper Kitchaman
ffeb^{ry} 23	Bur.	Ellen wife of Richard Carr
29	Bur.	Ellen wife of John Allott Wath

1692
Burialls 1693 are written at 8 page forward.
Baptisms in ye Year 1692.
1692

March	Baptlse^d^	Daniell sone of Daniell Twigge 29th day
Aprill	Baptis^d^	Ruth ye daughter of Robt Ellis 8th day
May	Baptis^d^	John ye son of Thomas Carr first day
	Bapt	Ann daughter of Wm Hoyland ye 30th day
	Baptis^d^	John son of Nicholas Tilney 31th day
June	Baptis^d^	John ye son of John Elam 5th day
	Baptis^d^	Mary daughter of Rich Gawtrey 19th
	Baptis^d^	Mary daughter of Andrew Smith 24
July	Baptis^d^	George son of Seth Gascoigne 3^d^ day
	Baptis^d^	Thomas and Hannah son & daughter of John Carr of Wath 10th day.
August	Baptis^d^	Thomas son of Joseph ffoulston 4th
Septemb^r^	Baptis^d^	Ann daughter of Robt Pinder 4th
October	Baptis^d^	Mary daughter of Edw Tinsley 7th
	Baptis^d^	Richard son of Richard Booth 10th
	Baptis^d^	Samuell son of Mr Burroughs 22th
	Baptis^d^	Richard son of Richard Pearson 23^d^
	Baptis^d^	Mary daughter of Richard Watson 24th
November	Baptis^d^	Martha daughter of Pet^r^ Law 6th
January	Baptis^d^	Ann daughter of Matthew Jackson 24th
February	Baptis^d^	Jonathan son of Martin Tomson 5th
	Baptis^d^	Margaret daughter of Thomas Cusworth 9th
	Baptis^d^	George son Nathaniel Ibitson 10th day
March	Baptis^d^	John son of John Hudson 19th day
	Baptis^d^	Thomas son of John Sheppard 24th day

Marriages in ye yeare 1692

August	Marryed	Nicholas Crosley & Eliz: Cutt ye 4th
	Marryed	John Glavill & Esther Moxon 29th
ffebruary	Marry^d^	Henry Hardcastle & Ellen Kay 23^d^
	Marryed	Thomas Kay & Sarah Taylor ye 28th

Baptisms in ye year 1693

March	Baptised	Richard son of John Arandall ye 26th
Aprill	Baptiz^d^	Ann daughter of John Holland 2^d^ day
	Baptis^d^	William son of John Birkes 7th day
	Baptis^d^	Ann daughter of John Campsall 12th
	Baptis^d^	Wiłł son of Joseph? Bingley 28th day
May	Baptis^d^	Thomas son of John Elam of Melton 7th
	Baptis^d^	Thomas son of Mr Twittey 7th 1727 He died at Mansfield & was buried there.
	Baptis^d^	William son of Wiłł Kempe 10th day
June	Baptis^d^	Ann daughter of Nehemia Wade 17th
	Baptis^d^	Thomas son of Daniell Broadhead 18th
July	Baptis^d^	Francis son of Edward Butterworth 7th
	Baptis^d^	Ann daughter of Robert Cutt 4th
August	Baptis^d^	Alice daughter of Thomas Lockwood 6th

1693

August Bapt: Martha daughter of Will Watkinson 13th
Bapt: William son of Ralph Stringer ye 27th
Septemb: Bapt Mary daughter of John Elam de Newhill 15th
Bapt Alice daughter of Godfrey Mathewman 21th
Octobr Bapt Elizabeth daughter of Richard Jackson 29th
Novembr Bapt Mary daughter of Thomas Carr ye 5th day
Bapt: Richard son of Robt Wharam ye 5th
Bapt Jane daughter of Michael Harrop 7th day
Decemb. Bapt William son of John Carr of Wath 24th
Bapt John son of Arcilaus Hoiland 9th

Marriages in ye year 1693

June 4 Marryed Thomas Gessop & Ann Sorby
July 30 Marryd Robt Sanderson & Ann Elam
Septembr 26 Marryd Jonathan Bullows and Ann Yates
October 22 Marryd Joshua Brook & Emmott Morton

Burialls 1693.

May 31 Buried Margaritt Taylour wid de Wath
August 29 Burd Edith Gawtresse de Wath vidua
Septemb. 2 Bur Elizabeth wife of Wm Carr de Wath
18. Bur. Grace Bingley de Swinton. vid.
Novembr 5 Bur. Alice wife of Robert Wharam
Decembr 8 Bur. Mary wife of Rich: Robbinson Wath
10 Bur Jane Wilkinson 10th day
11 Bur. Joseph son of Robt Pindar
12 Bur. Ann daughter of Mrs. Tolson
eod die Bur Robt Worrill de Melton
29 Bur John son of Jasper Citchaman
January 20 Bur John son of John Hudson Wath
ffebruary 5 Bur Thomas Gooddall de Melton
11 Bur William Wordsworth de Newhill
11 Bur Mathew ffoulston Bramton Bierley
15 Bur Martha daughter of Wm Watkinson
20 Bur Edward Brown de Wath
March 1 Bur. Mary Haslehurst de Wath.
1 Bur James Pennington de Brampt Birely
10 Bur Mary wife of Richard Beaumond
10 Bur Mary daughtr of Edw: Brown Wath
15 Bur: Richard Robbinson de Wath

Marriages in ye Year 1694

Aprill 10th Married Robert Watson & Mary Halmshaw
May 1st Married Jonas Pashley & Mary Beaumond
June 26 Married Robert Pearson & Alice Brigg
29 Married William Adamson & Sarah Bullowes
July 20 Married Jeremiah Langard & ffrances Cutt
September 27 Married Edmund Gervise & Widow Worrill
ffebruy 14 Married Thomas Howett & Ellen Whitakers de Adwick
License yr to

1694

Baptisms n year 1694

April	4	Baptised	John son of John Wood
	10	Bapt	Sarah daughter of Henry Kay
	10	Bapt	John son of Georg Bell
	16	Bapt	Daniell son of Wm Carniley
	21	Bapt	Jane daughter of John Arandal
	21	Bapt	John son of Wm Bentley
	29	Bapt	William son of Wm Stacey
• May	13	Bapt	Georg son of Richard ffoulston
July	8	Bapt	John son of Edward Tinsley
	10	Bapt	Mary daughter of Wm Hoyland
September	9	Bapt	Margaret daughter of ffrancis Trickett
	29	Bapt	Thomas son of Andrew Smith
November	25	Bapt	Mary daughter of Adam Hawksworth
December	9	Bapt	Thomas son of Richard Booth
	11	Baptis^d^	Martha daughter of Joseph Bingley
	14	Bapt	Georg son of Joseph ffoulston
	23	Bapt	Josias son of John Hudson
	27	Bapt	Elizabeth Daughter of Seth Gascoigne
January	1	Bapt	Elizabeth daughter of Wm Watkinson

Burialls 1694

April	10	Bur:	William ye son of Archilaus Hoyland Melton
	16	Bur:	Easther wife John Wood de Wath
	18	Bur:	Esther Rushworth de Wath
May	7	Bur:	Rich: Tilney son of Thomas Tilney de Wath
June	11	Bur:	Catherin Rushworth de Wath
	16	Bur:	Mary Tilney wife of Nicholas Tilney Wath
	25	Bur:	Richard Rymer de Wath
July	13	Bur:	William Smith junior de Wath
	20	Bur:	Alice Cusworth de Wath wife of Tho Cusworth
August	5	Bur:	Jane daughter of Nicholas Tilney Wath
	31	Bur:	Hannah wife of Thom: Tilney Wath
September	9	Bur:	Margaret daughter of John Eaton de Wath
	17	Bur:	Will: Smith sen^r^ de Wath
	17	Bur:	Marg^t^ Broadhead de Wath wife of Tho Broadhead
October	13	Bur:	Esthe1 wife of Nicholas Carr de Wath
	22	Bur:	Mary wife of Godfrey Shells de Swinton
	29	Bur:	Ann daughter of Will Smith de Wath
November	4	Bur:	Rich Ellison de Bramton Bierly
	6	Bur:	Andrew Smith de Wath
December	11	Bur:	Martha wife of Joseph Bingley
	26	Bur:	Thomas Trivie de Wath
	27	Bur:	Ann Yates vid de Wath
January	3	Bur:	Thomas Amcoate de Swinton
	14	Bur:	Daniell Broadhead de Wath
	14	Bur:	Mary daughter of Wm Hoiland de Wath
	23	Bur:	ffrances Smith a young woman
	27	Bur:	Thomas Wood
	29	Bur:	Mary ffoarge de Wath

1694

ffebruarie 3 Bur: Patience Wood de Swinton
6 Bur: Mary Addy de Swinton
15 Bur: Hanna daughter of John Lossiter Wath
March 3 Bur: ffrances Wills widd de Newhill
3 Bur: Joshuah son of John Birkes
5 Bur: Henrie Worril son of . . . . Worril Wath
14 Bur: Ellen Hill de Swinton widd

Baptisms in year 1695

May 5 Baptiz[d] Thomas son of Sylvanus Sykes
June 18 Baptiz[d] Mary daughter of Nathaniel Ibitson
23 Baptiz[d] John son of John Earnshaw
July 30 Baptiz[d] William son of M[r] Twittey
Septemb[r] 1 Baptized Margery daughter of David Stear
Septemb[r] 3 Baptized John son of John Bintliffe
5 Baptized Mary daughter of Charles Chevins
Octob[r] 24 Baptiz[d] Ann daughter of Edmund Gervise
31 Baptiz[d] Sharlot daught[r] of Philip Flint & Sarah daughter W[m] Horsfeild
Novemb[r] 10 Baptis[d] Stezick son of John Carr
30 Baptis[d] Richard & Ann son & daughter of Thomas Sharpe
Decemb[r] 15 Baptis[d] Jo: son of Thomas Gessop
January 2 Baptis[d] John son of Henry Kay
12 Baptiz[d] William son of Francis Trickit
19 Baptiz[d] Sarah daughter of Rob[t] Cutt
ffebruarie 2 Baptiz[d] Grace daughter of John Sheppard
26 Baptiz[d] Elizabeth daughter of Joseph Ant
March 5 Baptiz[d] Ann daughter of Archilaus Hoyland
8 Baptiz[d] Thomas son of Edward Tinsley
24 Baptis[d] Jane daughter of John Elam

Marriages 1695

June 18 Marryed Richard Beaumont & Susanna Smith Wath
July 4 Married Richard Slack of parish of Silkston & Jane Baxter of Par: of Wath
11 Married John Pole & Catherin Jackson of Par: of Wath
September 28 Married Anthony Readihough & Grace Rushworth of Wath
November 14 Married Robert ffoadge & Elisabeth Oldham Wath
21 Married Thomas Kay? & Elisabeth Carr Wath
21 Married Richard Chevins of Darfeild par: & Mary *(cut off)*
Februarye 2 169$\frac{5}{6}$ Married Robert Bingley & . . . . Torr

March the 26th 1695

Memorandum that John Holland of Newhill was Licensed and Authorized by us whose Names are Underwritten to erect one Pew or Seate in the West end of the Body of the Church joyneing to the Pew or Seate of Thomas Elam South and there to stand & be to him & his proper use under paine of Ecclesiasticall Censure

John Twittey Vicar of Wath
ffrancis Cleyton
mk of
John × Turner
John Elam Churchwardens

1695

Burialls 1695

March	30	Buryed William Cuseworth de Wath
April	11	Buryed Samuel Burton of Swinton
May	14	Buryed Adam Earle de Wath
June	10	Buryed Thomas Cusseworth of Wath
	11	Buryed Sarah wife of Thomas Kay of Wath
September	2	Bury^{d} George ffirth
	9	Buryed Elizabeth Wordsworth vidua of Wath
October	2	Buryed Elizabeth wife of Robt Bingley Wath
Novemb^{r}	29	Buryed Elizabeth Pate widdow de Melton
December	18	Buryed John Smith of Wath a young Man
	20	Buryed Mary Watkin
January	31	Buryed Ann daughter of ffrancis Watkin.
March	21	Buryed Ann daughter of Archilaus Hoyland
March	28	Buryed Mary Rymore a widdow of Wath

Christnings 1696

Aprill	14	Baptized Jane Daughter of William Hoiland de Wath
June	4th	Baptized Elisabeth Daughter of Richard ffoulston de Bramton
July	19	Baptised Thomas son of Thomas Wilkinson de Swinton
August	9	Baptized Richard son of Valentine Rodes de Swinton
	30	Baptised Thomas son of Martin Tompson
		Baptised Oswald son of Edward Butterworth
September	13	Baptised ffrancis son of George Addy
	27	Baptised Ann daughter of John Wilcocke
October	4	Baptised Robert son of Robert Byard
Novemb^{r}	13	Baptised Judith Daughter of Robert ffoarge
	14	Baptised John son of John Elam de Newhill
	22	Baptised Mary daughter of William Stacey
December	11	Baptised Samuell son of William Carniley
	24	Baptized Thomas son of Thomas Haslehurst
Januarie	5	Baptized Ann daughter of Thomas Carr
	16	Baptized William son of Robert Loveday
	18	Baptized John son of Robert Bingley
	18	Baptized William son of Richard Booth
February	2	Baptized Richard son of William Revell
	2	Baptized Thomas son of Thomas Kay
March	2	Baptized Martha daughter of Seth Gascoigne
	3	Baptized Martha daughter of Joseph ffoulston
	3	Baptized Ann daughter of John ffirth jun^{r}

Weddings 1696

May	1	Marryed John Ellison & Sarah Watson
June	3	Married Joseph Bingley & Jane Hutchinson
July	6	Married Charles Lightowler & Mary Amcoate
	16	Married William Revill & Dorothy Earle
	30	Marry^{d} Thomas Beaumont & Grace Cutt
Octob^{r}	8	Marry^{d} Adam Hawksworth & Ann Brown
	18	Marry^{d} Mr Richard Sherwood of City of York & Mrs Ann Burton of Doncaster

1696

November 26 Marry^d Thomas Hall & Ann Smith

Burialls 1696

March 31 Buryed Olive Ellison of Brampton Birely vidu
31 Buryed Elizabeth Roper Bierly
Aprill 11 Buryed ffrances wife of Adam Hawskworth Bierly
14 Buryed Alice Lockwood Bierly
May 2^d Buryed Susanna Beaumont wife of Richard Beaumont Wath
June 8 Buried John Sheppard of Melton Bierly
12 Buryed William Jackson of Wath
July 15 Buryed Elizabeth wife of Robert Tyas de Newhill Bierley
August 9 Buryed Ann Sheppard of Melton vid. Bierley
23 Buryed Dorothie Holmes of Melton Bierly
September 22^d Buryed Jonathan Walker of Wath
December 12 Buryed Tho Addye
12 Buryed Mary Halliwell of Bramton
January 1 Buryed Thomas Bawdison de Swinton
21 Buryed William Lovedall de Swinton
24 Buryed Thomas son of Stacey
30 Buryed Ann daughter of John ffirth.

Inchoat annus 1697

March 27 Baptized Joseph Twigge Bierley
28 Baptized Thomas son of John Hudson, Birly
29 Baptized John son of Wm Richardson, Wath
30 Baptized ffrances son of George Bell, Wath
Aprill 5 Baptized John son of John Arandall, Swinton
11 Baptized William son of John Arandal of hoober Bierley
26 Baptized Richard son of Nathaniel Ibotson Wath
June 21 Baptized Elizabeth daughter of Nicholas Morton Wath
21 Baptized William son of John Bintcliffe
July 4 Baptized Elisabeth daughter of Adam Hawksworth Birely
6 Baptized William son of Thomas Lockwood Birely
12 Baptised Richard son of Wm Couper Wath
18 Baptised George son of Richard Pearson, Swinton
25 Baptised George son of Charles Chevins Wath
26 Baptised John son of John Shertliffe Bierley
27 Baptised Margaret daughter of Ann Sisson Bierly
September 21 Baptised Sarah daughter of Wm Watkinson Wath
23 Baptised Danyell son of Thomas Hall Wath
23 Baptized William son of Richard Barber Wath
October 10 Baptized James son of Robert Oxley, Swinton
14 Baptized Mary daughter of John Dyson de Brampton
December 5 Baptised Richard son of Thomas Gessop Brampton
12 Baptized Mary daughter of John Roades Bierley
Jany 9 Baptized Mary daughter of Peter Law Swinton
19 Baptized Richard son of John Earnshaw Swinton
february 8 Baptized W^m son of Robert Byard. Wath
22 Baptized Ann daughter of John Carr de Wath
23 Baptized Mary daughter of John Carr de Bierly

1697
March 1 Baptized John son of John Kennerlay, Wath
10 Baptized Mary daughter of John Frost de Swinton
Weddings 1697
May 1 Marryed William Greaves & Dorothie day frō Darfeild
25 Marryed ffrancis Seaton & Esther Wright de Wath
June 18 Married John Hudson & Grace Wade de Bierly
August 5 Marry^{d} William Sales & Elizabeth Holmes, Wath
8 Marry^{d} Jasper Kitchaman & Ellen Bingley, Wath
27 Marryed George Whitaker & Martha Sheppard Bi^{r}eley
January 17 Marryed Robert Woodall & Sarah Litster, Licentia
27 Marryed Thomas Barker & Mary Hole, Wentworth
27 Marryed Henry Stables & Sarah Hutchinson
ffebruary 5 Marryed Thomas Hudson & Elizabeth Ellis, Wath
Burialls 1697
March 26 Buryed Ursula wife of John Turner de Wath
29 Buryed Joseph son of Daniell Twigge, Birely
Aprill 20 Buryed Thomas Holmes of Birely
21 Buryed Amos Shaw of Birely
30 Buryed Esther wife of Wm Stacey, Swinton
30 Bur^{d} John son of Wm Richardson Wath
May 30 Buryed Robert Champion de Wath
30 Bur. Mary daughter of Thomas Carr Wath
July. 30 Bur^{d} Darcy Stones de Swinton
August 2^{d} Bur^{d} Isabell wife of Wm Heyward Bierly
17 Bur. William Parrott & Brampton Bireley
September 21 Bur. Geo: Addy de Swinton
24 Bur. Margaret Bawdison de Swinton
28 Bur. Elisabeth wife of John Wood, Wath
October 12 Bur^{d} John ffirth junior de Bireley
30 Bur^{d} Richard son of Nathaniel Ibotson Birely
November 14 Bur^{d} Mary daughter of John Dyson Birely
$169\frac{7}{8}$
January 1 Bur^{d} William Smith de Wath
March 14 Bur^{d} John Elam senior de Newhill Grange Birely
13 Bur^{d} Jane daughter of Thomas Carr
*ffebruary 27th 1657. Buried George Mallinson of Wath
de eadem . . . . the daughter of Rich Oxley of Wath
Aprill ffirst 1659 Buried Will the son of Willm Wade of Swinton
June 26 1660 Buryed. Jervasse the sonn of Nathan Elison de Swinton
1698
March 27 Baptized John son of John Hicks
Aprill 3 Baptized Mary daughter of George Whitaker
4 Buried. John son of John Hicks
17 Buryed Elizabeth Jackson widdow.
26 Baptized Mary daughter of Wm Bentley
28 Married ffosterd & Dorothy Outwith
eo die Bury^{d} ffrancis Addy de Swinton

* These four entries which belong to a much earlier date are in this page in the register

1698

May 2 Marry^{d} Robt Fenton & Ann Tilney
7 Bury$^{d.}$ Elisabeth daughter of Joseph Halmsha
eo die Baptized John son of Widdo ffirth born after his father's decease
19 Buried Robt Wharam de Abdy
28 Buryed William son of Francis Tricket
29 Baptized Joseph son of John Birks.
June 6 Baptized ffrances son of Edward Smith
eo die Married John Briggs & Mary Sanderson
12 Married George Pearson & Mary Addie
19 Buried Elizabeth wife of Richard Bell
July 7 Baptized Peter son of Mary Ellis illegitimate
10 Buryed Andrew Robinson a Collyer
18 Baptised Elizabeth daughter of Wm Kemp
eod. die Buryd. Thomas Broadhead de Wath
31 Baptized Richard son of Robt Loveday
August 18 Baptized Thomas son of Wm Habsfeild
22^{d} Marryd John Waterhouse & Ann Joys
30 Baptised William son of Wm Hoyland
Septemb 1st Marry^{d} Mr John Pickard & Mrs Eliz: Tolson
11 Baptized John son of Jasper Kitchaman
13 Baptized Matthew son of Richard ffoulston

October 1698
Baptized John ye son Will: Stacy of Swinton ye 9th
Baptized Elizabeth ye doughter of Nathaniel Eberson ye 15th
Buried Peter ye son of Mary Ellis ye 16th
Buried Will ye son of Will Hoyland ye 17th
Baptized Mayry ye doughter of Edmond Jarvas ye 18th
Buried Easter ye doughter of Robert Wharam ye 21th
Baptized Hanna ye doughter of Daniel Twigg ye 24th
Buryed John ye son of Thomas Lockwood ye 28th
Buryed John Parrot of Newhill ye 29th

November
Buryed Will Addy of Swinton ye 4th
Married Samuell Waggstaf & Mary Wade of Swinton ye 6th
Buried Grace ffarburn ye 15th
Married George Wanhead and Ann Tilney ye 17th
Baptized Elizabeth ye doughter of Thomas Hudson 17th
Baptized Mary ye doughter of ffrancis Trickitt ye 24th

December
Buryed Will ye son of Tho: Lockwood ye 2^{d}
Burryed Sarah ye doughter of Thomas Robuck ye 4th
Baptized John ye son of Robert ffords ye 11th
Baptized John ye son of Thomas Tomson ye 15th
Buryed Chritobell Kitchinman ye 16th
Baptized John ye son of George Pearson y^{e} 27th
Baptized Mary y^{e} doughter of John dison y^{e} 27th
Baptized Mary y^{e} doughter of John Willkock y^{e} 27th

1698-9
January
Buryed John y^e son of Tho: Tomson y^e 10th
Baptized John y^e son of James Oxley y^e 15th
Marryed James Ghest and Jane Mawd y^e 18th
$ffeb^r$
Buryed John y^e son of Wiłł Stacy y^e 6th
Married John Burks and Elizabeth Addy y^e 16th
Married Thomas Betts & Mary Poplewell y^e 16th
Baptized Robert y^e son of Joseph ffoulston y^e 23^d
Baptized Mary y^e daughter of Joseph Bingley y^e 23
March
Buryed Joseph y^e son of ffrancis Carr y^e 2^d
Buryed Johanna Beckitt y^e 13

1699

Aprill	9	Marryed	John Otley & Elizabeth Watson de Highlaw
	11	Marryed	Thomas ffirth & Ann Mallinson de Bramtone Birely
	12	Buryed	John ffirth de Melton
	15	Buryed	Richard Carr de Brampto Birely
	16	Baptized	William son of Valentin Rodes, Swinton
	17	$Bury^d$	Elizabeth wife of Richard Beckit de Melton
	22	$Bury^d$	John son of Jasper Kitchaman de Wath
	26	$Bury^d$	John son of John Shertcliffe Bramto Birely
	30	Baptized	John son of John Elam de Melton
	30	Marryed	Thomas Bradbury & ffrances Bell Wath
May	7	Baptized	John son Richard Parken de Wath
	9	Baptized	Mary Daughter of Thomas Kay Wath
	14	Buryed	George ffoulston de Melton
	16	Buryed	Thomas Wilcocke de Swinton
June	1	$Baptz^d$	Ann daughter of Richard ffroggit de Melton
	11	$Baptz^d$	Susana daughter of William Carniley de Melton
	18	$Baptz^d$	John son of John Kay de Wath
	29	Buryed	Ann wife of John Rawwood be Bolton
July	11	$Baptis^d$	John son of William Revell de Wath
August	18	Buryed	Ann daughter of Richard ffroggitt Melton
	25	Buryed	William Carniley de Melton
	27	Buryed	Rachell supposed daughter of John Ward de Doncaster
September	1	Buryed	John son of John Kay de Wath
	5	$Baptiz^d$	Ann Daughter of Henry Kay Wath
	27	Buryed	Patience Dean of Wath
$Octob^r$	5	Marryed	Thomas Lambert of p^{sh} of Mexburg & Elisabeth Marsden de Wath
	12	$Baptis^d$	Elizabeth Doughter of John Shirtcliffe de Mexburgh
		Marryed	Wm Clarkson & Mary ffoulston Brampto Birely
	20	$Baptiz^d$	Abigaill Doughter of Edward Butterey de Wath
	26	Baptised	Thomas son of Robt ffenton de Wath
Novemb	2	Buryed	Hannah Daughter of ffrancis Carr de Wath
	5	Married	Rich Beaumond & Elizabeth Morton Bramton Birely

1699

Novembr	9	Buried	Tho Jessop. of Bramton byerley
	19	Baptized	Edward the son of Seth Gaskin of Wath
	24	Baptized	Elizabeth the daughter of John Elā of Bamt
	27	Buried	Abigall the daught of Edward Buter worth
	30	Maried	William Beardshaw and Helen Iredale ? Wath
Decemb̄	7	Baptized	Elizabeth the daught of Wiłł Hoyland
	15	Burd	John fforge of Wath
	31	Burd	Jane the wife of Thomas Sharp of Wath
Januā	1	Buried	Ralf. Stringer of Swinton
	2	Mard	John Wood and Jane Beamont of Skiers
	7	Buried	George Winterbotome of Bramton
	11	Bap:	Richard the son John Hick (*or Hill*) of Swinton
	16	Buried	Mary the wife of John Littlewood of Swinton
	16	Maried	Matthias ffarburne & Rosimđ Shaw of Mex
	17	Bap:	Tho: the son of Peter Law of Swinton
	27	Bu:	Wiłł Heward of Melton
	28	Bap:	Wiłł the son of John Brigs of Bramton
ffeb	4	Bap:	ffrances the daught of Tho: Hill Bramton
	5	Bu:	Ann the daught of Tho: Gilbert Bram
	6	Bap:	Katherine y dauh of George Wood Bramton
	6	Bu:	ye said ffrances Hill of Bramton
	6	Bap:	Tho ye son of Richard Watson Swinton
	18	Bap:	Mary the daughter of George Pearson
	28	Bap:	Tho ye son of Tho ffirth of Melton
March	1	Bu:	Ann ye wife of Tho ffirth of Bramton
	1	Bu:	Tho the son of Tho ffirth of Bramton Bierly
	3	Bap:	Wiłł ye son Wiłł Watkinson of Wath
	7	Bap:	John ye son of John Carr of Wath
	9	Bu:	Grace Hudson of Bramton bierley
	10	Bap:	Tho: the son of Wiłł Stacy of Swinton
	10	Bap:	Wiłł the son of Thos Hall of Wath
	11	Bu:	Ann The wife of ffrancis Carr of W.

1700

March	28	Baptizd	Elizabeth Daughtr of Ellen Barker of Bramt Birely
	29	Bur:	Joseph Bingley of Bramt: Bierly
Aprill	1	Buryd	John ffrost of Bramt: Bierly
	2	Baptizd	Elizabeth daughter of Richard Pearson de Swinton
	6	Buryd	John son of John Elam de Bramt Bierly
	21	Buryd	Elizabeth daughter of Ellen Burkes B. Bierly
	25	Baptizd	Mary daughter of Rich Ellis de Swinton
May	3	Burd	Thomas son of Edward Tinsley B. Bierley
	6	Buryd	William son of George Bell Wath
	9	Buryd	Alice daughter of Jasp Kitchaman Wath
	14	Baptizd	John son of Charles Cheuins de Wath
	12	Bur:	Elizabeth Chappell of Bramt: Bierley
	23	Bur:	Ana Wilson de Wath
	26	Buryed	William son of Thomas Hall de Wath
	29	Buryed	John son of Charles Cheuins de Wath

1700

May 30 Baptised Mary & Sarah daughters of Joñ Shaw, Swinton
June 28 Bur. Mary daughter of John Shaw de Swinton
30 Baptized ffrancis son of Thomas Wilkinson Swinton
July 4 Baptiz^{d} William son of Robt Cutt de Swinton
14 Baptizd Dorothy daught^{r} of Richd Beaumond Bierly
23 Marry^{d} James Whitakers & Ann Carnily Bierly
23 Marry^{d} John Littlewood, Swinton & Sarah Heyward Bierly
August 8 Baptiz^{d} John son of Wm Parrot of B. Bierley
Septemb^{r} 2 Bury^{d} Isabell Taylor vid. de Bramt Bierley
Octob^{r} 9 Baptized William son of John Kennerlay de Wath
12 Baptiz^{d} Elizabeth daughter of Jon Birks de Swinton
12 Baptiz^{d} Sarah daughter of Richd Booth. Melton.
20 Marryed John Allot & Margaret ffoarge.
28 Bury^{d} Edward Butterworth of Wath
Novemb^{r}: 5 Marryd John Gessop & Margarit Hall Mexburgh
12 Marryd George Wigfall & Sarah Nailor of Highland
12 Marryd. Richd Shaw & Hannah Leach Swinton
14 Baptiz^{d} ffrancis son of ffrances Trickit, Melton
27 Marryd. John Wood & Martha Offspring Swinton
Decemb^{r} 29 Baptiz^{d} Martha of Richar^{d} ffoulston Brampton Bierly
29 Baptized Edward son of Edward Smith Wath

1700-1

January 1 Baptized Thomas son of Thomas Hudson Wath
21 Marryed Mr Robert Banks, Minister of Hull & Mrs Millicent Hutton de Bramton Bierley
23 Marryed Robert Reiney de Wentworth & Mary ffosterd de Brampton Bierly
29 Baptized of Edward Butterworth de Wath. (*sic*)
ffebruary 1 Buryd William son of Robert Cutt de Swinton
16 Bury^{d} Jane daughter of Thomas Haslehurst Wath
March 2 Buryd Elizabeth daughter of John Hudson Melton
4 Marry^{d} James Smith of ye Parish of Hansworth & Mary Cloppenburgh
20 Baptized Thomas son of William Bentley de Melton
23 Buryed Thomas son of William Bentley de Melton
23 Bury^{d} John Sheppard de Wath
23 Baptized Jonathan son of Richard Gawtresse

1701

March 27 Bury^{d} Catherin daughter of Mrs Tolson Wath
29 Baptized Martha & Sarah daughters of George Whitakcr. Bramton Bierly
30 Buryed Matthew son of Peter Law de Swinton
30 Baptized Mary daughter of Henry Burne de Wath
Aprill 3 Baptized Joseph son of Joseph Bingley de Swinton
3 Buryed Ann Pheasant de Swinton widow
3 Buryed Mary daughter of Peter Law Swinton
6 Buryed Mary wife of Joshuah Mathewman Wath
7 Buryed Jonathan son of Thomas Sharp de Wath

1701

Aprill	9	Buryed	Thomas son of Anthony Smeaton Swinton
	14	Buryed	Jonathan son of John Thropp Swinton
	22	Marryed	John Stainton & Lettice Cook.
June	1	Baptised	Mary daughter of Richard Parkin Wath
	5	Baptised	Joseph son of Joseph ffoulston Bramto Bierly
	24	Marryed	John Jackson & Ann Wharam Wath
	26	Baptized	Mary daughter of John Bintcliffe Melton
	29	Buryed	Elizabeth daughter of Thom Hudson Wath
	30	Buryed	Mary daughter of Henry Burn de Wath
July	12	Baptised	Caleb son of Robt Bayard de Wath
	18	Buryed	Jasper son of Jaspr Kitchaman Wath
	28	Buryed	Thomas son of Thom: Hudson de Wath
August	17	Baptised	Ann daughter of John Elam
	24	Buryed	Elizabeth Mawhood of Bramton Bierly
	26	Buryed	Ann wife of Adam Hawksworth Wath
	31	Baptized	Robert son of Mr Twitty de Wath
Septembr	2.	Buryd	Robert son of Mr Twitty de Waђh
	6.	Buryd	Margery wife of Witt Carr, Wath
	16	Baptized	Ann daughter of James Whitaker Bramton Bierly
	18	Baptizd	Ruth daughter of John Trauise Bramton Birely
			examined ye 9th of 8th 1701 M. Cayley
Octobr	9	Buryd	Joseph son of Joseph Foulston Bramton Birely
	29	Baptisd	William son of Wm Revell Wath
Novembr	25	Baptisd.	John son of Robert Fenton Wath
	25	Marryd	John Townend of parish of Connisbrough & Mary Turner of Wath
	25	Baptizd	Ann daughter of George Rymer, Wath
	27	Baptizd	William son of Richd Palmer, Mexburgh
	27	Baptizd	William son of Thomas Kay de Wath
	30	Marryd	John Barber of Wentworth & Mary Sorsbye of Parish of Wath
January	6	Baptizd	Richard son of Robert ffoardge Wath
	22	Baptizd	Elizabeth daughter of Peter Law Swinton
	29	Marryd	Richard Trickitt & Martha Wainwright both of Wath
ffebruary	1	Baptizd	John son of Thomas Hopwood Swinton
	1	Marryd	James Ellis of Treeton & Mary Lambert Swinton
	8	Baptizd.	William son of George Pearson Swinton
	14	Baptizd	Elizabeth daughter of Matthew Jackson Swinton
	19	Buryed	Elizabeth daughter of Matthew Jackson Swinton
March	13	Baptized	Ann daughter of Thomas Hall Wath
			Examined 14th April 1702 M.C

Annus 1702

Aprill	7	Marryed	Edward Cartwright last Inhabitant wth in Gresbrok in parish de Rotherha & Mary Ellis de Wath
	7	Baptised	John son of John Wood de Swinton
	16	Baptised	William son of James Oxley de Swinton
	18	Buryed	Margaritt Bullowes de Swinton

1702

Aprill 21 Baptized Joshuah Mathewman son of Wid: Mathewman Bramton Birely
24 Baptized Sarah Turner of Bramton Bireley of ripe years
28 Baptized William son of Georg Bell Wath
30 Baptized Sarah Daughter of John Birkes sen Swinton
May 5 Baptized Margarett Daughter of William Hall Wath
14 Baptized Elisabeth Daughter of Robert Cutt Swinton
16 Baptized Hannah Daughter of John Carr de Wath
17 Baptized Sarah Daughter of John ffrost Swinton
25 Marryed John Otley & Ann Sorby of Chappelry Wentworth in p^sh^ of Wath
26 Marryed Charles Butler & Ann Pitt Brampton Bierly
June 19 Baptized Elizabeth Daughter of John Jackson Wath
25 Baptized Elizabeth Daughter of Thomas Hudson Wath
30 Buryed Elizabeth Daughter of Thomas Hudson Wath
July 2 Marryed William Stainton & Sarah Wigfall in Chapplry of Wentworth in p^sh^ of Wath
August 7 Bury^d^ Elizabeth Daughter of John Hill Swinton
16 Baptised John son of John Birks jun^r^ de Swinton
26 Buryed John Carr of Brampton Bierley
27 Baptised Willian son of Charles Butler Bramton Bierly
27 Baptised Hannah Daughter of John Shaw Swinton
Marryd Thomas Jackson & Ann Smith of Chapplry Wentworth.

May 7th 1702 Memdum that Joseph Wentworth of Wath is Lawfully Possessed of a Seat of ye South side of ye ffont in the Body of the Church of Wath which he Purchased of Robert Bingley of Wath aforesayd and the same he his to enjoy without any molestation and paine of Ecclesiasticall censure

Witnesse Jo: Twittey Vic De Wath

Thomas Kay
Thomas × Hudson his mark } Churchwardens

1702.

Octob^r^ 13 Baptized William son of William Parrot Bramt Birely
15 Baptised John son of William Watkinson de Wath
15 Bury^d^ James Lindsall de Wath
19 Bury^d^ Jane wife of John Trickett de Bramto Birely
Novemb^r^ 5 Marry^d^ Richard ffirth De Rawmarsh & Mary String^r^ Swinton
19 Baptised Sarah daughter of Thomas Pindarr de Wath
26 Baptised Ann daughter of Richard Gorrill de Bramto Birely
26 Marryd Luke Bradley & Rosamond Hudsone of Wath par
Decemb^r^ 7 Baptisd Samuell ye son of William Stacey Swinton
7 Buryd Mary daughter of Thomas Gawtry, Wath
20 Bapti'sd George son of Richard Shaw Swinton
20 Baptisd Thomas son of John Townsend Wath
27 Baptisd Joseph son of Richard Trickitt Bramt Birely
30 Buryd William son of Widdo Burton de Swinton

1702

January	5 Baptizd	Richard son of Jasper Kitchaman Wath
	5 Buryd	William ye son of John Bintcliffe Bramt Birely
	6 Buryd	Jane Hepworth of Wath widdowe
	14 Marryd	John Wright & Sarah Carr Bramto Birely
	26 Baptisd	Ann daughter of Thomas Hill Bramto Birely
February	4 Maryd	Symeon Pullen of Rotherham Par & Elisabeth Wharam de Brampton
	6 Baptisd	Robert son of Mr Twittey Miñ of Wath
	15 Buryd	Richard Beaumond de Brampto Birely
	18 Baptisd	Rachel daughter of George Wood, Birely
March	7 Baptisd	Ann daughter of Robt Oxley Swinton
	16 Buryd	Elizabeth Daughter of Widdow Burton Swinton

1703

March	30 Buryed	Sarah wife of Matthew Jackson, Swinton
Aprill	9 Buryed	John Allott de Wath
	16 Buryed	Elizabeth Knight vidua de Brampton
	29 Buryed	Elizabeth Baxter de Bramton vidu.
May	7 Buryed	Mary daughter of Thomas Sharpe, Wath
	18 Baptised	Hannah daughter of John Kennerly Bramt Birely
	26 Buryed	ffrancis son of ffrancis Trickitt
June	1 Marryed	Thomas ffirth & Mary Chappel? Bramt Birely
	15 Baptized	Joseph son of Richard ffoulston Bramto
	16 Buryd	Ann ye wife of Thomas Lockwood Melton
	27 Buryd	Richard Mathewman Bramt Bierly
July	1 Marryed	John March de Harthill & Mary Wade de Melton
	6 Baptizd	Robert son of Robert Fenton Wath
	20 Baptizd	Ann daughter of Thomas Jessopp Bramton Bierly
	29 Buryed	Godfrey Shelles de Swinton
August	6 Buryed	Elizabeth daughter of John Hudson Melton
	7 Buryed	Thomas Walker a Sojourner,
	29 Baptizd	Mary daughter of Joseph Ant de Swinton
Septembr	5 Baptizd	Richard son of Joseph ffoulston Bramt Bierly
	16 Baptizd	George son of William Hoyland Wath
	20 Baptizd	Catherine daughr of John Trickitt Bierly
	23 Baptized	Martha daughter of Thomas Hudson Wath
	24 Baptizd	John son of George Matthewman Brampton Bierley
		March ye 23d Examined ꝑ J. Lupton.
October	12th Buried	Catherine wife of Mr Emott de Bramt Bierly
	22 Baptizd	Sarah ye daughter of Wiłłm Revill Wath
	22 Buried	John Carr of Ranebarr Bramt Bierly
	28 Married	Phillipp fflint & Helen Chatburne Bierley
Novembr	11 Married	John Perrot & Dorothy Athey Bierley
	16 Married	Jonathan Beaumont & Elizabeth Beaumont Bierley
Decmbr	9 Baptized	Williã ye son of Nathañ Andrew, Bierley
	31 Buried	Elizabeth wife of Richard Elam, Bierley
January	5 Baptized	John the son of John Wilbraham, Bierley
	13 Baptized	George the son of John Carr de Wath
ffebruary	1 Baptized	John ye son of Francis Trickitt, Bierley

1703

ffebruary 7 Buried Elizabeth ye wife of John Loriter, Wath
8 Buried Jonas son of Richard ffoulston, Bierley
13 Bapptized Witte son of Stephen Kay, Bierley
Babptized Joseph son of Thomas Betts, Swinton
14 Babptized John ye son of John Jackson, Wath
24 Babptized Sharlott daughter of Luke Wood Bierley
Babptized Sarah ye daught^r^ of Susan Hurst Bierley
Examined pro J. Lupton
March 24th Buryed. Richard Barbar de Swinton

1704

Apl. 8th Buryed. Margarett wife of John Trickitt Bramton
11 Buryed. Thomas Bintciffe de Brampton

Memorand that Thomas Wade of West Melton in the Parish of Wath doe resign up his right to two Seates for two Persons which he hath in a stall or Pew adjoyning to the middle Alley & to the Seats of Richard ffoulston, ffrancis Trickitt. John Dyson on the East & also adjoining to a seate of Richard Jackson & Joseph ffoulston on the west to John Gorrill of Brampton Bierley, to Possess the same to Himselfe & heirs executors without Molestation or Disturbance In consideracon that he the sayd Thomas Wade shall have from John Gorrill aforesayd in exchange a Seat which adjoyned to the South Alley & a seate of Mrs Tolson on ye North & a seat of William Wharam & William Revell on the West. In witnesse whereof we have interchangeably sett o^r^ Handes the day & year above written

Thomas Wade John Gorrill

1704

Aprill 27th Marryed Joseph Halmshaw of Brampton Bierley & Catherine Crowther
30 Baptized Mary Daughter of John Travise of Bramton Bierly
May 21 Baptized John son of John Tomson—Swinton
12 Baptized Richard son of Richard Parken. Wath.
13 Buryed Henry Kay de Wath
14 Buryed Robert Bingley de Wath
25 Buryed John Ellis de Wath
28 Buryed Martha wife of Richard Tricket Bramton Bierly
June 4 Baptized Ann daughter of Georg Pearson Swinton
6 Baptized Ann daughter of Thomas ffirth Bramton
13 Baptized Matthew son of Peter Lawe Swinton
15 Baptized John son of Thomas Kaye de Wath
15 Baptized John son of John Elam de Bramton Bierly
29 Marryed George Speight & Margaritt Elliott Wath
July 4 Baptised John son of Edward Butteroth (*Butterworth*)
6 Marryed John Dyson & Sarah Birkhead Bramton Bierly
9 Baptized Ann Daughter of John Hudson Bierley
9 Buryed Margarett Wilson de Swinton
29 Baptised John son of John Carr de Melton
August 2 Buryed Richard Ellis de Wath

1704

August 1 Baptized Jonathan son of Nathaniel Ibotson
2 Baptized Ann daughter of John Wood, Swinton
10 Baptized ffrancis son of Richard Ellis of Swinton
25 Baptized Jervase son of Thomas Hall de Wath
25 Maryed John Roberts & Mary Matheman Bramton
26 Baptized Thomas son of Thomas Tilney Wath
Septemb^r 8 Baptized Samuell son of Robert Cutt de Swinton
14 Baptized Ann daughter of Richard Trickett de Swinton

A : D : 1704

Octob^r 19th day Baptized Ann daugt^r of Edward Smith Wath
22^d Buried Wid : Littlewood Bierly
31 Baptiz'd John ye son of Jon^n Swinden de Swinton
Novemb^r 18th Baptiz'd Thomas ye son of Ann Bentley, Bierley
19 Baptiz'd Elizabeth daught^r of John Birks de Swinton
23 Married Will dey of Bolton & Elizabeth Leach
Decemb^r 5th Buried Hannah ye daugh^r of Tho : Betts de Swinton
6 Buried Ann ye wife of Richard Watson de Swinton
10 Buried Henry Sanderson de Swinton
13 Buried John Eaton de Wath
13 Baptiz'd Elizabeth ye daught of John Wright de Cooly lane
21 Baptiz'd Edward ye son of Charles Butler, Bierly.

1705-6

January 3^d Buried Edward Butterworth de Wath
7th Baptiz'd Joseph ye son of Robt fforde de Wath
22^d Buried Nicholas Wright de Wath
24 Buried Margaret ye daught^r of Robt ffretwell Bierly
28 Baptiz'd Elizabeth daughter of Tho : Carr de Wath.
ffebruary 15th Baptiz'd George ye son of Willm Perrot Bierly.
March 2^d Buried Ann ye daught^r of Rich : Watson de Swinton
4 Buried George ye son of George Mathewman Bierly
16 Baptiz'd Richard ye son of Will Stacy de Swinton
18 Buried ye s^d Rich son of Will Stacey de Swinton
Survey, P.D

1705

Aprill 7 Baptized Elizabeth daughter of Richard Gorrill Bramton Bierly
8 Marryed William Cussworth & Joane Bower Wath
Baptized Elizabeth daughter of Mr Burroughs, Swinton
May 4 Buryed John Turner of Wath
21 Buryed Thomas Armroyd illegitimate Wath
30 Baptis'd Jane daughter of William Hall, Bramton
June 13 Baptisd William son of Robert ffenton Wath
19 Marryed Christopher Grey & Sarah Bullow
19 Maryed Abraham Heys & Beatrice Bingley
21 Marryd John Holland & Ann Ash tōday?
21 Baptizd Judeth daught^r of Willm Bentley Bramton
27 Buryd Mr William Marsden de Wath
28 Baptizd Elisabeth daught^r of John Twitty Wath

1705

June 29 Buryd Esther daught^r of Richard Gorrill Bramto Bierly
July 3 Baptized Sarah daught^r of Eliz : Wilson illegitimate Wath
3 Buryed William son of Robert ffenton Wath
25 Buryed Samuel son of William Stacey Swinton
Augs^t 16 Buryed Gervase son of Thomas Hall Wath
30 Bur^d Elizabeth daughter of Mr Twittye Wath
Septemb^r 16 Baptized son of Thomas Pindar de Wath
Octob^r 5 Baptized Mary daughter of Richard Trickit Bramto
Octob^r 9 Baptized James son of Georg Whitaker Melton
Novemb^r 4 Bury^d George Chappell of Bramton
5 Marryed Richard Allott & Margaret Flint Brampton Birely
10 Buryed Elizabeth Pitt of Bramton Bireley
10 Marryed Robert Chappell Susannah Hoyland Birely
21 Marryed ffrancis Mockson and Margaritt Needham
27 Baptizd ffrancis son of John Carr Wath
Decmb^r 9 Baptizd Sarah daughter of Stephen Kay Bramton
9 Baptizd John son of William Iredall Brampton
11 Baptizd Thomas son of William Revell Wath
11 Marryed William Carr & Grace Ormroyd
27 Marryd William Newbat & Elizabeth Willis
Decemb 8 Baptizd Thomas son of William Cusworth Wath
January 5 Baptizd John son of William Heald Melton
5 Buryed Mary wife of William Heald Melton
16 Baptizd Ann daughter of Jonathan Wilson Wath
24 Baptizd Margaret Daughter of Joshua Halmshaw Birely
28 Buryed Easther wife of Richard Jackson Wath
30 Married John Amory & Elizabeth Oxspring
ffebruary 3 Marryed Timothy Day & Esther Kay Wath
7 Baptizd Robert son of Thomas Hudson Wath
21 Baptizd John son of Richard Allott Birely
March 12 Baptizd John son of Thomas Hill Birely
Buryed John son of Thomas Hill Birely
14 Buryed John Robbinson de Wath
20 Baptized William son of John Shaw

1706

April 1st Buryed Sarah daughter of Elizabeth Wilson Wath
4 Bur^d Richard Sales of Swinton
7 Bur^d William son of John Shaw Swinton
8 Baptiz^d George son of Jasper Kitchaman
18 Baptiz^d Thomas son of Nathaniel Andrew
21 Baptis^d Thomas son of John Swinden Swinton
28 Baptis^d George son of Joseph Aut, Swinton
29 Baptis^d John son of Widdo Butterworth, Wath
29 Buryed Thomas son of John Swinden, Swint
May 4 Baptizd William son of William Stacey Swinton
5 Buryed Judeth daughter of William Bentley
11 Buryed Ann daughter of John Trickitt Birely
25 Bury^d a stranger ye dyd comeing to ye coale Pit Hall

1706

May 28 Marryed ffrancis Dyson & ffrancis Jackson
June 6 Buryed a child nursed by Thomas Hall wife in Wath
Married Peter Dawson of Doncaster & Ann Roebuck Birely
12 Baptized Ann daughter of John Jackson Wath
Baptized Mary daughter of Thomas ffirth Birely
12 Buried Thomas Pennington Birely
18 Baptisd Luke son of Luke Wood Bireley
July 4 Baptisd Samuell son of John Birkes Swint.
7 Baptisd Ann daughter of Richard Parkin Wath
14 Buried Valentine Roades de Swinton
28 Baptisd William son of Thomas Shaw Wath
August 4th Baptisd Ann daughter of John Kennerlay
11 Marryed Thomas Pēarson of Mexburgh & Elizabeth Robbinson de Wath
15 Baptisd George son of George Mathewman Birely
September 14 Buryed John Campsall de Wath
29 Baptizd Matthew son of John Tompson Swinton
Octobr 10 Baptizd Mary daughter of Wm Horsfeild Bierly
25 Buryd John Birkes of Swinton
27 Baptizd John son of William Newbatt Wath
Novembr 2d Baptisd William son of Timothy Dey. Wath
2 Baptisd Mary daughter of Richard Hill. Swint
7 Baptisd John son of John Travise Bierly
26 Buryed Elizabeth Carr de Rainbar Bierly
29 Buryed William Watson de Swinton
30 Buryed Elizabeth wife of Nehemia Wade Swinton
30 Marryd Thomas Mallison & Elizabeth Roebuck Birely
December 2 Baptisd John son of Richard Elam Bierley
19 Buryed Richard Mursden de Wath
Jany 1 Buryed Jane wife of Mr Thom: Baxter Bierly
18 Buryed Ann daughter of Richard Booth Bierly
23 Baptizd Mary daughter of Thomas Hutchinson, Youngr
24 Baptised Thomas son of Thomas Flecher de Swinton
ffebruary 2d Baptisd Sarah daughter of John Bintcliffe
5 Buryd John Carr de Hoober Bierly
6 Baptisd Hannah daughter of John Holland Bierly
9 Buryed Jane daughter of Richard Howgood
18 Buryed Jane daughter of Widdo Stones Swinton
23 Buryed Mary wife of William Hall Bierly
25 Buryed Elizabeth Stacey de Swinton
27 Baptisd Elizabeth daughter of John Elam Bierly
27 Baptisd Mary daughter of Daniel Twigge
March 2d Buryed Thomas Haslehurst Wath
2 Buryed John son of Richard Allatt Bierly

Ann dom. 1707
Aprill 13 Baptized John son of Thomas Hill, Brampton
14 Baptizd Thomas son of John Wood de Swinton

1707

May	22	Baptizd	Martha daughter of Williā North
June	5	Baptizd	William son of William Heald
	9	Baptizd	Richard son of Richd Gorrill jun^{r}
	11	Marryed	Nicholas Beardshall & Susan Robbinson
	12	Baptizd	Mary daughter of John Hudson, Melton
July	3	Baptizd	John son of Robert Ibotson
	5	Buryed	Elizabeth wife of Thomas Wilkinson
	9	Baptizd	Elizabeth daughter of Jonath^{n} Wilson
	18	Buryd	Bridget wife of Thomas Elam
August	3	Baptizd	William son of Thomas Tilney
	4	Buryd	Jane wife of Joseph Bingley
	8	Baptizd	Mary daughter of John Amorie.
	12	Buryd	Elizabeth & Mary wife & daughter of John Amorie
	13	Buryed	Ann wife of Phillip ffllinte
	17	Buryd	Jonathan Wilson & Margarit Lansdall
	19	Buryd	Ann wife of Wm Goddar^{d} de Adwick
	18	Baptizd	Thomas son of Thomas Mallison
	21	Buryed	Elisabeth wife of Thomas Mallison
	24	Buryd	Ann wife of Thomas Wade sen^{r}
September	4	Buryd	Thomas son of Thomas Mallison
	18	Baptizd	Ann daughter of John Shawe, Swinton
October	2	Baptizd	William son of George Addye
	26	Baptizd	Michaell son of Robert Fenton
	31	Buryd	Jane Matthewman, widdo.
November	2	Buryd	Hugh Shaw de Wath
	4	Baptizd	Mary daughter of Wiłł Newball
	13	Marryd	Nehemia Wade & Elizabeth Frost
	13	Baptizd	Hugh son of William Parrott
	16	Baptizd	John son of John ffrost
	19	Buryd	Richard Bell de Wath
December	5	Baptisd	Ann daughter of Charles Butler
	9	Baptisd	Henry son of Thomas Kaye
	18	Buryd	John Frost de Swinton
	22	Buryd	John Gawtrye de Wath
Januariè	2	Baptisd	Alice daughter of Wiłłiā Wharam
	5	Buryd	Elizabeth Parrott widow
	14	Buryd	Susannah wife of Thomas Carr junior
	14	Bnryed	Thomas ye son of ye sayd Thom: Carr
	15	Buryd	Elizabeth daughter of Mary Jackson de Swinton base Begotten
	20	Marryed	William Goddard & Alice Mattheman
	27	Baptysd	Thomas son of Thomas Andrewe
	29	Buryd	Joshua Matthewman Wath
ffebruary	1	Marryed	William Dewsnappe & Mary Jackson
	11	Buryed	John Elam of ye Grange
	12	Marryed	Thomas Gray & Mary Ellar
	13	Baptisd	Elizabeth daughter of Robert ffordge
March	4	Baptisd	Leah daughter of George Wood

1707			
March	7	Baptisd	Mary daughter of John Hickes
	14	Baptisd	Robert son of William Stacy
	19.	Buryd.	John son of Peter Mawoode
1708			
Aprill	3	Buryd	Sarah daughter of George Whitaker
	7	Buryd	Thomas son of William Cusseworth
	8	Baptisd	Mary daughter of William Revell
	13	Baptisd	Martha daughter of Richard Trickett
	15	Buryd	Elizabeth wife of Thomas Hall
	26	Buryd	William Hale of Bramton
	28	Baptisd	John son of Thomas ffirth
	30	Buryd	Thomas Tilney of Wath
May	5	Marryd	John Carr & Mary Armroid
	9	Baptisd	Jane daughter of Peter Lawe
		Buried	Elisabeth wife Wm Tickill
	10	Baptisd	Ann daughter of Richard Shore
	11	Baptisd	Mary daughter of Richd Froggett
	13	Baptisd	Mary daughter of Luke Wood
	13	Marryd	Thomas Mallison & Sarah Finche
	27	Baptisd	Ratcliffe son of Richd Gorrill
June	1	Baptisd	Mary daughter of Geo. Rymere
	3	Bur^d	George son of George Addye
	10	Bury^d	Ann daughter of Thomas Sharpe
	12	Buryed	Jonathan son of Thomas Gawtry.
June	27	Buryed	Richd Addy de Swinton
July	11	Maryed	Jonathan Marcroft & Ann *ffirth?*
	13	Buryd	Nathaniel Ibotson
	18	Buryd	Alexander Meridew
	25	Buryd	Richd Pearson de Swinton
	28	Baptized	Ann daughter of Widdo Wilson
August	8	Baptised	Susanna daughter of Robt Oxley Swinton
		Buryed	Samuel Burton
		Marryed	John Amory & Mary Peck
September	30	Baptized	William son of John Tattershall
October	3	Maryed	John Man & Mary Burton
	13	Buryed	Mary Loncaster
	21	Baptized	Mary daughter of Robert Ibetson
	24	Baptized	Ann daughter of William Iredall
Novemb^r	1	Buryed	Elizabeth wife of Francis Robbinson
	11	Baptizd	Henry son of William Hodkinson
	28	Baptizd	Ann daughter of Wm Cussworth
	29	Baptizd	Jane daughter of Thomas Pindarr
	25	Marry^d	William Baxter & Elizabeth Ellison
Decembr	5	Bur.	Ruth Bingley de Wath
	5	Bur	Elizabeth wife of Thomas Ellis de Wath
	13	Bur	Henry son of Wm Hodkinson
	15	Baptizd	Martin son of Martyn Tomson
	29	Bur^d	Margrett Cusworth wido

1708-9			
Januy	2	Baptisd	Thomas Cutt son of Eliz Cutt base begott
	6	Baptisd	John son of Thomas Gray
	8	Buryd	John Birks de Swinton
	20	Buryd	Elizabeth daughter of Robt Forge
	26	Baptisd	Mary daughter of Joshua Halmshaw
ffeb	1	Baptisd	Godfrey son of John Bintcliffe
	4	Bur:	Ann daughter of Nathaniel Andrew
	14	Baptisd	William son of John Carre
1709			
March	29	Buryd	Mary daughter of Widdo Kempe
	30	Baptisd	Mary daughter of John Kennerley
April	2	Baptisd	Mary daughter of Beniamin Hamond
	5	Buryd	Thomas Hewet of Brampton
	7	Buried	Susanna poor widdow of Newhill
	25	Baptisd	Mary ye daughter of John Fisher
	27	Baptised	Sarah ye daughter of Richard Gorril
May	19	Mar	John Smith & Ann Hoggard
	23	Buryd	Mary wife of . . . . Hammond
	2	Buryd	Mary daughter of Wm Hammond
	29	Baptizd.	William son of John Tompson
June	3	Buryd	ffrancis Carre
	14	Buryd	Thomas son of Thomas ffirth
	23	Baptised	John ye son of Nathanaell Andrew
	28	Baptised	Elizabeth daughter of John Travis
	29	Baptised	Henry son of William Heald
	30	Baptised	Elizabeth daughter of George Addey
July		(*Nil*)	
August	29	Married	Daniell Hall & Margery Martin
Septem:		(Nil)	
Octob:	20	Bap	Grace daughter of Wm Wharam
	26	Bap	John son of John Aman
	29	Bur	widdow Wadsworth of Newhlll
Novem.	11	Bur	Suanna ye daughter in Law to James Whitaker
	14	Married	Thomas England & Mary Golland
	17	Married	Andrew Speight & Sarah Harteley
		Mar	John Brooke & Hannah Parkin ye same day
		Bap	after Richard ye son of George Mathymā
December	3	Burd	Godfrey son of Thomas Hall
	27	Baptisd	Elizabeth daughter of Thomas Tilney
	29	Baptisd	Jane daughter of Robt Foradge
January	10	Baptisd	George son of William Burrough, Gentleman.
	14	Marryd	Thomas Addison and Sarah Flint
	19	Buryd	Ruth wife of William Wells
ffebuary	14	Burd	John Parkin son in Law to Geavase Lile
	21	Baptisd	Richard son of Robt Fenton
March	5	Baptisd	Mary daughter of Richard Shaw
	22	Buryd	Richard son of Robt Fenton
	28	Buryd	John son of Widdow Elam *(sic. See next entry)*

1710 Christnings, Weddings & Burials

March	28.	Buryed	John son of John Elam of Newhill Grange
May	4	Baptisd	Robert son of Timothy Day.
	5	Baptisd	Richard son of Richard Parken
	7	Baptisd	Joseph son of John Woode de Swinton
	7	Baptisd	John son of Thomas Mallison
May	7	Baptisd	Mary daughter of Joñ Birkes
	9	Buryd	Widdow Tinsley
	25	Baptisd	Jane Daughter of Richard Gorrill jun
	28	Baptisd	Izack son of William Hammond
June	15	Marryed	Phillipp Flint & Ann Shawe
July	2	Baptisd	Richard son of Richard Hill
	27	Baptisd	Mary daughter of Will: Hodgkinson
	27	Marryd	Charles Hill & Ann Thropp
August	8	Baptizd	Benjamin son of Luke Woode
	30.	Baptisd	John son of John Holland junio^{r}
Septemb^{r}	29	Baptisd.	Elizabeth daughter of Edward Hanson
	29	Marryd	Robert Hind & Eliz. Wilson
	30	Bury^{d}	Mary daughter of Wm Renell
Octob^{r}	5	Baptis^{d}	Mary daughter of Wm Parrott
	15	Baptis^{d}	Martha daughter of Jonathan Marcroft
	18	Baptisd	Ruth daughter of George Wood
	.'	Baptisd	Sarah daughter of John Jackson
Novemb^{r}	2	Baptisd	Son of William Foulston
	5	Baptisd	Mary daughter of George Battye
	10	Buryd	Thomas Gawtrey
	30	Baptis^{d}	Sarah daughter of Joseph Johnson
	30	Marry^{d}	Wm Pashley & Mary Oldham
December	6	Marry^{d}	ffrancis Bingley & Elizabeth Bell
	21	Bury^{d}	Jane wife of John Hall, Hoober
	22	Bury^{d}	Esther Denton
	26	Marryd	Joseph Sanderson & Sarah Kay
	27	Baptisd	Ann daughter of Richard Sales
January	4	Baptisd	Sarah daughter of Joseph Hill
	5	Baptisd	Sarah daughter of Thomas Gray
ffebruary	1	Baptisd	Robert son of Robert Ibotson
	2	Baptisd	John son of Mr Sugden Lecturer of Wath
	8	Baptizd	Ann daughter of Thomas Bingley
	14	Buryd	William son of Thomas Carre
	20	Buryd	Ann daughter of John Amorye
	21	Buryd	Widdow Butterworth
	22	Baptis^{d}	ffrancesdaughter of John Carre
March	1	Baptys^{d}	ffrances daughter of Richard Elam
	3	Buried	John son of Nathaniel Andrewe
	4	Baptisd	Margaritt daughter of Wm Cussworth.
	4	Baptisd	Joseph son of Will Stacey de Swinton
	11	Baptisd	Sarah daughter to Richd Gorrill
	13	Baptisd	Ann daughter of Richd Gorrill

1710			
March	14	Baptisd	ffrancis daughter of George Addy
	22	Baptisd	Mary daughter of Witt Revell
	23	Buried	Susannah wife of Joseph Wentworth
	24	Buried	John son of William Smith
	27	Baptis^d	Mary daughter of Joseph Foulston
1711			
Aprill	22	Baptis^d	John son of John Sheper^d Swinton
	22	Marryd	Richard Greenald & Isabell Haslehurst
May	10	Baptisd	Sarah daughter of Thomas Hudson
	10	Baptisd	Mary daughter to Richard Gorrill jun^r
	11	Baptisd	Savile son of Richard Froggett
	15	Baptisd	Sarah daughter of Gervase Carniley
June	3	Baptisd	Mary daughter of Andrew Speighte
	7	Buryd	Isaack son of William Hamōnd
	11	Buryd	Mary daughter of George Batty
July	5	Baptisd	Ann daughter of John Baxter of Bramton
	16	Baptisd	John son of John Hutchinson
	17	Buried	Ann daughter of Richard Sales
	17	Buryed	Ann daughter of Thomas Dingley
	24	Baptisd	John son of Richard Trickitt
August	2	Buryd	Elizabeth daughter of George Addy
	7	Buryed	Thomas son to Widdow Broadhead
	9	Baptisd.	William son of William Wharam
	11	Buryd.	John son of John Hutchinson
Septemƀ	25	Baptisd.	John son of James Smith
Novemb^r	6	Buried	Robert son of Robert Ibotson
	8	Baptisd	Mary daughter of Joshua Halmshaw
	8	Married	William Smith & Susanna Halmshaw
	12	Baptisd	Martha daughter of Mr. Eedes
	16	Buryd	Rich^d son of George Mathewman
	23	Baptisd.	Elizabeth daughter to Benjamin Hamond
	30	Baptisd	James son of John Fisher.
Jan^y	5	Buryd	James son of John Fisher
	17	Baptisd	Elizabeth daughter of William Flint
ffebruary	7.	Baptis^d	Elizabeth daughter to Nathaniel Andrew
	28	Baptisd	Richard son of Thomas Carr
March	24	Buryed	Francis daughter to John Carr
1712			
March	27	Buryed.	Widdow Bintcliffe
Aprill	7	Buryed	George Ellis of Bramton. Gentl^n
	21	Buryd	Widdow Addye
	27	Buryd	Elizabeth wife of William Smith
May	4	Baptizd.	John son of Robert Oxley
	27	Baptizd	John son of Richard Sales
	28	Buryd	William Smith
June	5	Baptisd	Mary daughter of George Mathewman
	24	Marr.yd	John Baxter & Thomasin Gawtrey
	15	Baptisd	Elizabeth daughter of William Heald

1712			
June	30	Buryd	Catherine wife to Richard Booth
July	14	Buryd.	John son to William Thacker
	16	Buryd	Thomas Sharpe of Wath
	17	Buryd	Widdow Mallison
	18	Buryd	Richard Foulston de Bramton Bierley
August	7d	Buryd	Thomas son of John Hutchinson
	7	Baptisd	Elizabeth daughter of Thomas Bingley
	9	Baptisd.	Hannah daughter of Richard Gorril junr
	10	Baptisd	John son of John Mann
	17.	Baptisd.	Richard son of Timothy Day
	17	Baptisd	William son to William Iredall
	30	Buryd.	Thomas Wade.
Septembr	14	Buryd	Richard Parker
	18	Buryd	Ann daughter of William Iredall
	20	Buryd	Ellen Linsley
	21	Baptisd	Ann daughter of William England
	24	Baptisd	Robert son of Robert Outram.
	29	Marryed	Hamond Hole & Ann Guest
October	3	Buryd	John Gorrill
	5	Baptisd	John son of Thomas Tilney
	15	Buryd	John son of Richard Trickitt
	28	Buryd.	Ann daughter of Robert Pindarr
November	7	Baptisd	Mary daughter of John Hutchinson
	20	Buryed	Thomas Hall
Decembr	7	Buryd	Edith wife to John Golthorpe
	17	Baptizd	John son of William Hamond
	28	Baptisd	Martha ye daughter of Edward Vanter
	30	Buried	Rosamond wife to Wm Robuck
Jan	5	Baptisd	Mary ye Daughter of Hammond Hole
	13	Baptisd	Mary ye Daughter to Tho: Grey ÷
	4th	Baptisd	Ann daughter to George Addy
	5th	Buried	Savil son to Richard Froggit
Feb		Buried	2 children of Wm Smith ye 1st 8th 2° 24th
	24th	Baptisd	Joseph ye son of Wm Parratt.
March	4th	Baptisd	Elizabeth daughter to Richard Gorrill
	12	Baptisd.	Jane daughter to Wm Thackrah
	1[illegible]	Baptisd	Mary daughter to John Carr
1713.			
	30	Baptisd.	Thomas son to John Baxter
		Burried	Thomasin wife to John Baxter aforesd.
April	7th	Baptizd	Susanna daughter to Gervas Carnaley
		Baptisd	Mary daughter to Wm Baxter eod die
	11	Buried	William son to Gervas Carnaley
	18	Bap:	Peter son to Thomas Taylor
May	28	Bap:	Thomas son to Tho: Hudson
June	2	Burried	Mary wife to John Briggs
	9	Buried	John Lossiter.
	24	Bap:	Mary daughter to John Holland

1713

July	5th	Bap:	William son to Wm Fowlston
	7	Bur:	Jane daughter to John Kennarley
	9	Bap	Henry son to Thomas Hill
	16	Bap:	Dorathy daughter to William Revell
	28	Bap:	Frances daughter to Joseph Hill
Augt		There was nothing to be Register'd this month	
Sep:	26	Buried	widow Wade
Octr	4	Bap:	Elizabeth daughter to John Amen
	10	Bur:	Mary daughter to Nehemiah Wade
	12	Buried	John Rodes.
Nov:	1	Bap:	Sarah daughter to Thomas Dodson
	24	Bap:	Elizabeth daughter to Mr Joseph Pearson
	25	Buried	Ann wife to Richard Gorrill
	30	Buried	Christian daughter to Thomas Elam
Dece	1	Buried	Widow Walker
	2	Bap:	George son to Richard Gawtry
	20	Bap:	Abel son to Robert Hides
	30	Bap:	Mary daughter to John Jackson
Jan		Bap:	Mary & Ann daughters to Wm Wharam 1st
	5	Buried	Mary wife to Gervas Lyall
	21th	Bap:	John son to Wm Flint
	28	Bap	Joseph son to Richard Hill
		Bap	Martha daughter to Richard Allen eodem die
February	3	Bapt.	Ann daughter to James Smith
	4	Mar:	Thomas Eaton Wharam & Jone Elam
March.	12th	Bapt	Mary daughter to Richard Gorrill
	13	Buried	Mary daughter to Wm Wharam
	22	Bur	John son to Wm Bentley
	23	Buried	Ann daughter to Wm Wharam
		Bur:	Wm son to Thomas Mallison eod die
1714			
	25	Bur	Mary daughter to Andrew Speight
	27	Bur:	Mrs Ann Tolson
	28	Buried	a child of Richard Booths
April	15	Buried	Milison daughter to John Baxter of Brampton
	24	Buried	John Tayler
	23	Buried	Milisent daughter to John Baxter
	28th	Bap:	Mary daughter to John Camsell
May	5th	Bap:	Ester daughter to Wm Cusworth
	9th	Buried	Stranger who died at Brampton
	10th	Married	Francis Poole & Sara Roads
	14	Bap:	Sarah Daughter to Richd Sales
	19th	Buried	Mary wife to John Hill.
	27.	Married	Francis Hardey & Elez: Steer
June	9th	Bur:	Margaret Crosland
	11	Bap:	John son Tho: Carr
	16	Buried	Joseph Fowlston
July—		*Nil*	

1714			
Aug^t^	8	Bapt	Mary daughter to Robt Ford
	26	Bap:	Mary daughter to Joseph Jonsō
	28	Bap:	Joseph son to Joshua Halmshaw
	31	Buried	Bettrice Hewit
Sept	26	Bap:	W^m^ son to Benjamin Hammond
	30th	Bap:	Ann daughter to Mr Burroughs
Oct,	6th	Bap:	Susanna daughter to John Kenerley
	19	Buried	Richard Frogget
	?	Bap.	Henry son to Luke Wood
		Married	John Cooke & Dorarthy Ellis eođ die
Nov	4th	Married	John Briggs & Ann Bower
	16	Buried	William Horsfield
	21	Bap:	Mary daughter to Thomas Carr
	29	Bap:	Jervas son to Gervas Carnaley
Dec^r^	14	Buried	William Carr
	16	Bap:	Thomasin daughter to Jane Wharam
	19th	Buried	Mary Mathewman
	30	Bap:	Mary daughter of Nath; Pepper
Jan:	14	Married	John Raby & Mary Tinsley
	20	Buried	James Hanley
Feb:	3	Married	Wm Taylor & Ruth Litster
	4	Bap:	Eliz: daughter to Timothy Dey
	6	Married	John Lial & Rebekah Laughton
	12	Buried	a boy of John Bentcliffes
	14	Buried	Eliz: wife to John Hicks
	24th	Bap:	William son of Wm Hamōnd
		Married	Leonard Stanley & Ann Holland eođ die
March	3	Bap:	W^m^ son to Robt Ibotson
	4	Bap:	George son to George Addey
	15	Buried	Francis Clayton
1715.		Christenings	
April	7	Baptizd	Mary Daughter to William Wharam & Margaret Daughter to Thomas Bingley
	12	Bap:	Sarah Daughter to John Aman
June	19	Baptizd	Ann daughter to Will: England
July	24	Bap:	Ann daughter to Thomas Booth
	28	Bap:	Elizabeth Daughter to Francis Hardy
August	7	Bap:	Sarah Daughter to William Iredal
	15	Bap:	Matthew son to John Jackson
	28	Bap:	Sarah Daughter to Richard Fowlston
October	4	Bap:	John son to John Liall
	16	Bap:	Benjamin son to William Parrat
	17	Bap:	John son to John Brigg
Nov^br^	24	Bap:	Mary daughter to Richard Gawtrey and Thomas son to William Kay
Dec^r^	29	Bap:	John son to John Campsal
Feb:	2	Bap:	Sarah Daughter to John Thompson
	9	Bap:	John son to John Wright

1715			
Feb :	15	Bap :	William son to William Cusworth
Burials			
June	15	Buried	Humphrey Jackson
Aug	29	Buried	Ester wife to Thomas Wilcock.
Feb	1	Buried	John son to John Campsal Afors[d]
March	23	Buried	Thomas son to Thomas Carr
1716			
April	12	Bapt	Sarah daughter to Thomas Adkinson
	15	Bur.	Eliz : wife to Daniel Twigg
	19	Bapt. :	Edward son to Edward Hanson
	24	Bapt. :	Francis son to Thomas Tilney
	26	Bur. :	Mary daughter to Will : Revel
May	3	Bapt :	Thomas son to Thomas Grey
	4	Bur :	Ann wife to Richard Bell
	25	Bur :	Richard Bell & John Hicks
June	3	Bapt	John son to Jonathan Marcroft
	23	Bur :	Antony Pawson ?
	24	Bur :	Richard son to Thomas Dodson
	26	Bapt	Ann daughter to George Mathewman
	28	Bapt :	Will son to Will Fowlston
July	4	Bapt :	Mary daughter to Thomas Hopkinson
	13	Bapt :	Robert son to Will : Wharam
	17	Bur	Will son to Will. Fowlston
	19	Bapt :	Ann daughter to Charles Butler.
Aug[t]	1	Bur :	Mary daughter to widow Horsfield
	2	Bapt	Ann daughter to Joseph Bingley
	3	Bur :	Robert son to Will : Wharam
	15	Bapt.	Will : son to Will : Flint
	19	Bapt	Sarah daughter Charles Hill
	21	Bur :	John Shaw
	22	Bur :	Joseph Wentworth
	24	Bapt	Eliz : daughter to Will : Newbat
Sept[r]	6	Bapt	Thomas son to John Carr
	9th	Bur	Martha daughter to Will : North
	23	Bur.	Eliz : Smeaton ? daughter in law to James Oxley
	24	Married	John Twittey & Mary Gawtrey
Nov[br]	6	Bapt	Joseph son to Joseph Hill
	9	Bur	George Hopton
	13	Bapt	Mary daughter to Richard Allen
	18	Bur	John Firth.
	29	Bapt	Sara daughter to Nicholas Murrey
Dec[br]	23	Bapt	Robert son to Haman Hole
		Married	Will Hurst & Sarah Bentley eodem diē
	27	Mar.	John Elam & Martha Hinch
	30	Bur :	John Trickit de Melton & Isabel Ant of Swinton
Jan	26	Bur :	Thomas son to Thomas Hudson
Feb—	5	Mar	Samuel Crummock & Mary Morton
	18	Bur :	Thomas Elam

1716

March	15	Bur:	Mrs Shepherd
	18	Bur:	wid: Hartley
	20	Bur:	Mary wife to Richard Ellis

1717

Christenings.

April	4	William son to William Gray &
		Catharine Daughter to Joseph Pearson
	7	Mary Daughter to Gervas Carnaley
	19.	Martha daughter to John Ammorey
	24	George son to George Addey
	26	Mary daughter to John Aman
May	3.	Mary daughter to Thomas Bingley
	8	Richard son to Richard Thomson
	9	Richard son to Richard Sales
	23	Mary daughter to Richard Watson &
		Catharine Daughter to Joshua Halmshaw
Augt	1st	Martha Daughter to George Wilkinson
	8th	Mary Daughter to Thomas Carr
	9	Ann Daughter to John Twittey
	11	Hannah Daughter to William Wharam
	22	Robt son to Robt Ibotson
	24	Benjamin son to Benjamin Hammond
Septbr	12	Eliz: Daughter to Will: Hammond.
Octobr	19	Sylvanus son to Thomas Taylor
	20	Rosimond Daughter to William Stacey
Novbr	14	William son to Thomas Booth
	17	Will: son to John Arthur
	24	Thomas son to Thomas Hartley
Decbr	2	John son to John Elam
	28	Eliz: Daughter to Will: Thackarey
Jan:	16	Wiiliam son to William Kay &
		Francis son to Francis Hardey
Feb:	18	John son to Richard Trickit
	25	William son to Luke Wood
	27	Mary Daughter to John Cooper
	29	Eliz Daughter to John Wright
March	7	Gervas son to John Liall
	13	Thomasin Daughter to Richard Gawtrey

Burials

March	29	Mary Daughter to Richard Gawtrey
	31	John Jackson
Apr:	5	John Wright
	7	John son to John Wilcock
May	8.	Martha daughter to John Ammory
July	2	John Kay
	25	Hannah Daughter to Robt Fenton
	30	Jane wife to Thomas Wade (*or August*)
Septbr	10	William son to Richard Booth

1717		
Septr.	23	Ann wife to Abraham Beaumont
Octo^{b}	13	John Roberts
	21	Widow Kay
	27	Thomas Huchinson
Nov^{br}	20	William son to Richard Harpam
	12	Mathew Fowlston
Feb	6	Mary Daughter to John Campsal
	25	Widow Sales
Marriages		
Oct^{br}	29	John Robinson and Susanna Broadhead
Novb^{r}	12	Abraham Beaumont & Martha Slack
1718.		Christenings.
March	27	Ann Daughter to John Carr.
April	24	John son to John Denton
	28	William son to James Smith
May	6	William son to John Arrundall
	9	William son to William Jackson
June	9th	Mary Daughter to John Huchinson
	28	Ann Daughter to Tho: Cawthorn
Sept^{br}	4	Joshua son to George Mathewman
	18	William son to William Baxter
	23	Abraham son to Abra: Beaumont
Oct^{br}	1	Martha Daughter to Thomas Gray
	3	Margaret Daughter to Thomas Hopkinson
	26	Philip son to William Flint
Nov^{br}	6	Joseph son to Joseph Pearson
Dec^{br}	2	Eliz: Daughter to John Carr
	26	Elizabeth Daughter to Mrs Martin
Jan:	1	Joseph son to John Robinson
	4	Samuel son to John Thomson
Feb	3	Paul son to Joseph Johnson
	6	Mary Daughter to Thomas Atkinson
	14	Mathew son to Peter Law jun^{r}
	15	Mary Daughter to Thomas Dodson
	26	William son to Richard Watson
Burials		
March	31	Jane wife to John Elam
May	11	Eliz Daughter to Will Parrat
	13	Thomas son to Thomas Hartley
Sept^{br}	25	John Clark
Oct^{br}	29	Nicholas Tilney
Dec^{br}	27	William son to William Baxter afors^{d}
Marriages		
April	15	Peter Law and Ann Campsal
May	22	Richard Smith and Jane Bingley
Nov^{br}	6	John Campsal & Eliz Finch
	9	Reginald Thompson & Charlot Beaumont
Nov	27	Daniel Twigg & Mary Baul

1718

Dec[br]	11	George Sanderson & Sarah Wilson	
	21	Thomas Bintcliffe & Eliz: Gascoign	
Feb:	17	John Wild & Margaret Roebuck	
March	3	George Wood & Widow Gorril	

1719.

Christenings

March	26	Baptized	Joseph son to Thomas Hartley
	30	Bapt	Richard son to Richard Smith
	31	Bapt:	Hannah daughter to Richard Allen
April	5	Bapt	Sarah daughter to Benjamin Bright
	19	Bapt	Daniel son to Gervas Carnaley
	29	Bapt	Elizabeth daughter to Will: Winter
May	3.	Bapt	Will: son to Thomas Dodson
June	18	Bapt	Sarah daughter to John Holland
Aug[t]	23	Bapt	Elizabeth daughter to Richard Sails
	26	Bapt	Mary daughter to William Hall
Sept[br]	24	Bapt	John son to John Campsal
Nov[br]	5	Bapt	Mary daughter to Thomas Lancashire
	14	Bapt	John son to John Cooper
	26	Bapt	Eliz daughter to John Twittey
		Bapt	Eliz daughter to Daniel Twigg
Dec[br]	26	Bapt	John son to Will: Gray
Jan.	27?	Bapt	Mary daughter to George Sanderson
Febr	4	Bapt	Tho son to Will Wharam
	11	Bapt	John son to Richard Dyson
	25	Bapt	Thomas son to Thomas Bingley
		Bapt	John son to John Carr
March	22	Bapt	Elizabeth daughter to William Greenbury?
		Bapt	Sarah daughter to Thomas Dodson
	24	Bapt	Mary daughter to Francis Hardey
		Bapt	Martha daughter to John Elam

Marriages 1719.

March	30	Married	Tho Wade & Martha Sorby
Apr	19	Mar.	Tho Elam & Mary Tilney
Aug	26	Mar.:	Samuel Fox & Theodosia Woodhouse
Sept	17	Mar:	Sylvanus Sikes & Ann Holland
Nov.	5	Married	Will Bawtry & Eliz: Hawksworth
	15	Mar	Tho Milner & Alice Bork
Dec	22	Mar.	John Wood & Mary Fostard

Burialls 1719

Aprill	22	Buried	Mary the wife of Sylvanus Sykes
May	8	Bur.	Will: Parrat of Coley lane
	13	Buried	Richard Ellis of Coley lane
	15	Bur	Mary the wife of Will Hoyland
	24	Bur	Will the son of James Smith
	28	Bur.	Daniell Twigg of y[e] Rhodes
Augt	11	Buried	John Gray of Rainbar
	17	Bur	Eliz Daughter to Jo: Carr

1719

Sep.	9	Bur	Mary wife to George Whitticar
	21	Bur	Mary wife to Thomas Beaumont
	25	Bur	a child of Nicholas Murrey
Oct.	5	Bur.	John son to Will Hammond
	11	Bur.	Ann Elam widow
	24	Bur	Mary daughter to George Burton
Nov	16	Bur	Francis son to Tho Tilney
	27	Bur	Richard son to Richard Watson
Dec	6	Bur	Sarah Daughter to Tho : Booth
	9	Bur	Will Bentley
	12	Bur	Widow Frost?
Jan.	14	Bur	Rosamond wife to Luke Bradley
	15	Bur	Tho son to Andrew Speight

March 21th 1719

Memorandum that we the Ministers & Churchwardens of Wath do give our Consent that John Carr of Wath Juniour Do erect a Pewe at the West End of the Church adjoyneing to the North Door & the Seate of John Elam of Newhill on the South to belong to his house in Wath and there to remaine, abide and be under paine of Ecclesiasticall Censure

John Twittey, Vic of Wath
John Wood
Tho : Carr
Tho Gray
William Wade } Churchwardens

Christenings in ye year 1720

March	26	Bapt.	Mary Daughter to Will Thackarey
	29		Faba daughter to Abraham Beaumont
Apr	6		Ann daughter to John Briggs
	14		Will. son to John Wright
	15		Sarah daughter to Will : Kay
	16		John son to Nathaniel Pepper
	19.		Joshua son to Joshua Green
			Eliz daughter to William Tompson
	21		Francis son to John Denton
May	1		Patience daughter to Mary Wood
June	2		John son to Thomas Bintcliffe
	7		James son to Benjamin Hammond buried ye 7th
July	7		Will : son to Charles Butler
Sept	9.		Robert son to Robert Fenton
Oct	20		Eliz : daughter to Tho. Cawthorn
	21.		Ruth daughter to Will Hammond
Nov	4		Eliz : daughter to Tho : Carr buried ye 12th
	17.		Margaret daughter to John Shepherd
	23		Eliz daughter to Richard Watson
Dec.	26		Thomas son to John Campsal
	28		Eliz daugther to Richard Lambert
Jan	11.		John son to John Arthur

1720			
Jan	19		John son to Will. Jackson
	26		Thomas son to John Robinson
Feb	1		Will : son to Will : Wilcock Buried ye 2
	23.		Joseph & Benj : sons to Will : Flint
Marriages in ye year 1720			
Ap.	19		John Firth & Martha Whitaker
	25		John Robinson & Mary Carr
Sept	22		Michael Armitage & Mary Ibotson
	29		Will Wilcock & Hannah Naylor
Nov,	13		Joshua Bingley & Martha Copley
	17		Samuel Birkes & Mary Steer
Dec	26		Richard Goodinson & Mary Cutt
	27		Henry Wilkinson & Ann Roberts
Burials in ye year 1720			
Apr.	12		Thomas son to Will Wharam
	23		Mary wife to Thomas Elam
May	27		Widow Barber
	27		Ruth Wife to Humphrey Jackson
July	12		Rebecca Wife to John Lyall
Aug	8.		Richard, Tolson, esquire.
Sept	6		Constance daughter to John Kempe
Oct	14		John Elam
Nov.	16		Will : Thompson
	29		Ab Cawthorn
Jan	2 :		Mary daughter to Robert Tyas
	10 :		John son to Thomas Carr
	12		Widow Heaton
Feb	1		Richard son to Francis Tolson Clerk
	13		Thomas Wilkinson
	26 :		Benjamin son to Will. Flint, Predict.
March	2		Robert Pindar
	16		Martha daughter to John Elam
	20		Jane Carr widow
1721			
March	31	Buried	Nicholas Hopkinson
April	9	Bapt	Will son to Peter Law
	20	Bapt.	Will son to Will Gray & Rosamond daughter to Wm Wharam
	25	Buried	Francis son to John Denton
	26	Buried	Joseph son to Will : Flint
May	7	Bapt	Sarah daughter to Gervas Carnaley
	11	Buried	Eliz daughter to John Twittey
	16	Buried	Robert & Ann son & daughter to Robt Fenton
June	4	Bur	Wil. Roebuck
	23 :	Bur	Samuel Hanson
	29 :	Bur	Robert son to Haman Hole
July	14 :	Bur	Thomas Lancashire
	26	Bapt	Sarah daughter to Brian Eleot

1721			
Sept^{br}	3	Bapt	Thomas son to Will: Tingle
	6	Buried	Eliz wife to Robert Ford
	17	Bur	Will Cusworth
	18	Bur	Eliz wife to Thomas Bintcliffe
Oct:	4	Bapt	Thomas son to Thomas Booth
	12	Bapt:	John son to Daniel Twigg
	14	Bapt	John son to John Rodes
	24	Married	John Crossland & Mary Trickit
	25	Bapt:	Thomas son to Thomas Hopkinson
	27	Bur:	Sarah wife to Daniel Cawton
	29	Bur:	Eliz wife to John Throp
Nov^{br}	1	Bur	Thomas Carr
	16	Bur	Peter Law
	30	Bapt	Thomas son to Thomas Fowlston
Dec	14	Bapt	William son to Richard Smith & Rachel daughter to Thomas Bingley
	18	Bur.	Will son to Will Hall.
	22	Bur	Richard Gawtrey & Jennet Parrat
	25	Bur	Will: Sales
Jan	16	Bur.	John son to Will: Winter
	27	Bur.	Widow Tompson
Feb.	2.	Bapt	John son to Thomas Dodson
	11	Bur	Mary wife to Richard Trickit
		Bapt	Francis son to Richard Trickit eod: die
	13	Bur.	Will Carr & Francis son to Rich Trickit predict
		Bapt	Mary daughter to Will Tompson eod die
	14	Bapt	Mary daughter to John Carr Buried ye 19
	23	Bapt	Martha daughter to John Elam
March	4.	Bapt	Thomas son to Wid Loncashire
	8	Bapt	Mary daughter to John Twittey and George son to Geo Sanderson, Gent.
	15	Bapt	Hannah daughter to Will Wilcock.
	19	Buried	John Baxter.
1722			
March	27th	Bapt	Tho: son to Thomas Carr
	30th	Buried	Mary daughter to Willm Thompson
April	3.	Bur:	Willm son to John Denton
		Buried	John Broadhead eodem die
	15th	Baptiezd.	George son to Haman Hole
	17th	Bapt	Thomas son to Abraham Horsefield
	24th	Bur:	Will: Burroughs Gent
May	3^{d}	Buried	Elizabeth Thompson of Swinton widow
		Bapt	Will son to Will: Iredal eodem die
	16th	Bapt.	Ann daughter to Thomas Wade
	15	Bur:	Thomas son to Will. Tingle
	20th	Married	Thomas South & Eliz. Jackson & John Hurst & Judeth Carr
	27th	Bapt.	Mary daughter Abraham Beaumont

1722			
	29th	Bapt	Ann daughter to Rich. Allen
June	30th	Bur.	John son to John Elam of Melton
July	2	Married	Richd Hunt
	17	Bur.	Helen Burton (widow)
Aug^{t}	10th	Buried	Will: Richardson
	16.	Bapt.	Will son to Richard Thompson of Swinton
	22	Bur:	Nicholas Murrey
	23	Bur	John son & Ann daughter to John Carr
Sept^{br}	21	Bapt	Margaret daughter to Jo. Crossland
Oct	2^{d}	Bur:	Jonathan Marcroft of Swinton
	28	Bapt	Michael son to John Campsal
Nov^{br}	6	Bur	John Arundel & Helen his wif ye 9th or 10th
	22	Bapt	Ann daughter to Tho; Hartley
	23	Bur:	Thomas Ellis
Dec^{br}	7th	Bapt	Sarah ye daughter of Rich. Hicks, Illegitimate
	11th	Married	Willoughby Thompson & Ann Wilson.
	22^{d}	Buried	Sarah daughter to Jo: Huchinson
	24th	Buried	Ann wife to Thomas Wood
	26	Bapt	Mary daughter to Will. Gray.
Jan	1^{s}	Bapt	Mary daughter to John Kemp
	10th	Bur:	John son to John Turner
	27	Bapt	Will son to Gervas Carnaley
	25	Buried	John Hudson of Melton
Feb.	2	Bapt.	Will. son to Will Hall
	21st	Married	Geo White & Ann Whitaker by license
		&	Thomas Elam & Ann Sylvester
March	3^{d}	Buried	Daniel Cawton of Swinton
1723.			
March	26	Bur	John son to John Cowper
	29th	Bur.	Eliz daughter to Rich Lambert
May	9th	Bur	Ruth & Rebecca daughters to John Wright of Wath
	27th	Bapt	Ann daughter to Will Wharam
June	18th	Marr	Philip Vincent Esqr & Mrs Elizabeth Tolson
	24th	Buried	Mary wife to Tho ffowlston & Bp his son
	27	Bapt	Hanna daughter to Will. Thompson
		Bur	Sarah daughter to Richard Booth eod̄ die.
July	7th	Bur.	Ann wife to Thomas Ward
Aug	18th	Bapt	Francis son to John Adin
Sept	6th	Bur.:	Will Pit.
	15th	Bur	Will: son to Will: Wharam
	22	Mar.	Thomas Stephenson & Mary Hague
		Bapt.	Eliz. daughter to Daniel Twigg eodem die
Oct	10th	Bapt	Mary daughter to Will. Winter
	13th	Buried	Will: Wharam above written
	16th	Buried	Thomas son to Thomas Booth
	17th	Bur:	Eliz daughter to Richard Hill
	25th	Bur.	Margaret daughter to Rich: Allen

1723

Nov^{br}	2	Bur	Mary daughter to Robert Fenton
	3^{d}	Bur	Will. Thackarey
	6th	Bur	Thomas Crossland
	8th	Bur	Thomas son to Joseph Pearson
	14th	Bur	Susanna wife to Robert Chappil
	18th	Bapt	Eliz daughter to Tho : South
	20th	Bapt	Ann & Mary daughters to Will Flint
	23	Married	John Swift & Mary Ellis
	26th	Marr.	John Denton & Ann Rymer
		Bapt	Rich son to Will Jackson of Swinton & Mary daughter to Will Kay of Wath
	27th	Bapt	Ann daughter to Thomas Gray
	30th	Bapt	Ann daughter to John Arthur & Sarah daughter to Abraham Horsfield
Jan.	1	Bapt	Ann daughter to John Robinson
	4th	Buried	Francis Mokeson.
	7th	Bapt	Sarah daughter to Rich Watson of Swinton
	23	Bapt	Ann daughter to Francis Hardey
Feb.	5th	Buried	The Reverend Mr Thomas Ackroyd, Lecturer of Wath
	13th	Mar	Joseph Roe & Judith Ford
		&	John Harrison & Catherine Barker
March	1st	Bapt	Sarah daughter to Henry Walker &
		Bur :	Will Wilcock
	6th	Buried	George son of Will. Hoyland & Mary daughter to Rich : Gorril.
	12.	Bapt :	Jonathan son to John Twittey
	24th	Bur	. . . . . . son to Tho Fowlston

1724. Baptisms

March	25	Sarah daughter to Tho : Dodson
April	9th	Will son to John Campsal
	12	George son to Rich : Stead
	17th	John son to Mr Sanderson
May	17th	Will : son to Will : Wilcock
July	2^{d}	Margaret daughter to John Shepherd
	9th	Tho son to Thomas Cawthorn post morte fratris
Sept^{br}	10th	Tho : son to Tho : Wade & Will : son to Richard Sales of Swinton
	20th	Joseph son to Joseph Tasker
	24th	Rich : son to John Wright
	25th	Will son to Will : Tingle
Oct	22	Sarah daughter to Joseph Bingley of Swinton
Nov^{br}	8th	Jonathan son to Jonathan Bentley
	12th	Will : son to John Elam
	17th	Will son to John Carr
	19th	Ann daughter to Tho : Gray & Ann daughter to John Denton
	24th	Will : son to Rich Thompson
Dec^{br}	11th	Joshua son to Joshua Halmshaw

1724

	26	Eliz : daughter to Thomas Booth
Jan	21st	Ann daughter to Rich : Fowlston
	28th	John son to Rich : Russel & Francis son to Rich : Trickit
Feb	2d	Ann daughter to Rich Gawtrey
	9th	Rich son to Rich Allen
March	17th	George son to Geo : Chevines

Marriages. 1724

March	26	Jeremiah Pybus & Mary Bentley
April	5th	John Kennerley & Martha Gascoign
	7th	Rich Russel & Jane Elam.
May	17th	Will : Wood & Mary Watson
	28th	Tho Ubanks & Mary Wood
June	25th	Tho : Wood & Sarah Hopkinson & John Rodes & Ann Marcroft
Oct	22d	Rich Booth & Sarah Lodge

Burials

March	26th	Jane ye wife of Reg : Burdyn Schoolmaster of Wath
	29th	John son Abraham Beamont
April	5th	Sarah wife to John Clarkson
	19th	John son to John Adin
	29th	Ann Kay who was brought from Haslington in ye Parish of Barnbrough
July	17th	Eliz : ye wife of Philip Vincent Esqr
Aug	8th	Mary wife to Rich. Huchinson of Swinton
	11th	Joseph son to Tho : Carr
Septr	8th	Mary daughter to Will : Tickhill
	12	Robert Loveday
	24th	Robert Ford or Forge
	30th	Magdalen Gascoign
Oct	9th	Will son to Richard Sales
	26th	Thomas Hudson
Novbr	10th	Jonathan son to Jonathan Bentley
	30th	George Bell.
Decbr	3d	Mary daughter to Eliz Thackerey (widow)
	9th	Helen Kitchenman, (widow)
	11th	Cartherine wife to Joshua Halmshaw
	13	Thomas Lockwood
	14th	Eliz : Marsden widow
	22	Henry Hoggard & Ann Addy
	31	Ann wife to Thomas Baxter
Jan	21th	Nicholas Carr
Feb	1st	Mary Fosterd (widow)
March	8th	Ann wife to Charles Butler.
	20th	John Littlewood

N.B.—In the 2 Vol of the Registers there are three duplicate paper leaves for the years 1722, 1723, 1724 where it is stated

May 28 Mar. Philip Vincent Esq & Mrs Eliz Tolson

1723 June 8 Bapt John son to John Carr (Editor).

The Register Book

for the

Parish of Wath

Bought ye 18th day of March, 1723.

John Twittey, Master of Arts of Ch : Church in Oxford.	Vicar
Jonathan Gawtrey, John Kay, Tho Baxter (of Abty) junr, Jonathan Gascoign, Abraham Beaumont	Churchwardens

This Register contains all ye Chrytenings, Marriages and Burials within the Parish of Wath (the Chappelry of Wentworth excepted) since the 20th day of March 1724

A Schedule or Inventory of all the Books, Vestments and Vessels belongin to ye Parish Church of Wath-upon-Dearne in the County of Yor taken the 21st day of June 1726 By order of ye Reverend Doct Blake Arch-Deacon of York at his Parochial Visitation that day hel in the s^d^ church

Books

A new Great Bible best edition
An old. Do (new bound 1736)
A new Common prayer Book
Two old Do.
Book of Homillys
Bishop Jewels Apology
Exposit^n^ of ye Ep. to ye Thessalon^ns^ } very old and out of the Binding (bound new 1736)
Erasmus on the New Testament
Table of Consangu^ty^ & Affinity.

Vestments

A new Surplice & one very old one & a Hood
A new Carpet, a linnen Cloath & Napkin for Comun^n^ Table
A green Shag Cushion for the pulpit.

Vessells

Two Flaggons of pewter } For Communion Table
Chalice and Paten of Silver
Two boxes of Wood for the offertory.

An Inventory of the above Books, Vestments, & Vessells was given to Arch-Deacon the day and year above mentiond signd Joh Twittey, Thomas Key & William Ottley, Francis Trickett & Richar Smith.

A counterpart wherof was returnd the same day signd by the sam persons being the Vicar & Church wardens for the sayd year as als thus.

Ric- Brathwait Regrãrius.

Provided since for ye use of the sayd Church viz

A new Communion Table.
A Carpett to cover it of Crimson Cloath trim'd wth Gold
A Diaper Cloath & Napkin for the time of Ministration
A Cushion for the Pulpitt of Gold & Silver Brocade trim'd wth Gold Crimson & Gold Tassells.
A Bitt to go round the Desk-part or Board of ye Pulpitt under ye say Cushion made of Crimson Cloath & trim'd wth Gold. Given in th year of our Lord 1727
An arm Cain Chair to stand on ye North side of ye Communion Tabl for ye ease of ye officiating Minister
All but the Table given by Mrs. Sarah Tolson

---

21 June 1736

Wath. at the parochial Visitations of the Reverend Doctor Blake Arc Deacon of York it was order'd & decreed as follows vizt That th rubbish & shrubs lying near the church walls be taken away, Th the Roof of the Vestry & the Window be repaird, That the Flo of the Church as well in the Isles as in the Seats be new lay'd & made plain and even where wanting, That ye Skreen betwixt ye Church & Chancell be taken down & the Ten Comãndm^s^ & King's Arms be plac'd else where. That the pulpit be remov'd & set forward unto that pew call'd Mr Ellis's and that a new Sounding Board be provided for it. That the Reading Desk be made more convenient for the Minister That new rails be made to the Communion Table & to be return'd at each end to be certified on or before Martinmas next

Chancell. That the Roof on the South East corner be repair'd

Table of Benefactions to be hung up in some convenient place in ye Church. } Signed Ric: Brathwaite
Regr̃arius

In obedience to which Order & Decree the sayd Repairs & Alterations were made accordingly as also a new pulpit & Reading Desk & South Window giving Light to them But some Dispute arising concerning the Article of paving & repairing theer said respective Seats a Citation was procur'd at the Instance & Request of the Minister, Churchwardens & principal Inhabitants of ye sayd parish from the Court of York to y^t^ purpose & after due publicat^n^ thereof & notice given in the said parish church the following Decree was obtein'd thereon, Viz—

John Audley, Doctor of Laws Vicar gen'al & official principal of the most reverend Father in God Lancelot by divine providence Lord Arch-Bishop of York Primate of England & Metropolitan. To our well-beloved in Christ Thomas Key, William Ottley, Francis Trickett, Richard Smith & Thomas Fosterd pres^t^ Churchwardens of Wath within the County and Diocess of York greeting—Whereas we lawfully proceeding have lately issued out a Citation under the Seal of our office against all and singular ye Parishioners & Inhabitants of and within the parish of Wath aforesd to appear before us or our lawful Surrogate at a certain Time therein assign'd to shew Cause if they had or knew any why an order should not be issued under the Seal to the effect hereafter mentioned which sayd Citation has been duely publish'd in the sayd Church & return'd in open Court where the sayd parishioners & Inhabitants being then publickly call'd upon and none appearing to shew cause to the contrary Wee have Decreed and Do by these presents grant unto you the said Thomas Key, William Ottley, Francis Trickett, Richard Smith & Thomas Fosterd, Churchwardens aforesaid to take and pull down all and singular the Seats or Stalls or Pews scituate within the said Church of Wath & to rebuild & erect the same for the better convenience & use of the Parishioners & Inhabitants of the said Parish requiring all persons whatsoever not to attempt to molest or disturb you the sayd Thomas Key &c in the performance of this our order, And what you shall do or cause to be done on the premises you shall certify us as soon as conveniently may be together with these presents. Given at York under the Seal of our office this 21st day of November 1726.

Concordat cum Decret Tho Jubb.

Which Decree being duly publish'd in the Parish Church of Wath aforesaid was shewn to John Tucker of Moregate in ye Parish of Rotherham & County of York aforesaid Esqr Lessee under the Dean and Chapter of Christ Church in Oxford Impropriators of the Rectory of Wath aforesaid for his Concurrence therewith in relation to what pews are erected in ye Chancell of ye said Church. But he refus'd to comply therewith or to suffer the said chancell pews to be meddled with till such time as the Churchwardens & some of the principal Inhabit^{ts} should sign the following Instrument viz

Whereas the Church Wardens & the major part of the Inhabitants of the parish of Wath intend to make some alteration in the seats contain'd in ye Body of the parish Church of Wath & for the purpose have obtain'd a Decree from the Ecclesiastical Court of York for the doing thereof and whereas there are diverse Seats in ye Chancell of the sayd church which do belong to the owners of the Impropriation of Wath and whereas the said seats are irregularly plac'd & not so much to the advantage & ornam^t of ye chancell & convenience of ye Seats as the same might be plac'd therein the said Churchwardens & Inhabitants have desir'd leave of John Tooker of Moregate in the parish of Rotherham in the County of York Esq^e who holds the Rectory of Wath of the Dean & Chapter of Christ Church in Oxon to make & place the said Seats more regularly wch the sayd John Tooker as far as lyes in his power doth grant so that no greater Quantity of the ground belonging to the sayd Chancell be taken for making the said regulation and so as the persons who shall be plac'd in the Seats after ye regulation thereof shall not have any other Right or Title to the new Seats y^n what they had before to their old seats and so as there shall be no prejudice done to the Dean & Chapter of Christ Church or to the s^d John Tooker as to their respective Rights in the sayd Chancell and so as the same be not done by any Decree or by any other Authority but from and by the said John Tooker & the sayd Dean & Chapter which the sayd Churchwardens & Inhabitants do hereby declare is not nor ever was intended and as a Testimony of our agreement to make the sayd new Regulations in the said Chancell upon the Terms & in the manner aforsayd Wee the Church Wardens & Inhabitants have set our hands the 12^h day of December in the 13^h year of the reign of our Sovereign Lord King George Anno Dom. 1726.

A Counterpart of ye above written Instrument of Agreem^t was deliv'd to ye sayd Church Wardens sign'd by ye sayd Mr. Tooker the same day.

Signed Thomas Key
Francis Trickett
Willm + (his mark) Ottley
Sar: Tolson

The above are true Copies of the several Papers, Instruments & prociss to wch they respectively relate taken the 31^s Day of December 1726

By me

Frs. Tolson.

Examin'd & compared with their respective originals with which we find them exactly to agree By us	Will Twittey Cur Ibm Thomas Kay Sar : Tolson

A Register

of the several respective claims of every particular Parishioner & Inhabitant of and belonging to y[e] parish of Wath aforesayd to the Seats & Pews in the sayd Church according to the new regulations thereof by virtue of the above written process as appropriated to every one's respective Farm or Freehold in the sayd Parish this 25[h] day of March 1730.

Lady Choir

No of Pews		No of Seats
No 1	M[rs] Tolson for Wath Hall	all
2	The same for the same	1
	Rob Hudson for y[e] house	1 s
	M[r] Sanderson lives in	2 s
	R. Elam his property	3
	Jn[o] Kay for his house	2
3.	R[t] Hon[ble] Lord Malton for Newil Grainge	all

Chancell

No of Pews		No of Seats
No 1	Wid Gawtres for her house at Brooke	all
2	L[d] Malton for Ester Maud's house	all
3	J[no] Hall for his house at Hoober	all
4	L[d] Malton for Newell Grainge	5
	Tho[s] Tilney for R[d] Jackson's house	1
	Jn[o] Jackson for his own house	1
	Wid Gawtres for her house at Brooke	1
	Wid. Marsden for J[no] Amery's house	1
	R[d] Gawtres for his own house	1
5	The Parish for the Vicar	all
6	The Reading Desk	all
7	The Impropriators seat	all
8	L[d] Malton for Wid Cawthorn's house	all
9	The Parish for y[e] Vicar's Serv[ts]	
	Tho Harpham his property	
	Roberts for his house	2
10	H. : Jackson for his house	2
	Tho Tilney for R[d] Jacksons	:
11	Tho Carr for his house at Newall	
	Carr of Brampt. his property	:
12	Hu : Jackson for his house	
13	R[d] Gawtres for his own house	all

Body of y[e] Church
Middle Allè.

No of Pews		No of Seats
No 1	The Parish for y[e] Clerk's desk	all
	M[r] Ellis's Trustees for Bramp[n]	all
3	Mrs Tolston for Wath Hall	all
4	Mrs Wharam for her house at Abdy	all
5	L[d] Malton for Fr. Hard'y's house	:
	The same for R[d] Bingleys house	:

No of Pews		No of Seats
6	The Same for Jn° Bentclif's house	2
	Ja^s Whitacre for his own house	2
7	Ld Malton for Jo Gascoign's house	2
	R^d Gawtres for Jn° Twitteys house	2
8.	Mr Jackson for his house	all
9	Mrs Tolson for Wid Smith's house	2
	Jno Shepherd for his own house	2
10	Tho Wade for his own house	2
	Wm Baxter for his house	2
11	Jno Ford for his house	2
	Robt Cutt his own property	2
12	Ld Malton Jno Campsal house	2
	Jo. Townend for his house	2
13	Luke Wood for his house	2
	Phil Flint for his house	2
14	R^d Scargill for R^d Heeler's house	
	J^{no} Wright for Geo: Chevins house	[illegible]
15	Ld Malton for Wid Holmshaw	2
	Mr Stevenson for Wid: Hurst house charged wth Ld Malton for y^e in No 6 North Allé	1
	Jn° Denton his property	1
16	Revd Mr Greenwood for Jno Wright	2
	Tho. Firth for R^d Elam's house	1
	Wid. Gawtres for Oxclife house	1
17	Ld Malton for Hen Dyson's house	2
	The same for Willm Grey's house	2

No of Pews		No of Seats
18	The same for J^{no} Jackson's house	all
19	The same for Tho Kay's house	2
	The same for Jona Gawtres house	
20	The same for R^d Towlston's ho.	
	The same for F^{rs.} Trickets ho.	[illegible]
21	Mr Shipden for Wm Jackson's ho.	all
22	Ld Malton for Jn° Hutchinson's Ho.	all
23	The Parish for Christenings	2
	Wm Frettle for R^d Scailes house	2
24	Mr Baxter for his house at Abdy	all
25	Ld Malton for R^d Thompson's ho.	4
	The same for Jos^h Bingley's house	[illegible]

North Allé

No of Pews		No of Seats
1	All the upper part of the seat which extends beyond ye pillar to Swinton seat conteining	3
	Thos Kay for his freehold all that part of ye seat wch is under ye pillar conteining	3
2	Jn° Denton for his freehold	all
3	Mr Silvester for Ed Foster's ho.	2
	Tho. Carr of Wath. The upper end.	2
4	Mr Ellis Trustees for Wm Healds	2
	The same for J^{no} Clark's house	2
5	Mr Fenton for Wm Kay's house	[illegible]

No of Pews		No of Seats
	Wm Wade for his house	4
6	Ld Malton for R^d Lamberts house	2
	The same for Robt Allen's house	[illegible]
7.	Ld Malton for Thos Kayes upper House	all
8.	The same for John Lisle's house	all
9	Mr Stevenson for Jno Denton	2
	Jno Denton for R^t Ibersons hou.	2
10	Mr. Savils Charity Hanson's ho.	2
	Robt Hudson for Jno Hudson's hou.	2
11	Th^o Tilney for R^d Jenkinson's house	all
12	Fine with the pillar	all
13	Tho. Hutchinson for R^d Smith's hou.	all
14	Wm Kay for his freehold	all
15	Fra. Tricket for Shepherds house	all
16	R^d Tricket for her own house	all
17	Jno Denton for his freehold	all
18	Jno Kay for his own house	all
19	Mr Shipden for Nath. Laws house	all
20	Mr Ellis's Trustees for Tho Firths ho	2
	The same for Matt. Reiner's house	2
21	Tho Baxter for Ro Twittey's house	all
22	Tho Townend for his own house	all
23	Tho Kay for Geo Batty's house	all
24	Ld Malton for Fra Trickets house	all
25	Jn Denton for his freehold	all

No of Pews		No of Seats
1	Mr Hoyland for Wolton Croft	
2	Thomas Harpain & Will Baxter of Morton	

South Allé

No of Pews		No of Seats
No 1	Ld Malton for Ro^t Fenton's house	all
2	The Same for Thornhill Hall	all
3	Will Wade for Tho. Dodson's house	all
4	Geo. Henworth for his own house	2
		2
5	Jno Green for his own house	all
6	Wm Kay for his freehold	all
7	M^rs. Tolson for Ro^t Budson's house	all
8	Ld Malton for Jona Gawtres his farm at Melton	2
	Martin Thompson his property	1
9	Lꞌı Malton for Pet. Maud's house	all
10	The same for R^d Sharp's house	2
	Mr Jackson for Wm Tomson's house	1
11	Robt Hudson Senr for his house	all
12	Ld Malton for Jno Beaumont	2
	The same for Wm Iredal	1
13	Ld Malton for Jno Arundell's house	2
		2
14	Wm Kay for Thom^s South's house	all
15	Jerv. Carneley for his own house	all
16	Geo: Wood for Geo Whitacre's house	2
—	Wm Wade for Jno Willcox's house	2

No of Pews		No of Seats
17	Jno Wood for his own house	2
—	Mr Law for Wid Wade's house	2
18	Mr Shipden for Wm Jackson's house	2
—	The same for Jn° Birks house	2
19	Mr Ellis's Trustees for y° house late Th° Baxter's burnt down	2
—	Ja^s Inman for Robt Chappell's	2
20	Hum. Jackson for his own house	all
21	Danl Carnally his property	2
	Ld Malton for Wm Revell's house	2
	Jona^n Bingley for Tho. Bingley's ho	2
22	Thos Wade for his own house	all
3	R^d Gorrell for his own house	all
24	Mr Astlin for Newell house	all
25	Mr Ellis's Trustees for Brampton School	
—	The same for Wm Hodgkinson's	

Cross Allé

No of Pews		No of Seats
No 1	Ld Malton for G. Matthewman's house	2
	The same for Thos Grey's house	2
	The same for Jn° Shepherd's house	2
2	Poor house at Melton	2
	Robt Iberson for Benj Bamond's	3
3 / 4	The Parish for y° Singers	all / all
5	Jn° Ball for his house on Boober	all
6	Jn° Tewson his property	3
	M^rs. Wharam for her house	2
7	Jn° Thompson his property	2
	Ric^d Watson his property	2
		2
8	Mr Morver for Wm Baxter's house	2
	Ric^d Smith his property	2
	Thos Firth for Elam's house	2
9	Mr Astlin for Robinson's house	2
10	Jn° Carr for his own house	

The above & before written Regulation of Seats in y° parochial Church of Wath upon Dearn in the County of York was made and agreed upon by virtue of the foregoing Decree & with the consent & approbation of the R^t Honble The Lord Malton and Mrs Sar: Tolson joint Lords of the Mannor of Wath aforesaid & the Rest of y° Parishioners & Inhabitants of y° said parish by us the Minister & Churchwardens thereof for y° time being. Wittness our hand y° 25th day of March 1730

Will Twittey } Vic. ibid

} for Wath

Wittness. } for Byerley

} for Swinton.

The Revnd Francis Tolson Drew all the above writings and Instruments concerning the new Pewing of the Church and ye plan of it; & a many more writings & plans during the carrying on of ye work & perfected everything so admirably well as appears plainly by the work itself & the above Register of it by wch all the Rights of the Parishioners will be ascertained for ye time to come & he was so zealous in every particular & took so much Pains about it, that he deserved well of God (if I may so say) & it was acknowledged universally that the Parish of Wath could not mak him too great a comple^{mt} for it and yet made him none at all. Quœre whether this be not a Paradox or no. In my opinion it is & I always told him so & sent him a Letter to York of thanks in my own name & of Complaint for such a Contempt of the Religion of Holy Places of the Parish.

Witness my Hand

Will Twittey

A Memorandum that Thomas Atkinson bought of John Bintcliffe a seat in the Middle Alley Numb. 6. in y^{e} year 1731 Witness my Hand. Will. Twittey, Vica$^{r.}$

Memorandum That in the year 1742 Mr John Jackson Bought of Joseph Pearson three Seats in a Pew in the Cross Alle' Number 6

Memorandum that in the year 1741 Mr John Jackson and Mr Thomas Baxter did jointly purchase of Tooker Tooker Esquire of Mooregate near Rotherham a Pew in the Chancel Number seven.

Memorandum that William Wright bought of Thomas Harpam half of that Seat No 2 in the Lady Choir which Seat was built by the said Thomas Harpam and William Baxter of Melton this was entred Nov^{br} 1st 1763

Jno Rowley Vic^{r}

Memorandum that William Wright bought of Thomas Harpam's Widow 1 Seat in No 9. in the Chancell Nov^{br} 1st 1763

Witness. Sarah × Harpam's Mark

Jno Rowley, Vic^{r}

Memorandum That John Elam of Melton, Taylor, has three Seats and the Clap-seat in the Pew No 2 in the Lady Choir which his Father Richard Elam bought of Mrs Tolson this has been related to me by Persons of Credit. Witness my hand this 17th Day of April 1765 Jno Rowley Vic$^{r.}$

Memorandum that Thomas Watson bought of Martin Thompson one Seat or Sitting in No. 8. in the South Allé April the 8th 1767 Jno Rowley Vicr.

Be it remembered that the half of that seat No 2 in ye Lady Choir built by William Baxter of Melton is now become the property of Thomas Lancashire of Melton. Witness my hand this 12th Day of April 1770 Jno Rowley, Vicr.

Be it remembered that two Seats in the Pew No 7 in the Cross Alley which were erected at the Expense of John Thompson of Swinton are become the Property of Samuel the Son of the said John Thompson of Swinton and that the said Samuel Thompson hath sold and disposd of the said two Seats in the said Pew No 7. to John Evas of Wath upon Dern in the County of York to be held and enjoy'd by him his Heirs or assigns for ever. As Witness my Hand this 9th day of April 1781

Samuel his × mark Thompson

Witness Jno Rowley, Vicr

Be it remembered that Mr Thomas Tuke bought of Richard Smith, William Smith, William Wood of Swinton & James Roberts of Stubbing Lane two Seats in the Pew No 8 in the Cross Alley the property of Richard Smithson in the year 1779 As witness my hand this 4th day of November 1786

Jno Rowley Vicr

Be it remembered that Daniel Smith of Thrunscoe has purchas'd one Seat or Sitting of the Devisees of Sarah Harpum, Widow, in No 9 in the Chancell November the twenty-fourth 1791

Jno Rowley Vicr

I Thomas Trebeck, Vicar of Wath upon Dearne do hereby certify that Doctor W. Kaye hath bought of his Brother John Kaye Esqr. a Moiety of a Pew or Seat in the Church of Wath aforesaid called the Wath-Hall-Pew No 3 in the Middle Isle. Witness the hand of the said John Kaye the 24th of March 1812. When the purchase money was paid to the said John Kaye

J. Kaye

Witness

Thos Trebeck, Vicar
Josh Blythman Atty at Law, Bawtrey.

BAPTISMS.

1725

Apr. 15 Eliz ye daughter of Abraham Beaumont
July 1 Jane ye daughter of Rich : Smith
Aug 29 Will. son of Will : Hall
Sept 23 Ann daughter to Will Thompson
Dec 9 John son to John Ford
16 Geo : son to John Campsal
21 Ann daughter to Tho : South
Jan 6 George son to Benjamin Hammond
Feb. 1 Hannah daughter to Daniel Twigg
5 Ann daughter Will. Hardware
19 George son to Abraham Horsefield
Mar 10 Mary daughter to John Trickit

1726

Mar 29 Thos son to Richd Jackson
31 Eliz daughter to Thomas Ostliffe
Apr 13 Jane daughter to Thomas Bingley
28 Mary daughter to Will Jackson
May 5 Sarah daughter to Gervas Carnaley
28 Ann daughter to John Wood
June 4 Godfrey son to Thomas Bintcliffe
27 Hannah daughter to Daniel Schorey
July 7 Ann daughter to John Carr
Aug 3 Mary daughter to John Trickit
29 John son to Richard Booth
Sept 18 Lydia and Susanna daughters to John Robinson
21 Thomas son to Henry Walker
22 Mary daughter to John Ammorey
Nov. 7 Mary daughter to Jonathan Bentley
Dec 15 Sarah daughter to Joshua Halmshaw and Susanna daughter to John Shepherd
26 John son to Benjamin Albright and Mary daughter to Thomas Elam
27 George son to Samuel Rodes and Richard son to Joseph Bingley
29 John son to John Twittey
Jan 1 Mary daughter to Thomas Dawer.
6 Benjamin son to Thomas Grey

1727

May 4 Ann daughter to John Denton
11 Robert son to John Ford
17 Thomas son to Joshua Roberts
23 Will : son to Will Hardware
June 6 Sarah daughter to Thomas Booth
10 Mary daughter to Richard Russel
July 20 Will : and Joseph sons to Mr Sanderson & Will : Son to John Dickson

1727		
Aug	5	Sarah daughter to Richard Smith
	12	Will : son to Richd Bingley
Sept	5	John son to Thomas Birkinshaw
	26	Sarah daughter to Will: Baxter and Eliz daughter to Richd Gawtrey
Oct	29	James son to John Campsal
	31	Ann daughter to Rich: Shaw
Nov	18	Will: son to Richd Dyson & Thomas son to John Elam
Dec	27	Sarah dau to Saml Carnaley
Jan	4	Margaret, daughter to John Trickit
	28	Robt son to Will: Hall
Feb	2	Rich^{d} son to Richd Jackson
	29	Sarah daughter to Joseph Tasker
Mar	17	Rich^{d} son to Thomas Daur
	21	Mathew son to Will: Jackson
1728		
Apr	4	Jane daughter to John Kennerley
	7	Tho son to Samuel Rodes
	23	Henry son to Will: Olley
May	29	Sarah daughter to Andrew Speight
June	16	Hannah daughter to Richard Heeler
	23	Margaret daughter to Rich: Allen
Aug	11	Joshua son to Benjamin Hammond
	15	Will son to Francis Hardey
	29	Ann daughter to Thomas Dodson
Sept	26	Samuel son to Daniel Twigg
	27	Rich^{d} son to Richd Stead
Feb	2	Eliz: daughter to Richd Ford
1729		
April	15	Joseph son to Joseph Roberts
May	15	Will son to Saml Carnaley & John son to John Wood.
	22	Thomas son to Will: Tingle
July	2	Eliz: daughter to Mr Burtwizell
	11	Thomas son to Thomas Bintcliffe
	13	Martha daughter to Widow Halmshaw (post mortem patris.)
	17	James son to Haman Hole
Aug	1	Mary daughter to John Robinson.
Sept	25	Will: son to Will Fisher
Oct	11	Sarah daughter to Will: Flint
Nov	15	Michael son to John Ford.
	28	Eliz: daughter to Tho: Hopkinson
Jan	20	Eliz: daughter to John Twittey
Feb.	6.	Thomas son to Richard Sharp
1730		
Mar	29	Richard son to Richard Trickitt
Apr	8	Gilbert son to John Hamerton

1730

May 19 Samuel son to Will[m] Hall
24 Mary daughter to Joshua Roberts
June 11 John son to Thomas Carr
26 Sarah Daught[r] to Abraham Horsefield
28 Thomas son to Richard Sharp
July 5 Elizabeth Daught[r] to W[m] Baxter
26 Thomas son to Thomas Elam
Aug 27 Godfrey son to Josias Hudson
Oct 13 Jonathan son to Jonathan Gawtress
20 Martha Daughter to John Kennerley
25 Elizabeth Daught[r] to George Chevins
Nov 3 Ann Daught[r] to Daniel Carnaley
5 Elizabeth Daughter to John Shepherd and Ann daught[r] to Richard Thompson
Dec 5 Martha Daught[r] to Jonathan Ibotson
22 Mary Daughter to William Fisher
Jan 8 William son to William Wolton
9 Sarah Daughter to Richard Ruswell
17 John son to Henry Walker and
Elizabeth Daughter to Will[m] Banks
Feb. 14 Samuel son to Samuel Carnaley
23 Mary Daughter to Daniel Twigg
Mar 11 George son to George Foulston and
John son to William Kennerley

1731

Apr 29 Rich[d] son to Rich : Bingley
May 6 Sarah daughter to Joseph Bingley
20 Hester daughter to Rich[d] Dyson
June 6 Thomas son to John Elam.
15 Thomas son to John Crossland
July 4 Eliz : daughter to Will : Rawson
9 Jane daughter to Tho Dodson
14 Mary daughter to Rich[d] Smith
Aug 8 Eliz daughter to Tho Smith
Sept 9 Eliz daughter to Henry Pullan.
23 Will son to Joseph Roberts
Oct 23 Mary daughter to James Wolton
Nov 2 George son to Will : Flint
Dec 13 Sarah daughter to Thomas Booth
Jan 1 Eliz daughter to Will : Jackson
6 Sarah daughter to Will Heald
Feb 24 Martha daughter to Joshua Roberts &
Will son to Will : Hall
Mar 5 Mary daughter to John Campsal
7 Sarah daughter to Joseph Tascar
9 Robert son to Will : Winter
12 Eliz daughter to John Robinson

1732

Apr. 10 Ann daughter to John Elam
May 14 Elizabeth daughter to Rich[d] Healey
June 6 Helen daughter to Francis Hardey
11 Samuel son to widow Stead post patrem patris & John son to John Turner & Ann daughter to Matthew Newsom
25 Mary daughter to John Ford
26 Jane daughter to Manwaring Arthur, of Doncaster, gentleman &
buried y[e] s[d] daughter to Mr Arthur y[e] 28th day
July 1 John son to John Adin
2 John son to Daniel Carnaley
23 Willoughby son to John Wood
30 George son to Will: Bell
Aug 12 Ann daughter to Tho[s] Fenton
30 Will son to Henry Pullan
Sept 9 Dorothy daughter to Rich[d] Bingley
14 Will: son to Jonathan Gawtress
15 Ann daughter to John Hargreve
17 Ann daughter to Tho: Hopkinson
Oct 5 Tho[s] son to George Foulston
Dec 17 Mary daughter to John Carr Jun[r]
26 Will son to Edward Fosterd
Jan 1 John son to Samuel Carnaley
11 Martha daughter to M[r] Wainman
Feb. 10 Ann daughter to Abraham Horsfield

1733

Mar 27 William son to Rich Hicks
May 3 Ann daughter to Jonn Trickit &
Sarah daughter to George Brammald
15 Joseph son to Joseph Slater &
John son to James Bower
27 Thomas son to Will: Kay
June 24 Ann daughter to Will Wolton
July 8 John son to John Iredal &
Sarah daughter to John Cut &
Grace daughter to Joseph Tasker
15 Elizabeth daughter to Thomas Dodson &
Olive daughter to Daniel Twigg &
Sarah daughter to Will Fisher
Sept 4 John son to John Shepherd &
Will son to Will: Heald jun[r]
13 John son to Edward Smith
23 Rebekah daughter to Will Shaw
Oct 6 John son to Thomas Wood
19 Susanna daughter to Tho Hopkinson
Nov 8 Martha daughter to John Elam

1733		
Nov	11	Sarah daughter to John Robinson
	23	Thomas son to John Twittey
	28	Martha daughter to John Campsal
Jan	1	George son to James Whitaker & Ann daughter to Richard Dyson & Thomas son to Richard Bingley
	3	Elizabeth daughter to Will Baxter
	31	Eliz : daughter to Richard Sharp
Feb	3	John son to Richard Ford
	19	John son to Joseph Roberts
Mar	21	Robert son to Henry Pullan
1734		
May	30	John son to Thomas Foulston Schoolmaster of Brampton
June	2	John son to Will: Watkin
	26	Joseph and Benjamin sons to John Crossland
July	11	Joshua son to Joshua Roberts
	23	Ann daughter to Jonathan Gawtrey
Aug	18	Sarah daughter to Richd Gorril
Sept	26	Ann daughter to Will: Hilton
Oct	1	Sarah daughter to John Kennerley
	17	Alice daughter to Rich: Russel
	22	Hannah daughter to Richd Gildin
	24	Michael son to Joshua Earnshaws
	28	Thomas son to George Kay
Nov	3	Sarah daughter to John Hargreavs
Dec	1	Ann daughter to Will Kemp
	13	Will son to John Morton
Jan	2	John son to Joseph Sadler
	16	Joseph son to Thomas Hopkinson
	19	Mary daughter to George Brammald
	30	Ann daughter to Ann Dodson, illegitimate
Feb	2	Martha daughter to Daniel Carnaley
	6	Joseph son to Joseph Bingley
	18	Will: son to Peter Law
Mar	6	Eliz: daughter to Henry Dyson
1735		
Mar	28	Mary daughter to Richard Birkes
Apr	6	John son to Richd Hicks & Ann daughter to Rich Booth
	13	Ann daughter to James Hartley
	20	Ann daughter to John Adin
May	8	Tho son to Saml Carnaley
June	26	Will & Ann son & daughter to John Jackson
July	6	Ann daughter to John Elam
	13	Tho son to John Trickit & Ann daughter to John Cut
	15	Martha daughter to Richard Bingley
	17	Sarah daughter to Will Winter
	20	Benjamin son to Mathew Law
	27	Will son to Will Kay
Aug	1	Ann daughter to Will Heald

1735		
Aug	28	Martha daughter to Thomas Dodson
Oct	12	Dorithy daughter to Will Iredal
Nov	12	John son to Thomas Everit
Dec	27	Thomas son to John Mallison
	28	Thomas son to John English
Jan	1	Ann daughter to Tho Bintcliffe
	8	Eliz daughter to Mathew Batterwood
Feb	3	Elizabeth daughter to John Ford
	4	John son to James Bower
	10	Francis son to Tho Hardey
Mar	6	Thomas son to Tho Oufield
	12	John son to Henry Pullan
1736.		
Mar	27	Will son to John Hussy
Apr	2	Sarah daughter to John Campsal
	4	Will son to Joshua Earnshaw
	27	Francis son to Edward Smith
May	18	Abraham son to Abraham Horsfield & Jonathan son to Thomas Townend
June	1	Martha daughter to Rich: Ford
	2	Hannah daughter to Rich. Tasker
	11?	Mary daughter to Will. Watkin
	18	Sarah daughter to John Fisher
Aug	3	John son to Richard Sharp
	22	John son to Ratcliffe Gorril & John son to Thomas Jenkinson
Sept		Nothing
Oct	5	Samuel Savile son to Will Wade of Swinton junr
	9	John son to Samuel Smith
	27	John son to Richard Gorril
Nov	13	Sarah daughter to Daniel Twigg
	30	Ann daughter to Joseph Roberts
Dec	7	Gervas Creasey son to Mr Gildin
	19	Thomas son to Richard Dyson
	23	Elizabeth daughter to Thomas Smith
	25	Elizabeth daughter to Thomas Dyson
Jan	13	Susanna daughter to Edward Fosterd
	27	Joanna daughter to Will Banks & Elizabeth daughter to John Birks
Feb	3	Will: son to Will: Hilton
	4	Paul son to John Ely
	9	Will son to Will Kemp of Swinton
1737		
Mar	27	Eliz: daughter to George Bell
May	8	~~Saml son to~~ John Crossland & Daniel son to Daniel Carnaley
	29	George son to Thomas Hopkinson
	5	Eliz daughter to Richard Hicks (*June crossed out*)

1737		
June	17	John son to Mr John Jackson
	19	Joseph son to Sam[l] Smith
	26	Mary daughter to Joseph Sadler
July	18	Tabitha daughter to Will[m] Mann
Sept	4	John son to John Cut
	19	Elizabeth daughter to Will : Heald
	25	Mary daughter to George Kay
Oct	5	Henry son to Henry Pullan
	23	Mary daughter to Will Iredal
Nov	12	Mathew son to Will Rawson
	23	Mary daughter to Mr Joseph Wainman
Dec	10	Eliz : daughter to Will Wharam
	16	Robert son to John Morton
	17	Mary daughter to Thomas Oufield
	26	Eliz daughter to Will Kay
	30	Joseph son to Mathew Butler
Jan	1	John son to James Hartley
	22	Sarah daughter to John English
	26	Isaac son to Will : Winter
	29	Mary daughter to Thomas Bintcliffe
Feb	7	George son to George Bramald
Mar	2	Robert son to Mr Richard Bingley
	12	Eliz : daughter to Abraham Horsefield
1738		
Apr	3	Alice daughter to Thomas Ledger
	11	John son of Thomas Pain a Quaker
	25	Ann daughter to Ratcliffe Govril
May	6	Sarah daughter to John Trickit
	25	Thomas son to Thomas Baxter
	29	Thomas son of Joshua Hernshaw
June	22	Ann daughter to Sam[l] Carnaley
	26	Eliz daughter to George Bell
July	2	Eliz daughter to Richard Russel
	9	Richard son to Thomas Worril
Aug	24	Jane daughter to Thomas Guest
Sept	25	James son to Joseph Roberts
	28	Thomas son to Edward Smith
Oct	20	Eliz. daughter to Will Wade jun[r]
Nov	7	Martha daughter to Richard Sharp
	12	Eliz : daughter to John Birks
	15	Richard son to Thomas Townend
	27	Ann daughter to James Bower
Dec	4	Abraham son to Stephen Yoyle
	26	Ann daughter to Will : Watkin
	28	Benjamin son to John Eylee
Jan	1	Will son to Will Kay
	6	Joseph son to Edward Lowley
	28	John son to Thomas Tyson

1738		
Feb	22	Rachel daughter to Richard Lambert
Mar	6	Sarah daughter to John Mallison
	12	Martha & Mary daughters to Will: Mann
1739		
Apr	8	Matthew son to Matthew Speight
	23	Joseph son to William Banks
	24	John son to Mary Beit?
	28	Martha Daughter to Joseph Monday
May	11	Will: son to John Kennerley
June	3?	Sarah Daughter to Joseph Wainman
	9	John son to John Smith
	10	Sarah Daughter to George Bell
	12	Richard son to Richard Wilson of Clay lane
July	1	Hannah Daughter to Daniel Carlington
Aug	5	Elizabeth Daughter to William Eastwood
	12	John son to Joseph Tasker of Newel
	16	Mary Daughter to Mr John Jackson
	26	Elizabeth Daughter to John Lyal of Melton
Sept	9	Margaret Daughter to Thos Smith of Rhodes
	16	George son to Joseph Sadler of Coley lane
	23	Martha Daughter to Tho Worrel
	26	William son to John Forge
Nov	18	Joseph son to Zechariah Frogget
Dec	19	Richard son to Richard Hicks of Swinton
Jan	4	John son to Matthew Butterworth of Newel
	20	Richard son to Richard Dyson
	26	Benj son to William Rowson of Swinton
	31	John son to William Heald
Feb	1	Ratcliff son to Ratcliff Gorril of Melton
	2	Sarah Daughter to Richard Tompson
	10	Sarah Daughter to Joshua Gill
	12	Mary Daughter to John Wood
	24	William son to Thomas Bintcliff of Newel
Mar	7	John son to John Morton
	16	Elizabeth Daughter to George Kay
	23	Sarah Daughter to William Iredal of Coley Lane
	24	Richard son to Richard Bingley.
1740		
Apr	3	John son to George Trout of Street
	4	Wm son to Wm Wharam of Wath
	8	Martha Daughter to Tho. Howfield of Hobberthy
	13	Tho. son to Samuel Smith of Hobberthy
May	6	Robert son to Abel Hyde, Clark of Wath
	22	Wm son to Tho Baxter of Wath
	27	Joseph son to Samuel Carnley of Melton
June	15	Elizabeth Daughter to Johua Earnshaw of Wath
	15	Abraham son to James Hartley of Wath
	22	Wm son to Edward Smith of Wath

1740		
June	24	James son to Henry Pullen of Wath
	24	Ann Daughter to Henry Pullen of Wath
July	6	Sarah Daughter to James Whitaker of Melton
Aug	20	Tho : son to Tho. Worril of Wath
Sept	21	Sarah Daughter to John English of Wath
Oct	30	Tho : Son to Joshua Hilton of Wath
Nov	27	Sarah Daughter to John Kay of Wath
Dec	10	W^{m} son to Jonathan Darwin of Swinton
Feb	1	John son to Richard Bingley of Wath
Mar	8	W^{m} son to Richard Booth of Melton
	11	Tho. son to Joseph Roberts of Hoober
	15	John son to Wm Jackson of Swinton
Nov	16	Omitted by neglect Thos son of Thomas Kemp
1741		
Mar	31	Thomas son of Richard Sharp
Apr	5	Ann Daughter to George Bell
	12	Elizabeth Daughter of Joseph Booth
	26	Elizabeth Daughter of John Wood
May	3	Mary Daughter of William Fisher
	10	Thomas son of Thomas Everard
	17	Betty Daughter of William Kay
	29	Mary Daughter of Robert Stead
July	12	Ralph son of Thomas Sedgwick
Sept	24	William son of Thomas Townend
Oct	10	William son of William Eastwood
	12	Ruth & Olive daughters of George Trout
	13	Robert son of John Jackson
Nov	14	John son of John Lyell
Dec	1	Thomas son of Thomas Sharp
	20	Thomas son of Thomas Tyson
	26	William son of Abraham Horsfield
	29	Mary Daughter of Abel Hyde
Jan	26	Mary daughter of William Pearson and
		Mary Daughter of Thomas Howworth
Jan	28	Alice Daughter of Henry Pullen
Feb	17	Betty Daughter of Edward Bool
	21	Ann daughter of Edward Smyth and
		John son of John Darton a Stranger
	28	Edward son of Edward Peace
Mar	2	Samuel son of Richard Thompson
1742		
Apr	2	Joseph Son of Daniel Twigg
	4	Joseph Son of Joshua Gill
	25	Amos Son of Joseph Roebuck
May	4	Joseph Son of William Rawson
	27	John Son of Richard Bingley
June	13	Jane Daughter of Joseph Hill
July	11	John Son of Jervice Kernley

1742

Aug 22 Ann Daughter of John Forge
26 William son of John Tricket
28 Jonathan Son of Richard Sharp
31 Elizabeth Daughter of Robert Hudson
Sep 18 Jonathan Son of John Marcroft
19 Matthew Son of Matthew Butterworth
23 Ann Daughter of John Smith.
John Son of Joseph Robinson &
Mary Daughter of Joshua Hilton
24 Robert Son of Robert Steads
Oct 3 Thomas Son of Thomas Bincliff
24 Ann Daughter of William Hyerdle
31 Edward Son of Edward Fosterd
Nov 5 Mary Daughter of Zechariah Frogget
Charles Son of Mary Twittey
30 William son of John Crosland
Dec 7 Ann Daughter of John Kenneley
Jan 23 Robert Son of William Kemp
31 John son of Joshua Hernshaw
Feb 2 William Son of William Fisher
6 John Son of William Eastwood
27 William Son of George Bell
Mar 6 Nancy Daughter of Thomas Smyth
12 Tommy Son of Thomas Owfield
13 Sarah Daughter of John Ely
16 Abel Son of Abel Hyde
20 Jane Daughter of Richard Bellamy

1743

Apr 1 Henry Son of William Heald
5 Joseph Son of John Cutts
May 21 Betty Daughter to George Swift
27 Ann Daughter of Thomas Inman
June 26 John Son of William Kay of Rhodes
July 31 Martha Daughter of John English
Aug 11 Mary Daughter of Thomas Kay.
Sept 18 Edward Son of Edward Bool
22 Joseph Son of Susanna Wheedling
23 Martha Daughter of Thomas Day of Kilnhurst
Oct 18 Richard Son of John Jackson
Nov 8 Ann Daughter of George Kay
13 Sarah Daughter of John Wood
14 Thomas Son of Matthew Law
20 Joshua Son of Thomas Worrill
Dec 8 Hanna Daughter of John Wingfield
26 Sarah Daughter of Joseph Sadler
28 Edward son of George Brammald
Jan 2 John Son of John Shertcliff
3 George Saville Son of William Wade

1743		
	5	John Son of Thomas Baxter
Feb.	7	Sarah Daughter of John Lyell
Mar.	8	John Son of Robt Woodall
1744		
Mar	30	Dorothy & Ann twin Daughters of Joshua Hilton of Wath
Apr	26	Sarah Daughter of Richard Bingley of Wath
	29	Elizabeth Daughter of Ratcliff Gorrel of West Melton
May	15	Richard son of Richard Thompson of Wath
	27	Jervase Son of Jervase Kernley of West Melton and William Son of Richard Wright
	28	William Son of Joseph Hill of Swinton
June	1	Mary Daughter of George Gawtrees of Wath
	6	Betty Daughter of Thomas Hammond of Brampton
	14	John Son of William Pullen of Swinton
	17	John Son of Elizabeth Whittles of Wath Illegitimate
Aug	9	Mary Daughter of Samuel Kernley of West Melton.
	12	Joseph Son of Edward Peace ofWath
	24	John Son of Joshua Matthewman of Wolsey Croft
	26	Henry Son of Joshua Wood of Melton Green and John Son of Matthew Speight and Ann Daughter of John Mallison of West Melton
Sept	23	Thomas Son of Henry Pullen of Wath
	27	Ann Daughter of Joshua Gill of Wath and Elizabeth Daughter of John Kay of Wath, Tanner
Oct	4	George son of Joseph Monday
	11	Betty Daughter of George Trout of Street
	25	Mary Daughter of Henry Wood of Hoober
	27	William Son of Nelly Bower widow, Illegitimate
Nov	4	Mary Daughter of Samuel Foulstone of West Melton, Taylor
	8	Francis Son of John Lutterel, Gardener to the Earl of Malton
	17	William Son of Thomas Worral of Wath
	25	John Son of Zeckariah Frogget of Wolsey Croft
Dec	2	John Son of Thomas Bintcliff of Coley Lane
	26	Ann Daughter of William Fisher of West Melton
	27	Mary Daughter of William Wilson of Newhill
Jan	11	Mary Daughter of Matthew Butterworth of Newhill
	20	William Son of Thomas Tyson of Swinton Common, Collier
Feb	4	George Son of George Bell of Wath
	10	Elizabeth Daughter of John Smith of Wath
	14	Alice Daughter of Joseph Sadler of Coley Lane
	16	Sarah Daughter of William Bingham late Coachman to Mr Ward of Hooton Pannel
Mar	2	Jane Daughter of Richard Lambert of Linfit
	8	Hannah Daughter of Joseph Gilliat of Melton Green
	10	George son of Joseph Robinson of Wath, Blacksmith
	11	Alice Daughter of Edward Bool of Wath

1744

20 William Son of George Brammeld of Swinton

John Empson Cur[te] of Wath
Tho Kay } Church Wardens
Robert Hudson }

1745
Mar 31 Thomas Son of Thomas Colburn of Kilnhurst
Apr 15 Hannah Daughter of William Jennet of Hoober, Blacksmith
And Mary Daughter of William Eastwood of Wath, Labourer
May 1 Ann Daughter of William Cusworth of Wath
11 Hannah Daughter of Thomas Howfield of Hoober
19 William Son of William Iredle of Coley Lane
24 Mary Daughter of William Heald of Abdy
26 Richard Son of Joseph Shaw of Swinton
June 6 John Son of Thomas Adin of Swinton
13 Thomas Son of Robert Hudson of Wath
July 4 Elizabeth Daughter of Thomas Kay of Wath
14 Robert Son of Edward Smith of Wath
And Ruth Daughter of William Kay of Rhodes
Aug 3 James son of Thomas Inman of West Melton
15 Mary Daughter of Robert Woodall of Swinton
Sept 23 Mary Daughter of Joshua Grey of Rainbrough
29 William Son of John Smith of Hoober
Oct 6 Martha daughter of Jonathan Darwent of Swinton
13 Ann Daughter of Stephen Alender of Swinton
16 John Son of Abel Hyde of Wath
And Thomas Son of John Lyell of West Melton
20 Elizabeth Daughter of William Pullen of Swinton
And Ann Daughter of Joseph Hill of Swinton
Nov 7 Jeremiah Son of Jeremiah Lightowler of Newhill
13 Mary Daughter of John Lydster of West Malton
15 John Son of Jonathan Gaskin of Coley Lane
Dec 15 Ann Daughter of Isaac Tomlinson of Hoober
Jan 5 Ann Daughter of Samuel Smith of Newhill
6 Edward Son of Richard Sharp of Wath
And Ann Daughter of John Kay of Wath, Tanner
15 Elizabeth Daughter of John Hall late of Hoober
Feb 21 Mary Daughter of Richard Revel of Wath
28 Sarah Daughter of Joshua Hilton of Wath
Mar 7 Martha Daughter of Thomas Smith of Rhodes

John Empson Curate of Wath

1746
Mar 29 Martha Daughter of John Cutt of Newhill
Apr 6 Abraham Son of John Wood Junior of Wath Barkchopper
16 Mary Daughter of Richard Becket of Swinton Wharf

1746

Apr 20 Elizabeth Daughter of John Tricket of West Melton
& Ann Daughter of Thomas Worral of Wath
27 John Son of John English of Wath
May 4 Mary Daughter of John Ely of Newhill
11 Robert Son of John Marcroft of Swinton
18 Ann Daughter of Henry Pullen of Wath
& Ann daughter of Henry Slater of Newhill
27 William Son of George Gawtrees of Wath
June 1 Mark Son of Edward Hill of Wath
5 John Son of John Pepper of Coley Lane
At the same time received into the Church Sarah Daughter of Joseph Charlesworth of Moorhouse in the parish of Hutton Pannel who had been baptized in private by the Minister of Hutton Pannel before her removal hither
17 Benjamin Son of Jervase Carnaley Junr of West Melton
22 Sarah Daughter of Thomas Hammond of Brampton
July 20 George Son of Edward Fosterd of Swinton
Aug 24 John Son of Luke Worral of West Melton
29 John Son of Richard Foulstone Junr of Brampton &
Hellen Daughter of George Trout of Street
Oct 3 Ann Daughter of Martha Butterworth of Newhill
17 Sarah Daughter of Thomas Kay of Wath
18 Martha Daughter of John Babb of Swinton
Dec 4 Jane Daughter of Joseph Sadler of Coley Lane
12 William Son of William Hargreaves of Swinton
28 Stephen Son of the late Stephen Alendar of Swinton
Jan 6 Thomas Son of Joshua Gill of Wath
23 Mary Daughter of Richard Bingley of Wath
25 John Son of Mary Rhodes of Swinton Illegitimate
Feb 12 Charles Son of Henry Wood of Hoober
Mar 1 William Son of William Hartley of Swinton
8 Ann Daughter of Edward Bull of Wath

John Empson Curate of Wath
Jonathan Twittey } Church Wardens
William Baxter }

1747

Mar 31 Richard Son of Robert Stead of Wath, Mason
Apr 8 Sarah Daughter of Joseph Hudson of Newhill
16 William Son of Samuel Smith of Newhill, Labourer
May 7 James Son of John Lutterel, Gardiner
9 George Son of William Cusworth of Wath &
8 Jonathan son of William Fisher of West Melton
11 George Son of Abel Hyde of Wath, Parish Clerk.
June 14 John Son of James Hartley of Wath, Labourer &
William Son of John Lydster of West Melton
June 17 Sarah Daughter of Robert Woodall of Swinton
21 John Son of Samuel Foulstone of Melton Green

1747

July 5 Henry Son of Henry Slater of Newhill, Collier
19 John a child found in the Fields
27 Martha Daughter of John Smith of Wath, Joyner
Aug 6 William son of Thomas Lonkeshire of West Melton
11 Godfrey Son of Thomas Bintcliff of Coley Lane
14 Mary Daughter of Joseph Robinson of Wath, Blacksmith
28 Mary Daughter of John Lyell of West Melton.
Sept 13 Ann Daughter of Joseph Gilliot of Melton Green
18 Robert son of Robert Hudson of Wath
29 Jane Daughter of Thomas Inman of West Melton, Blacksmith
Oct 18 Ann daughter of Joseph Roebuck of West Melton
29 Richard Son of Richard Sharp of Wath
Nov 6 Joshua Son of Joshua Matthewman of Rhodes
& Sarah Daughter of George Dyson of Wath
Dec 10 Anne Daughter of Joshua Grey of Rainborough
26 George Son of George Trout of Streat
& Sarah Daughter of William Heald of Abdy
Jan 1 Thomas son of Richard Foulstone Junior of Brampton
2 Sarah Daughter of Joseph Monday of Brampton
15 William Son of Richard Lambert of Linfit
21 Ann Daughter of Wilham Pullen of Swinton
30 John Son to Joshua Hilton of Wath
Feb 2 Martha Daughter of John Kay of Wath, Tanner
7 Martha Daughter of John Wood Junr of Wath, Bark chopper
11 Elizabeth Daughter of Henry Wood of Hoober, Mason
& Richard Son of Thomas Oldfield of Hoober Labourer
23 Ann Daughter of William Wharam Wath, Labourer
Mar 9 Thomas Son of Richard Beckit of Swinton Wharf
& Joseph Son of Joseph Hill of Swinton
11 Thomas Son of Thomas Worril of Wath, Taylor

N.B.—We are informed that some children belonging to Wath Parish were baptized the year above written at Swinton Chappel whose names have not been transmitted to us April 16. 1748

John Empson Curate of Wath
William Ibotson } Church Wardens
Timothy Rhodes }

1748

Mar 27 William son of John Denton Junr of Wath, Malster
& Francis Son of George Brammald of Swinton, Blacksmith
Apr 1 Joseph son of Luke Worrall of West Melton, Wheelwright
11 Mary Daughter of Joseph Haigh of Newhill, Labourer
& Ann Daughter of William Eastwood of Wath, Labourer
May 1 William Son of William Arundel, Wheelwright, of Hoober at present, but whose usual abode is at Thorn
19 William Son of William Rogers of Brampton, Blacksmith

1748

June	24	John Son of Jonathan Gaskin of Coley Lane, Farmer
Aug	28	Joseph Son of Joseph Sadler of Coley Lane
		& James son of William Iredle of Coley Lane Labourer
Sept	11	Ann Daughter of John Shaw of Swinton, weaver baptized at Swinton Chapel
	19	Received into the Church John Son of Richard Gildon of Thriberg after he had been baptized in private at Thriberg
	22	Elizabeth Daughter of John Shirtcliff of Wath, Shopkeeper
	23	Sarah, Daughter of Richard Revel of Wath, Farmer
	27	Ann, Daughter of Timothy Swift of Wath, Labourer.
Oct	6	Joseph Son of Thomas Hammond of Brampton, Farmer
	13	William Son of John Robinson of West Melton, Skinner
Nov	15	Sarah Daughter of Thomas Bintcliff of Coley Lane, Labourer
	17	Mary daughter of Jervase Carnaley Junr of West Melton, Weaver
	20	John son of John English of Wath, Labourer
Dec	27	Katy Daughter of Thomas Smith of Roydes, Farmer
	31	Benjamin Son of Edward Bool of Wath, Mason
Jan	5	Mary Daughter of Richard Dodson of Wath, Hatter
	7	Ann Daughter of George Hoyle of Wath, Taylor
	12	George Son of Mr Benjamin Broadhead of Wath, Apothecary
		& Jonathan Son of Samuel Carnaley of West Melton
	26	Richard Son of George Gawtrees of Wath, Malster
Feb	7	Martha Daughter of Abel Hyde Parish Clerk
		& Campsal (illegitimate) son of Ellen Bower of Wath
	17	Joshua Son of Joshua Gill of Wath, Mason
	26	Sarah Daughter of John Lewis of Roydes, Labourer
Mar	1	Martha Daughter of George Dyson of Wath Taylor
	10	Hannah Daughter of James Beaumont of the Schoolhouse Labourer
	17	Ann Daughter of Thomas Kay of Wath Farmer and Malster

John Empson Curate
John Denton Junr } Church
Joseph Roberts } Wardens

1749

Mar	27	Godfrey Son of Matthew Speight of Swinton
Apr	13	Betty Daughter of John Wright of Wath, Hatter
	25	Mary Daughter of John Mallinson of Melton, Weaver
May	4	Richard Son of John Russel of Melton, Taylor
	24	Richard Son of Robert Parker of Seacroft in the parish of Whitchurch near Leeds, Collier
	28	John Son of Richard Thompson of Wath, Shoemaker
June	6	Richard Son of Henry Slater of Newhill, Collier

1749

July 6 William Son of John Pepper of Coley Lane, Farmer
8 William Son of John Lydster of Melton, Cobler
Aug 1 Richard Son of Robert Woodall of Swinton
6 John Son of John Baumforth of Hoober, Labourer
8 William Son of William Watkin of Melton, Labourer
Aug 15 Joseph Son of William Fisher of Melton, Labourer
26 Mary Daughter of Major Munton of Newhill, Joiner
Sept 24 Thomas Son of John Parkin, Cook to a Gentleman in London
Oct 5 Mary daughter of Edward Smith of Wath, Butcher
8 Sarah Daughter of William Harrison of Wath, Labourer
Nov 2 Francis Son of George Brammald of Swinton, Blacksmith
4 Ann Daughter of Richard Foulstone Junior of Brampton
5 Elizabeth Daughter of Joseph Hudson of Newhill, Flax Dresser
20 Mary Daughter of Edward Fenton of Wath, Shoemaker
30 Sarah Daughter of Joseph Robinson of Wath, Blacksmith
Dec 26 Betty Daughter of Joseph Monday of Brampton
Jan 6 Hannah Daughter of John Smith of Wath, Joiner
& Mary Daughter of William Cusworth of Wath, Flax Dresser
8 John Son of Timothy Swift of Wath, Labourer
21 Sarah Daughter of Robert Hudson of Wath, Farmer
Feb 6 Mary Daughter of George Trout of Street
25 William Son of Luke Worrall of Melton, Carpenter
28 Sarah Daughter of William Eastwood of Wath, Labourer
Mar 2 Ann Daughter of John Denton Junior of Wath
23 Olive Daughter of Richard Lambert of Linfit

John Empson Curate
John Denton } Church
Joseph Roberts } Wardens

1750

Mar 27 Samuel Son of Samuel Foulstone of Melton
Apr 16 William Son of John Shaw of Swinton, Weaver
May 3 Ann Daughter of John Lyell of Melton, Farmer
13 Esther Daughter of Joseph Hill of Swinton, Labourer
24 Edward Son of Benjamin Thicket of Wath, Hatter
& Thomas Son of Thomas Lonkeshire of Melton, Weaver
June 5 Richard Son of Richard Becket of Swinton, Wharf
6 Martha Daughter of Richard Revel of Wath, Farmer
10 Mark Son of Henry Pullen of Wath, Joiner
11 Sarah Daughter of William Pullen of Swinton, Farmer
18 Sarah Daughter of William Hartley of Swinton, School master
July 25 Sarah Daughter of Richard Dodson of Wath, Hatter
Aug 4 Rosamond Daughter of Thomas Owfield of Hoober, Labourer

1750		
Sept	23	John Son of Thomas Dobson of Roydes.
		& Elizabeth Daughter of Henry Slater of Newhill, Collier
	27	William Son of Joshua Hilton of Wath, Carpenter
	28	Mary Daughter of John Wright of Wath, Hatter
	30	George Son of Thomas Worral of Wath, Taylor
Oct	2	Ann Daughter of Joseph Sadler of Coley Lane
	7	Anne Daughter of William Trippet of Swinton, Labourer
Nov	12	Sarah Daughter of John Swinden of Swinton
Dec	14	Elizabeth Daughter of John Howard of Swinton, Farmer
	16	Jane Daughter of Abel Hyde of Wath, Parish Clerk
Dec	25	Elizabeth Daughter of Thomas Dyson of Swinton Common
Jan	1	Mary Daughter of John Kay of Wath, Tanner
	3	Ann Daughter of George Foulstone of Brampton
	6	Richard Son of Francis Tricket of Wath, Blacksmith
Feb	19	Ann Daughter of Thomas Campsal of Wath, Labourer
		& Mary Daughter of Jervase Lyell of Melton
	22	George Son of George Dyson of Wath
Mar	8	Martha Daughter of Joshua Grey of Rainbro', Farmer
	15	Elizabeth Daughter of Thomas Silcock of Wath, Flax-dresser
	20	Ann Daughter of Richard Glasby of Denaby, Farmer
		John Empson, Curate,
1751		
Apr	8	Ann Daughter of Gervas Carnally of Melton
	8	Elizabeth Daughter to William Dyson
	8	William Son of Jonathan Gaskin
	12	Ruth Daughter of William Bisby
May	5	Ellen Daughter of John Lidster
	9	Ann Daughter of Thomas Hammond
July	7	Joseph Son of Joshua Hampshire of Royds
Aug	2	Elizabeth Daughter of George Gawtry of Wath
	8	Elizabeth Daughter of John Pepper of Coley Lane
	10	Elizabeth Daughter of Joseph Robinson of Wath
	11	Thomas Son of John Lewis of Simondwood gate
	11	Thomas Son of Michael Bisby of Woolsey croft
	15	Hannah Daughter of Robert Woodhall
Sep	22	Mary Daughter of Joshua Gill of Wath, Mason
	26	Mary Daughter of William Wharum, Labourer
	26	James Son of Henry Slater of Newhill, Collier
	29	Mary Daughter of John Balmfirth of Hoober, Labourer
Oct	27	Hannah Daughter of George Bell of Wath, Carpenter
Nov	10	Ann daughter of William Harrison of Wath, Labourer
	11	Philip Son of Philip Hepstone of Swinton, Labourer
	14	Sarah Daughter of John Matthewman, Farmer
	23	Richard Son of Henry Pullen jun^r^
Dec	26	John Son of John Denton of Wath
	27	Elizabeth Daughter of Mr Benj Broadhead of Wath

1751		
Dec	29	John Son of John Shaw of Swinton, Weaver
Jan	6	Thomas Son of Timothy Swift, Labourer
	18	Elizabeth Daughter of John Hewitt, Labourer
	30	Ann Daughter of John Wright, Hatter.
Mar	4	. . . Son of Edward Birks, Collier
	13	Joseph Son of Joseph Crowder of Melton, Labourer
	15	Thomas Son of Thomas Jackson, Collier
	15	Ann Daughter of John Woodcock, Labourer
	24	Benjamin Son of William Fisher, Labourer
	1.	Will Son to Francis Yates
1752		
Mar	30	William Son of John Smith, Joyner
	,,	Hannah Daughter of Luke Woonl, Carpenter
	,,	Mary Daughter of Thomas Lonkishire, Weaver
May	17	Richard Son of Thomas Bincliff, Labourer
	,,	Joseph Son of Joseph Hudson, Lime-dresser
	,,	Mary Daughter of Thomas Campsall, Labourer
	28	Margaret Daughter of John Heward of Swinton
	29	Sarah Daughter of Samuel Baddely, Skinner
		Mary Daughter of John Law of Kilnhirst & Elizabeth Law
June	7	Joseph Son of Joseph Roebuck, Labourer
		Charles Son of William Eastwood
		Elizabeth Daughter of Richard Thompson of Swinton
July	5	John Son of William Hyerdale, Labourer
	30	Elizabeth Daughter of Joseph Sadler of Coley Lane
Oct	5	Thomas Son of Martha Kenerly
	15	Martha Daughter of Richard Becket
	27	John Son of John Russel of Melton, Taylor
Nov.	24	William Son of Hannah Twigg. 2 Alice daughter of Will: Pullen of Swinton (*inserted*)
Dec	3	Hannah Daughter of Elizabeth Tallow-pot
	15	Ann Daughter of George Gawtrey
	26	Henrietta Daughter of Henry Wood, Mason
Jan	17	Elizabeth Daughter of John Crossland, Skinner
1753		
Mar	6	Ann Daughter of William Bisby, Shoemaker
	9	George Son of Richard Lambert, Farmer
	10	William Son of William Scorah, Farmer
	16	John Son of Francis Tricket, Blacksmith
	18	Joseph Son of John Hampshire, Labourer
	23	John Son of Michael Ford, Mason
	25	Robert Son of Henry Slater, Collier
1753		
Apr	5	Martha Daughter to John Lyall, Farmer
	8	Mary Daughter to Thomas Worril, Taylor
		Abel Son to Abel Hyde, Parish Clark
	23	Hannah Daughter to John Campsall, Labourer
May	11	Richard Son to Richard Foolstone, Farmer

1753		
May	28	Joseph Son to George Parkin
	29	John Son to John Wright, Hatter
June	13	Rhoda Daughter to William Green
	16	Edward Son to Robert Stead, Mason
	28	Ellen Daughter to Thomas Kay, Farmer
July	7	Joseph Son to Joseph Munday Labourer
	29	Sarah Daughter to Edward Johnson
Aug	12	William Son to Joseph Robinson, Blacksmith
	30	John Son to George Dyson, Taylor
Sept	6	Thomas Son to Gervas Carnalley, Weaver
	9	William Son to William Hammond, Breeches-maker
	28	William Son to John Ward, Hoober, Malster
	30	John Son to John Woodcock, Newhill, Labourer
Oct	4	Ann Daughter to Thomas Silcock, Line-dresser
	5	Elizabeth Daughter to Joshua Hilton, Carpenter
	28	Ann Daughter to Abraham Ely, Labourer
		Matthew Son to Thomas Dyson, Collier
Nov	10	Benjamin Son to Thomas Hammond, Farmer
Dec	6	John Son to Joshua Hampshire, Labourer
	9	Joseph Son to John Shaw, Swinton, Weaver
	20	Elizabeth Daughter to John Denton, Malster
1754		
Jan	1	Joanna Daughter to William Cusworth Line-dresser
	6	William Son of John Lewis, Collier
	11	William Son of William Stead, Taylor
	20	Sarah Daughter of William Parkin, Hatter
Feb	8	William Son of Joseph Campsall, Labourer
	9	William Son of Thomas Oldfield, Nailor
	24	John Son of George Bell, Carpenter
Mar	2	John Son of Joseph Crowder, Labourer
	3	Mary Daughter of Timothy Swift, Labourer
	8	Mary Daughter of John Pepper, Farmer
	26	James Son of James Beaumont, Labourer
	31	Mary Daughter of William Trippit
Apr	5	Mary Daughter of Joseph Kenshaw, Labourer
		Mary Daughter of Henry Slater, Collier
	16	Thomas Son of Gervase Lyall, Labourer
May	5	Samuel Son of Samuel Badely
	16	William Son of Elizabeth Mollard
	23	Elizabeth Daughter of Richd Wildsmith, Sadler
June	2	Ann Daughter of Abraham Turton, Hatter
	16	Ann Daughter of Joshua Matthewman
	30	Elizabeth Daughter of Thomas Jackson, Collier
July	7	Thomas Son of William Dyson, Mason
	28	Mary Daughter of Samuel Brown
Aug	1	Thomas Son of William Eastwood
		Ann Daughter of Thomas Campsall
S^br^	3	John Son of George Asque

1754		
	3	Catherine Daughter of Joseph Hudson
	4	George Son of Joshua Gill
	20	Joseph Son of John Balmfirth
	do	John Son of Thomas Mann
Nov	3	Michael Son of Elizabeth Wright
	17	John Son of Benjamin Spencer
	20	William Son of William Green
	24	John Son of William Schorah
	28	William Son of William Pullan
Dec	1	George Son of William Wharam
	3	Nancy Daughter of Henry Beet
	26	Mary Daughter of John Heward
	27	William Son of John Wright
1755		
Jan	1	William Son of Michael Ford
	4	Timothy Son of Martha Beardshall
	6	John Son of Richard Becket
	12	Richard Son of Thomas Bincliff
	do	William Son of George Dyson
	19	Mary Daughter of Hannah Tingle
	26	Elizabeth Daughter of Thomas Lonkishire
Feb	4	John Son of John Crosland
	11	Elizabeth Daughter of Abel Hyde
	16	Stephen Son of Benjamin Senior
Mar	1	William Son of John Parkin
	6	Ann Daughter of William Wade
	25	Lydia Daughter of Ann Hartley
	31	George Son of Richard Laycock
Apr	25	Jane Daughter of Joshua Holmshaw
May	4	Rachel Daughter of William Bisby
	13	Elizabeth Daughter of William Gray
June	1	John Son of John Holmshaw
	27	Samuel Son of Mary Clark
July	19	Elizabeth Daughter of William Fisher
Aug	16	John Son of William Stead
	28	Sarah Daughter of Richard Fowlstone
Sept	21	Thomas Son of William Hyerdale
Oct	6	Luke Son of Henry Wood
	10	Sarah Daughter of James Beaumont
	11	Sarah Daughter of Richard Wildsmith
Dec	7	Grace Daughter of Henry Slater
	25	Jonathan Son of Jonathan Charlesworth
1756.		
Jan	18	William Son of Michael Bisby
	29	Sarah Daughter of Thomas Briggs
Feb	1	Richard Son of William Tingle
	2	Mary Daughter of John Shaw.
	do	Samuel Son of Gervas Carnally

1756		
Feb	19	Philip Son of Philip Flint
Mar	2	Jonathan Son of Thomas Silcock
	9	George Son of George Gawtres
Mar	28	Thomas Son of Joseph Robinson
Apr	9	William Son of Joshua Gray
	18	John Son of Thomas Padmore
	19	Abraham Son of Abraham Ely, Labourer
	20	William Son of William Dyson
May	25	Mary Daughter of Robert Hudson
June	6	Isaac Son of William Hammond
	do	George Son of Samuel Foulstone
	8	Betty Daughter of John Campsall
	20	John Son of John Mallison
	do	John Son of John Lewis
	25	Elizabeth Daughter of George Asque
	27	George Son of William Hicks
July	9	Thomas Son of John Pepper
	15	Mary Daughter of Francis Tricket
	18	Margaret Daughter of John Woodcock
	25	Sarah Daughter of Giles Batteson
Aug	4	Sarah Daughter of John Bell
	8	Elizabeth Daughter of Abraham Turton
	12	Ann Daughter of Thomas Carr
	29	William Son of William Harrison
Sept	1	Joseph Son of Gervas Lyell
	5	Susan Daughter of William Tingle
	19	Peggy Daughter of John Woodcock
	30	Richd Son of Joseph Crowder
	do	Sarah Daughter of Thomas Jackson
Oct		Thomas Son of John Wright
Nov	14	Thomas Son of Samuel Badeley
	25	Martha Daughter of John Denton
	26	Sarah Daughter of William Wood
Dec	21	Mary Daughter of Thomas Hartley
1757		
Jan	4	John Son of Joseph Bentley
	17	Ann Daughter of Michael Forde
	28	William Son of John Swinden of Swinton
Feb	20	Thomas Son of William Bingley
	22	Joseph Son of William Cusworth
	6	John Son of Isaac Tomlinson
	21	William Son of William Wade
Mar	27	Ann Daughter of John Heward
May	5	Richard Son of Richard Wildsmith
	15	Sarah Daughter of Thomas Lonkey
	18	Mary Daughter of John Crossley
June	5	George Son of George Asque
	26	William Son of William Trippit

1757		
July	31	Mary Daughter of William Lun
Aug	27	Abigail Daughter of Abel Hyde
Oct	6	Willoughby Son of William Stead
	7	Sarah Daughter of Richard Laycock
	17	Mary Daughter of George Dyson
Nov	6	John Son of William Dyson.
Dec	25	Fanny Daughter of George Bell
	26	Sarah Daughter of John Wade
	27	Mary Daughter of Joshua Holmshaw
1758		
Jan.	15	John Son of Joseph Roebuck
Feb.	20	Ann Daughter of John Shaw
Mar	17	Martha Daughter of Benjamin Senior
Apr	6	William Son of Robert Hudson
	23	Sarah Daughter of William Malpas
May	3	Sarah Daughter of Henry Wood
	7	Margaret Daughter of John Walker
	7	Mary Daughter of William Bisby
	11	Mary Daughter of William Pulleyn
	15	John Son of Abraham Ely
	17	Johathan Son of John Twittey
	20	Thomas Son of Joshua Padmore
	28	John Son of John Kay, Tanner
June	11	Mary the Daughter of Joseph Bentley
	30	Susanna Daughter of Thomas Tyson
July	23	Thomas Son of Thomas Silcock
Aug	20	John Son of John Button
Sept	5	Joseph Son of Joseph Robinson
	5	Thomas Finch Son of Elizabeth Thompson
Oct	21	John Son of John Betts
Nov	12	Elizabeth Daughter of John Wright
	19	Joseph Son of Joseph Kitson
	23	Ann Daughter of Thomas Briggs
Dec	3	George Son of Joseph Campsall
	27	Jonathan Son of William Wade
	30	Mary Daughter of Richard Lambert
1759		
Jan	1	James Son of John Hampshire
	7	Mary Daughter of John Woodcock
	25	Mary Daughter of Major Monton
	28	William Son of John Hewit
	28	Ann Daughter of William Hammond
Feb	3	John Son of Thomas Jackson, Collier
	22	John Son of Henry Otley
Mar	1	Sarah Daughter of John Pepper
	3	Richard Son of William Hyerdale
	3	Betty Daughter of Samuel Crowder
	8	Thomas Son of John Denton

1759		
Mar	15	Elizabeth Daughter of Edward Radcliff
	22	Richard Son of John Crosley
	25	Ann Daughter of John Lewis.
Apr	8	George Son to Timothy Swift
	16	John Son of John Smith
	17	Mary Daughter of George Moor
	17	John Son of John Cudworth
	24	Elizabeth Daughter of William Lun
	29	Joseph Son of John Blake
May	6	James Son of James Hartley
	6	Abraham Son of Abraham Turton
	20	Sarah Daughter of Joseph Bingley
June	3	Thomas Son of Michael Ford
	3	Mary Daughter of William Tingle
	16	Thomas Son of Thomas Carr
July	1	Thomas Son of William Gillot
	15	Sarah Daughter of George Asque
	22	Ann Daughter of Francis Garlick
	29	Benjamin and Susanna Son and Daughter of Susanna Widdup
Aug	3	John Son of William Trippit
Sept	2	George Son of John Warin
	29	John Son of Thomas Lonkey
	29	Thomas Son of John Russel
	30	George Son of Henry Slater
	30	Hannah Daughter of Thos Dyson
Oct	4	John Son of Thomas Powles
	4	John Son of Robert Bailey
Nov	25	Margaret Daughter of Thomas Silcock
	25	Ann Daughter of Mary Hall
1760.		
Jan	8	Sarah Daughter of Francis Tricket.
	12	Thomas Son of Richard Wilson.
Feb	2	George Son of William Harrison
	3	Mary Daughter of James Woodcock
	16	Mary Daughter of Thomas Malpas
	26	Sarah Daughter of George Gawtrees
Mar	2	Thomas Son of Matthew Maslin
	5	John Son of Thomas Watson, Swinton
	7	Dorothy Daughter of Joshua Grey
	9	Elizabeth Daughter of William Bizby
	18	Elizabeth Daughter of John Smith, Butcher
Apr	10	William Son of John Twittey
	24	Hannah Daughter of William Pulleyn of Swinton
May	1	George Son of William Malpas
	do	George Son of John Wright
	15	Ann Daughter of Richard Wildsmith
	25	Joseph son of Joseph Bentley

1760		
May	26	Ann Daughter of Henry Otley
	29	Mary Daughter of Mr Webster, Schoolmaster
June	22	George Son of William Tingle
	24	Richard and Sarah Son and Daughter of William Stead
	25	Mally Daughter of Joseph Hill
July	16	Nanny Daughter of John Hopkinson, Swinton.
	20	John Son of John Firth
Aug	9	Martha Daughter of John Wade
	10	John Son of William Smith
	24	William Son of William Cusworth
	do	George Son of John Ward
Oct	9	Edward Son of Edward Radcliff
	do	John Son of William Hammond
Nov	8	James Son of Sarah Carr
	9	Martha Daughter of Wm Burley
Dec	26	Elizabeth Daughter of William Hardy
	28	Emilia Daughter of Mary Linfit
1761		
Jan	2	John Son of George Foulstone
	6	Richard Son of Peter Dean
	do	Robert Son of John Pepper
	17	Thomas Son of Thomas Cusworth
	18	John Son of Jonathan Hargreave
	do	Sarah Daughter of Richard Wilson
Feb	2	Joseph Son of John Russel
	24	Martha Daughter of William Wade
	27	Thomas Son of John Cudworth
Mar	20	John Son of Samuel Crowder
	22	Ann Daughter of John Appleyard
	23	Sarah Daughter of John Campsall
	24	James Son of Abraham Ely
	do	Sarah Daughter of Joseph Bingley
May	10	Thomas Son of Thomas Gass
	10	Major Son of Major Mountain
	12	William Son of George Moor
June	14	Joseph Son of John Warin
	17	Richard Son of Joseph Hunt
July	8	Benjamin Son of Joseph Robinson
	24	Sarah Daughter of Mr William Watson
Sept	1	Martha Daughter of Richard Foulstone
	3	Mary Daughter of William Newsom
Oct	1	Joshua Son of Joseph Crowder
	do	William Son of Thomas Jackson
	do	Elizabeth Daughter of John Halmshaw
	8	Martha Daughter of Joseph Hudson
Nov	15	Ann Dyson Daughter of Mary Gleadhill
	19	Sarah Daughter of John Smith, Butcher
	27	Elizabeth Daughter of John Lewis

1761		
Nov	28	Elizabeth Daughter of Benjamin Grayson
Dec	11	George Son of William Trippit
	27	William Son of Henry Otley
1762		
Jan	3	Elizabeth Daughter of Robert Bailey
	30	Ann Daughter of Joseph Bentley
	31	Hannah Daughter of John Firth
Feb	7	Ann Daughter of Thomas Lonkey
	22	Elizabeth Daughter of Michael Ford
Feb	23	Elizabeth Daughter of Peter Dean
	23	Frances Daughter of Henry Wood
Apr	8	Thomas Son of Thomas Roberts
	17	Elizabeth Daughter of Thomas Briggs
	25	Martha Daughter of Timothy Swift
June	6	Jane Daughter of Joshua Sympson
	20	Mary Daughter of Thomas Silcock
July	9	Thomas Son of Thomas Dyson
	11	George Son of Richard Laycock
	18	George Son of John Blake
Aug	1	Elizabeth Daughter of William Linfit
	—	Charlotte Daughter of William Pulleyn
	—	Sarah Daughter of Thomas Watson
	—	Martha Daughter ol William Wade
	2	Henry Son of James White
	11	Charles Son of William Malpas
	15	William Son of Joseph Hunter
	—	Richard Son of George Asque
Sept	5	John Son of William Rodger
	26	John Son of William Burland
	—	Maria Daughter of Thomas Gibson, London
Oct	6	Richard Son of Richard Wilson
	7	Mary Daughter of William Stead
	—	Thomas Son of William Hammond
	28	Ann Daughter of Edward Radcliff
	31	Sarah Daughter of Widow Harrison
Dec	16	John Son of Phinehas Holdroyd
	24	Thomas Son of John Wright
1763		
Jan	1	Mary Daughter of George Moor
	12	Samuel Son of John Smith
	30	John Son of Robert Pulleyn
		Joseph son of Sarah Broomhill
Feb.	2	Richard Son of John Russel
	22	William Son of William Hicks
	27	Francis Son of William Hardy
Mar	13	Daniel Son of Daniel Twigg
	6	Elizabeth Daughter of Richard Hague
Apr	14	Sarah Daughter of John Smith, Butcher

1763		
Apr	28	Thomas Son of John Carr
	29	Sarah Daughter of Joseph Bingley of West-Melton
May	9	Benjamin Son of Benjamin Gray
	12	John Son of William Bizby
	22	Catherine Daughter of William Malkin
	do	Mark Son of Jonathan Hargreave
	do	William Son of Edward Sooter
June	7	Ann Daughter of William Denton
	16	John Son of John Twittey
	28	William Son of William Hall
Juy	6	Joseph Son of Joseph Hunt
	10	Ann Daughter of Henry Ledger of Swinton
	17	Hannah Daughter of John Cutt
Aug	7	John Son of Thomas Hartley
	21	Hannah Daughter of Joshua Lockwood
Oct	5	Richard Son of Richard Jackson
	9	Martha Daughter of Joseph Bentley
Nov	4	John Son of John Jackson
	6	Ann Daughter of William Tingle
	20	William Son of Abraham Turton
	27	Elizabeth Daughter of Thomas Cusworth
Dec	26	Mary Daughter of Henry Otley
	27	William Son of Richard Wilson
	do	John Son of William Linfit
1764		
Jan	1	John Son of Peter Dean
	7	Mary Daughter of Enoch Thompson
	12	John Son of James White
	22	David Son of William Butler
	do	John Son of Thomas Earnshaw
Feb	12	Benjamin Son of Benjamin Grayson
	17	John Son of Henry Wilkinson
	18	George Son of John Child
Mar	14	Joshua Son of Thomas Roberts
	18	Sarah Daughter of George Hobkins
Apr	15	Sarah Daughter of John Halmshaw
	22	Lucy Daughter of John Smith of Swinton
May	3	John Son of Thomas Briggs
	13	Martha Daughter of Major Mountain
	20	Martha Daughter of Abraham Ely
June	10	John Son of John Warin
	24	Samuel Son of Thomas Whitehouse
July	22	John Son of Giles Battison
	29	Joseph Son of William Pulleyn
	do	John Son of Francis Cliff
Aug	5	Joseph Son of Thomas Jackson
	11	Mary Daughter of George Fowlstone
	16	Sarah Daughter of Benjamin Gray

1764

Aug	26	John Son of Thomas Rose
	do	Martha Daughter of John Cudworth
Sept	5	Josias Son of Richard Laycock
	21	George Son of Samuel Stenton ?
	23	Edward Son of John Wade
	do	Mary Daughter of John Russel
	24	Ann Daughter of Joseph Crowder
Oct	4	Robert Son of Michael Ford
	7	Thomas Barker Son of Sarah Cuseworth
	16	——— Daughter of William Hall
	25	John Son of John Smith
Nov	25	John Son of Jonathan Ely
Dec	13	William Son of John Jackson
	do	Martha Daughter of John Pepper
	26	Thomas Son of George Robinson
	do	Thomas Son of William Wade

1765

Jan	1	Mary Daughter of John Hewit
	20	Fanny Daughter of Henry Ledger
	do	John Son of Mary Charlesworth
Feb	7	George Son of Thomas Cusworth
	3	Mary Daughter of Thomas Watson
	17	James Son of Joseph Hunter
	19	William Son of Joseph Bentley
Mar	10	Elizabeth Daughter of Timothy Swift
	14	John Son of John Wright of Kilnhurst
Apr	2	John Son of William Denton of Wath
	8	Joseph Son of Thomas Dyson of Wath
	8	Joseph Son of Daniel Twigg of Brampton-byerly
	8	John Gilberthorp Son of Elizabeth Shaw
	14	Mary Daughter of William Hardy of Brampton byerley
May	27	Sarah Daughter of William Linfit of Melton
	27	Ann Daughter of Thomas Wardingly
June	2	George Son of Grace Lauton
	30	Ann Daughter of Bryan Clarkson
July	10	Sarah Daughter of Edward Radcliffe
	12	Charlotte Daughter of William Malpas
Aug	1	Sarah Daughter of Richard Hague
	4	Samuel Son of William Rodger
	4	John Son of Edward Sooter
	4	Martha Daughter of Thomas Silcock
	19	Ruth Daughter of William Hammond
	25	Martha Daughter of Abraham Turton
Sept	26	Ann Daughter of William Newsom
Oct	3	Martha Daughter of John Woodcock
	4	Ann Daughter of John Cutt
Nov.	17	Mary Daughter of Peter Dean
	23	Ann Daughter of George Tingle

1765		
Nov.	27	Benjamin Son of Joseph Gill
Dec	5	Ann Daughter of William Tricket
	15	William Son of Joseph Birks
	27	John Son of John Child
1766		
Jan	1	Mary Daughter of Joseph Hunt
	12	Thomas Son of Thomas White of Swinton
Feb.	1	John Son of John Sailes of Swinton
	13	William Son of Thomas Roberts
	21	Charles Son of Thomas Cusworth
	22	Samuel Son of Samuel Crowder
	22	Thomas Son of Benjamin Gray
Mar.	2	Jonathan Son of Jonathan Ely
	31	Robert Son of Thomas Jackson
	31	Charles Son of Joseph Gibson
Apr	2	Jane Daughter of John Rowley, Vic^r^
	6	John Son of William Hicks
	29	John Son of Thomas Wade
May	8	Thomas Son of Richard Jackson
	20	Edward Son of John Smith at Swinton Warehouse
	26	John Son of Richard Laycock
June	8	Hannah Daughter of George Asque
	22	Hannah Daughter of Mary Senior
	29	Henry Son of Henry Otley
July	18	Lucy Daughter of Henry Ledger
	21	William Son of William Malkin
	24	Jonathan Son of Jonathan Hargreave
	27	Thomas Son of Thomas Bramhall
Aug	7	Thomas Son of Edmund West
	19	Hannah Daughter of William Trippit
Sep	7	Elizabeth Daughter of Frances Tricket
	19	Maria Daughter of Thomas Kay
Oct	9	Joseph Son of Michael Ford
	9	Martha Daughter of Major Mountain
	12	Richard Son of Richard Hepworth
Nov.	9	Ann Daughter of William Carr
	13	Mary Daughter of Ann Fisher
	18	John Son of William Wade
	23	George Son of John Russel
Dec	11	John Son of Thomas Carnalley
	27	Francis Son of John Smith
1767		
Feb.	6	Samuel Son of James White
	8	Mary Daughter of Francis Cliff
	20	William Son of Henry Heald
Mar	3	Samuel Son of Thomas Dyson
	3	John Son of George Robinson
	8	Joseph Son of William Fisher

1767

Mar	12	Edward Son of William Trickit
	21	Thomas Son of George Tingle
	22	Mary Daughter of Joseph Hunt
	30	Abel Son of Henry Hill of Sheffield
	13	Richard Son of Richard Hague
Apr	10	John Son of Mary Wilson
	12	William Son William Burland
	20	William Son of William Vickars
	21	Nancy Daughter of John Smith of Barnbro
	26	Hannah Daughter of Abram Turton
June	7	Richard Son of John Halmshaw
	8	Richard Son of John Sailes
July	5	Hannah Daughter of Giles Battison
	19	Ann Daughter of William Hicks
	19	Elizabeth Daughter of John Wright
	26	John Son of John Hall
Aug	2	John Son of John Robinson
	2	Thomas Son of Thomas Rose
	9	Michael Son of Robert Ford
Sep	6	William Son of William Linfit
Oct	5	Joseph Son of Thomas Roberts
	6	Dorothy Daughter of John Ward
	23	Mary Daughter of Benjamin Law of Swinton
Nov	22	Joseph Son of George Shaw
Dec	7	Frances Daughter of Willoughby Wood
1768		
Jan	1	Ann Daughter of Joseph Gill
	25	William Son of Richard Laycock
	25	Catherine Daughter of Heny Birchby
	31	David Son of Nicholas Pilley
Feb	17	Mary Daughter of William Smith
	21	Barnabas Son of John Blake
	27	Elizabeth Daughter of William Rodgers
Mar	2	John Son of Henry Heald
	6	Ann Daughter of Joshua Longley
	20	William Son of Jonathan Ely
	26	Martha Daughter of Catherine Fisher
	20	George Son of John Wharin
Apr	4	Sarah Daughter of Thos Brammer
		John Son of Joseph Gibson
May	15	Elizth Daughter of Thos Wade
	17	Ann Daughter of William Malpas of Kilnhurst (*Inserted see again below.*)
June	12	Joseph Son of John Cutt
	19	Thomas Son of Wm Campsall
	—	Martha Daughter of Peter Dean
July	10	Ann Daughter of Robert Bizby
	21	Ann Daughter of Wm Malpas

1768

July 24 Eliz^th Daughter of John Russel
30 John Son of Miles Ledger
Aug 1 Betty Daughter of Thos White
7 John Son of Willm Malkin
8 Mary Daughter of John Smith, Swinton Warehouse
Sept 13 Philip Holmes 17 years of age
Oct 2 Joseph Son of Benj^m Gray
— Abra^m & Isaac sons of Daniel Twigg
6 Willm Son of Thos Kay, Junr
Mich^l Son of Michael Ford
9 Thos Son of Wm Huntington
17 Ann Daughter of John Twittey
27 Ann Daughter ol Thos Carnelley
No. 11 George Son of Thos Birkinshaw
— Martha Daughter of Wm Trickett
24 Mary Daughter of John Smith, Butcher
26 George Son of Wm Wright of Swinton
— William Son of Joseph Hunt

1769

Jan 6 Richard Son of John Jackson
16 Sarah Daughter of John Askew
Feb 7 George Son of Henry Ledger
9 John Son of Thos Cusworth
10 Eliz^th Daughter of Edward Radcliffe
Mar 8. Martha Daughter of Wm Linfitt
Hannah Daughter of James White
27 Francis Son of George Askew, Labourer
Apr 9 Ann Daughter of George Moore, Hatter
11 William Son of Thomas Brammah, Labourer
16 Charles Son of William Hix, Taylor
16 Ann Daughter of William Fisher, Labourer
16 Joseph Son of William Vickers, Wheelwright
16 Thos Son of Thos Worral, Mason
30 Mary Daughter of Robert Ford, Taylor
May 6 William Son of John Sailes of Swinton, Farmer
9 Mary Daughter of John Sorby, Labourer.
14 George Son of George Shaw, Labourer
28 Joshua Son of John Matthewman, Labourer
28 John Son of John Ward, Farmer
June 11 Ann Daughter of Michael Bizby, Butcher
8 Richard Son of Benjamin Law of Swinton
13 Sarah Daughter of Robert Smith, Butcher
July 9 Sarah Daughter of Joseph Nailor, Weaver
24 Charles Son of Thos Dyson, Cordwainer
Sept 24 Eliz^th Daughter of Thos Smeaton of Howber, Collier
Oct 5 Wm Son of Ann Beaver's Bastard.
5 Joseph Son of Abra^m Turton, Hatter
5 John Son of Wm Blake, Collier

1769		
Oct	6	Peter Son of Peter Dean, Labourer
	9	Mary Daughter of Wm Carr, Farmer
Dec	11	Elizth Daughter of Elizth Gorrell, Bas^{d}
	28	Elizth Daughter of Joshua Longley, Labourer
1770		
Jan	7	John Son of David Clarke, Labourer
	14	Mary Daughter of Wm Burley, Labourer
	18	Elizth Daughter of Richd Stead, Mason
	30	Mariah Daughter of Tabitha Wilson, Bast^{d}
Feb	2	Wm Son of Thos Hilton, Joiner
	4	Martha Daughter of John Smith of Swinton
	8	Wm Son of Edw^{n} Radcliffe, Shopkeeper
	28	John Son of Joseph Bingley, Farmer
Mar	4	Benjn Son of Robert Bizby
	6	Mary Daughter of Jno Wright
	13	Ann Daughter of Wm Cartridge, Potter
	16	Mary Daughter of Benjn Gray, Farmer and Malster
	18	Ann Daughter of Charles Wood, Potter
1770		
Mar	25	Sarah Daughter of Joseph Jones, Potter
Apr	1	John Son of Richard Hague, Labourer
	16	Mary Daughter of Wm Hix of Swinton
	22	Fanny Daughter of John Halmshâw, Labourer
May	4	Samuel Son of Wm Malkin, Potter
	5	Joseph Son of John Whitehead
	20	John Son of Thos Gill, Cordwainer
	20	Martha Daughter of John Gill, Mason
	24	Hannah Daughter of Thos Durham
June	4	Elizth Daughter of Thos Roberts, Farmer
	5	John Son of Edward Lindley, Collier
	5	Olive Daughter of Giles Battison, Labourer
	24	John Son of Henry Slater, Joiner
July	8	Saml Son of Saml Malkin, Potter
	5	John Son of George Wrongham, Excise Man
	15	Hannah Daughter of Jonat^{n} Hargreaves, Labourer
	29	Richd Son of Ann Carr, Bast
Aug	12	Elizth Daughter of John Sorby, Labourer
	19	John Son of Anthony Jackson of Howber, Farmer
	24	Margaret Daughter of Wm Trickett, Farmer
Sept	2	Joseph Son of Wm Rogers, Blacksmith
	30	Thomas Son of Henry Ottley, Labourer
Oct	4	Alice Daughter of Joseph Hunt, Cordwainer
	20	Hannah Daughter of George Tingle, Labourer
Nov	4	Ann Daughter of Thomas Worral
	27	Sarah Daughter of John Smith, Butcher
Dec	6	Thos Son of Thos Briggs.
	9	Mary Daughter of John Cutt
	10	William Son of John Twittey, Tanner

1770		
Dec	20	Charles Son of Ann Cusworth, Bast
	28	John Son of Thomas Kay, Farmer
1771		
Jan	1	Abraham Son of Thos Cusworth of Hoober
	1	Samuel Son of Michael Ford, Mason
	17	Mally Daughter of David Stone, Currier
Feb	7	Ann Daughter of Wm Linfitt, Cordwainer
	10	Sarah Daughter of George Shaw, Labourer
	12	Wm Son of Wm Fisher, Labourer
	24	Sarah Daughter of Robert Ford, Taylor
Mar	22	Ann Daughter of Mich^l^ Bizby, Butcher
	24	Thos Son of John Wharin, Collier
Apr	1	Mary Daughter of Thos Webster, Maltster
	1	Sarah Daughter of John Sailes, Farmer
	2	James Son of Ann Baley, Bast.
	4	Thos Son of John Jackson, Farmer & Maltster
	21	Sarah Daughter of Wm Coope, Potter
		Bapt
Apr	28	Hannah, Daughter of Richd Thompson, Taylor
May	7	Lucy Daughter of Wm Malpass
	17	Hannah Daughter of John Hopkinson, Swinton
June	2	Martha Daughter of Wm Dawson, Labourer
	16	John Son of Benjn Clarke
July	5	Thos Son of John Ward, Farmer
	14	George Son of Thos Downend, Cordwainer
	14	Richd Son of James White, Farmer
Aug	3	Eliz^th^ Daughter of Saml Wells, Labourer
Sept	8	Wm Son of John Mawson, Labourer
	29	John Son of John Smeaton, Collier
Oct	3	Robert Son of Richd Steads, Mason
	3	Thos Son of Thomas Kemp, Labourer
	3	Ann Daughter of Thos Brammah, Labourer
	3	Sarah Daughter of Peter Dean, Labourer
	17	Mary Daughter of Richd Ducker, Farmer
	20	Thos Son of John Tysap, Labourer
Dec	1	Wm Son of Anthony Jackson, Farmer
	8	Hannah Daughter of Joshua Longley, Labourer
	26	Thos Son of Wm Cartridge, Potter
	26	Sarah Daughter of James Walker, Weaver
	27	Sarah Daughter of Thos Hudson, Farmer
1772		
Jan	12	Emanual Son of Jonat^n^ Hargreaves, Labourer
	27	James Son of Thomas Cusworth, Maltster
Feb.	2	Martha Daughter of Joseph Fisher, Labourer
Mar	1	Wm Son of Enock Thompson, Collier
	3	Mariah Daughter of Robert Smith But^r^
	3	Wm Son of George Crowder, Blacksmith
	3	Paul Son of George Askew, Labourer

1772		
Mar	15	Sarah Daughter of Josh Gill, Mason
	22	Ann Daughter of Wm Huntington, Labourer
	28	Elizabeth Daughter of Benjamin Law of Swinton
Apr	5	Wm Son of John Brameld
	19	Hannah Daughter of Benjn Gray
	20	Martha Daugh^r^ of Wm Burley
	—	Dorothy Daught^r^ of Jno Smith of Swinton Wharehouse
	—	Joshua Son of Wm Barker
	22	Ann Daughter of Thos Hillton
	—	Thos Son of Thos Roberts
May	3	John Son of Samuel Locker
	—	Martha Daugh^r^ of Thos Worrall
	—	Hannah Daught^r^ of Wm Linfitt
	15	Thos Son of Wm Malkin
	17	Hannah Daughter of John Hopkinson
June	14	Ann Daugh^r^ of Jonathan Fisher
	28	Hannah Daugh^r^ of Josh. Jones
July	4	Benjamin Son of John Lyster
	5	Nancy Daughter of Thos Durham
	9	John Son of John Whitehead
	19	Jonathan Son of John Russel
Aug	2	Thos Son of Paul Garfitt
	—	Ann Daughter of Wm Blake
	6	Mary Daught^r^ of Wm Trickett
Sept	27	Eliz^th^ Daught^r^ of Jno Rodgers of Rotherham baptiz^d^ at Swinton
Oct	6	Charlotte Daught of Thos Dyson
	8	John Son of John Sorby
	—	Wm Son of Thos Watson of Swinton
	25	Stephen Son of Richd Shaw
Nov	12	Hannah Daught^r^ of John Smith
	15	William Son of Wm Turner
	21	John Son of Geo Tingle
Dec	3	John Son of Thos Downend
	—	Hannah Daughter of John Revill
	12	Jacob.—Widdow Son of David Stones
	26	Joseph Son of Thos Roberts Junr
1773		
Jan	1	John Son of John Matthewman
	31	Charles Son of Charles Wood
Feb	13	Thos Son of Wm Hall
	18	Ann Daughter of Richd Thompson
	28	Hannah Daughter of Wm Rodgers
	24	Luke Son of Henry Ledger
	28	Ann Daught^r^ of Eliz^th^ Hudson (Illegitimate)
Mar	4	Charles Son of Miles Ledger
	16	Mary Daught^r^ of Richd Steads
	21	Mary Daught^r^ of Jonat^n^ Eley

1773		
Mar	26	Thomas Son of Joseph Taylor
Apr	2	Sarah Daughter of Benjamin Law of Swinton
	11	Elizabeth Daughter of William Fisher, Junr
May	9	William Son of William Smith
	23	William Son of Robert Ford
	23	Samuel Son of John Ramsden
	27	George Son of William Fox
	30	Joseph Son of Robert Bisby
June	13	John Son of George Shaw
	20	John Son of John Slater
	20	Ann Daughter of George Auty
July	3	Joseph Son of John Sayles
	11	Abraham Son of James White
Aug	1	Mary Daughter of John Woodcock Junr
	1	Joseph Son of Joseph Fisher
	8	Ann Daughter of Thomas Andrew
	8	Joseph Son of John Robinson
	22	William Son of John Ward
Sept	26	Ann Daughter of Wm Wharin
Oct	3	Rebecca Daughter of Samuel Hague
	7	Joseph Son of Thomas Brammah
	7	John Son of James Saville
	7	Mary Daughter of Michael Ford
	7	Betty Daughter of Joseph Matthews
	17	Martha Daughter of Mr John Cooke
	17	Elizabeth Daughter of Jonathan Hargreaves
Dec	8	William Son of John Kemp
	12	William Son of John Smith of Swinton Wharehouse
	26	Jonathan Son of John Hawke
1774		
Jan	1	John Son of Benjamin Gray
	14	Mary Daughter of Thomas Goulding
Feb	20	Edward Son of Edward Radcliffe
Mar	13	George Son of George Cusworth
	20	John Son of William Rodger Junr
	21	Elizabeth Daughter of John Twittey
	26	Wm Son of Jno Smith
	30	Mary Daughter of Richd Shaw
Ap	3	Mary & Eliz^th Daugh^s of Geo Linley
	4	Matthew Son of Thos Roberts Jun
	7	Wm Son of Sarah Wells a Bastard
	17	Jno Son of Jno Cutt
	17	Jno Son of Joshua Longley
	24	Jno Son of Jno Lyster
May	1	Eliz^th Daughter of Willoughby Wells
	22	Wm Son of Thos Kemp
	22	Ann Daugh^t of Wm Mellard
	26	Joshua Son of Joshua Hunt

1774		
June	5	Sarah Daugh^{t} of Robert Mower Esqr
	9	Ann Hill Dau. of Mark & Mary Hill of Swinton
	19	Hannah Daugh^{r} of Thos Durham
	23	Jno Son of Wm Trickett
	26	Joseph Son of Joseph Gill
	30	Mary Daugh^{r} of Thos Cutt
July	3	Joseph Son of Henry Ottley
	24	Mary Daugh^{r} of Thos Roberts Senr
	24	Lydia Daugh^{r} of Paul Garfitt
	31	Elizth Daugh^{r} of Jno Ward
Aug	14	Mary Daugh^{r} of Wm Dodgson
	28	John Son of Wm Vickers
Sept	22	Wm Son of Richd Gawtress
	22	Jno Son of Wm Crosley
Oct	6	Hannah Daugh^{r} of Richd Wilkinson
	6	Robert Son of Robert Ford
	6	Martha Daughter of Josh Nailor
	24	Benjamin Son of Benjamin Law of Swinton
	24	Marinnae Daugh^{tr} of Christopha Schafe
Nov	6	Jno Son of Eliz^{h} Stenton a Bastard
	13	Thos Son of Bartholemew Wood
Dec	4	John Son of John Revel
	26	Ann Daugh^{r} of Geo. Crowder
	27	Olive Daught^{r} of John Smith
	27	Wm Son of Wm Dawson
1775		
Jan.	1	Sarah Daught^{r} of Sarah Mitchel
	2	Saml Son of Richard Thompson
	3	Nancy Daught^{r} of Geo Dickenson
	9	Robert Son of John Mawson
	10	Ellen Daught^{r} of John Broone or Browne
	19	Eliz^{h} Daugh^{r} of John Evers
Feb	16	Mary Daugh^{r} of John Hyde
	26	Dorothy Daugh^{r} of Josh Bower
Mar	3	Benjamin Son of Wm Addey
	4	Sarah Daugh^{r} of Jonathan Eley
	19	Thos Son of Thos Andrews
	19	Ann Daughter of John Bramhall, Swinton
	10	Sarah Daughter of William Carrier
	15	Lucy Daughter of Henry Lodge
April	2	John Son of John Swallow, Wath
	9	Mary Daughter of George Autey
	16	Elizabeth Daughter of John Earnshaw
	16	Elizabeth Daughter of Joseph Robinson
	16	Sarah Daughter of Edward Lindley
	17	Robert Son of Thomas Cusworth
	17	Joseph Son of George Frost
	17	Mary Daughter of Joseph Fisher

1775		
April	17	Sarah Daughter of William Sympson
	25	Mary Daughter of William Moor
May	7	John Son of Thomas Worrall
	8	Elizabeth Daughter of John Hilton
	13	William Son of Thomas Bates
June	4	Elizabeth Daughter of John Blake
	6	Mary Daughter of John Sailes
	11	Richard Son of Joshua Matthewman
	28	John Son of William Fisher
July	8	Isaac Widdup Son of David Stones
	28	George Son of Miles Ledger
Aug	6	William Son of Thomas Downing
	13	William Son of John Crowder
Sep.	7	Godfrey Son of John Bingley
Oct	1	Moses Son of Elizabeth Sadler
	5	William Son of Thomas Golding
	5	Martha Daughter of John Campsall
	5	Sarah Daughter of William Rogers
	6	Bartholomew Son of George Asque
	8	Jane Daughter of Thomas Bramhall
	15	Joseph Shaw Son of Richard and Mary Shaw of Swinton
	19	William Son of John Blackburn
	29	Christopher Son of Christopher Scaife
Nov	20	Elizabeth Daughter of John Cook
	29	Stephen Son of John Whitehead
Dec	7	Joseph Son of Benjamin Gray
1776.		
Jan	14	Isaac Son of James White
	21	Jane Daughter of Mark Cooper
	30	John Son of Joseph Hunt
Feb	19	Sarah Garner Daughter of Ann Bizby
Mar	6	John Hill son of Mark and Mary Hill of Swinton (*inserted*)
	30	Sarah Daughter of John Warin
	31	William Son of Francis Cliff
Apr	21	Samuel Son of George Shaw
	21	Joseph Son of James Saville
	28	Mary Daughter of Thomas Bramhall
May	14	Esther Daughter of William Malkin
	26	Richard Son of Joshua Longley
	26	Elizabeth Daughter of John Hawke
June	13	Mary Daughter of Richard Gawtrees
	16	Sarah Daughter of Robert Marcroft
	23	Ann Daughter of John Mawson, Brampton
	27	Mary Daughter of George Dickinson
July	3	Olive Daughter of Elizabeth Campsall
	14	Martha Daughter of Willoughby Wells
	16	Hannah Daughter of John Hyde

1776

July	21	John Son of Thomas Dyson
	21	Lydia Daughter of John Slater
	27	Thomas Son of John Lydster
	28	James Son of Jonathan Hargreave
	29	Lucy Daughter of Thomas Dunnel
Aug	11	Ann Daughter of John Evas
	25	John Son of Thomas Kemp
Sept	26	Sarah Daughter of John Burlay
Oct	1	Joshua Son of John Ward
	3	William Son of John Cutt
	3	Joseph Son of George Cusworth
	3	Josehn Son John Sorsby
	3	Hannah Daughter of Campsall Bower
Nov	13	Charlotte Daughter of William Trickit
	16	Eli Son of Eli Anely
	21	Ann Daughter of Thomas Roberts Son of the late Joseph Roberts
	29	Charles Son of William Firth
Dec	26	Ann Daughter of John Earnshaw

1777.

Jan	1	Sarah Daughter of Thomas Roberts Son of the late Joseph Roberts
	1	George Son of John Sailes
	3	Thomas Son of Richard Thompson
	11	Benjamin Son of Jonathan Ely
	11	William Son of William Rogers, junr.
	19	John Son of Thomas Aden, Swinton
	20	Peggy Daughter of William Crossley
	25	Richard Son of Richard Stead
	26	John Son of William Mellard
Mar	28	Ann Daughter of William Conyers
	20	William Son of Thomas Worrall
	31	Luke Son of Richard Shay
	31	Mary Daughter of Thomas Durham
Apr	1	Ann Daughter of Matthew Tyson
	8	George Son of Henry Ledger
	3	George Son of George Awtey
May	7	John Son of John Clarkson of Swinton
	10	John Son of Joseph Fisher
	19	George Son of George Frost
	25	Ann Daughter of Thomas Nailor
June	1	William Son of Mary Bailey
	4	Martha and Susan Daughters of John Smith, Butcher
	8.	John Son of Thomas Cutt
	8	Alice Daughter of John Swallow
	22	Martha Daughter of Thomas Wright
	29	Elizabeth Daughter of George Fostard
July	7	Henry Son of William Addey of Barnsley

1777		
Aug	5	Mary Daughter of John Trickit
	26	Ann Daughter of Robert Smith
	27	John Son of William Thompson
Sept	17	Charlotte Daughter of George Crowder
Oct	9	William Son of William Allott.
Nov	23	John Son of Richard Smith
	27	Thomas Son of Elizabeth Crossley
Dec	18	Mary Daughter of John Evas
	24	Jonathan Son of William Wright
	29	Sarah Daughter of William Dawson
1778.		
Jan	18	Joseph Son of Jonathan Lilley
	24	Susanna Daughter of William Carrier, Swinton
	22	Elizabeth Daughter of Thomas Watson of Swinton
	29	Mary Daughter of William Watson, Gent
Feb	8	John Son of Robert Ford
	13	George Son of John Mawson
	14	Benjamin Son of John Blackburn
	22	Thomas Son of Joshua Longley
	22	Thomas Son of Thomas Downing
Mar.	4	William Son of William Barker
	4	Mary Daughter of John Bell
Aug.	24	Betty Daughter of John Smith of Swinton Wharehouse
1780		
May	6	John Son of John Smith of Swinton Wharehouse
1781		
Oct	16	Thomas Son of John Smith of Swinton Wharehouse

MARRIAGES.

1725		
Aug.	17	Tho: Bintcliffe and Martha Fowlston
Sept	16	John Jackson and Rebecca Birkes
Oct	18	Robert Needham and Hanna Fowler
	31	John Ward and Mary More also
		John Parkin and Sarah Thompson
Nov	2	Will: Hardware and Ann Hudson
	7	Charles Butler and Margaret Parret
Feb	10	Samuel Rodes and Elizabeth Dodson
1726		
June	28	Joshua Roberts and Martha Rawlin
Sept	22	Robert Walker & Mary Kay, widow
Nov	10	Will. Baxter & Mary Lancashire, widow &
		John Bell & Eliz: Thackarey, widow
Dec	1	Daniel Carnaley & Ann Firth &
	4	Joseph Windsor & Ann Thompson
	11	Mr Reginald Burdyn & Frances Bell, widow
	30	Richard Sharp & Mary Hanson
Feb	9	Samuel Carnaley & Mary Firth.

1726		
Mar	3	Thomas Tyas of Mexbrough and Ann Hall wth Licence
1727		
June	11	Samuel Freeman & Jane Rawlin
	18	Richard Ford & Eliz: South
July	20	Will: Cudworth & Ann Hartley.
1728		
May	28	Will: Beardshaw & Alice Brigg
		Thos Bromeld & Susanna Trippit
		Joshua Culpan and Mary Morley
1729		
May	25	Mathew White & Ann Pool
Aug	24	John Elam & Martha Foulston
Nov	15	Anthony Alsop & Mary Mougham
Dec	23	John Hamerton & Sarah Bintcliffe
	26	Jonathan Rials & Sarah Lockwood &
		Thos Wanhead & Martha Ramsden
1730		
Jnne	25	John Iredal and Sarah Jones
	29	Joseph Milner & Ann Flint
July	5	Benjamin Trippit & Eliz: Elam
Aug	13	Thomas Smith & Elizabeth Halmshaw
Sept	24	Mr John Horncastle & Mrs Eliz: Jackson
Oct-	24	Francis Robinson & Sarah Slack
Nov	30	William Thompson & Elizabeth Cowper &
		Thomas Jub & Mary Rimer
Dec	17	Bartholomew Hattersley & Ann Carr
	22	Samuel Hall & Hannah Kennerley
Feb	4	Matthew Ward & Martha Trickitt and
		John Arthur & Elizabeth Pinder
1731		
June	8	George Foulstone and Mary Hodkinson
June	10	Will: Bell and Hannah Rayner
Sept	24	Joshua Gray and Eliz Dyson
Nov	4	Jonathan Woodhead and Martha Lambert
	18	Will: Thompson and Sarah Battirwood
Jan	24	James Walton & Mary Moras
Feb	10	John Carr & Ann Briggs
1732		
Oct	26	Joshua White & Marth Cowwood &
		Philip Flint & Mary Hurst
Nov	5	Will Olley & Mary Coe
	15	Joseph Glossop & Sarah Shaw &
		Mr George Kent & Ann Gibson
	19	John Cut & Ann Holland
Dec	24	Philip Flint & Martha
Jan	4	John Abdy & Sarah Loserf
Feb	13	Rich Ax & Sarah Mathewman
Mar	13	George Gill & Eliz: Samson
	12	Mathew Speight & Mary Newbot

1733

1733		
June	27	Will Tingle & Eliz. Hamond
Aug	14	Will Hilton & Sarah Frost
	23	Will Watkinson & Sarah Wood
Sept	25	Sam[l] Foulston & Eliz Ashley.
Oct	19	Richard Norlem & Dorothy Kirkby
	24	Will Armitage & Hannah Beal
Nov	2	Jonathan Cocks & Eliz Low
	20	George Kay & Eliz Hanson
Dec.	6	Richard Sikes & Mary Rodes
	18	Francis Smith & Mary Brooksbank
	26	Thomas Tingle & Sarah Wingle
Jan.	28	William Kemp & Jane Ford
Feb.	4	John Crawshaw & Mary Hudson
March	17	Rich[d] Womack & Sarah Harrison
1734		
Apr	25	John Jackson & Grace Wharam
July	9	Thomas Beaumont & Mary Hopton
Aug.	29	Rich[d] Gildin & Elizabeth Wood
Sept.	30	James Parkinson & Elizabeth Firth and John Hattersley & Elizabeth Chadwick
Oct.	28	Rich[d] Sales & Sarah Mallison
Dec.	27	Will: Iredal & Dorothy Guest
Jan	14	Thomas Everet & Mary Rogers
1735		
Apr	27	Thomas Swift & Martha White
Jun	24	Mr Housely Freeman & Mrs Ann Wharam
Aug	19	John Samson & Catherine Woodal
	23	Tho: Hardey & Eliz Hardey
Sept	8	Jonathan Pashley & Elizabeth Kirkby
	22	Tho Jenkinson & Eliz: Mathewman
Nov.	12	Sam[l] Gillatt & Eliz Walker
Dec	4	Sam[l] Slubbin ? & Sarah Roberts
	11	Jonathan Burgin & Mary Dobson
	26	Joseph Monday (a souldgier) & Sarah Foulston
Jan.	1	Will: Goldsborough & Mary Armstead
Feb.	8	George Bell & Mary Brook
	9	Ezra Hobson & Ann Addy
Mar	8	John Birks & Eliz Cox
1736		
	28	Will Kay & Ruth Mathewman
Apr.	25	Robert Hill & Sarah Cowper
May	20	Dan Hargreave & Mary Kay
June	13	John Hill & Dorothy Steer
Sept	12	Thomas Baxter & Mary Wharam
	19	Will Man & Mary Gray
1737		
May	13	Godfrey Wainright & Mary Kay

1737		
June	23	John Firth & Dorothy Swift
	30	Richard Wilson & Sarah Battison
Aug	8	Antony Rose & Alice Hudson
	2	John Wigfield & Sarah Burgin
Nov	21	Will : Moras & Agnes Tingle
Dec	25	Joseph Milner & Sarah Gregson
	27	Joseph Stanfield & Ann Hague
	29	John Elam & Mary Ley & John Cusworth & Mary Bullos ?
1738		
May	21	Stephen Yoyle & Mary Holt
June	29	Thomas Beaumont & Frances Wingle
July	31	John Gill & Eliz : Addy
Oct	5	Richard Rodison & Jane Gorrill
Nov	14	Will Eastwood & Hannah Brook
Dec	26	James Burgin & Margaret Parkin
Feb	6	James Couper & Ann Bower
	13	Stephen Kay & Hannah Howeth
	25	Richard Thompson & Frances Elam
1739		
Apr	23	Joseph Burgon & Sarah Hill were married
	24	Samuel Hall & Sarah Elam
Mar	29	Jonathan Dobson & Elizabeth Richardson
June	19	James Bower & Ellen Cunningam
Nov	5	Joseph Bingley & Martha Allinder
Feb	14	Jonathan Halley & Mary Hill
1740		
May	27	John Norburne & Sarah Elam
June	17	John Oxley & Ann Swift
July	13	Wm Fisher & Ann Carnley
Aug	10	Joseph Heaton & Elizabeth Arthur
	28	Tho Poles & Mary Birk
Sept	11	Wm Tingle & Dorothy Parrott
Oct	19	Samuel Dink and Mary Brook
Nov	25	Wm Mossly & Anne Thompson
Jan	1	Wm Newsom & Elizabeth Butler
1741		
Apr	16	Benjamin Epworth & Alice Goddard
	19	Edward Bool & Alice Bailey
May	11	Jonathan Swift & Margaret Hoyle
Nov	12	Joseph English & Mary Joys
		also James Ellis & Mary Hill
Dec	13	George Bailey & Sarah Stead
	26	James Wood & Martha Watson
Jan	9	Richard Hicks & Mary Watson
	21	Richard Massey & Katherine Bingley
Feb	2	William Clerk & Martha Couper ?
		also Benjamin England & Elizabeth Leversidge

1741		
Feb	25	Benjamin Haycock & Alice Wharam
1742		
Apr	29	Edward Fox & Susannah Birks
June	27	Nathan Birkin & Mary Armitage
July	22	John Dixon & Grace Ibberson
Sept	19	Joseph Birk & Mary Hellaley
Oct	13	John Fox & Mary Button
Nov	28	Henry Wood & Ann Goglin
Dec	9	John Wingfield & Hannah Grey by a licence signed by the Revd Wm Steer
Jan	2	Robert Jennet & Martha Button
Feb	20	Thomas Hammond & Elizabeth Patteson
1743		
Apr	14	James Wigfield & Mary Hinchliff
June	16	John Sheepshank & Mary Cutts
July	20	John Bullous & Rachel Hallaley
Oct	13	Joshua Matthewman & Sarah Atkinson
	18	William Morley & Catharine Bower
Nov	13	John Cooper & Rosamond Craven
Dec	26	John Hanson & Hannah Baldwin
Feb	2	William Wilson & Mary Wright
	6	Henry Turner & Hannah Wigfield
	7	John Gaskin & Sarah Cusworth
		John Stancel & Sarah Matthewman
1744		
May	15	Henry Hurst & Esther Rainey * both of this parish after Banns duly published
June	11	Richard Becket of Bolton & Elizabeth Jubb of this parish Married by Mr Ibbotson
July	11	Thomas Ellis & Ann Moulson
Aug	14	George Copley & Mary Clarkson
	19	John Archdale of the parish of Darfield and Ann Abbott of this parish after banns certified by Mr Marriott
Oct	21	John Swift & Elizabeth Bashford
Nov	11	William Wood & Mary Butter
Dec	17	John Lydster & Martha White
	18	Isaac Tomlinson & Sarah Walker
	30	William Vains & Sarah Sunderland
Jan	1	Stephen Alender & Elizabeth Watson
	10	Richard Pilley & Mary Bullous
Jan	24	Jonathan Gaskin & Sarah Goddard
Feb	24	Joseph Graceson of the parish of Bradfield & Mary Woodhead of this parish married by Mr Thompson
	25	Paul Dobson & Sarah Wodsworth
March	3	Samuel Butcher & Mary Hague

John Empson Curate of Wath

Tho: Kay
Robert Hudson } Churchwardens

* Note—This is after each entry.

1745		
May	2	William Copley and Sarah Horsfield
June	9	Samuel Smith and Hannah Wilcock
July	20	John Coe and Martha Beaumont
Aug	4	John Pepper and Mary Rhodes
Sept	19	Richard Beardshall and Martha Wigfield
Oct	14	John Hague and Mary Elam
	29	Luke Worral and Hannah Arundel
Nov.	5	John Walker and Sarah Senior
	17	John Blake and Ann Baley
Dec	24	George Willey and Elizabeth Armitage
1746		
May	13	Robert Stead and Elizabeth Kay
June	12	Matthew Fornace and Elizabeth Birks
Sept	8	John Adin and Martha Argreaves
Dec	11	William Bingley and Ann Wager both of this parish married by Mr Banks at Swinton Chappel after Banns duly published in Wath Church
1747		
May	7	Thomas Moulson & Ann Allot
	21	John Brook of this parish & Ann Falding of the parish of Ecclesfield after banns certified by the Curate of Ecclesfield
June	15	John Denton & Ann Wade
Aug	...	John Lewis & Martha Hartley married by Mr Ibotson
	23	John Robinson & Sarah Whitaker
Sept	1	Thomas Norburn & Elizabeth Yeardley
Oct	15	William Hague & Jane Darwin
Nov	12	Timothy Swift & Mary Elam by Mr Ibotson
also		Thomas Man and Elizabeth Nelthorp
also		Benjamin Mallendar & Martha Osliffe
	26	William Rogerson & Ann Ibberson by Mr Ibotson
Dec	1	John Shaw & Ann Wood
	31	William Mallendar & Margaret Adin
also		John Baumforth & Sarah Smith
Jan	17	George Hoyle & Mary Harrison
Feb	2	William Rogers & Elizabeth Booth by Mr Ibotson
also		Richard Glasby of the parish of Mexbrough and Esther Carr of this parish

John Empson Curate of Wath
William Ibotson, Timothy Rhodes } Churchwardens

1748.		
Apr.	24	John Barber of the parish of Sheffield & Elizabeth South of this parish after banns certified by Mr Dossie
May	29	John Wright and Mary Appleyard both of this parish
July	18	John Wigfield and Martha Denton

1748		
Aug	14	Thomas Inman & Mary Carnelly by Licence from Mr Bright
	21	Abraham Ellis and Jane Beaumont
Sept	8	John Russell & Mary Bower
Oct	16	Joseph Copley of Pennistone & Elizabeth Sales of this parish after Banns certified by the Curate of Pennistone
	23	Thomas Osliffe of Barnborough & Alice Blythe of the parish by banns certificated by Mr Ayde
Nov	21	William Harrison & Mary Horsfall
Dec	29	William Mudd of St. Saviours York & Ann Ibotson of this parish married by Mr Ibotson by Licence from Mr John Blanshard, Proctor
Jan	16	William Robinson of Ranfield & Rebecca Bartholomew of this parish by Banns certified by Mr Lawson.
1749.		
Apr.	9	David Audin of Ecclesfield & Ruth Armitage of this parish by Banns certificated by Mr Bailiff
May	16	Edward Fenton & Mary Kennerley
Juue	13	John Cowper & Mary Rotheray
Aug	14	John Utley & Mary Wing
	31	Samuel Brook & Mary Burgen
Nov	27	John Swinden of Mexbrough & Mary Beet of this parish by Banns certificated by Mr Perkins
Dec	11	Thomas Dobson & Elizabeth Twigg
	31	John Beaumount & Frances Beaumont
Jan	9	Francis Tricket & Elizabeth Hewit
	14	Richard Axe of Rawmarsh & Hannah Lightowler of this parish by Banns certified by Mr Stephenson
1750		
July	16	Thomas Harpham & Sarah Wodsworth both of this parish by Banns
Aug	11	William Bisby & Ann Goss both of this parish married by Mr Twittey
Sept	2	Joseph Crowder & Ann Foulstone
	30	William Doe & Ann Michaelthwaite
Nov	26	John Owram of the parish of Knaresborough & Mary Varah of this parish married by Mr Barber at Swinton Chapel by Banns
Dec	18	John Senior of the parish of Darfield & Ann Stead of this parish.
	26	Thomas Silcock & Mary Hanby
	27	Rowland Burkit & Frances Darby
Jan	1	George Stear & Alice Beaumont
Feb	5	Joseph Campsal & Ellen Bower
	21	Robert Swift & Ann Mellors both of this parish married by Mr Twittey by Banns

1751.

Apr.	24	Thomas Arundale and Jane Smith
June	9	Matthew Clayphan and Sarah Bingley
July	7	George Harrison & Margaret Townend
Oct	17	Joshua Beevers & Ann Whiteley
Nov	5	John Hewitt & Mary Tasker
	10	John Hampshire & Elizabeth Sanderson
	21	Thomas Turner & Elizabeth White
Dec	5	Richard Hesom & Sarah Armstead
	8	William Green & Ann Roads
	12	Abraham Ely & Ann Wilson
1752.		
May	3	Michael Ford & Ann Ledger
June	16	Benjamin Senior & Catherine Revel
July	5	Isaac Cundey & Elizabeth Alinder
Nov	30	Bejamin Spencer & Ann Hargreave
1753.		
Jan	1	Edward Hey & Mary Sharp
		John Smith & Jane Kemp
Feb.	13	William Marshall & Margaret Hobkison
1753.		
Apr	26	Nathaniel Bower and Dorothy Heden
July	16	Richard Wildsmith and Sarah Clayton
Aug	14	George Goddard and Hannah Senior
Oct	29	Thomas Penter and Sarah Bailey
Nov	1	William Downing and Mary Hicks
	29	George Asque and Sarah Russel
Dec	6	Thomas Cliff and Elizabeth Jackson
	10	Joseph Kershaw and Elizabeth Fisher
	23	James Hirst and Mary Rhodes
	27	William Clarke & Elizabeth Beaumont
	30	George Blackmore & Mary Bowers

BURIALS.

1725		
Mar	28	Richard Kay
Apr	24	Two children of Thomas Hopkinson
July	14	Will: Hudson
Sept	18	Will: Hoyland
	19	Widow Roberds
Oct	12	Widow Rodes
	24	George Gawtrey
Dec	21	Eliz: wife to Tho: South & John son to John Ford
Jan	2	Ann daughter to Tho: South
	10	Tho: son to Abraham Horsefield
	25	Eliz: wife to Will. Baxter
Mar.	13	Nathaniel Pepper

1726		
Apr	3	Nathaniel Pepper (*sic*)
	12	George son to George Addy
May	17	Jane daughter to Thomas Bingley
June	28	Ann daughter to John Wood
July	12	Ann daughter to John Denton
	16	George son to George Chevings
	23	Ann daughter to Abraham Horsefield
Aug	8	Mary wife to William Kay
	23	Richard son to John Wright
	26	Will: & John sons to Thomas Dodson
Oct	27	Margaret daughter to Mr. Reginald Burdyn
	30	Mary daughter to William Jackson
Nov	7	Mary wife to Jonathan Bentley
Dec	24	Joseph son to John Rodes
Jan	8	Eliz daughter to Richard Thompson
	15	Samuel son to John Man
	17	John Hall
	18	George son to Daniel Schorey
Feb	19	John Wood
Mar	24	Charles Hill
1727		
Mar	27	Hannah daughter to Daniel Schorey
Apr	17	Will: son to Thomas Dodson
July	4	The Schoolmaster of Swinton
	17	Widow Lovedey
	20	Lydia daughter to John Robinson
Aug	20	Robert Tyas
Sept	7	John son to John Wood
	10	Reginald Burdyn Schoolmaster of Wath
	14	Ann wife to Will: Flint
Oct	12	Will son to John Briggs
Nov	3	A Stranger
	20	John Hurd
	26	Nicholas Willis
Feb	8	John Tooker Esqr of Moor-Gate in ye Parish of Rotherham
Feb	23	Margaret wife to Willm Rawson
Mar	8	Richard Jackson
	18	Tho Baxter of Brampton who was burnt to death in his own house
1728		
Mar	30	Sarah Littlewood, widow
Apr	5	John Bell
	23	Isaac Wade
May	5	Mary Hoggard
	13	Mary wife to John Arthur
	23	Ann Gawtress, widow

1728		
Aug	4	Sylvanus Sykes
	11	Edward Hanson
Oct	13	Ann Sykes, widow
	20	George son to Richard Stead
	24	Tho son to Tho: Baxter of Abdy G[t]
	29	Joseph Bingley
	31	Will son to M[r] George Sanderson
Nov.	12	Mary daughter to Will: Iredale
	27	Margaret Hawksworth
Dec	7	Abigail Adran
	8	Eliz: Gant
	13	John son to Rich Loveday
	27	John son to John Howith?
	30	Mary wife to Rich Lambert
Jan	7	Edward Smith
	12	John Twittey Master of Arts & Vicar of Wath
	14	Margaret daughter to John Trickit
	17	Eliz: wife to Will Newbat
July	7	Edmund Brumflit
	14	Thomas Beaumont
	14	Thomas Kay
	25	Ann wife to James Roberts
Mar.	2	John Hill
	7	Ann Wilkinson
1729.		
Mar.	29	Susanna Fosterd
Apr.	2	Joshua Halmshaw and John Sykes
	18	John Huchinson
	19	Lydia his wife
	23	Grace wife to Will: Wade
May	2	Richard Huchinson
	7	Thomas Fosterd
	27	Thomas Wilcock
July	11	Martha wife to Thomas Bintcliffe
	25	John Lyall
	27	Hannah daughter to Richard Heeler and Ann wife to Haman Hole
Aug	1	Eliz daughter to W[m] Burtwizell
Sept.	2	Widow Hammond
Oct.	6	Grace wife to Joshua Shepperd
	25	Ruth daughter to Will Hamond
Nov.	18	A poor traveller that died at Swinton
	25	Joseph Halmshaw
Dec.	4	Widow Hill
Jan.	22	Will: Bingley
	23	Thomas son to Widow Fowlson
Feb.	5 or 15	Robert Oxley
	22	Sarah daughter to Thomas Grey

1729

Mar. 8 Thomas Jessop
12 Philip Flint
23 Widow Sales

Memorandum April 24th 1729 Mr Will: Twittey was inducted Vicar of Wath.

1730.

Mar. 28 Widow Sales
Apl. 2 Richard son to Richard Trickitt
25 John Wood
26 Gilbert son to John Hammerton
May 5 Margaret wife to Thomas Hopkinson
June 8 Thomas son to Richard Sharp
July 3 Elizabeth Heaton
5 Mary wife to Francis Robinson
16 Widow Oxley
Aug. 2 Mr Baxter and Richardson to Thos Elam
4 Widow Halmshaw
26 James Oxley and John Briggs de Bramptō Bierly
Sept. 18 Michael son to Widow Hill
Oct. 26 William Iredal
Nov. 2 William son to Willm Hall
7 Thomas son to Mr Thoms Jackson
11 Alice Pullen
29 Richard Gorril
Dec. 15 Sarah wife to Richard Lambert
Jan. 9 William son to Wm Walton
12 John son to Wm Revel
13 Mary wife to John Townend
19 Mary daughter to William Flint
24 Jonathan Battie
24 Samuel son to William Rawson.
Finis Anni Prœdicti Wm Prickitt, Curate.

1731.

Apr. 5 Benjamin Hammond
12 Robert Stell of Ulley
June 12 Mary daughter to John Carr
17 Thomas son to Thomas Ostcliffe
19 Ann daughter to Richard Stead
July 9 Mary daughter to John Crossland
13 Richd son to John Crossland supra dict
Aug. 6 Ann daughter to Daniel Carnaley
8 Sarah daughter to Richd Russel
18 Sarah daughter to Will Fisher
Sept. 5 Ann daughter to Richd Sharp
25 Rosamond daughter to Mrs Wharam
Oct. 7 Mary daughter to Will Baxter
14 Martha wife to Michael Fenton
19 Thomas Shepherd from Mexborough

1731		
Oct.	23	Hannah wife to Thomas Walton
	26	Widow Rodes from Swinton
Nov.	4	Ann wife to John Morton from Wickersley
Dec.	19	Sarah daughter to Thomas Booth
	22	Valentine son to John Rodes
Jan	25	John son to James Bower
Feb.	2	Eliz daughter to Richd Forge
	3	Richd Watson of Swinton Senr
	20	Thomas Dowar
	23	Sarah Daughter to Will: Heald Junr
Mar.	14	George Hepworth
1732		
Apr	12	Ann wife to Thos Booth
	13	Martha daughter to Tho: Dodson
	15	Sarah wife to Richd Booth
	16	Widow Pinder
	28	George Batty
May	10	Widow Law
	14	Richard Stead
	16	Frances Trickit & Joh: Beaumont & Ann wife to Robert Fenton
Aug	3	Thomas Grey
	10	Grace daughter to Joseph Tasker
	16	Mary daughter to Matthew Newsom
	23	Thos Sales
Sept	7	George son to George Brammald
Oct	16	Ann daughter to Tho: Hodkinson
	19	Two daughters of Will Swinden
	21	Lydia Doughty
Nov	8	Thomas Wood
	24	Mary daughter to Tho: Hodkinson
Jan	21	Mary Hanson
	26	Ann wife to John Carr
	28	Mary daughter to John Carr
Feb.	4	John Amorey & Sarah daughter to Thomas Atkinson
	14	Widow Carr
	16	Ann daughter to Will Butler
	18	Widow Burdin
Mar	6	Agnes wife to Will Tingle
1733		
Apr	17	John Carr
May	1	James Brooksbanks
	17	Hannah wife to Richd Healey
June	12	Joseph son to Joseph Battison
	17	Ann England (a widow)
July	14	Mary daughter to Thomas Dodson & Sarah wife to John Hamerton

1733		
Sept	3	Richard Gorrill
	22	Henry son to Bart Hattersley of the Houndhill in y[e] Parish of Darfield
Oct	6	Eliz wife to Thomas Wood & Elizabeth Smith
Nov	23	John Redale
	24	Ann wife to Hugh Elison
Dec	23	Susanna daughter to Tho Hopkinson
Jan	14	Nehemiah Wade
Feb	2	Josias Hudson
	15	Joseph Milner
	20	Widow Gawtrey
	24	John Bintcliffe
1734		
Apr	25	Ann wife to Sam[l] Cut
	28	Thomas Mallison
May	2	Eliz: wife to Martin Thompson
	30	Will son to Will: Banks
	31	John Kennerley
June	3	Sarah wife to Rich[d] Sales
	13	Ann daughter to John Trickit
	15	John Elam
	27	Ann daughter to Will: Shaw
Aug	6	John Moreley
	14	Hannah Shaw (widow)
Sept	17	Joseph son to Joseph Sadler
Oct	7	John Arundel
	24	Martin Thompson
	31	George son to George White
Nov	8	Joshua Shepherd
Jan	15	a poor Traveller
	26	a poor woman from Brampton
Mar	13	Widow Wade of Swinton
1735		
Apr	23	Jane wife to James Smith
May	3	Elizabeth daughter to Edward Smith
Aug	19	A Stranger from y[e] Rhodes
Oct	20	Joseph son to Edward Fosterd
	22	Will: son to Henry Walker
Dec	8	Ann daughter to John Adin
	11	Martha daughter to Tho Dodson
Feb	15	Sam[l] son to Robert Cut
Mar	9	Thomas Elam
1736		
Apr	18	Robert Hudson
May	24	Elizabeth Gessop
June	1	Edward Braithwait
Sep	12	Eliz daughter to Will Kay

1736		
Sep	12	John son to Thomas Carr
Oct	23	John Hargrave
Nov	5	George son to George Brameld
	10	Samuel son to Widow Stead
	18	Elizabeth daughter to Will Banks
	20	Susanna wife to Robert Cut
Dec	10	Joseph Battison
	23	Ester wife to Peter Maud
	24	Mary wife to George Whitaker
Jan	2	Thomas son to Richard Lambert
	24	Widow Horsfield
Feb	6	Ann daughter to Widow Elam
Mar	6	John Turner and his son
	8	Thomas son to John Trickit
1737		
Mar	27	Richard Thompson of Swinton
	31	Thomas son to Will: Wood
Apr	21	Thomas son to Will: Kay
May	3	John Birks of Swinton
	8	Joanna Cusworth
	15	Jonathan son to Thomas Townend
	25	Jane wife to John Thompson
	30	Robert Dobson, stranger from Swinton
June	30	John Dickson
	19	Francis son to Edward Smith
July	15	Joseph son to Samuel Smith
	16	Ann daughter to Joseph Roberts
	18	Thomas son to Thomas Oufield
	30	John Arthur
	31	Ann daughter to Will: Winter
Aug	24	Eliz: daughter to George Bell
Sept	7	Hugh Elison
	20	George son to Thomas Hopkinson
Nov	4	Eliz: wife to George Bayley
	14	Rich[d] Allen
	23	Sarah wife to Will Stacey
Dec	30	Susanna wife to Robert Ibotson
Jan	7	Sarah wife to Thomas Roebuck
	29	Robert Cut
Feb	10	Ann daughter to John Adin
Mar	18	Esther daughter to Rich: Dyson
1738		
Apr	8	Sarah Wood
June	15	Jane wife to John Wilcock
	27	Eliz: daughter to George Bell
July	5	Richard Hudson
	10	Richard son to Thomas Worrill
	18	Eliz: wife to Will: Tingle

1738
Aug 15 Will Hamond
Nov 13 Jonas Archer, a stranger from Burdet Flat-House, Swinton
30 Ann daughter to James Bower &
John Parrat
Dec 6 Abraham son to Stephen Yoyle
10 Esther wife to Will: Fisher
Jan 20 Joseph Lee & John son to Joshua Gill
Feb 8 Alice wife to Will Hodkinson
Mar 9 Joseph son to Edward Lowley
19 John Rodes
21 Mary daughter to Will: Mann
23 Elias Mathewman

1739
Mar 29 Richard Tricket, clark
30 John Hudson of Newel
Apr 10 Margaret wife to James Bower of Newel
21 Mary Gray
28 Richard son to Richard Hicks of Swinton
29 William North of Melton
Sept 27 Charles Jenkin, serv[t] to Will[m] Heald
Oct 9 Joseph Hammond of Brampton
30 John Tompson of Swinton
30 Martha daughter to Thomas Worrel
Dec 19 Mary wife to Richard Hicks of Swinton
Jan 22 Thomas Firth of Brampton
Feb 21 Mary daughter to John Wood

1740
Apr 6 Ann Hill of Swinton
2 John son to Matthew Low of Swinton
11 Mary Frith of Brampton
11 Ann wife to Joseph Sadler of Coley lane
Aug 21 Tho. son to Tho. Worrill of Wath
Dec 2 Wm son to Tho. Hopkinson of Swinton
10 Mary wife to Jonathan Darwin of Swinton
Jan 29 Eliz: Hammond of Wath
Feb 21 John son to Richard Bingley of Wath
27 Ann daughter to Henry Pullan of Wath
Mar 1 W[m] son to John Forge of Wath
9 Elizabeth daughter to W[m] Kay of Wath

1741
Mar 28 James son of Henry Pullen
29 Edward son of Edward Fosterd
Apr 6 John Birks
27 Tabitha daughter of William Man
May 6 Joseph Johnson
10 William son of Edward Smyth
June 6 Francis Robinson
7 William son of Jonathan Darin

1741		
June	14	Sarah daughter of Richard Thompson
July	21	Ann Sissens
	24	Joseph son of Matthew Law
	26	Richard son of Richard Sharp
Aug	7	Elizabeth wife of William Kay
	25	Elizabeth daughter of William Eastwood
Oct	31	Richard Lambert
Nov	21	William Farrer. Afternoon Preacher
	26	Ruth wife of Henry Walker
Dec	12	Robert Fenton
	22	John Townend
	29	Mary wife of John Man
Jan	2	Richard Booth
	14	William son of Thomas Watson
Feb	5	Sarah Bintcliff
	21	Betty daughter of Edward Bool
	23	Ann Ainley a stranger
	28	Ann wife of William Hall
Mar	16	Sarah Tuck
1742		
Mar	31	Peter Mawd
Apr	27	William Carr
	29	Richard son of Richard Dyson
May	20	John Wilcock
	22	James Bower
July	2	Mary daughter of Robert Stead
	11	George Chevin
Aug	11	William Tinley
Nov	17	Ann Thompson
Jan	25	Thomas Hartley
Feb	9	John Shepherd
	22	Sarah daughter of John English
	26	Ann daughter of Edward Smyth
Mar	11	John son of John Denton of Hoober
	17	William Heald
1743		
Apl	5	George Rymer
	10	Margaret Daughter of Thomas Smyth
	18	Olive Daughter of Daniel Twigg
	19	Thomas Roebuck
	21	Edward Box
	24	Ann wife of James Whitaker
	27	Richard Son of Richard Bingley
		Thomas Hobkinson
		Charles Son of Mary Twittey
May	5	Robert Chappel
		Joshua Culpin
	8	Elizabeth Hudson

1743

May 13 John Son of John Ely
14 William Son of William Wharam of Wath
15 Ann Foulstone
31 Betty Daughter of George Swift
June 10 John Son of Jeremiah Lightowler
July 24 Dorothy Wife of John Adin
Oct 7 Sarah Wife of Thomas Bingley
20 Mary Wife of Mr Mower of Nottinghamshire
Dec 3 Margaret Wife of Joshua Shepherd
31 Elizabeth Wife of Michael Fenton
Jan 15 Mary Hawksworth
22 Elizabeth Birks
29 John Wright
Feb 3 Ann Wife of Richard Birks
15 Mary Daughter of George Brammald
19 John Woodall
23 Robert Ibbotson
Mar 11 William Kemp
Edward Son of George Brammald

N.B.—William Jackson of Swinton was buried about midsummer the Day forgotten. I have heard it was on July ye 13th.

1744

Apr 1 William Hall of West Melton
May 12 William Son of the late William Kemp of Swinton
17 George Lovedy of Wath
June 3 Joshua Jackson of Swinton, Miller
8 William Son of Joseph Hill of Swinton
July 25 George Kay of Wath, Collier
Aug 2 Mary the wife of Jonathan Gaskin of Coley Lane
22 Ann Daughter of William Thompson of Wath, Butcher
Sept 14 Mary Hudson of West Melton
19 Thomas Foulstone of Brampton, Schoolmaster
Oct 7 Richard Son of John Jackson of Wath
Nov 22 William Son of Thomas Worral of Wath
Dec 8 Thomas Bagshaw of Newhill
29 Sarah Daughter of John Lyell of West Melton
Jan 4 John Son of John Lyell of West Melton
Feb 3 John Son of Mary Sharp of Wath, widow
15 Elizabeth Beaumont of Newhill, widow
18 Ruth Lockwood of West Melton
Mar 21 Richard Hicks of Swinton, Taylor

John Empson, Curate of Wath
Tho: Kay } Church
Robert Hudson } Wardens

1745

Apl 29 Mary Tricket of Melton, widow
May 20 John Dalton of Wath
and Richard Sales of Swinton

1745

June 26 Ann wife of Daniel Kernley
Sept 2 Frances wife of Richard Elam of West Melton
5 Elizabeth Daughter of Thomas Kay of Wath
12 Mary Ibbotson of Wath
17 John Wharam of Swinton
Oct 13 Olive Daughter of James Ellis of Hoyland
Nov 1 Ann Swift of Wath
23 Sarah Arundel of Swinton
Dec 31 Ann Daughter of Stephen Alender of Swinton
and Sarah Hartley of Rhodes, widow
Jan 15 John Hall of Hoober
19 Ann Daughter of Samuel Smith of Newhill
28 Mary Wife of Robert Stead of Wath
Feb 2 Edward Son of Richard Sharp of Wath
12 Martha Daughter of Thomas Booth of Brampton
17 John Son of Richard Dyson of Wath
20 James Smith of Wath
23 Ann Pindar of Newhill, widow
Mar 11 Mary Daughter of William Watkin of Melton
18 Sarah Woodall of Swinton, widow
23 Elizabeth Kay of Wath, widow

John Empson, Curate of Wath

1746

Apr 2 Joseph Son of Joseph Tasker of Newhill
May 6 William Grey, Senr of Rainbrough
8 Mary Wife of William Bingley of Swinton
July 5 Ann Jackson of Wath, Widow
16 William Son of Ellen Bower (illegitimate)
Aug 5 Rachael Wife of Thomas Man of Swinton
& Hannah Daughter of Joseph Gilliot of Melton Green
6 Ruth Daughter of William Kay of Elsecar
17 Stephen Alendar of Swinton
Sept 2 Daniel Scora of Swinton
8 Dorothy Rymer of Wath, widow
18 Hellen Daughter of George Trout of Street
Oct 19 Ann Daughter of Joseph Hill of Swinton
29 Thomas Son of John Lyell of West Melton
Dec 6 John Son of Richard Foulstone, Junr of Brampton
22 Sarah Daughter of Joshua Hilton of Wath
29 William Son of Thomas Tyson of Swinton Common
& Frances wife of Richard Thompson of Wath
Jan 18 Mary Twittey of Wath, Widow of the Rev^d^ Mr John Twittey
22 John Son of John English of Wath
23 Abraham Son of John Wood Junr of Wath, Bark Chopper
Feb 9 Mary Daughter of George Gawtrees of Wath
12 Ann Daughter of William Newbold of Swinton

1746

Mar 19 Humphrey Jackson late of Wath but died in the parish of Rotheram
& Elizabeth Oxley of Swinton, Widow

John Empson, Curate of Wath.
Jonathan Twittey } Churchwardens.
William Baxter }

1747.

May 11 Mary Daughter of John Ely of Newhill
June 1 Mary Amorey of Wath, widow
3 William Baxter of West Melton, Labourer
July 13 Benjamin Son of William Rawson of Swinton
& Elizabeth Daughter of the late John Wharam of Swinton
21 John a Child found in the fields
27 John Son of John Smith of Wath, Joyner
Aug 16 Godfrey Son of Thomas Bintcliff of Coley Lane
23 John Son of Robert Woodhall of Swinton
29 Mary Daughter of Samuel Carnaley of West Melton
Sept 7 Sarah Heald of Brampton, Widow
15 William Son of Thomas Bintcliff of Coley Lane
& Thomas Arundel of Wentworth House, Butcher
30 Jane Daughter of Thomas Inman of West Melton, Blacksmith
Oct 8 Ann Wife of Thomas Ledger of Wath, shoemaker
11 George Son of Abel Hyde of Wath, Parish Clerk
13 James Whitaker of West Melton
16 Thomas Son of Widow Loveday of Wath
19 Jane Wife of Thomas Inman of West Melton, Blacksmith
20 William Revel of Wath
27 Elizabeth Wife of Jonathan Darwin of Swinton
30 Mary Wife of Jervase Carnaley of West Melton
Nov 7 Ann Daughter of Matthew Speight of Swinton
8 Elizabeth Daughter of John Mallison of West Melton
Dec 1 Sarah Daughter of John Ely of Newhill
17 Susan Shepherd of Coley Lane, Widow
Feb 11 John Arundel of Hoober, Mason.
12 John Lutterel, Gardiner
Mar 13 Sarah Daughter of George Dyson of Wath.

John Empson, Curate of Wath
William Ibotson } Church
Timothy Rhodes } Wardens

1748

Mar 25 George Bailey of Wath
Apr 10 Francis Son of George Brammald of Swinton, Blacksmith
17 Jeremiah Lightowler of Newhill, Collier
24 William Son of William Hartley of Swinton, Schoolmaster
May 11 Sarah Wade of Wath, Widow

1748		
June	3	Ann Daughter of Robert Stead of Wath, Mason
	5	William Kay of Wath, Feltmaker & Farmer
Oct	11	Elizabeth Wife of William Rogers of Brampton, Blacksmith
	12	William Wade of Swinton
Jan	2	Joshua Green of Swinton
	20	John Smith a poor Traveller
Feb	9	Lydia Wife of John Ely of Newhill, Collier
Mar	8	Elizabeth Bell of Wath, Widow
	14	Elizabeth Wife of Robert Hyde of Wath

John Empson, Curate
John Denton Jun[r] } Church
Joseph Roberts } Wardens

1749		
Apr	7	Thomas Dodson of Melton, Clothier & husbandman
	11	Joshua Shepherd of Swinton, Farmer
	25	John Carr of Wath, Farmer
May	13	Francis Smith of Wath, Farmer
June	26	Ann Daughter of Thomas Kay of Wath, Farmer & Malster
Aug	6	Edward Fosterd of Swinton, Farmer
	30	George Whitaker of Melton
Oct	1	Richard Son of Henry Slater of Newhill, Collier
	2	Edward Son of Edward Smith of Wath, Butcher
	29	Ann Elam of Newhill, Widow
Nov	20	Mary wife of Edward Fenton of Wath, Shoemaker
Jan	8	Mary Daughter of Robert Woodall of Swinton
	30	Elizabeth Wharam of Swinton, Widow
Feb	13	Mary Wife of Daniel Twigg of Roydes
	18	Thomas Bingley of Swinton
	22	Joshua Wood of Melton, Mason
Mar	17	Martha Wife of Henry Walker of Newhill

John Empson, Curate
John Denton } Churchwardens
Joseph Roberts }

Buried in the Year 1750.

March	29	Ann Gorril, Widow
Apr.	9	Elizabeth wife of Thomas Harpam of Wath
May	11	Robert Son of Robert Hudson of Wath, Farmer
	30	John Wade of Swinton
June	9	Abigail Jackson of Swinton, a Servant
	20	Ann the Wife of Samuel Hurst
July	13	Ann Bradshaw, a Traveller
	14	Jervase Carnaley of Melton, Farmer
	27	Ann Daughter of John Shaw of Swinton, Weaver
	30	John Dyson of Brampton
Aug	2	Sarah Daughter of William Harrison of Wath, Labourer

1750
Aug 9 William Baxter of Roydes, Gentleman
Mary Daughter of Major Munton of Newhill, Joiner & Thomas Carr of Wath
16 Robert Son of Robert Stead of Wath, Mason
Oct 15 Sarah Daughter of Joshua Swallow of Barnsley
20 George Son of Thomas Worral of Wath, Taylor
Nov 10 John Son of John Baumforth of Hoober, Labourer
Jan 13 George Matthewman of Thiefhole
28 Thomas Hopkinson of Swinton, Tinker
Feb. 12 Mrs. Sarah Tolson, of Rotherham
Mar 7 Ann Daughter of Thomas Campsal of Wath, Labourer
John Empson, Curate.

1751.
April 5 John Son of John Woodcock of Newhill
May 1 Ann Daughter of Richard Birks, of Swinton, Taylor
18 Ann Wife of John Hardwick of Swinton
June 18 All Church Son of John Coleburn, of Kilnhurst
July 3 Elizabeth Wife of John Tyas of Hoober
27 Ann Daughter of Ann Jessop of Melton
31 John Son of John Wood of Wath
Aug 1 Ann Daughter of John Denton of Wath
4 Martha Daughter of Thomas Jackson of Melton
30 Benjamin Thicket
Sept 18 John Hunt of Thorn, Waterman
27 Mary Daughter of William Wharam
Oct 17 Mary Jubb
Nov 16 Mary Ellis
24 Sarah North
30 Martha Daughter of Robert Hudson
Dec 12 Thomas Pinders
Feb 6 Jonathan Son of William Best of Swinton
9 Martha Wife of Joshua Roberts of Hoober
Mar 1 Ann Daughter of John Wright, Hatter
3 William Son of John Lidster of Melton
7 Benjamin Son of Widow Thicket
16 Richard Son of Thomas Worril

1752.
Apr 7 Mr. John Jackson
13 Ann Daughter of John Lyall
23 Mary Daughter of Richd Sharp
May 4 Alice wife of Richard Hill
13 Richard Sharp
15 Edward son of Susan Thicket
19 Richard Revel
31 Mary daughter of John Law
June 1 Elizabeth daughter of John Law
7 Sarah daughter of Mr Jo. Smith
11 Charles son of William Eastwood

1752		
July	8	Dorothy Revel
Aug	18	Jane wife of Richard Russel
Sept	24	John Twittey, Tanner
Nov	5	Ann daughter of John Woodcock
	16	Francis Hardy, Mason
	22	Dorothy wife of William Flint, Hoober
	23	Martha Revel
Dec	5	Ann daughter of Gervas Carnally, Weaver
	18	Sarah daughter of Richard Dodson, Hatter
	19	Elizabeth daughter of Thomas Silcock, Line-Dresser
	22	Jonathan Gascoign, Farmer
	25	A child of Joshua Hampshire's
	31	John son of John Littlewood of London
1753		
Jan	3	Richard son of Thomas Bincliff, Labourer
	6	Mary and Elizabeth daughters of John Wright
	14	Ann daughter of Samuel Baddely, Skinner
	23	Martha wife of Jonathan Charlesworth
	28	Richard son of John Russel, Taylor
Feb	14	James son of William Hyerdale, Coley-lane
	24	William Thompson, Butcher
	28	Mr Robert Woodall
Mar	2	Ann daughter of George Foulstone
	13	Thomas son of Timothy Swift
Apr	22	Richard Foolstone, Farmer
May	14	Sarah wife to Isaac Tomlinson, Shoemaker Daughter to William Hartley
	23	Richard Wilson, Farmer
	27	John Crosland, Farmer
Aug	8	Samuel son to William Eastwood, Labourer
	29	Martha wife to John Kennerley, Hatter
Sept	13	Elizabeth daughter to Thomas Dyson, Labourer
	28	William Carr of Swinton, Mason
Oct	8	John Carr, Farmer
Nov	4	John Jackson, Farmer
	6	A Child of William Marshall, Taylor
Dec	26	Mary wife to Richard Jackson, Farmer
1754.		
Jan.	12	Richard Jackson
	14	William son of Matthew Law
Feb.	10	Alice Carr
Mar.	4	John son of Joshua Hampshire
	20	Richard son of Thomas Oldfield
	24	Jonathan son of John Twittey
	Do.	Mary daughter of Joseph Kershaw
	31	James son of James Beaumont
Apr.	2	Ann Oates
	28	Thomas Oldfield

1754		
June	2	James Rollin
	10	Joseph son of George Parkin
July	15	Elizabeth daughter of Richard Thompson
Aug.	19	William son of William Athron
Sept.	8	Sarah Wilson, Widow
Nov.	21	Mary Ellis
Dec.	13	Elizabeth wife of Richard Watson
	28	Sarah wife of Richard Lambert
1755.		
Feb.	13	Hannah wife of John Holland
	25	Sarah wife of John Bell
Mar.	31	William Eastwood, Labourer
Apr.	20	Rebecca Green
	28	Ann wife of William Otley
May	3	Ann wife of Benjamin Spencer
	4	John Babb
	6	Mary wife of David Froggit
	11	Richard Thompson
	20	Dorothe wife of William Tingle
June	11	Hannah wife of William Wharam
	14	Mary Trickit
Sept.	5	Mary Carr, Widow
	11	Rich: Wildsmith
	18	Sarah daughter of Richard Wildsmith
	26	Luke Worril
Nov.	1	Robert Hyde
	1	John son of John Law
Dec.	1	Richard Canby, Gentleman
	17	Sarah Ellis, Widow
1756.		
Jan.	15	Richard Watson
	26	Susanna Hyerdale, Widow
Feb.	10	Mary Parkin, Widow
	23	Thomas Harpen
Mar.	4	Philip Flint
	19	John Chetham
Apr.	10	Philip son of Philip Flint
June	13	Joseph son of John Cutt
	25	Mary Calpin
	28	Elizabeth daughter of George Asque
July	7	Thomas son of John Wade
	16	Stephen son of Benjamin Senior
	30	An old Soldier
Aug.	12	Charles Butler
Sept.	1	Mary daughter of Gervas Lyall
	8	Mary wife of Joseph Birkes
	26	Thomas son of William Dyson
Oct.	7	Abel son of Abel Hyde

1756		
Oct.	24	Edward son of James Butler
	28	Mary daughter of John Cutt
Nov.	7	Jane wife of Richard Smith
Dec.	22	George son of William Bell
	23	George son of George Gawtrees
	30	Mary wife of George Foulstone
1757.		
Jan.	2	Mary Colledge, a Foundling
	3	Sarah, daughter of Joseph Munday
	14	Ann Wilcock
Feb.	2	John son of William Stead
Mar.	3	Thomas South
May	18	Mary daughter of Joshua Gill
June	17	George son of William Wharam
July	14	William Newbolt
Sept	8	Mary daughter of William Swinden
	12	William son of William Fish of Hooton Pagnell
	do	Elizabeth wife of Major Mountain
Dec.	22	Mary Gray, Widow
1758.		
Feb.	15	William son of William Dyson
	19	Dorothy wife of Joshua Hylton
	20	daughter of Joseph Hill
Mar.	5	Samuel Thompson
	9	Elizabeth wife of Richard Forde
	10	Richard son of Mrs Dolby
	19	Martha Oldfield
	26	Hannah Cock
Apr.	8	Richard Lambert, Swinton
	14	Thomas son of Philip Heptonstall
	19	Mary daughter of Hannah Tingle
	21	Ann daughter of Joseph Sadler
	28	Sarah wife of Joseph Dickinson
May	23	Sarah daughter of Richard Laycock
	31	George son of Richard Laycock
June	17	John son of John Scott of Haxworth
June	22	John Green, Swinton
July	8	John Son of William Schorah
Aug	18	A child of William Morley's
Sept	1	William son of Robert Hudson
	13	Matthew Speight, Swinton
Oct	1	Martha daughter of Mary Slater
	8	Richard Gawtrey
	19	A Foundling
	29	A Foundling
Nov	19	Thomas son of Thomas Silcock
Dec	11	John Heward
	29	Sarah Daughter of Ann Law

1758		
Dec	29	Elizabeth Daughter of Catherine Fisher
1759		
Jan	10	Abraham Son of James Hartley
	17	Sarah Daughter of Joseph Munday
	19	William Son of William Tingle
Feb	5	Sarah Daughter of Thomas Briggs
	18	William Morley
Mar	21	John Denton
	21	Sarah Pinder
	22	James Hartley
May	13	Ann Wife of Peter Law
Aug	7	Ann daughter of John Anley
	14	Eleanor Daughter of Thomas Kay
	19	John Son of Mr. Manby
	27	Joseph Turner
Nov	25	Jonathan Charlesworth
	29	John Son of James Beaumont
	31	Matthias Reynald
1760		
Jan	6	Sarah Thompson, Widow
	16	Ann Daughter of Thomas Worril
Feb	22	Sarah Sailes, Widow
Mar	26	William Otley
	28	Mrs Cleator, Wife to the Revd Mr Cleator, Lecturer
Apr	2	Mary Daughter of Robert Hudson
	21	Mary Twittey
	30	Thomas Adkison
May	13	John Wood
	16	John Rhodes
	20	James Son of Henry Slater
June	7	Thomas Son of Richard Wilson
	11	Mary Cowley
July	20	Rebecca Daughter of Gervase Lyall
Aug	11	Ann Wife of Samuel Griffin
	30	John Son of Revd Mr Empson of Scawby, Lincolnshire
Sep	1	Thomas Carr
Oct	1	Sarah Wife of Robt Hudson
	25	Margaret Crosley
1761		
Jan	20	Elizabeth Wife of Moses Evas
	23	John Lum belonging Huthersfield
Feb	10	Sarah Wife of Joseph Munday
	15	Sarah Watson
Apr	11	Richard Fowlstone, Hoober
	14	The Rev Mr William Twittey, Vicar
	22	Elizabeth Fowlstone, widow
	24	Elizabeth Wilson, widow
	28	Mary Wife of Edward Smith

1761		
May	15	Elizabeth Daughter of Edward Radcliff
	16	Peter Law
	23	Eleanor Bramhall
	27	Edward Son of Edward Radcliff
June	3	Ann Daughter of James Beaumont
	16	Eleanor Moor, a Scotch Woman
	18	John Howorth
July	8	Thomas Son of Joseph Robinson
	30	Thomas Carr, Tanner
Aug	13	Samuel Son of John Cudworth
	14	Mary Daughter of George Moor
	20	Ann Daughter of Richard Wildsmith
	22	John son of John Cudworth
	30	Ann Wife of William Butler
		George Son of Timothy Swift
Sept	8	Jonathan Son of William Wade
	23	William Son of John Twittey
	25	Martha Daughter of William Wade
Oct	1	Martha Daughter of William Burland
Nov	11	Samuel Crossley
1762		
Jan	3	William Hodkinson
	3	Rosamond Wife of John Wood
	10	Ann Carr of Brampton, widow
	16	Joseph Son of Joseph Sadler
	26	Jane Daughter of John Bell
Feb	12	Thomas Rodger
	24	John Wood
	25	George Son of William Malpas
Mar	6	John Son of John Wright
	25	George Son of John Wright
Apr	7	Elizabeth Loveday
	8	John Campsall
	20	Charlotte Wife of Richard Dyson
June	3	William Harrison
	6	Sarah daughter of John Smith, Butcher
	10	Richard Becket
	20	Henry Pulleyn
July	8	Esther daughter of the Revd Mr Webster
	14	Hannah daughter of the Revd Mr Webster
Aug	7	George Fowstone
	8	John son of Thomas Cusworth
	29	Elizabeth daughter of Matthew Law
Sept	5	Jonathan Gawtrees
	23	Ann Hardy
Oct	31	Daniel Carnally
		Margaret daughter of William Ossop
Nov	1	Mr John Smith

1762		
Nov	18	Richard son of Richard Wildsmith
	21	William Fenton
Dec	11	Thomas Dodson
	14	Edward Bolton, a Soldier
	31	Sarah wife of Thomas Brook
1763		
Jan	1	John son of William Bingley
	2	Richard son of Richard Wilson
	4	Mary wife of John Littlewood
	14	Edward Butler
	31	Mary Twittey, widow
Feb	5	Mary wife of Jonas Beet
	21	Mary daughter of George Moor
	23	Richard Russell
	27	Leah Gray, widow
Mar	27	Martha wife of John Trickit
Apr	10	Hannah Worril, widow
	20	John Mercer of Swinton
June	2	Mary wife of George Bramhall
	10	John Holland
	14	Martha Wood, widow
	17	George son of John Woodcock
	23	Sarah daughter of John Hobkison
July	6	Sarah wife of Joseph Hunt
	8	William son of John Wade
	21	Ann Chetham, widow
	Do	William Bisby
Oct	3	Thomas son of William Hyerdale
Nov	2	Matthew Mazlin
	24	Thomas Malpas
	30	Elizabeth Hardy, widow
Dec	1	John son of Joseph Bentley
	8	Hannah daughter of John Best
	21	Thomas son of Major Mountain
	29	Richard Elam
1764		
Jan	10	Martha daughter of William Wade
Feb	25	Sarah Fowlstone
Mar	16	Robert son of Robert and Hannah Woodall
Apr	3	Jonas Beet
	15	John Tricket of Melton
May	21	Martha wife of John Lewis
June	10	George son of John Warin
	18	Thomas Townend
July	5	Dorothy Dodson, widow
	22	Ann wife of William Heald
Aug	1	Henry Walker
	20	Nancy daughter of Thomas Smith

1764		
Sept	8	Elizabeth Fowlstone
Oct	15	Mary daughter of John Appleyard
	29	Margaret Allen, widow
1765		
Jan	3	William son of William Kay
	22	Joshua son of Thomas Worril
Feb	8	George son of Richard Laycock
Mar	1	George son of William Trippit
	2	Elizabeth Daughter of William Lunn
	3	Robert Ibbotson
	5	Hannah Thompson, Widow
Apr	11	Mary Harrison, Widow
	13	Betty wife of Thomas Bolden
	25	George Son of Thomas Cusworth
	25	Nancy Daughter of Thomas Dunnel
May	4	Elizabeth Daughter of Thomas White
	8	Mary Jackson, Widow
	13	Josias Son of Richard Laycock
June	19	Dorothy Smith
July	7	William Son of Abraham Turton
	16	George Bell
Aug	16	Joseph Roberts
	19	Richard Wilson
	29	Elizabeth Campsall
Sept	1	Martha Daughter of Major Mountain
	1	William Son of Joseph Bentley
	16	John Son of William Denton
	22	John Wood
Nov	19	Sarah Daughter of Robert Hudson
Dec	4	Thomasin wife of William Ibbotson
	23	Elizabeth wife of Samuel Griffith
	24	Timothy Rhodes Esq
1766		
Jan	3	A Child of William Fishers Junr of Melton
	7	Sarah Daughter of William Linfit
	31	John Son of Thomas Aden
Mar	19	George Asque
	26	William Burn, a stranger
May	3	Robert Son of Major Mountain
	11	Sarah Harrison, Widow
	12	Ann Daughter of William Trickit
	22	Robert Stead
June	6	John Son of William Linfitt
	14	Elizabeth Daughter of Joshua Earnshaw
	15	Charles Son of Thomas Cusworth
	24	George Son of Philip Hepinstall
July	22	George Gawtrees
	23	Lucy Daughter of Henry Ledger

1766		
July	24	Hannah wife of Jonathan Hargreaves
	30	Elizabeth Daughter of Thomas Bates
Sept	17	Thomas Son of Richard Jackson
Oct	3	Elizabeth Butler
	11	Major Mountain
	16	Susanna Parker
	22	Joshua Roberts of Nether Hough
Dec	2	Thomas Son of Thomas Roberts
	4	John Son of George Moor
	23	Martha Daughter of Joshua Roberts of Nether Hough
1767		
Jan	15	Thomas Booth
	16	Richard Bacon
Feb	3	Andrew Speight
	9	Elizabeth Hammond
	10	Samuel Smith
Mar	29	Mary Wharam, widow
	29	John Son of John Smith
Apr	8	Hannah Wife of Joseph Hunter
	19	William Hammond
	27	Ann Daughter of Richard Thompson
May	2	Martin Thompson
	5	Mary Daughter of William Grey
	31	Martha Daughter of Zilpah Mountain
June	3	Martha Elam, Widow
	8	Ann, wife of Edward Radcliff
July	19	Hannah Goddard, widow
	28	William Gawtrees
Aug	15	Margaret wife of John Woodcock
	19	Mary Daughter of Thomas Kay
	27	Martha Daughter of John Elam
Sept	9	Lucy Wife of Richard Rollin
	30	Robert Son of Joshua Dickinson
Oct	1	A child of Joshua Sympson's
	24	Mary Hopkinson
Nov.	4	William Son of George Bramhall
	5	Ann wife of Joshua Dickinson
	18	William Allsop
Dec.	7	Frances, wife of Willoughby Wood
	23	Ann Rhodes
1768		
Feb.	17	John Son of Gervas Lyell
Mar	12	Mary Hartley, Widow
	22	Ann Tyas, Widow
	27	Mrs Hannah Rhodes, Widow
May	13	Eliz[h] Wife of W[m] Ibbotson
		Martha wife of Rich[d] Dodson
June	22	Ann Matthewman, widow

1768		
June	30	John Son of Wm Hargreaves
Aug	24	Sarah Speight, Widow
Oct	9	Charles Son to Joseph Gibson at Lock Side
	21	$Eliz^h$ wife of Edward Salter
	25	John Son of Robert Bayley
Nov.	4	Martha daughter of Peter Dean
	22	Richard Townend, Yeoman
Dec.	4	Ann Denton, Widow
	13	John Brook (Newhill)
1769.		
Jan.	16	Mary wife of John Ashey
Feb.	12	Sarah wife of $Rich^d$ Thompson
Mar.	24	Elizabeth Arundel of Hoober
	31	Mary daughter of George Fowlstone
May	4	John son of Thos Briggs
June	15	Sarah daughter of $Rich^d$ Wilson
July	6	Mary daughter of $Rich^d$ Wildsmith
	14	Ann daughter of Wm Newsom
	24	Matthew son of Godfrey Speight
	26	$Rich^d$ Dyson
	27	Mary wife of Wm Wright
Sept.	2	Ann daughter of George Moore
	8	Mary wife of James Wilson
	29	John Steads
Oct.	2	$Eliz^h$ daughter of Thos Jackson
	9	Sarah wife of Wm Carr
	11	Ann Pullen, Widow
	12	Eliz wife of Thos Carnelly
	22	A child of John Cowper's
	24	Ann wife of Thos Crosly
Nov.	26	Samuel Malkin
	30	Abel Hyde
Dec.	24	Edward Heys
	29	The Revd Mr Steer
1770.		
Jan.	4	Robert son of $Mich^l$ Ford
	14	$Eliz^h$ wife of Enoch Thompson
Feb.	13	Hannah daughter of Abram Turton
Apr.	28	Mary wife of John Tysap
	29	Ann wife of Thos Worral
May	2	Susannah wife of Wm Muss
	7	John son of John Holland
	8	Ann daughter of Michael Bisby
	26	Thos Jackson
	31	Joshua son of John Matthewman
June	3	Martha wife of John Adin
	26	Catharine wife of $Benj^n$ Senyor
	27	Joseph son of Thos Roberts

1770		
Aug	1	Eliz^h daughter of John Lewis
	15	Richd Smith
Oct.	10	Joseph Birks
Nov.	18	Joseph Cliffe
Dec.	14	Wm Iredale
1771.		
Jan.	5	Wm Baxter
	5	Mary wife of Wm Schisms
	6	Joseph son of Benjn Askew
	18	Martha daughter of Joshua Gray
	21	George son of George Dyson
	22	Joshua son of Joshua Gill
Feb.	5	Alice wife of Thos Wood
	23	Abram son of Thos Cusworth
Mar.	20	David Clarke
May	3	Mary wife of Thos Baxter
	14	W^m son of Thos Hilton
June	26	Sarah wife of Joshua Gill
July	3	Ann Rhodes, Widow
	4	Mary Baxter, Widow
	17	John son of Thos Downend
	22	John son of Jonat^n Eley
Aug.	8	Martha Kennerley, Widow
	11	Grace Jackson, Widow
Sept.	26	A child of Thos Watson's of Swinton
Oct.	7	Ann daughter of Charles Wood
	9	A child of Josh Birks
Nov.	5	Grace Prince, Widow
	24	Rich^d son of Ann Carr
Dec.	2	A child of John Robinson's
1772.		
Jan.	12	Giles Pattison
	28	Sarah Penter, Widow
Feb.	4	Hannah daughter of Wm Linfitt
Mar.	3	Thos son of Benjn Grayson
Apr.	4	Hannah wife of Thos Webster
	23	Thos son of James Saville
	25	Martha wife of Peter Dean
May	6	Mary daugh^r of Wm Carr
	26	Richd Birks
	27	James son of Thos Cusworth
June	2	Robert Hudson
	7	Sarah wife of Abra^m Horsfall
	9	Samuel Wells
	20	Ann wife of John Cooper
	27	George son of John Blake
July	10	Mary Sewyer
	19	John Kay, Tanner

1772		
July	30	Eliz^{h} daugh^{r} of Saml Wells
Aug.	17	Thos Hading
Sept.	15	Henry Slater's child
1773		
Jan	3	Bridget Haworth
		Martha Daughter of John Allen
	11	Ann Wife of Thos Hillton
Feb	24	Thos Whites, Child of Swinton
	26	Jane Pindar
	28	Ann Wife of John Adams
Mar	9	Mary Wife of Mr Robert Watson
	12	John Son of John Taylor
	13	Martha Daughter of John Wright
	14	Richd Son of Thos Cusworth
	27	Ann Cusworth
Apr	11	Betty Daughter of William Hall
	11	Hannah Daughter of George Tingle
	18	Martha wife of John Allen
	18	George Son of Henry Ledger
	19	John Holland
	22	William Steads
	22	John Son of George Tingle
May	5	A Child of Joseph Nailers
	11	Maria Daughter of Thomas Kay, Junr
	26	Ann Daughter of William Addey
June	1	Joseph Staten
	2	Mary Wife of William Wood
	2	Ann Daughter of William Cartridge
	14	A Child of William Cartridge
	15	Thomas Son of Paul Garthfitt
	23	A Child of Henry Slaters
	25	Francis Son of John Smith
July	6	Sarah Daughter of Francis Trickett
	12	Hannah Daughter of Thomas Durham
	30	Joshua Roberts
Aug	10	Ann Daughter of William Linfitt
Sept	2	David Froggett
	5	Isaac Widdup son of David Stones
Oct	19	Elizabeth Wells, Widow
Nov	14	Mary Bingley
	15	Richd Cookeson
Dec	14	Martha Wife to John Elam
	17	Benjamin Shaw
1774		
Jan	10	Elizabeth Bacon, Widow
Mar	12	A Child of Thomas Cusworth's
	30	Thos Crosley
Apr	13	A Child of Thos Worral's

1774		
Apr	17	Ann Wife of Wm Fisher
	23	Mary Wife of Geo Wright
May	23	A child of Wm Huntington
July	1	Thos Kay Senr
	17	Hannah wife of Wm Bell
Aug	14	Daniel Twigg
Sept	1	Sarah Malkin, Widow
	29	Elizh Townend, Widow
Nov	9	Alice Aden Widow
	13	Geo Fowlstone
Nov.	16	Ann Gawtress, Widow
Dec.	5	Thos Kay, Junr
1775.		
Jan.	2	Joseph son of Joseph Gill
	7	Elizh wife of Richard Wright
	16	Benjamin Burton
Mar.	4	Wm Dodson
	15	Joseph Gill
	23	John son of John Slater
Apr.	25	Michael Fenton
May	4	Robert son of Thomas Cusworth
	10	Lydia wife to William Conyers
	13	Grace wife to Thomas Bates
	17	Joseph son of William Malkin
	19	Jonathan son of Jonathan Ely
June	3	Ann wife to Richard Smith
	12	John son of John Lydster
	15	Benjamin son of John Lydster
July	7	William son of Thomas Bates
Aug.	28	Mary daughter of John Sailes
Sept.	11	Elizabeth Carr, Widow
	11	A child of George Cusworth's
	24	Mary wife to John Woodcock
	25	Grace Rodgers, Widow
Oct.	13	Joshua Earnshaw
Nov.	19	Mary Worral, Widow
Dec.	10	Elizabeth Finney, Widow
	19	William Taylor
	22	William son of William Carrier
1776.		
Jan.	12	Mary Hirst, Widow
	22	Mary Swinden, Widow
Feb.	5	A child of William Rodgers, junr
	12	A child of William Huntington's
	18	Joseph Tasker
Mar.	14	Mary daughter of William Fisher, senr
Apr.	15	William Fisher, junr
	18	Paul Garthwait

1776		
April	29	Nicholas Morton
May	14	Ann wife to John Sharey
June	16	Ann wife of William Jackson
July	6	Mary daughter of Richard Stead
Aug.	10	Jane wife of Joseph Ritson
	17	Daniel Twigg
Sept.	15	Sarah Garner daughter of Ann Bizby
	30	Mary Mercer, Widow
Oct.	2	Thomas Collyers
	3	John son of John Cutt, Junr
	20	Bartholomew Wood
Nov	4	Joseph Bingley
	4	Matthias Kemp
	9	Francis Trickit
	15	John Son of Joseph Hunt
	24	John Son of William Rogers
Dec	30	Thomas Smith
1777		
Jan	24	Mary Shay
Feb	24	Catherine Wife to William Lunn
Mar	13	William Bell
	25	Martha Allen, Widow
	26	Jonathan Frudd
Apr	1	Mary Wife of John Ford
May	7	John Hay
	15	John Carnalley
	19	Widow Bingley
	30	Richard Firth
June	27	Leonard Towers
Aug	18	Elizabeth Wife of Joseph Blackburn
	22	John Son of John Twittey
	27	Catherine Wife of William Thompson
	28	William Bingley
Oct	3	Thomas Carr
	14	Sarah Daughter of William Stead
Nov	15	Thomas Son of Thomas Andrews
	16	Thomas Bartholomew
Dec	2	Mary Daughter of Thomas Andrews
	21	Ann Shepherd
	24	Richard Wright
1778		
Jan	7	Richard Lambert Linfitt
Feb	16	Thomas Carnalley
Mar	2	Mary Wife of Thomas Kemp
	18	Ann Wife of Henry Otley

VOL. III.

MARRIAGES.

1754		
May	21	William Fletcher and Jane Kennerley of Wath
Aug	5	James Wright and Mary Mare (Mayer) of Wath
	18	John Nell of Pontefract and Eliz: Pashley of Wath by Licence
	18	Jonathan Bucher and Mary Ditch of Wath by Licence
	28	Isaac Tomlinson and Mary Oates of Wath by Licence
Sept	25	John Walker and Ann Clarkson of Wath
Dec	12	Robt Goddard of Peniston and Mary Law of Wath
1755		
Jan.	16	Philip Flint of Wath and Frances Roebuck of Hooton Roberts
	27	Thomas Broadhead and Eliz: Parkin of Wath
Feb.	17	John Broughton of Campsal and Mary Ford of Wath
Mar	17	Will: Norman and Sarah Bagshaw of Wath
	17	Joseph Kitson and Jane Parkin of Wath
Apr	8	Joshua Padmore and Jane Butterworth of Wath
	14	John Bett and Jane Robinson of Wath
May	19	Giles Battison and Martha Fowlston of Wath
Aug	26	Tho: Thompson and Mary Beamond of Wath
Sept	2	Will: Tingle and Alice Ibberson of Wath
	4	Tho: Shaw and Hannah Wager of Wath by Licence
	9	Benjamin Spencer and Sarah Speight of Wath
Oct	28	Will: Wharam and Eliz: Chevings of Wath
	30	William Wild and Ann Booth of Wath
Nov	25	Will: Gessop of Darfield and Sarah Beamont of Wath
Dec	11	Thos Arundel of Rotheram and Sarah Bingley of Wath
1756		
Jan.	1	Thomas Gaunt Barber of Hansworth in the County of York and Ann Freeman of Wath by Licence
	6	William Wood and Mary Smith of Wath
	7	Mathew Stephenson and Sarah Flint of Wath
	18	Tho: Priestley of Rotherham and Hannah Hill of Wath
Feb.	10	Joseph Bentley and Hannah Fenton of Wath
Apr	19	Will: Jackson and Mary Hanson of Wath
May	25	John Smith and Mary Mathewman of Wath
July	13	Joseph Parkin and Eliz: Wharam of Wath
	1	Will: Medley of Darfield and Sarah Booth of Wath
	25	John Otter of Cleyworth in the County of Nottingham and Ann Jackson of Wath
Sept	12	Francis Wilks and Eliz: Mosforth of Wath
Nov	23	John Pool and Joye Beamont of Wath
1757		
Jan	18	George Whitaker and Hannah Thompson of Wath
	31	John Key and Eliz. Carr of Wath

1757		
June	21	Will Walker and Phœbe Hall of Wath
	23	John Twittey and Eliz: Jackson of Wath
Aug	1	Will: Thackrey of Wickersley and Mary Foster of Wath by Licence
Oct	31	Will: Brook of Rawmarsh and Martha Role of Wath
1758		
Jan	29	John Marsden of Sandal and Ann Poles of Wath
	30	Rich: Hague of Hooton Roberts and Sarah Windsor of Wath
Feb.	7	Isaac Hanby of Coningsbrough and Mary Twigg of Wath
June	11	Thos Crosley of Wath and Ann Walker of Barnsley by Licence
	22	Will: Duke and Mary Vains of Wath
July	16	James Hartley and Alice Jubb of Wath
Sept	28	John Hopkinson and Mary Gregory of Wath
Oct	2	Will: Garlick and Ann Fowlston of Wath
	12	Joseph Halley and Ann Hinchlife of Wath
	31	Robert Bagley and Ann Hartley of Wath
Nov	27	Thomas Smith of Darfield and Ann Grey of Wath
	30	Thomas Dyson and Mary Ax of Wath
Dec	12	Samuel Crowder of Darfield and Mary Iredal of Wath
	25	Joseph Hobson and Ann Taylor of Wath by Licence
	26	Thomas White and Elizabeth Burks of Wath
1759		
Jan	29	William Dale of Warmsworth and Sarah Twigg of Wath by Licence
Feb.	13	Thomas Watson of Wickesley and Rachel Lambert of Wath
Apr	27	Thos. Poles and Alice Pullen of Wath by Licence
May	20	William Smith and Ann Elam of Wath
	27	Thomas Malpas and Wath and Martha Hobson of Rawmarsh
June	10	Will. Thompson of Rotherham and Martha Booth of Wath
	11	John Jenkinson and Eliz: Clarkson of Wath
July	5	John Firth and Mary Mathew of Wath by Licence
	5	Rich. Wilson and Dorothy Green of Wath
June	29	Will. Hardey and Eliz: Varah of Wath
Sept	10	John Darley of the Parochial Chappel of Wooley and Sarah Warron of Wath
	11	David Frogget and Hannah Thompson of Wath
Oct	1	James Roberts of Rawmarsh and Sarah Smith of Wath
	22	Joseph Jenkinson and Elizth Ashforth of Wath
	24	John Smith and Eliz. Horsfall of Wath by Licence
Nov	22	Samuel Stenton and Sarah Wilby of Wath
	27	Peter Dean and Martha Ford of Wath
Dec	20	Joseph Burley of Bolton and Sarah Baxter of Wath
	25	Wm Burland and Sarah Hargreave of Wath
	27	John Rhoades and Elizabeth Armstead of Wath

1759		
Dec	27	John Grimshaw and Sarah Siar of Wath
1760		
Jan	5	John Hague and Mary Harrison of Wath
Feb.	14	Benjn Kay and Hannah Howland of Wath
Mar	5	Thos Roberts and Elizabeth Barker of Wath by licence
Apr	7	Joshua Wormel of Woodchurch and Sarah Dean of Wath
	10	Thos Cusworth and Eliz: Allot of Wath
May	11	Jonathan Hargreaves and Hannah Tingle of Wath
	12	Major Monton and Zilpah Staton of Wath
	27	Joseph Butterworth and Anne Heaton of Wath
June	12	Thos Brooke and Sarah Green of Wath
July	7	Jonathan Carr and Ann Laycock of Wath
	27	Thomas Whitehouse and Catherine Morley of Wath by Licence
Aug	3	Joseph Hunt and Sarah Malkin of Wath
	3	Richard Wright and Mary Ledger of Wath by Licence
	24	John Ward and Elizth Mellard of Wath
Oct.	8	Wm Newton and Mary Hurst of Wath
Nov.	10	James Whitwam of the Chapelry of Barnsley and Margaret Butler of Wath
	30	Benjamin Grayson and Alice Russel of Wath
Dec	16	Samuel Dawson of Doncaster and Ann Munday of Wath
	28	Joseph Darin and Mary Earnshaw of Wath
1761		
Feb.	3	John Carr and Elizabeth Watson of Wath
Apr	2	Joseph Bucher and Ann Robin of Wath
	7	James Abson of Bolton and Mary Wilson of Wath
	9	Joseph Bower and Dorothy Swift of Wath
	20	Samuel Griffin of Wath and Elizabeth Bingley of Rotheram
June	4	Joseph Newton and Mary Heward of Wath by licence
Aug	3	William Foulstone and Mary Birks of Wath
	9	George Scholey and Ann Wadkin of Wath
	25	William Linfit and Joannah Robinson of Wath by licence
Sept	21	George Golding and Hannah Birkinshaw of Wath
Nov.	6	James White and Elizabeth Dyson of Wath by licence
	24	Robert Pullen and Susan Wilkinson of Wath
	30	John Utley and Ann Booth of Wath
Dec	3	Benjamin Coldwell of Ackworth and Ann Ibetson of Wath
1762		
Jan.	5	Joseph Hunter of Felkirk and Hannah Burland of Wath
Feb.	14	Richard Becket of Badsworth and Catherine Kemp of Wath
Apr	22	Thomas Fostard and Francis Bingley of Wath by licence
May	24	John Hardwick and Martha Wilkinson of Wath by Licence
	24	James Wigfield and Sarah Hyerdale of Wath

1762

Aug	2	John Burgin and Ann Tottie of Wath
	15	James Utley and Susan Thicket of Wath
Oct	1	John Smith and Elizabeth Andrews of Wath by licence
	10	Benjamin Gray and Hannah Birks of Wath by licence
	28	William Denton and Eliz: Gawtress of Wath by licence
Nov	4	John Broomhead of Royston and Elizabeth Silverhood of Wath by licence
	15	Robert Swift and Ann Crooks of Wath
	23	Thomas Earnshaw and Mary Brown of Wath
Dec	30	Richard Jackson and Mary Thompson of Wath
1763		
Feb	7	Jeremiah Pickard and Alice Ledger of Wath
	15	Thomas Dunill of Rawmarsh and Eliz: Carr of Wath
May	19	Samuel Nelson of Ecclesfield and Ann Mallison of Wath
	23	John Knight and Frances Carr of Wath
Aug	8	Joseph Hall of Rawmarsh and Mary Burland of Wath
Sept	26	John Child and Martha Munday of Wath by licence
	27	John Harrison and Martha Clark of Wath
Oct	10	Thomas Rose and Hannah Bower of Wath
	13	Henry Wilkinson and Mary Blackburn of Wath by licence
	25	John Atkinson of Mexbro' and Deborah Fostard of Wath by licence
Nov.	14	John Raines of Wheldrake and Catherine Savage of Wath by licence
	24	Jonathan Heeley and Ann Ford of Wath
	24	Thomas Wigfield and Sarah Skelton of Wath
	27	Benjamin Battye and Sarah Newton of Wath by Licence
	29	Thomas Birkinshaw and Anne Shay of Wath
Dec.	29	Richard Marshall and Hannah Robinson of Wath
1764		
Jan	31	Thomas Kay and Elizabeth Sharp of Wath by Licence
Feb.	7	John Fretwell of Snaith and Alice Wharam of Wath by Licence
May	8	Bryan Clarkson and Mary Munday of Wath by Licence
June	18	Joseph Charlton and Mary Robinson of Wath
July	8	George Thompson and Elizabeth Halley of Wath
Aug	6	Richard Stenton and Ann Hoyland of Wath
Oct	15	William Hunt and Sarah Addy of Wath
(*No date*)		Nathan Burgund and Ann Taylor. Banns published Sept 30th, Oct 17th and 14th. 1764. The above persons were married in Wentworth Chapel with my consent Jn° Rowley Vic^r^
Oct	29	John Goddard and Hannah Evas of Wath
Nov.	8	Joseph Cook and Elizabeth Parkin of Wath
	29	Francis Avison and Grace Green of Wath
Dec	4	Jonathan Higgins and Martha Cooper of Wath
	17	George Tingle and Elizabeth Goss of Wath

1765

Jan	31	Thomas Shaw and Elizabeth Speight of Wath
Feb	*3	John Smith of Barnbrough and Ann Bell of Wath
	19	John Sailes and Ann Renny of Wath by Licence
Mar	26	Jonathan Dickinson and Sarah Dobson of Wath by Licence
Apr	7	Joseph Gill and Mary Malkin of Wath
	8	William Wood of Clayton and Sarah Rimington of Wath
	28	William Carr and Sarah Nicholson of Wath
May	1	John Knowles and Hannah Wigfield of Wath
—	6	Joseph Gibson and Martha Butler of Wath
June	6	Joseph Twigg and Ann Vickers of Wath
July	14	Joseph Hunt and Elizabeth Rodgers of Wath
Aug	4	John Auslin and Martha Bower of Wath
Sept	12	Thomas Taylor and Sarah Shaw of Wath
Nov	25	John Beaumont and Hannah Sympson of Wath
	26	Benjamin Ward and Martha Allott of Wath
Dec	16	William Butcher of Wath and Susanna Smith of Armthorp
	30	Joseph Emerson of Staveley and Ann Allen of Wath by Licence

1766

Jan	23	Henry Heald and Sārah Kay of Wath
Mar	31	John Swindhill and Henrietta Butcher of Wath
Apr	1	Joseph Wigfield and Leah Ryley of Wath
	27	John Shilleto and Mary Dyson of Wath
	29	Joseph Burgund and Hannah Parkin of Wath
May	12	John Duke and Ann Wood of Wath
	29	John Ward and Dorothy Wilson of Wath
	29	William Haxworth of Darfield and Martha Carnally of Wath by Licence
June	19	Francis Brothell and Jane Andrew of Wath
July	18	John Robinson and Ann Sheppard of Wath
	31	William Vickers and Sarah Bell of Wath
Nov	23	Thomas Goddard and Mary Sykes of Wath
	23	Robert Ford and Hannah Sharpless of Wath
	30	Jonas Bell of Rotherham and Mary Dixon of Wath
Dec	1	Miles Ledger of Mexbro and Ann Forde of Wath
	7	Richard Smith and Mary Mellard of Wath
	11	Abraham Hawksworth and Sarah Ducker of Wath by Licence
	11	John Wood and Mary Wigfield of Wath
	25	Richard Shaw of Wickersley and Elizabeth Jackson of Wath

1767

Jan	1	William Campsall and Ann Bincliff of Wath
	20	John Cooper of Rotheram and Ann Gill of Wath
Apr	20	Joshua Longley and Mary Machant of Wath
	20	George Shaw and Sarah Warburton of Wath

* This marriage is entered in the wrong place perhaps to fill up a vacant place. It is dated 3 Feb., 1767, the banns being published 23 and 30 Nov. and 7 Dec., 1766.

1767

Apr	25	John Smith and Elizabeth Wesnage of Wath
June	1	John Elam and Elizabeth Roddey of Wath
	11	Thomas Cooper and Mary Burley of Wath
	17	James Haigh and Sarah Wallhead of Wath
	21	John Watson of Wath and Frances Houghleton of Chapelry of Cawthorn
Oct	1	Robert Bizby and Ann Roebuck of Wath
	19	Willoughby Wood and Frances Wilkinson of Wath
Dec	1	Samuel Walker and Martha Pool of Wath
	9	Benjamin Hague and Mary Smith of Wath
	16	William Pearson and Sarah Loy of Wath

1768

Jan	19	Thomas Hagar of Rawmarsh and Ann Flint of Wath by Licence
Feb.	1	Richard Beardshall and Elizabeth Wigfield of Wath
	9	John Otley and Hannah Beardshall of Wath by Licence
Mar.	13	John Matthewman and Eliz: Ford of Wath
Apr	5	George Fisher of Sheffield and Phœbe West of Wath
	12	Thomas Worral and Elizabeth Fisher of Wath by Licence
	24	William Ibbotson and Elizabeth Gawtrees of Wath by Licence
June	2	George Denton and Mary Barker of Wath
	2	William Wright and Ann Ward of Wath
	23	George Davis of Rotheram and Mary Burrow of Wath by Licence
July	7	Thomas Hague and Ann Bailey of Wath
Aug	23	John Eastwood and Hannah Hoyle of Wath
Nov.	22	John Sorby and Elizabeth Barrot of Wath
	24	Godfrey Speight and Rachael Ryley of Wath
	24	John Bullhouse of Wath and Margaret Rawson of Rotheram
	27	William Firth and Ann Hutchinson of Wath

1769

Jan	5	Michael Bisby and Elizabeth Pepper of Wath by Licence
	16	George Dyson and Martha Davidson of Wath
	29	Charles Wood and Hannah Beaumont of Wath
Mar	3	Henry Slator and Mary Scholey of Wath by Licence
	8	John Lockwood and Elizabeth Beardshall of Wath by Licence
Apr	23	William Jackson Esq and Sarah Kay of Wath by Licence
May	22	William Hague and Ann Green of Wath
	25	Thomas Coldwell and Ann Pullen of Wath by Licence
June	1	Thomas Hilton and Ann Kay of Wath
	18	George Wrangham and Thomasin Ducker of Wath by Licence
	29	Richard Harrison of Darfield and Hannah Bashford of Wath
July	20	James Haigh and Sarah Hading of Wath by Licence

1769

Aug 4 John Harrison and Elizabeth Hill of Wath

31 Matthias Hartley of Ecclesfield and Martha Butterworth of Wath

Nov 27 John Whitehead and Mary Ford of Wath

30 Robt Watson and Sarah Butler of Wath

Dec 12 David Stone and Susanna Widdup of Wath by Licence

14 Jonas Wilson of Wath and Mary Russell of Mexbro by Licence

17 William Cartlidge and Elizabeth Slater of Wath

24 John Adams of Rotheram and Ann Green of Wath

28 Edward Linley and Esther Senior of Wath

1770

Jan 15 William Flint of Rotheram and Elizabeth Bartholomew of Wath

Feb 8 William Thompson of Mexbro' and Catherine Lum of Wath by Licence

22 James Utley and Elizabeth Mitchel of Wath

25 William Hoult and Mary Denton of Wath

Mar. 12 Edward Dickinson and Mary Wigfield of Wath by Licence

Apr 3 Robert Vickers of Hooton Roberts and Grace Armstead of Wath

May 7 Godfrey Hirst of Sheffield and Ann Wigfield of Wath

10 Jonathan Hargreave and Catherine Fisher of Wath

13 John Harrison and Mary Butcher of Wath

15 Jonathan Bashford of Rawmarsh and Ann Shaw of Wath

15 William Sympson and Mary Mallinson of Wath

June 17 Joseph Wilkinson of Rotheram and Sarah Bashforth of Wath

Aug 5 Thomas Downing and Mary Worral of Wath

23 Enoch Thompson and Ann Jackson of Wath

26 Richard Firth of High Melton and Mary Cusworth of Wath

Sept 16 John Mercer and Elizabeth Heward of Wath by Licence

Oct 7 John Mawson and Frances Oats of Wath

11 Thomas Webster and Hannah Hill of Wath

18 Matthew Blacksmith of Rawmarsh and Ann Hill of Wath by Licence

18 John Hague of Rawmarsh and Hannah Carnelly of Wath by Licence

25 Joseph Wigfield and Katy Smith of Wath by Licence

Nov 11 Charles Bower and Sarah Lewis of Wath

12 Joseph Rowe of Ecclesfield and Ann Dyson of Wath

26 Samuel Wells and Sarah Addy of Wath

Dec 23 John Jessop and Zilpah Mounton of Wath

1771

Jan 6 Richard Thompson and Sarah Revell of Wath by Licence

Feb. 10 James Cooper and Elizabeth Lockwood of Wath by Licence

1771		
Mar	5	John Wilkinson of Felkirk and Mary Silverwood of Wath by Licence
Apr	7	James Nightscales and Hannah Gill of Wath by Licence
	25	William Berwick and Mary Hirst of Wath
May	5	Thomas Cliff and Ann Hague of Wath
June	16	William Lancashire and Elizabeth Birkinshaw of Wath
	25	Thomas Kemp of Wath and Martha Wood of Mexbro
July	7	William Shaw of Rawmarsh and Ellin Carrier of Wath
	28	Thomas Hudson and Elizabeth Gawtress of Wath by Licence
Nov	4	Jonathan Parkin and Ann Morley of Wath
	5	Joseph Fisher and Ann Eastwood of Wath
	26	Jonathan Fisher and Hannah Roddinson of Wath
Dec	2	Thomas Campsall and Gertrude White both of Adwick
	26	Richard Shaw and Mary Hatock of Wath
1772		
Jan	2	Samuel Dyche and Ann Wigfield of Wath
Feb	11	William Barker and Ann Matthewman of Wath
Mar	3	Jonathan Stead and Alice Watson of Wath
	3	William Rawlin and Mary Carr of Wath
	22	Thomas Sorsby of Thribergh and Sarah Holdsworth of Wath by Licence
Apr	20	Luke Ogden and Mary Burgund of Wath
	21	George Norton of Rotheram and Ann Turner of Wath
May	5	Joseph Butcher and Grace Hoyle of Wath
June	9	William Poles and Ann Mouldson of Wath by Licence
July	7	Thomas Roberts and Mary Duke of Wath by Licence
Nov	17	John Kemp and Mary Trippitt of Wath by Licence
	23	Matthew Middleton of Rawmarsh and Margaret Hopewell of Wath
Dec	7	Neddy Green and Hannah Green of Wath
	10	Willoughby Wells and Ruth Bizby of Wath
1773		
Jan	7	John Carnally and Ann Fisher of Wath
	12	David Jubb and Mary Rawlin of Wath
	17	Edward Pailthorpe and Hannah Oldfield of Wath by Licence
	25	Joshua Matthewman and Ann Foulstone of Wath
Feb.	23	Samuel Hartley and Ann Cooper of Wath
Mar	7	Samuel Hague of Rawmarsh and Elizabeth Lyell of Wath by Licence
	23	Thomas Andrew of Darfield and Ann Gillott of Wath by Licence
May	11	George Cusworth and Martha Beckitt of Wath
	30	Richard Gawtress and Ann Denton of Wath by Licence
June	6	John Evas and Mary Bingham of Wath
	28	James Wright and Rebecca Wright of Wath
July	5	William Hodgson and Ann Woodhead of Wath

1773		
July	27	Robert Moor and Sarah Woodall of Wath by Licence
Aug	26	Jonathan Gascoigne and Mary Hague of Wath
Oct	12	William Bottom and Betty Dearden of Wath
	19	Edward Sarter and Mary Stead of Wath
Nov	4	Joseph Sylvester and Ann Marshall, widow of Wath
	21	John Hyde and Frances Wilson of Wath by Licence
	22	George Frost and Elizabeth Hudson of Wath
	22	William Dodgson and Sarah Durdy of Wath
	22	William Mellard and Sarah Norton of Wath
Dec	2	George Hoyland and Hannah Milner of Wath
	5	William Rogers and Mary Lonkishire of Wath
1774		
Jan	17	Samuel Smith and Martha Cooper of Wath
	14	Richard Denton and Mary Beaumont of Wath
Feb	26	Robert Williamson of Gainsbro' and Mary Cawkwell of Wath
Mar	19	Joseph Colton of Great Driffield and Mary Beardshall of Wath by Licence
	22	George Dickenson and Mary Fisher of Wath
Apr	21	John Earnshaw and Mary Parkin of Wath
May	29	Benjamin Senior and Ann Horsfall of Wath by Licence
	30	Thomas Nettleton and Jemima Cooper of Wath
June	26	John Blake and Ann Parkin of Wath
July	25	William Dawson and Martha Allender of Wath by Licence
Aug	26	William Ax. and Ann Radley of Wath by Licence
Sept	11	John Rhodes and Martha Dickinson of Wath
	22	John Mawson and Jane Hyde of Wath
Oct	17	John Young and Ellen Froggit of Wath
	17	Benjamin Taylor and Mary Hague of Wath
	18	John Swallow and Hannah Campsall of Wath
Nov.	7	Jonathan Moor and Ann Rogison of Wath
	27	William Coggin of Rawmarsh and Elizabeth Matthews of Wath
Dec	8	Thomas Wadsworth of Barnbro' and Sarah Balmfirth of Wath
	25	George Skelton of Rotheram and Jane Sadler of Wath
	25	John Kay and Margaret Cooper of Wath
1775		
Jan	19	Charles Sidebottom of Sheffield and Sarah Goddard of Wath
	30	Thomas Smith, widdower, and Elizabeth Goddard of Wath
Feb	6	William Otley, widdow, and Ann Swallow, wid. of Wath
	16	Richard Dickinson and Sarah Barns of Wath
	19	Thomas Smith and Esther Sylvester of Wath
Mar	21	William Brooke and Ann Bulhouse of Wath
Apr	16	George White and Sarah Hall of Wath
May	4	John Hilton and Ann Trippit of Wath

1775		
June	5	Campsall Bower and Mary Walker of Wath
	8	John Blackburn and Martha Senior of Wath
	27	Mark Cooper and Olive Lambert of Wath by Licence
July	3	John Bales and Ann Wallhead of Wath
	23	William Carr and Hannah Curtis of Wath
Aug	1	Robert Marcroft and Ann Hopkinson of Wath
	3	Richard Lambert and Martha Fenton of Wath by Licence
	14	William Lyster and Elizabeth Lyell of Wath by Licence
	23	James Copley and Phœbe Wood of Wath
Nov	28	John Trickitt and Sarah Staton of Wath
Dec	5	Thomas Wallhead and Mary Vickers of Wath by Licence
	28	John Burlay and Sarah Jackson of Wath
1776		
Jan	25	Thomas Hanson and Mary Beaumont of Wath
Feb.	25	Nathan Bark and Martha Duke of Wath by Licence
Mar	24	John Singleton and Lucy Lum of Wath by Licence
Apr	9	Joseph Utley and Sarah Dickinson of Wath by Licence
May	5	Matthew Tyson and Margaret Woodcock of Wath
	19	John Belk and Sarah Downs of Wath
	26	Edward Goddard and Sarah Sykes of Wath
June	13	George Barnsley of Sheffield and Mary Moulson of Wath by Licence
July	3	Thomas Nailor and Elizabeth Crowder of Wath
Aug	22	John Woodcock and Sarah Swift of Wath
	26	Joseph Darwin of Darfield and Alice Saxby of Wath
	27	George Godly of Braithwell and Mary Revel of Wath
Oct	1	Robert Taylor of Sutton, Nottingham and Mary Hampshire of Wath
	3	Edward Shaw and Ann Forde of Wath
	15	Edward Hall, widower, and Grace Grimshold of Wath
Nov.	13	John Burgan and Ann Mitchell of Wath by Licence
	22	John Slack of Rawmarsh and Susanna Tingle of Wath
Dec	17	John Burgund and Ann Smith of Wath by Licence
	29	Thomas Wright of Sandall Magna and Sarah Beaumont of Wath by Licence
	31	Jonathan Lilley and Hannah Revil of Wath
1777		
Jan.	7	George Spencer of Mexbro and Elizabeth Lancashire of Wath
	9	John Cooper and Mary Gill of Wath
	13	William Allott and Joanna Cusworth of Wath
	23	Thomas Bocock and Elizabeth Stead of Wath
	23	John Bintliff of Peniston and Tabitha Tinker of Wath
	23	William Wilson of Hooton Roberts and Ann Barratt of Wath
Feb	2	Robert Turner of Rawmarsh and Elizabeth Kay of Wath
	6	John Gordon and Martha Butheroyd of Wath
	21	Richard Harrison of Rawmarsh and Alice Barker of Wath

1777

Mar 17 John Bagshaw and Sarah Shaw of Wath
23 Joseph Blackburn of Sheffield and Elizabeth Hall of Wath by Licence
Apr 7 George Fostard and Mary Woodcock of Wath
7 Robert Beaumont and Hannah Swift of Wath
8 Mark Megson of Wath and Mary Burgund of Arksey
May 20 Joseph Dean of Sheffield and Mary Firth of Wath
July 3 John Cropper and Ann Walker of Wath
Sept 15 William Cooper and Mary Goddard of Wath
24 John Iredale and Ann Ostrich of Wath by Licence
25 Richard Waterton of Hemsworth and Mary Vanes of Wath by Licence
Oct 2 John Burgund and Jane Tinley of Wath
9 Thomas Bool of Rawmarsh and Sarah Parkin of Wath
13 Richard Smith and Sarah Wade of Wath
Nov. 9 Joseph Beevers and Mary Coe of Wath
24 William Freeman of Sheffield and Hannah Walker of Wath
25 Willoughby Methley of High Melton and Martha Coe of Wath
27 Joseph Smith and Mary Swift of Wath
30 John Bell and Sarah Lancashire of Wath
Dec 1 John Hoyle and Elizabeth Saxby of Wath
14 Benjamin Ford and Sarah Spencer of Wath
25 Thomas Grundy of Handsworth and Caty Carr of Wath
25 William Chapman and Mary Pilley of Wath
27 Samuel Carr and Mary Spalding of Wath
30 William Longley and Mary Pilley of Wath

1778

Jan 20 Thomas Jackson and Elizabeth Cook of Wath
25 John Tyne and Martha Smith of Wath by Licence
Feb. 12 George Beaumont and Frances Pashley of Wath by Licence
Mar 3 John Smith and Mary Wood of Wath by Licence
16 John Saville and Margaret Hague of Wath
Apr 6 John Mann and Mary White of Wath
13 Joseph Cusworth and Ann Maugham of Wath
19 Richard Rhodes and Hannah Ellis of Wath
20 Edward Swallowof Bolton upon Dern and Lydia White of Wath by Licence
June 8 William Watson of Doncaster and Mary Gee of Wath
22 Joseph Newton and Esther Hill of Wath
July 12 Joshua Hague and Mary Butler of Wath
16 William Rhodes and Elizabeth Oates of Wath by Licence
Aug 6 Thomas Webster, Widower and Ann Pulleyn Spinster of Wath by Licence
17 Joseph Smith and Mary Kay of Wath
17 Charles Unwin and Ann Coats of Wath
21 John Nettleton and Elizabeth Longley of Wath

1778		
Oct	15	Thomas Smith of Tankersley and Betty Robinson of Wath by Licence
Nov	23	Thomas Shirtcliff of Hooton Roberts and Mary Swift of Wath
	26	Thomas Leeke and Ann Dixon of Wath
	29	John Oldfield and Hannah Cookson of Wath
	29	Joseph Deplidge and Emilia Hattersly of Wath
Dec	6	Joseph Hargreaves and Elizabeth Appleyard of Wath
	17	Samuel Brooke and Ann Parkin of Wath
	20	Thomas Hobson of Kirkheaton and Ann Appleyard of Wath by Licence
	24	John Parkinson of Darfield and Margaret Carr of Wath by Licence
	24	John Mabson and Mary Smith of Wath
1779		
Jan	5	Thomas Eastwood and Ann Morton of Wath
	17	Dollif Rollison of Sheffield and Elizabeth Hatfield of Wath by Licence
	31	Thomas Rayner and Catherine Kemp of Wath
Feb.	14	John Hepworth of Wath and Frances Maria White of Mexbro'
Mar	25	William Ellis and Elizabeth Hyde of Wath
	28	Mark Allott and Ann Sorsby of Wath
May	24	Edward Hind and Mary Hartley of Wath
	31	John Wigfield and Sarah Parkin of Wath
June	3	William Bulhouse and Sarah Vickers of Wath
	7	Job Longley of Mexbro and Mary Bizby of Wath
	8	Joseph Parkinson of Sheffield and Mary Armytage of Wath by Licence
July	4	John Laughton of Mexbro and Mary Lunn of Wath by Licence
	26	William Ford and Elizabeth Fisher of Wath
Aug	19	David Coe and Elizabeth Maugham of Wath
	23	William Senior of Darfield and Elizabeth Coward of Wath

N.B. The marriages in this Volume from 1754 were mostly by the Revd Wm Twittey, Vicar. up to 10 Nov 1760. except in a few instances by the Revd John Rowley, Curate. Mr Twittey was buried in Apr 1761 and Mr Rowley seems to have succeeded him, his first entry as Vicar being 3 Aug 1761. He was still in office at the close of the volume.

(EDITOR).

INDEX OF PERSONS.

(An asterisk after a number means more than one mention on the page.)*

INDEX OF PLACES.

* *These place names usually occur more than twice on the pages quoted.*

WAKEFIELD:

W. H. MILNES, RADCLIFFE PRINTING WORKS.

Printed in Great Britain
by Amazon

20195365R00190